Jane Austen on Screen

Jane Austen on Screen is a collection of essays exploring the literary and cinematic implications of translating Austen's prose into film. Contributors raise questions of how prose fiction and cinema differ, of how mass commercial audiences require changes to script and character, and of how continually remade films evoke memories of earlier productions. The essays represent widely divergent perspectives, from literary "purists" suspicious of filmic renderings of Austen to filmmakers who see the text as a stimulus for producing exceptional cinema. Theoretical issues are explored in balance with the practical concerns of literature-to-film conversions: casting choices, authenticity of settings, script "amputations" of the original prose, anachronisms, relevance for modern mass audiences, and the intertextuality informing the production of much-remade works. This comprehensive study, including an exhaustive Austen bibliography and filmography, will be of interest to students and teachers alike.

GINA MACDONALD teaches at Nicholls State University in Thibodaux, Louisiana. Her books include *James Clavell* (1996) and *Robert Ludlum* (1997). She has just edited a *Dictionary of National Biography* volume *British Mystery and Thriller Writers since 1940* (2003).

ANDREW MACDONALD teaches at Loyola University in New Orleans. He is the author of *Howard Fast* (1997).

Together the Macdonalds have published *Mastering Writing Essentials* (1996), *Shapeshifting: Images of Native Americans in Recent Popular Fiction* (2000), and *Shaman or Sherlock? The Native American in Recent Detective Fiction* (2001). They were coeditors of the *TESOL Intensive English Newsletter*, and they are regular contributors to *Creative Screenwriting*.

Colonel Brandon's (Alan Rickman's) quiet, gentlemanly courtship of Marianne Dashwood (Kate Winslet) in a scene from Columbia Pictures/ TriStar Pictures' 1995 *Sense and Sensibility*

Jane Austen on Screen

Edited by

Gina Macdonald

Nicholls State University, Thibodaux, Louisiana

and

Andrew Macdonald

Loyola University, New Orleans

CAMBRIDGE
UNIVERSITY PRESS

PUBLISHED BY THE PRESS SYNDICATE OF THE UNIVERSITY OF CAMBRIDGE
The Pitt Building, Trumpington Street, Cambridge CB2 1RP, United Kingdom

CAMBRIDGE UNIVERSITY PRESS
The Edinburgh Building, Cambridge, CB2 2RU, UK
40 West 20th Street, New York, NY 10011–4211, USA
477 Williamstown Road, Port Melbourne, VIC 3207, Australia
Ruiz de Alarcón 13, 28014 Madrid, Spain
Dock House, The Waterfront, Cape Town 8001, South Africa

http://www.cambridge.org

First published 2003

Printed in the United Kingdom at the University Press, Cambridge

Typeface Plantin 10/12 pt.   *System* LATEX 2$_\varepsilon$ [TB]

A catalogue record for this book is available from the British Library

ISBN 0 521 79325 4 hardback
ISBN 0 521 79728 4 paperback

Contents

vi   Contents

Illustrations

Contributors

ELLEN BELTON is Dean of Undergraduate Studies and Professor of English and a former Chair of the English Department and of the Faculty Council at Brooklyn College of the City University of New York; she is the author of poetry and articles on the plays of Shakespeare, John Webster, and Thomas Heywood and on "The Detective Plots of Jane Austen," and the recipient of the 1998 Theodore M. Hesburgh Award for Faculty Development to Enhance Undergraduate Teaching and Learning and of the 1999 Noel-Levitz Retention Excellence Award.

KATE BOWLES is Lecturer in Communication and Cultural Studies at the University of Wollongong, South Wales, Australia; she has published on the legal and cultural implications of the Internet, on television soap opera, and on television fandom.

JAN FERGUS is Professor in the Department of English, Lehigh University, Bethlehem, PA, USA, author of several essays on Austen and two books (*Jane Austen and the Didactic Novel* and a biography, *Jane Austen: A Literary Life*) as well as a number of articles on the reading public during Austen's time.

ROGER GARD is an English Austen scholar, author of *Jane Austen's Novels: The Art of Clarity* and *Emma and Persuasion* (Penguin Critical Studies).

PENNY GAY is an Associate Professor, Department of English, University of Sydney, Australia; she has published on the theatrical performance of gender (*As She Likes It: Shakespeare's Unruly Women*, Routledge, 1994), with monographs on Jane Austen (*Jane Austen's "Emma,"* 1995, and *Jane Austen's "Pride and Prejudice,"* 1990, and with articles on the three *Emma* films. She has recently published *Jane Austen and the Theatre* (Cambridge University Press, 2002).

JOCELYN HARRIS is the holder of a personal chair at the University of Otago, New Zealand. She edited Samuel Richardson's *History of Sir*

Charles Grandison (Oxford University Press, 1972); she has explored the Grandison link in *Jane Austen and the Art of Memory* (CUP, 1989), reviewed the Jane Austen film versions, written on eighteenth-century women poets, and introduced Richardson's published commentary on *Clarissa* for Pickering & Chatto (1998).

ANDREW F. MACDONALD is an Associate Professor at Loyola University, New Orleans, LA, USA, with a Ph.D. from the University of Texas, Austin, in Renaissance; he has published widely on popular fiction for Bruccoli Press, Salem Press, St. Martin's and St. James Press, among others; he is the author of *Howard Fast*, coauthor of *Shapeshifting* and *Shaman or Sherlock?*, and a regular reviewer for *Creative Screenwriting.*

VIRGINIA (GINA) L. MACDONALD is an Assistant Professor at Nicholls State University, Thibodaux, LA, with a Ph.D. from the University of Texas, Austin, in Renaissance and Nineteenth-Century British Fiction; she has published widely for Bruccoli Press, Salem Press, St. Martin's and St. James Press, among others, including several books for Greenwood Press on popular fiction (*James Clavell, Robert Ludlum*, and is coauthor of *Shapeshifting* and *Shaman or Sherlock?*), editor of the Bruccoli Press edition *of British Mystery and Detective Fiction since 1960*, and a regular reviewer for *Creative Screenwriting.*

HARRIET MARGOLIS is a senior lecturer in film at Victoria University of Wellington, Aotearoa New Zealand, who previously taught film, literature, women's romance novels, and related subjects at various universities in the USA; she is the author of *The Cinema Ideal: An Introduction to Psychoanalytic Studies of the Film Spectator*, and articles on film or literature that have appeared in various books and journals internationally; she is the editor of *Jane Campion's "The Piano"* (Cambridge University Press). She is on the editorial board of *Screening the Past*, an electronic journal available at http://www.latrobe.edu.au/www/screeningthepast

DAVID MONAGHAN is Professor of English at Mount Saint Vincent University, Halifax, Nova Scotia, author of *Jane Austen: Structure and Social Vision* (1980), and editor of *Jane Austen in a Social Context* (1981) and the New Casebooks volume on *Emma* (1992). His teaching and research interests have expanded in recent years to embrace popular literature, film, and cultural studies. His most recent book, *The Falklands War: Myth and Countermyth* (1998), combines all of these interests through a study of written and visual texts that range from Margaret Thatcher's speeches, through Steve Bell's cartoons to films such as *The Ploughman's Lunch.*

JOHN MOSIER is a Professor at Loyola University, New Orleans, USA, where he regularly teaches Jane Austen; a member of the Camera d'Or Jury at Cannes; author of articles on film adaptations for *Kino*, *Americas*, *PMLA*, the *New Orleans Review*, and the *New Orleans Art Review*, where he is currently a contributing editor; a founding member of Film Historia (Barcelona), whose essays on film have appeared in Russian, Italian, Spanish, French, Slovak, German, and Portuguese; author of *Men and Women Together* (1986), *The Myth of the Great War: A New Military History of the First World War* (2000), and *The Blitzkrieg Myth* (2003).

GAYLENE PRESTON is a New Zealand director, producer, and screenwriter known for *Ruby and Rata*, 1989; *War Stories our Mothers Never Told Us*, 1995, among other films.

PAULETTE RICHARDS is an Associate Professor at Loyola University, New Orleans, USA, where she teaches African-American Literature and Creative Writing; author of *Terry McMillan* (1999), articles on French, Spanish, and Romance novels, translations in *Callaloo*, and papers on African-American Science Fiction for National Popular Culture Association conferences; an avid romance fan with a Certificate in Multimedia Production from Georgia Tech University.

HILARY SCHOR is an Associate Professor of English at the University of Southern California, Los Angeles; a specialist in Victorian and feminist studies; author of *Dickens and the Daughter of the House* (Cambridge University Press, 1999) and *Scheherezade in the Marketplace: Elizabeth Gaskell and the Forms of the Heroine's Plot* (1992). She has contributed a chapter to a critical study entitled *Great Expectations* (1995), and articles in *Carlyle Studies Annual*, *Dickens Studies Annual*, and *Novel*.

TARA GHOSHAL WALLACE is an Associate Professor of English at George Washington University, Washington, DC, editor of Fanny Burney's *A Busy Day* (Rutgers University Press, 1984), coeditor of *Women Critics, 1660–1820* (1995), and the author of *Jane Austen and Narrative Authority* (1995). She has also written articles on Austen, Walter Scott, and Dr. Johnson in *Eighteenth-Century Fiction*, *European Romantic Review*, *South Central Review*, and *Studies in the Novel*, among others.

Acknowledgments

This book is dedicated to the memory of Roger Gard, a contributor to this text, a respected scholar and teacher, and an eighteenth-century specialist whose critical books (*Jane Austen's Novels: The Art of Clarity* and *Emma and Persuasion*) continue to engage readers.

Our thanks go to professional screenplay writer Bill Witliff and novelist and screenplay writer Hugh Selby, Jr. for sharing with us their experience with their craft, and to Andrew Horton for his encouragement and support. Thanks too go to Erik Bauer, editor of *Creative Screenwriting*, Jim Shepard at Collectors Book Store, Hollywood, Hollywood Book & Poster Co., Miramax, MGM, Sony Pictures Classics, the BBC, and A&E for the photographs which grace this book. The front picture from *Sense and Sensibility* is with the permission of Columbia Pictures/Tristar Motion Picture Group; our thanks to Margarita Medina for arranging this permission.

Editors' note

Throughout the text, quotations from Jane Austen's novels are designated by book and chapter, with, for example, *Persuasion*, I.i referring to Book I, Chapter 1 of that work.

Introduction

Gina Macdonald and Andrew Macdonald

Timothy Corrigan has argued that the relationship between the two media of film and literature has "a history of ambivalence, confrontation, and mutual dependence,"[1] succinctly summing up the range of critical reaction to film productions of Jane Austen novels. The "mutual dependence" is evident: Austen films have brought her novels a far wider readership than she herself could have imagined. Undeniably, at least some viewers experience the films and then turn to the books for a deeper, richer, much more extended experience. Certainly, given modern proclivities, without the film as bait to attract more general readers and to help justify including the novels in school reading lists, Austen's readership might well be a far more limited, esoteric group than it is today. Perfectly worthy writers of Austen's time have been far less lucky than she; the enthusiasm for the redoubtable Henry Fielding that followed the wonderful Albert Finney screen version of *Tom Jones*[2] was brief and unsustainable once readers faced up to unfamiliar literary sensibilities and leisurely, extended texts. The story of Robinson Crusoe is made and remade (as in *Castaway* featuring Tom Hanks),[3] but it is safe to predict there will be no boom in Defoe book sales. Generally speaking, Austen is unique among writers of her period for none of her contemporaries transcend the narrow precincts of "classic literature" bookshelves. Modern interest in gender issues, of course, has much to do with this, allowing screenwriters to use her novels as valuable launching pads for filmic vehicles that track changing notions about women's roles in society, with the virtue of no copyright restrictions. The symbiosis between Jane Austen's prose fiction and its silver screen versions is a phenomenon worth exploring, for it is unique and rich in messages about current thinking, and not just about gender; the adaptations touch nerves concerning authenticity, social class, and literary sensibility.

The "ambivalence" that Corrigan sees in the literature–film relationship is also very true of scholarly attitudes toward the Austen films. One double-edged sword is Austen's feminism, the very ambiguity of which has attracted some screenwriters: is she or isn't she? Where does she

1

make her stand among the dug-in positions occupied in the current gender wars? There is room enough in the novels to swing the sword either way, cutting down male arrogance, duplicity, and outright chauvinism on one stroke yet also deftly drawing blood in the satire of women's ways and women's culture when the sword turns back. Ambivalence reigns in the readership as well: Austen's inspirational effect on feminist thought is apparent throughout the pages of this book, yet her readers also include the mirror images of feminists, legions of young women attracted by visions of traditional roles amid romantic settings. These latter are evident in myriads of fanzine reviews and Internet articles occupying Austen space; Pemberley is both a literary setting and a website, two manifestations of the imagination, traditional and contemporary, but mutually dependent. Ambivalence also permeates responses to the very filming of Austen's novels. Literary people – traditionalists and purists in the eyes of many practitioners of the youthful cinematic form – have at best felt reservations about the ability of a visual medium to measure up to the novels, regarding film as anything and everything from a presumptuous upstart to a manipulative commercialized instrument serving the lazy and vulgar. What begins as ambivalence can end as confrontation. The interjection, "But it wasn't as good as the book!" is often loaded with assumptions about culture high and low, and may reflect complex positioning of the speaker with regard to social class, education, taste, and sensibility. (Or the interjection may simply be true: many films, complex creations involving scores of makers and huge amounts of money, are not worthy of the unified prose which gave them life.)

If many literary people range from defensiveness to sure superiority when they evaluate a movie made from a literary work, film advocates tend to see adaptation differently. Just as theatrical producers and directors may understand dramatic scripts as instructions for putting on a play, and just as literary translators may regard the original work in the language of its creation as the jumping-off point for their own efforts, so film artists typically view the art of making a film from literature as a creative process in itself. The artist working in prose chooses her words and, editors aside, regards them as final. The artist working in celluloid dances a complex minuet involving the efforts of dozens of others, including craft workers with varying commitments and skill levels. Commands can be given, but results depend on cooperation and a joint vision. That film is a collaborative medium is driven home whenever the credits roll, but film people have a particular sensitivity to that fact: in the eyes of many producers and directors, it is a wonder that films get made at all.

Thus, the movement from literature to film is a translation from one medium to another, and, as with all translations, something is lost and something gained. Film advocates assert that the final film product has as much validity and worth as, say, the translation of a poem from one language to another: the words will never be the same as the original, yet a careful, imaginative treatment can shed new light on the text and open up a new readership that brings new perspectives and new responses to the source. Traditionalists uncomfortable with this concept assert that no brief film can measure up to the subtlety, complexity, and intertexuality of an Austen novel, that even lengthy mini-series have proven wanting, and that, perforce, screenwriters and directors must slash the text to a manageable size and scale down the complexity of Austen's subtle and complex narrative voice to produce a focused, manageable "product" suitable for the screen. For the orthodox, cutting even minor characters and scenes means the destruction of the original. Traditionalists may fall in love with a particular visual moment where the filmmakers "get it right," but inevitably they miss their personal reading of Austen. Roger Gard in "A Few Skeptical Thoughts on Jane Austen and Film" effectively voices this skepticism about the limits of film productions, and Jan Fergus in "Two *Mansfield Park*s: Purist and Postmodern" compares the 1983 and 1999 versions of *Mansfield Park*, seeking a formula for "purist" productions, ones that come as close as the film medium can to Austen's novelistic intent. Paulette Richards, in turn, in "Regency Romance Shadowing in the Visual Motifs of Roger Michell's *Persuasion*," finds film misrepresenting Austen, employing Regency romance conventions to make Austen familiar and even comprehensible to a mass audience. However, the remaining contributors argue forcefully that, whether or not the film versions of Austen's novels truly reflect her authentic world and vision, they are exciting and intriguing artistic works themselves, employing intertexuality and blending the commercial and the literary into a composite creative vision encompassing rich visual and aural experiences.

Herein, then, lies the "controversy" of which Corrigan spoke. Harriet Margolis in "Janeite Culture: What Does the Name 'Jane Austen' Authorize?" and Jocelyn Harris in "'Such a Transformation!' Translation, Imitation, and Intertextuality in Jane Austen On Screen" provide quite different but thoroughly informed takes on the controversy, raising and exploring the significant issues of translation versus imitation, problematic reader/viewer response, intertextuality, the profit motive, and exchange-value ethics. The chapters which follow extend the controversy in highly specific contexts. Penny Gay's "*Sense and Sensibility* in a Postfeminist World: Sisterhood is Still Powerful" and Tara Wallace's "Filming Romance: *Persuasion*" counter Jan Fergus's purist plea with a challenge for filmmakers to find the visual language and a reading of the original that will speak to modern viewing audiences. Agreeing with Gay and Wallace that the filming of Austen's novels is subject to the fashions of our time and that the process of adaptation demands a recognition of the historical distance between the original text and its new audience, Ellen Belton, in "Reimagining Jane Austen: The 1940 and 1995 Film Versions of *Pride and Prejudice*," explores the role of audience, culture, and time in affecting the celluloid vision. In "Emma, Interrupted: Speaking Jane Austen in Fiction and Film" Hilary Schor explores the change in narrative voices in the move from novel to screen, but finds Douglas McGrath's *Emma* to a surprising degree capturing the complexity of subjectivity and realism Austen's text (and narrative voices) provide to its canniest readers, leaving them, as does the novel, unsure of what they are hearing, caught up in the complexity of contradictory, interactive voices with several dimensions of meaning. In short, Schor's audacious claim is that a commercial filmmaker has successfully duplicated the rich experience of literature. David Monaghan, in *"Emma* and the Art of Adaptation," is less impressed by McGrath's *Emma* but also takes on the literary purists. Arguing against adaptations of Austen's novels made according to the conventions of the BBC classic drama house style, he defends the ITV/A&E *Emma* and *Clueless* as creative endeavors, new works of art that enrich appreciation and understanding of their source text.

This text begins with a contrarian pronouncement by Roger Gard, who argues a traditionalist position; it ends with a contrarian manifesto. John Mosier's "Clues for the Clueless" turns the controversy on its head, taking on both purists and their opposite numbers. Mosier looks back to European scholarly traditions to undercut the negativism of traditionalists with his assertion that "the primary objective of good adaptation, like that of any good interpretative reading of a text, is to make us go back to the text and reconsider it anew": filmmakers are simply doing what critics do, but in a more creative form. However, when he asserts that a basic measure used to evaluate an adaptation is the extent to which the filmmaker seems to understand the author, he distinguishes between fidelity to text and understanding, noting that a film can be faithful to the details and totally empty of the author's wit, irony, satire, and meaning. Authorial intention thus rears its shaggy head. Finally, when Mosier measures modern productions by whether the film is any good as film, or whether its interest is completely a function of its relation to the text, he finds all of the film productions of Austen wanting, except the two most on the periphery, *Clueless* and *Mansfield Park* (1999), and of these two, only *Clueless* is deemed both faithful to the spirit of Austen and good as a film, in and of itself.

The controversy over how to convert any piece of literature to a screenplay and then a film is an engaging one for scholars interested in the uniqueness of different media and the variety of ways available to artists to express their ideas. Andrew Davies, screenwriter of the 1996 ITV/A&E *Emma*, believes adaptations of Jane Austen require great restraint. "You can't change the actual story," he asserts. Despite this purist attitude, he admits that the scriptwriter must take "a certain amount of liberty," justifying this presumption as filling in "little gaps," especially where there are "hidden scenes . . . that Austen didn't get around to writing herself."[4] Here is authorial intention again: we know what she meant, so let's do it better than she did. Since the film must be coherent to communicate successfully with a mass audience, improvising with the original materials is required. Roger Michell, director of *Persuasion*, went further than filling in "little gaps"; lacking a unifying thematic middle, he found the center of his understanding of *Persuasion* in an age-old theme: "It's a Cinderella story," he asserts. "It's boy meets girl. Girl loses boy. Boy finds girl."[5] For director Ang Lee, the secret to a unified vision of *Sense and Sensibility* was his discovery of Jane Austen as "a wonderful painter of family rituals and social customs." Seeing in Austen's work qualities which he has tried to achieve in his own work enabled him to depict *Sense and Sensibility* as a combination of "warmhearted romance and drama with a sense of social satire." "Sense and sensibility, pride and prejudice, eat drink man woman – I like . . . getting to the bottom of life itself!" says Lee.[6] Where, we might be forgiven for asking, is Jane Austen in all this? We have come very close to the position screenwriter Bill Wittlif attributes to Texas writer J. Frank Dobie: "Every story belongs to whoever can tell it best."[7]

In a diametrically opposed fashion, Emma Thompson found the novel *Sense and Sensibility* "so complex" and so full of so many different stories "that bashing out a structure was the biggest labour." She reports that she would write a version which producer Lindsay Doran would then read; then either he would send her notes or they would "sit down together and talk out the problems." After crying for a while, she would then go back to work – a pattern repeated for three years. Ultimately, her approach was to find a thematic center that would provide a unity to the materials, in this case, the question of economic survival:

We plunge into their [the Dashwoods'] stories at a time when the whole question of survival is entering their lives because they don't have any money. When their father dies and they lose the family estate at Norland, they are edging towards the abyss of genteel poverty. If something happens and they lose what little they do have, there's nothing at all to fall back on, except the kindness of relations – an unreliable business at best. The whole question of finding somebody to marry becomes a great deal more essential to their financial and social survival.[8]

Thompson's approach was clearly most respectful of Austen's intention, but whether it produced a better end result than more cavalier improvisation we will leave to our contributors to sort out.

While screenwriters fret about character and coherence, some directors and producers obsess over details. Sue Birtwistle, producer of film versions of both *Pride and Prejudice* and *Emma*, compares filming a period drama to marshaling "a battle campaign," with all its potential for chaos and disaster.[9] Lindsay Doran, the producer of *Sense and Sensibility*, claims to have searched ten years to find a screenwriter who could translate Austen's combination of satire and romance equally well to the screen; Doran is tormented about being "true to the period," and worries, for example, that a beautiful little yellow flower in a scene with Emma Thompson and Hugh Grant riding horses "wasn't introduced into England until 1879," not really a problem of much literary moment.[10] In contrast, Diarmuid Lawrence, director of the 1996 ITV/A&E *Emma*, sees his job as a practical one: how to create the illusion of weather, season, and crowds:

If it's a blue sky, we can make it look autumnal, it's not really a problem. To make snow, we use a mixture of salt and foam. The foam is a bit of a problem when you run carriages over it, because it just comes up like soap bubbles. [In carriage scenes] you can't get as many people as you'd like in [the scene]. I find myself running along beside the coach trying to watch the actors.[11]

The many specialists involved in adapting a literary work to the screen have widely divergent agendas, not all of them aesthetic, literary, or intellectual. The cinema, as many of our contributors stress, is a collaborative medium, as complex in its teamwork as a symphony orchestra or an operatic production; what is seen by the audience is only a small part of the enterprise.

Novelist and screenwriter Hugh Selby, Jr., when asked how difficult it was to turn his novel *Requiem for a Dream* into a screenplay, replied that a screenwriter has to simply accept limits, as if doing a translation into a new language: screenwriters should try to get to the "essence" of the source text and amputate everything else. "This simply comes with the screenwriting territory," says Selby. In fact, the process of translating novel to screen necessitates "amputating" the book so much that most authors can't cope and admirers of the book feel that too much has been lost in the shift in medium. By its nature, says Selby, a screen treatment is an exterior or "voyeur" experience, and as a result much depiction of inner life must be cast aside. Besides, he goes on to note, there is something ineffable in the language of a good book, in the unspoken voice of the writer, something that cannot be carried onto the screen. Selby advises putting the goal of making a good film first and forgetting about being "true" to a literary text. Being true to the heart of the work, its essence, is, to him, of far more importance and value.[12]

By this definition of scriptwriting, Amy Heckerling's script for *Clueless* does what all good scripts should do, provide broad opportunities for actors, directors, set decorators, costume designers – the whole cast and crew – to realize a modern vision of Austen's original story. Heckerling sets up a surprisingly parallel milieu, develops a character that is both the object of satire and of sympathy, and then draws on parallels of plot, with the similarity in plot events relatively less important than the parallel settings – privileged and isolated worlds obsessed with status and manners – and parallel characters – immature young women moving from self-love to a more mature awareness of others. Heckerling looked back to *Emma* to find the present and to argue that the human condition, especially that of young people entering adult society, does not change. Yet, she evokes and satirizes every cliché of youthful California life. The power and staying power of *Clueless* comes from Heckerling's sense that people and place matter, that character and situation are meaningful. This intuitive and creative approach to translating literature to film is in direct contrast to the more historically respectful, restrained BBC productions that attempt a reconstruction of Austen's time and place. What is gained by a creative parallel is a new work of art, one resonant of an early masterpiece, yet one which retains its own character. Once again, however, we must ask: where is Jane Austen in this fresh milieu?

A source novel and film can echo back and forth in a satisfying way, their intertextual relationship reminding us of virtues in each medium that might remain unnoticed otherwise. The intimacy of Austen's narrative voice and of our recreation of her characters in the private theaters of our minds are not necessarily violated by seeing the collaborative visions of talented artists on screen: their Jane Austen may not be ours, but may speak to us nevertheless. We agree with John Mosier's dictum that a good adaptation should take us back to the original work – what more could we ask from a couple of hours of entertainment than to be reintroduced to past pleasures with a new perspective?

NOTES

1 Timothy Corrigan, *Film and Literature: An Introduction and Reader* (Upper Saddle River, NJ: Prentice Hall, 1999): 1.
2 *Tom Jones*, Writers Henry Fielding and John Osborne, Director Tony Richardson. United Artists, 1963.
3 *Castaway*, Writer William Broyles, Jr., Director Robert Zemeckis. Twentieth Century Fox, 2000.
4 David Goldman, "Jane Austen's *Emma*: Meet the Production Team" (1996): www.pemberley.com/janeausten
5 "Lindsay Duran [*sic*]" at www.archive.salon.com

6 Ibid.
7 Personal communication, 2000.
8 Emma Thompson, *The "Sense and Sensibility" Screenplay and Diaries: Bringing Jane Austen's Novel to Film* (London: Bloomsbury, 1995).
9 "Lindsay Duran."
10 Ibid.
11 Goldman, "Meet the Team."
12 Personal communication, 2000.

1 Short "takes" on Austen: summarizing the controversy between literary purists and film enthusiasts

The following three short essays briefly and clearly establish the boundaries of the academic argument over Jane Austen's novels made into film, with Professor Roger Gard taking the conservative, or purist, position, with New Zealand filmmaker and scriptwriter Gaylene Preston taking the liberal, film community position, and with Kate Bowles looking to the future and the ways in which technology will change our relationship to Jane Austen, the historical figure, and her works, which speak to us today in ways Austen never imagined. The longer essays which comprise this text explore these broad questions, answering them through the case studies of individual novels and the film productions associated with them.

Roger Gard's eloquent defense of the uniqueness of literary experience is both dismissive of film's claims – the "artistic paucity of mere looking" at surfaces – and systematic in enumerating the special gifts of prose – at creating subtlety and perspective, psychological deftness, irony, and a sense of context in time. Gard articulates what most impassioned readers feel after viewing a screen version of a favorite work; appearances may be wonderfully particularized (though at a great loss to imagination and variety), plot may be dutifully unfolded in basic outline, but the essence of what makes the work worthy is lost, or at least, sadly depleted. Professor Gard's stout defense will stand for one pole in the discussions which follow, the high ground of literary sensibility, which many feel can only be approached, not occupied, by cinema.

As a filmmaker, Gaylene Preston speaks of Jane Austen finding the characters "directly living and breathing" in the director's "framed images." The artistic perspective is that of the theater rather than of the literary experience, the prose exposition. This stance is a defensible position given Austen's frequently remarked-on theatricality, her palpable "voice," and even the historical fact of her domestic "shows." As in great pictorial art, exteriors capture inner states; the heart of the matter inhabits the look of people and things. Film captures these surfaces perfectly, even controlling the "thespian posturing" of the boards.

Kate Bowles asks a question for the future: will networked communication change everything, including our roles as readers and viewers of literature and film? (The question has been asked before about other presumed paradigm shifts, usually with muddled answers.) The Internet negates the passivity of "audience," creating participatory, egalitarian connections between "art" and "consumers"; while, as Roger Gard argues, film may dilute the essence of a text down to mass-culture tastes, shared electronic dissemination creates a new beast entirely. As Bowles perceptively points out, fandom challenges even the commercialization that has long been the ultimate literary rebuke of the movies. Fandom is hardly new, existing in recognizable forms in Austen's time – will the Internet empower it and transform its progenitors?

A few skeptical thoughts on Jane Austen and film

Roger Gard

The tremendous success the camera has with appearances can be a great asset – for instance, in giving instantaneous and powerful landscapes, and so on, in place of lengthy Walter Scott-style descriptions – but this asset, even in simple storytelling – let alone the intertwined narratives of complex souls – is limited and can distort. It is so difficult not to be bowled over by the glamor and instant apparent reality of vivid shots of striking people in beautiful places (or ugly ones for that matter) that the artistic paucity of mere looking is too easily forgotten.

Of course, films also use music to suggest, direct, and enhance emotion, often quite potently; and dialogue can be lifted straight from the text to specify dramatically. But any filmmaker will quickly tell you that the camera is King.

The crucial difficulty lies in this camera's inability to discriminate easily and swiftly within a given appearance. Because of this, the adaptation of subtler effects is very hard to achieve. Moreover, the possible advantages of a camera-enforced objectivity are duly paid for by the difficulties of establishing a particular point of view. The camera has no narrative voice.

These drawbacks are felt to be particularly acute, and damaging, when one considers the clumsiness of psychological notation in anything other than words. Not only in famous direct insights such as, "It darted through her with the speed of an arrow, that Mr. Knightley must marry no one but herself!" (*Emma*: III.xi) – how do you film that? – but in all those glittering pages of strong and delicate exposition through free indirect speech, a resource so brilliantly developed by Jane Austen.

But there are hundreds of other ways in which pictures can't do easily what language does easily. They can't establish an ironic context: "It is a truth universally acknowledged, that a single man in possession of a good fortune, must be in want of a wife" (*Pride and Prejudice* I.i). You could use a voice-over, but in pictures the irony has to be much simpler even than that.

Pictures cannot, while contextualizing, manage time, or summarize. Consider the bravura opening of *Mansfield Park*:

About thirty years ago, a Miss Maria Ward of Huntingdon, with only seven thousand pounds, had the good luck to captivate Sir Thomas Bertram of Mansfield Park, in the county of Northampton, and to be thereby raised to the rank of a baronet's lady, with all the comforts and consequence of an handsome house and large income. All Huntingdon exclaimed at the greatness of the match, and her uncle, the lawyer, himself, allowed her to be at least three thousand pounds short of any equitable claim to it . . . But there certainly are not so many men of large fortune in the world, as there are pretty women to deserve them. Miss Ward, at the end of half a dozen years, found herself obliged to be attached to the Rev. Mr. Norris, a friend of her brother-in-law, with scarcely any private fortune, and Miss Frances fared yet worse . . . Miss Frances married, in the common phrase, to disoblige her family, and by fixing on a Lieutenant of Marines . . . did it very thoroughly. (I.i)

The deft authoritative larger span with all its rich implications – how lumbering, how impossibly drawn out, an attempt to film this would be!

Pictures can tell only of the surface of things. Even when visual phenomena themselves are in question, a mere picture of them may tell us little or nothing. We need the associations from inside and outside the novel that words convey; as, for example, in *Mansfield Park* again, when we read the touching description of poor Fanny's "nest of comforts" in the East Room, where "Every thing was a friend" – her transparencies of Tintern Abbey, her sketch of brother William's ship, HMS *Antwerp*, and a "collection of family profiles thought unworthy of being anywhere else" (I.xvi).

The mess of things that pictures can't easily do – or can do only so cumbersomely as to be prohibitive in some way or other – seems to me dauntingly large. They can't make jokes, or pun, or allude to the Bible, or Shakespeare or Cowper; their pace is very inflexible – they can't easily be fleeting or dismissive; they can't comment; they can't say things like "Let other pens dwell on guilt and misery"; they can't affectionately adjust attitudes by following that up with "my Fanny" – they just don't have a voice; they can't span the years; they can't condense; they can't moralize; they can't conduct sustained arguments without cluttering the mind with irrelevant visual detail – that chair, that dress, that tree are always demanding equal attention unless we're to be shown mere talking heads; their bold definiteness and specificity – their great virtue, that is – is also a hand of stone, it leaves no room for mystery, for imagination about, for example, someone's appearance, or for reflection about the nuances of their actions and motives. However good the casting and the acting, that particular face or presence may seem wrong, or limited. And so on.

Finally, however much one quite enjoys this or that filmed piece with a title from Jane Austen (like the BBC's 1995 *Pride and Prejudice*), and however excited one temporarily gets at there being a large public out there doing the same, isn't it unfortunately the case that none of them remains in the mind as even a minor work of art?

It is surely no surprise that what is often held to be the best film adaptation is of Austen's least complex work, *Sense and Sensibility* – though I suspect that the palm should go to *Clueless*, precisely because it abandons all pretensions to be more than a good-natured romp.

It is a truth widely acknowledged that mediocre books often make good film or television; great books do exactly the same.

Sense and Sensibility: Ang Lee's sensitive screen interpretation of Jane Austen

Gaylene Preston

It is at once ironic and somehow predictable that it takes a male Chinese director to capture on film the overriding constrictions and formality of the world Jane Austen's characters inhabit. In the film *Sense and Sensibility*, aided by Emma Thompson's innovative script, Ang Lee presents a painfully small community preoccupied with unspoken social rules, which to modern eyes would be almost laughable if the price paid for them by the characters on screen were not so high. Their larger world outside the cold little borrowed cottage is made smaller and the range of social choices frighteningly constrictive. The framed images of a hopeful mother and a protective aunt nervously watching the seedling romance of their young charges from closed walls, the claustrophobic sets, and the visual contrasts of wealth with genteel poverty bring to life the harsh social realities of daily life, and the complex interplay of decorum, propriety, class, and desire. England has never looked damper or greener or so English.

Unlike many Jane Austen adaptations to the screen, the actors do not appear to be carrying the posthumous weight of the great Jane Austen. The heavy responsibility of transposing an important literary work does

1. Elinor Dashwood (Emma Thompson) with Edward Ferrars (Hugh Grant) from Columbia Pictures/TriStar Pictures' 1995 *Sense and Sensibility*

not taint this quietly passionate rendering of an inviting and deeply human story. Sedately attired, her body language tightly controlled, Emma Thompson communicates the quiet burden of sense and restraint as effectively as Kate Winslet, with her bouncing curls, lush clothing, pastel shades, dramatic intonations, and rippling emotion, embodies sensibility. The performances don't reek of self-conscious thespian posturing. We get Jane Austen's characters directly living and breathing. *Sense and Sensibility* visibly inhabits the very heart of the piece, defining every characteristic.

What creates this lively art, this bringing-to-life of centuries-old prose? It is more than performance, though of course the hard-and-fast line between prose and its staging would have been blurred in Jane Austen's time by public reading aloud, group theatricals, and other failures to maintain an opposition between solitary reading and the spoken word. Our time sees such reading as a privilege of the individual; earlier periods shared poetry, printed plays, and even parts of novels as family, church, and community reading events, opportunities for an almost sensual enjoyment of language. (The pleasures of John Milton's *Paradise Lost*, for example, can only be fully experienced through a dramatic reading of text.) But what of Austen's famous narrative voice, which perforce disappears on screen except in brief voice-overs? What equivalent can cinema claim?

Professor Gard speaks of "the paucity of mere looking," the fact that even vivid film shots may inhabit the memory only temporarily. Certainly, films can be limited in scope and intensity, just as novels can be. However, the process of seeing a projected image (as opposed to the self-created image projected in the theater of the mind) need not be dismissed with "mere." The carefully wrought images created by artists over the centuries inhabit the memory of every student of European art, and meet and surpass all Professor Gard's tests of subtlety, wit, irony, and so on. True, some filmmakers scant the visual in favor of plot and dialogue, but not Ang Lee, or Douglas McGrath, whose lushly shot *Emma* makes the decor speak louder than words. Some directors are famously painterly, drawing as much inspiration from the picture gallery as from the reading room.

The best painterly filmmakers, in fact, go beyond showing us what to look at to show us how to look. By revealing and highlighting the unexamined that surrounds us in our everyday life, they do exactly what Jane Austen's prose does in the social arena, bring to notice manners and behavior. While all filmmaking is collaborative, depending on location scouts, set dressers, musicians, costumers, make-up artists, cameramen, and so on, the shaping force of the director's vision gives a "look" that is as distinctive and personal as a prose style and one that, like such a style, can convey a worldview.

Actors too are part of the look of a film. Casting is simply the beginning of a process that can release a full palette of effects, depending on the complex and mysterious synergies of acting with and against others in the service of a common vision. Like a sentence, paragraph, or chapter, unforeseen chemistries can make a scene work or fail, but the effects can be as rich as prose, and can withstand repeated viewings. That these processes are collaborative and public, as opposed to the singularity and privacy of prose read silently, should not trouble us. The effects may be different, but they offer the same wealth as reading does – only in a different medium.

Commodifying Austen: the Janeite culture of the Internet and commercialization through product and television series spinoffs

Kate Bowles

> *Before I got on-line, I thought writing fan fiction was as fundamental to anyone with an imagination as eating chocolate is to anyone with a mouth . . . It seemed to me the most natural thing in the world to want more of what I liked.*[1]

Film and television adaptations of Jane Austen's novels are not new; neither is the Internet any longer the novelty that it was in the early 1990s. The Internet in particular has shifted its weight from being primarily a medium of communication to being an exponentially expanding networked archive of data. It's the global superstore of the information age, but as governments, moral lobbyists, and commercial entrepreneurs are discovering, the Internet is wholly dependent on *use*, and apparently independent of the normal rules of cultural, industrial, and economic *production*. Economic, political, and social theories fall short of describing its range; in terms of cultural and media studies, it is neither unequivocally mass culture nor popular culture. Networked communication has not done away with real political and social power, but it has transformed the way in which these can be talked about; theories which depended narratively on category discriminations between producers and consumers, artists and audiences, buyers and sellers, governments and the governed, find themselves in a kind of epistemological crisis. Has everything changed? Or has the Internet revealed the ways in which the whole gamut of interpretive positions – developed throughout the nineteenth and twentieth centuries for explaining the way things are – were less adequate to the task than we thought?

This essay confronts these questions by rethinking the assumption that the cycle of Austen screen adaptations at the end of the 1990s produced an effect which retro-nostalgic Marxism seems to call "commodification," and which may or may not be related to Deborah Kaplan's observation that Hollywood has "harlequinized" Jane Austen.[2] True, adaptation from the novel form to the screen media has repackaged Austen's elegant, detailed, ironic tales, making plot more important than narrative, displacing withering authorial tone with dialogue, partially decommissioning the author's critique of eighteenth-century materialism by making a fetish of costuming and set design, and selectively buffing up her subtle characterization with the gleam of small-screen stardom. While the Internet has greatly expanded the territory and potential of scholarly exchange, making archives of annotated texts and historically contextual information available without involving the tyranny of travel, it has at the same time played host to that growing horde of fans for whom the dark and difficult nature of misunderstood Mr. Darcy seems inseparable from the mop-headed appeal of Colin Firth. Worse, the Internet has actively encouraged fans to engage in the self-publication of fan fiction, sequelization, pastiche, and general amateur expansion of the *œuvre*. It is one thing for family members and scholarly historians to recover an author's juvenilia and unfinished works, and perhaps even for established writers to have a go at finishing them off; quite another for a new generation of enthusiasts for whom Jane Austen is synonymous with film and television to condemn her to the hamster-wheel of posthumous productivity, publication (if not quality) guaranteed.

At first glance, therefore, it does indeed seem that, thanks in particular to popular television serialization and global electronic Janeitism, Austen has become the victim of her own celebrity. What the laws of trademark and copyright recognize as moral ownership of ideas is being convincingly violated in her case. From this position, it's hardly a stretch to suggest that Austen has not been so much commercialized as floated, and the multiple shareholders of Austen Inc. are engaged in a substantial restructuring of the company. However, as James Collins argues in his persuasive rethink of Jamesonian theories of the postmodern:

> The contention that commodification suddenly tainted all cultural production starting somewhere in the nineteenth century, and then just plain ruined it in the twentieth century, is fraught with a number of historical problems. The argument that art has become commodified, and therefore less aesthetically and politically pleasing than it had been before, has been made by innumerable critics from a wide variety of critical perspectives and has been located, interestingly enough, at different time periods . . . Such discrepancies suggest that the impact of commodification is hardly as far-reaching or one-dimensional as many would have it, since its impact and temporal dimensions appear to depend more on the scenario of the historian than any kind of *episteme*-shattering moment in the evolution of material production.[3]

I am substantially in agreement with Collins here: if commodification exists, it is in the eye of the beholder. It's a political metaphorization of change as a process of transforming the *essence* of a thing under specific (regrettable) material and economic conditions, whereas what seems more likely is that the indeterminability of meaning and cultural value is always already part of that essence. For example, I am neither an Austen scholar nor an Austen fan, but this does not mean that the idea "Jane Austen" fails to convey meaning to me, nor that that meaning is less dynamic, volatile, or interesting than others. This personal scenario will of

course predispose me differently than others on the matter of commercialization or harlequinization – but it may not necessarily predispose me
less, as I am certainly not proposing here the model of the disinterested
ethnographer of others' enthusiasms and cultural practices. Thanks in
larger part to Emma Thompson, the BBC, Colin Firth, and the Internet
than to the works of Jane Austen herself, disinterest is not an option. For
me, as for all fans and non-fans, it's a matter of working out where and
how my interest is being mediated, and for whose benefit.

With this as my scenario, I set off in search of Jane Austen on the
Internet. Sifting through hundreds of references to discussion sites,
archive sites, large scholarly sites maintained on expensive university
servers, individual school and college study sites, small personal sites
constructed by amateur readers for other readers, reviews of sites, jour-
nalistic mentions of sites, and sites which gateway to all the other sites
in the manner which dooms all online searches to the labyrinth of self-
referentiality, I kept finding myself reading the same two small consoling
pieces of advice: "The Republic of Pemberley: Your haven in a world
programmed to misunderstand obsession with things Austen," and "No,
you've not lost your way. You remain safe, within the borders of the
Republic of Pemberley." Indeed, at times during my search it seemed
that the Republic of Pemberley[4] was exerting the same lure as the Hotel
California: you can check out, but you can never leave. Each time I returned, the site's discreet but personalized welcome, noting how long it
had been since my last visit and summarizing the traffic since then, reminded me that panoptical surveillance is as much a means to feeling in
control, as a means of being controlled: Foucault meets the cookie monster. It is in large part this capacity to use Internet technology so fluently
and yet so discreetly that makes the Republic of Pemberley one of the
most effectively registered, regularly revised, well-regulated, and productive amateur sites on the Internet dedicated to Jane Austen fandom.

Since its "secession" from the now defunct Internet discussion list
Austen-L in July 1996,[5] the Republic of Pemberley has offered a generous
and reassuring haven to Austen fans stumbling through the Internet in
search of quick answers to frequently asked questions, and a community
of like-minded enthusiasts ("we tightly define the appeal of the site to Jane
Austen obsessives").[6] First impressions count on the Internet, and the
Republic of Pemberley works hard to control its reputation as both serious
and easy-going, exclusionary and welcoming. Its FAQ (Frequently Asked
Questions) makes clear that this is a community, not a service: there are
strict policies on posting and cross-posting; on topic appropriateness and
safety for minors; on helping with homework; on etiquette as much as
netiquette. It tackles the harlequinization slur head on: "The roots of

this community were a support group for people addicted to P&P2 ... because we wanted to feel free to gush. It's since become something more than that; however, we still honor our gushing roots, and the Austen-for-the-masses feel that a demonstrative love of the adaptations brings to the site."[7] Nevertheless, the deliberate, ironic, and playful deployment of an Austenesque pastiche of social regulation means that this populist freedom to gush at TV adaptations is not a free-for-all; the community's blue marbled charter members have, in their own words,

> a bit of an attitude, which could be characterized as polite with a bite. We mirac-ulously manage, even within this odd framework, to remain one of the most civil places on the Internet, a distinction we prize, but one which is cultivated through an emulation of Jane Austen's own honest, moral and forthright ways, as opposed to sprinkling artificial sweeteners on our words.[8]

None of this so far amounts to much evidence of commercialization. The nearest that the Republic swings in this direction is in its sponsorship and co-promotion arrangements with Amazon.com, who return a small percentage of all sales achieved via Pemberley links, to help this volunteer community defray its server traffic costs. But I suspect that the real provo-cation of the Republic of Pemberley to the more puritanical traditions of scholarly Janeitism (greater even than the very metaphorically challenged site map, which reconceptualizes the Pemberley estate as a treasure is-land republic) may be its expansion into the territory made so unpopular by Emma Tennant and others: what literary scholarship calls sequeliza-tion, postmodern theory calls pastiche, and the Internet calls fanfic, or fan fiction. A very substantial part of the site is given over to publishing, discussing and then archiving community members' own epistolary, nov-elish, undoubtedly harlequinesque, even soap-operatic speculations as to the further life of Jane Austen's characters beyond the closed narratives of her original novels. Of course, this practice is not new; Jane Austen herself indulged in it.[9] It is a process of renovation, and as a characteristic of media fandom it has provided one of the clearest rebukes to the myth of the fan as passive, indifferent cultural dupe.

Henry Jenkins's extensive work on television fandom defines this play in the field of cultural production as "textual poaching," following de Certeau, and like many others, he identifies in it a carnivalesque tradi-tion of dodging, and defying authority – in the cases he has studied, this means the hardcore legal authority of copyright, big business, and cor-porate protection of media product. Jenkins's fans stand up to Lucasfilm and Paramount, asserting their participatory right to rethink the relation-ship between *Star Trek* or *Star Wars* characters in sexual terms. It is logical for our sympathies to lie with the little guy in this case. But the question

of who wins, who loses, who is violated, and who is loyal is far more perplexing when it comes to electronic self-publication of twentieth-century
adaptations of the work of a long-dead English novelist. Jane Austen is
scarcely a multinational media corporation with corporate lawyers swing-
ing to her defense. The struggle here seems to be between fans and fans –
literary fans, scholarly fans, television fans. The accusation that Jane
Austen has been commercialized may turn out to be a way of avoiding a much less dignified dispute over the moral quality of interpretation,
as Jenkins observes:

Fan interpretive practice differs from that fostered by the educational system and
preferred by bourgeois culture not simply in its object choices or in the degree of
its intensity, but often in the types of reading skills it employs, in the ways that
fans approach texts. From the perspective of dominant taste, fans appear to be
frighteningly out of control, undisciplined and unrepentant, rogue readers.[10]

It is in fact the very practices of fandom that rebuke the accusation of
commercialization. As Jenkins has also recognized, fandom's impetus is
toward networking, sharing, and collaboration rather than marketing,
sales, and cash; fandom explicitly challenges the proprietorial rights of
some to profit at the expense of others.[11]

In return, fandom is challenged by what amounts to a crisis of
legitimation.[12] Pierre Bourdieu's close analysis of the field of cultural
production as a site of struggle over meaning, identity, and value, rather
than simply a site of mechanistic output, positions the dispute over who
counts as a writer or an artist as central to this struggle:

The artistic field is a *universe of belief*. Cultural production distinguishes itself
from the production of the most common objects in that it must produce not
only the object in its materiality, but also the value of this object, that is, the
recognition of artistic legitimacy. This is inseparable from the production of the
artist or the writer as artist or writer, in other words, as a creator of value.[13]

However, as Bourdieu further argues, the struggle does not stop once it
is decided who qualifies as a writer, but continues into a struggle over
the value of an audience: "The hierarchy by degree of real or supposed
dependence on audience, success or the economy itself overlaps with
another one, which reflects the degree of specific consecration of the
audience, that is, its 'cultural' quality and its supposed distance from the
centre of the specific values".[14] In these two statements, Bourdieu offers
a useful way of seeing through the politico-economic conspiracy theory of
commodification to a much more primitive struggle over cultural power.
What is at stake when fans of the second film production of *Pride and
Prejudice* (*P&P2*) gather to gush on the Internet is their legitimacy as true
Janeites, as both fan-consumers and fan-renovators of the mediated Jane.

Furthermore, Bourdieu slyly takes a third helpful step in suggesting why it is that these intergenerational contestations represent such a tactical challenge to the old guard: "One of the difficulties of orthodox defense against heretical transformation of the field by a redefinition of the tacit or explicit terms of entry is the fact that polemics imply a form of recognition; adversaries whom one would prefer to destroy by ignoring them cannot be combated without consecrating them."[15]

The fourth and final elaboration of this crisis of identity, in terms of the paradoxical *textual* status of the pastiched copy, comes from art historian and philosopher Arthur C. Danto, reflecting on the example of Hans van Meegeren, "the remarkable forger of Vermeers in the 1940s.'[16] According to Danto, van Meegeren's pique at not being recognized as a great painter in his own right led him to produce paintings which were not direct copies of existing Vermeers, but which were so convincingly Vermeerish that fooled Vermeer experts would be compelled to grant van Meegeren the same status as Vermeer. However, as Danto points out, the march of art history had already condemned van Meegeren's efforts to establish his own painterly reputation by these means, in that by the 1940s it was no longer possible to recapture the essence of being Vermeer in the seventeenth century, only to reproduce Vermeerishness as a twentieth-century quotation from the past, at best a small conceptual success in the field of postmodern cultural production. Elsewhere, Danto suggests provocatively that, although the motives have changed, the idea of a material copy of something which asks to be taken seriously in a different ontological category to the original has become a commonplace of art, to the extent that history as a meaningful guarantor of the value of things is done with: "To say that history is over is to say that there is no longer a pale of history for works of art to fall outside of. Everything is possible. Anything can be art." Far from being pessimistic about this, however, Danto remains upbeat, populist, even perhaps gushing: "But the situation is far from bleak... Rather, it inaugurates the greatest era of freedom art has ever known."[17]

So does the metaphorical muddle of the self-avowedly conservative republican treasure island of Pemberley signal the end of the history of great works being written only by great, sanctioned writers, appreciated only by audiences endowed with certain, sanctioned literacies? With so many new reader-writers emboldened by the accessibility and intimacy of television adaptations, all wanting more of what they like, in Clerc's terms, and throwing themselves at the task of extending even the works which Austen herself had assumed to be complete, it does seem that anything can now be sufficiently Austenesque to meet the needs of Austen's fans. If so, then isn't this the greatest era of freedom Janeitism has ever known?

Of course, it is a flippant and unfair question. However, at the heart of it lies the proposition that the reason Janeitism on the Internet is after all not fully conducive to commercial interests is because fandom is not mere consumerism – it is the game of cultural production itself.

NOTES

1 Susan Clerc, "Estrogen Brigades and 'Big Tits' Threads: Media Fandom On-line and Off," in *The Cybercultures Reader*, eds. L. Cherny and E. Reba Weise (London: Routledge, 2000): 218.
2 Deborah Kaplan, *Jane Austen among Women* (Baltimore, MD: Johns Hopkins University Press, 1992).
3 James Collins, "Jane Reactions," *Vogue* (January 1996): 124–125.
4 www.pemberley.com
5 Republic of Pemberley, FAQ ("Frequently Asked Questions"): 2.
6 FAQ: 3.
7 FAQ: 4.
8 FAQ: 3.
9 www.pemberley.com
10 Henry Jenkins, *Textual Poachers: Television Fans and Participatory Culture* (New York: Routledge, 1992): 18.
11 Ibid.: 279.
12 Jim Collins, *Unknown Cultures: Popular Culture and Post-Modernism* (New York: Routledge, 1989): 2.
13 Pierre Bourdieu, *Distinction: A Social Critique of the Judgement of Taste* (1979; London: Routledge, 1984): 164.
14 Ibid.: 46.
15 Ibid.: 42.
16 Arthur C. Danto, *After the End of Art: Contemporary Art and the Pale of History* (Princeton, NJ: Princeton University Press, 1997): 206.
17 Ibid.: 114.

2 Janeite culture: what does the name "Jane Austen" authorize?

Harriet Margolis

"I can't guarantee that Janeite business, excep' 'e never told a lie since 'e was six. 'Is sister told me so. What do you think?"

"He isn't likely to have made it up out of his own head," I replied.

"But people don't get so crazy-fond o' books as all that, do they? 'E's made 'is sister try to read 'em."

Rudyard Kipling, "The Janeites"[1]

Opinions express values, and values may change, but where do we learn them in the first place?

A study of her heroes shows that Jane Austen changed her opinion of gentlemanly deportment, concluding that the active life of service to others should be most valued. From valuing, in principle, the life of leisure because it was necessary to a gentleman's development as a model for lesser citizens, she came to value the active life of industrious service to others.[2] Austen's governing principles of life were generally those espoused and promulgated by the influential conduct books of her youth. Such books, unlike the novels of their time, taught young women how to behave properly as well as told women what society expected of them. From such books Austen learned what her society respected and valued. In contrast, then, as now, many people have expressed concern that young women will be misled by what they read in novels, especially since some novels – romances, for example (then and now) – are unrealistic and may lead to false expectations of what life offers. Besides, reading such novels is a waste of time that could be better spent in practical activities affecting real people in the real world.

Or is it? This essay explores what some people value and why, specifically, the values currently associated with Jane Austen's name and the reasons these associations make her name a valuable commodity.[3] Why, on the one hand, are some people horrified when current adaptations show more sexually explicit material than Austen herself provides, or when these adaptations are marketed in ways that evoke romance novel packaging? Why, on the other hand, is it amusing as well as apt that Jim Abrahams – whose films have satirically commented on current media fads since *The Kentucky Fried Movie* (1977) – entitles a film with no obvious Austen connection *Jane Austen's Mafia* (1998)?[4] The one extreme sets up Austen as canonic material to be treated reverentially; the other sees Austen as cannon fodder for pop culture comedy. Perhaps more accurately, the second extreme sees the phenomenon of Austen adaptations for what it is: an effort to capitalize on people's desire for a stable, recognizable world – a cultured world – such as we associate with Austen, whose world was guided by rules for proper conduct and social structures determining people's relations, on the basis of which one can identify good and bad characters (however charming a Willoughby or a Wickham might be).

Austen wrote at a time when novels themselves had an ambiguous cultural status. Condemned at least for being a waste of time and at worst for inculcating immoral behavior, false hopes, and unrealistic expectations, novels were perceived as particularly bad influences on young women.[5] Over time, moralists, Platonists, and others opposed to escape into fiction have had to cede ground. Novels have gained in social status; certainly, they are no longer seen as being particularly dangerous to women. They have even come to be held in higher esteem than other forms of leisure-time activities, as, for example, when women speak of reading romance novels as being a more valuable activity than watching television.[6]

Of course, Austen's novels are nothing like women's romance novels. Or are they? They seem to be almost as popular, along with their television and film adaptations, and their audiences, while not excluding males (neither do women's romance novels), are predominantly female. It isn't even safe to generalize about such things as educational background, since Ph.D.s read romances and nonreaders enjoy the Austen adaptations. Both phenomena – the popularity of women's romance novels and the Austen adaptations – are sufficiently complex to reward investigation; investigation into the two phenomena in tandem also turns out to be rewarding.

Feminist scholars from various disciplines have considered women's romance novels, sometimes inquiring into and exploring, rather than condemning, a phenomenon that encompasses a diversity of writers, readers, and novels. Yet, several authors in *Jane Austen in Hollywood*[7] criticize some of the more recent Austen adaptations for their "harlequinization" of Austen's heroes. "Harlequin," or "Mills and Boon," as these novels are known outside the States, once referred to a specific type of book, but are now applied by non-cognoscenti to other books that do and do not share common characteristics. Though recognizing many of the nuances of the phenomenon, I shall largely ignore them in order to refer to the broad phenomenon of women's romance novels as such, by which I shall mean (unless otherwise indicated) the entire phenomenon, united by underlying assumptions about ethical behavior played out in domestic settings in terms of heterosexual romance. Generally, the "harlequins" have been denigrated for failing to satisfy many of the evaluative criteria by which Austen's novels are academically judged to be successful. Romance novels are bad because they are mass-produced, formulaic, limited in scope, accepting of a patriarchal status quo, overly concerned with sex, almost exclusively concerned with heterosexual sex, and appealing only to an unintelligent readership incapable of appreciating better writing. In 1987 an unsympathetic male editor working for Harlequin even accused romance novels of the near-impossible in the postmodern era: the absence of irony.[8]

Some of these criticisms are untrue, and the others are at least debatable, but the point is that such criticism derives from a system of values embedded within an ideology to which Jane Austen herself arguably did and did not subscribe. The aesthetic standard this ideology generates has a history of being unkind to women's work. If one approaches the women's romance novel phenomenon in other terms – for example, via the discourse of use-value and exchange-value ethics that figures significantly in Austen's novels as well as in women's romance novels – they easily score higher.

After all, romance novels usually focus on a female protagonist – she is the center of the universe – and they do so at some crucial moment in that character's life when her relations with the world around her are about to undergo as significant a change as the change in her sense of self, of her own identity.[9] Her decisions pretty consistently rest on a sense of moral behavior that can be associated with use-value ethics rather than exchange-value ethics. That is, the good characters value people's happiness and well-being and often base decisions on how other people will be affected, while the bad characters evaluate people and objects in materialistic terms, selfishly preferring potential personal gain over communal benefit or consideration for other individuals.

Romance author and Ph.D. Jennifer Crusie Smith, among others, declares women's romance novels to be actively feminist: "The romance heroine not only acts and wins, she discovers a new sense of self, a new sense of what it means to be female as she struggles through her story, and so does the romance reader as she reads it."[10] Often such characters must assert themselves in the face of male attitudes that assume an exchange-value-based behavior; in other words, the novels set up an opposition between two value systems, each associated with gender as well as class. Thus, if "aesthetic value . . . [coincides] with social value," as David Monaghan asserts,[11] then the women's romance novels should rate high. In fact, a type of ideological ambiguity associated with women's romance novels (roughly equivalent to an opposition to the effects of capitalism on human interaction) can also be found in Austen's novels. For example, John Wiltshire describes *Emma* as uniting "erotic longing . . . with a conservative political and social agenda."[12] Consequently, there is neither contradiction nor dishonor in arguing for similarities between Austen's novels and contemporary women's romance novels.

In fact, when Deborah Kaplan mocks those apparently oxymoronic Austen admirers who argue that contemporary women's romance novels trace their lineage back to Austen – "Jane Austen as one of the mothers of the Harlequin or Silhouette novel? This genealogy should amuse many of Austen's admirers, who know her novels to be much more culturally and linguistically complex than the mass-market romance"[13] – she is merely expressing an opinion, one that likely originates in a learned distinction between high and low culture, often associated with medium of delivery as well as subject matter and style.[14] It is a distinction prepared to condemn one text simply for appearing on television and to praise another for appearing in print. It holds that cultural and linguistic complexity are clear-cut characteristics of works of art waiting to be revealed by sensitive and/or well-trained scholar-critics. It accepts tradition, and because tradition is associated with a male-dominated past, it tends to reject interventions by women who may even work within the tradition yet manage to challenge it. Worst of all, it asserts the validity of one opinion over another, without justifying that validity, because it refuses to acknowledge that what is at issue is merely a matter of opinion.

If authors criticize Austen adaptations for harlequinizing Austen, then they must think that the adaptations have in some way betrayed Austen's intentions. As this essay's epigraph from Kipling suggests, being "so crazy-fond o' books" as virtually to idolize them is not only not a good thing, it is the sort of thing that Austen herself would make sport of. The possibility also exists that if these phenomenally successful adaptations have harlequinized the Austen novels, such changes have even been enabled by similarities of some sort that connect the Austen novels with our contemporary phenomenon of women's romance novels. The greatest similarity has to do with gender, power, and relations, all perceived from a female point of view.

The most significant common factor is that both groups of novels consider a world of women's concerns, framed by the perspective of use-value ethics. The success of both the current women's romance novel phenomenon and the phenomenon of current Austen adaptations derives from this grounding in use-value ethics. The name "Jane Austen" in front of one of her adaptations assures audiences of such a worldview. Her name even carries over into other films that explore the distinction between use-value and exchange-value ethics in situations far from nineteenth-century British settings. For example, Austen's name is invoked in Nora Ephron's *You've Got Mail*,[15] a film set in modern Manhattan that links the moral-ethical economic debate about competition in the retail book trade to issues of love and romance. Tom Hanks and Meg Ryan meet by email, but the substance of the film has nothing to do with modern epistolary communication but rather with sentiment intervening when "big box" franchise retailer Hanks drives Ryan's mom-and-pop bookstore out of business. He stands for modern, rationalized best-seller marketing, pleasing a mass audience first and foremost; she is fuzzier, representing literary quality, eccentricity, and taste, a "heritage" summed up by Austen's worldview even in end-of-millennium New York.

Branding Jane: commercial culture

Hollywood or even BBC producers, however, think less in terms of ideology and aesthetics than of financial success. For that, their production needs to be popular. Why does Austen's name seem to function as a guarantor of such success? Much of the answer lies in branding, primarily in terms of Austen herself but secondarily in terms of the producers' own perceived cultural status. Branding involves simple name recognition as well as recognition in terms of identifiable qualities associated with the name (or face or whatever). Thus, marketing can use branding in various ways, which helps explain the success of spin-off products (the net value of which may be greater than that of the original source material, *Star Wars*[16] being a case in point).

Authors as diverse as Lynda Obst and Jesse Algeron Rhines speak of the significance of marketing factors such as stars and genres for gaining producers' approval of film projects.[17] Christina Lane's study of Kathryn Bigelow provides one example of the argument that *auteurist* status can help market a film and thus get it greenlighted in the first place.[18] In the case of the BBC and A&E productions of Jane Austen's novels, the use of her name suggests that it is Austen herself who guarantees a project's viability, for example, *Jane Austen's Persuasion* (1995) and *Jane Austen's Emma* (1996).

As with stars, genres, or *auteurs*, this identification of a project in marketing terms through Austen's name is meant to identify an audience. Presumably what appeals to this target audience is a type of experience that Austen's name leads spectators to expect. That expectation has been exploited since the nineteenth century as a market phenomenon. Henry James noted that a "body of publishers, editors, illustrators, [and] producers of the pleasant twaddle of magazines" found "their 'dear,' our dear, everybody's dear, Jane so infinitely to their material purposes." As Claudia L. Johnson explains, Janeitism, "the self-consciously idolatrous enthusiasm for 'Jane' and every detail relative to her which James is alluding to," is a late nineteenth-century product of changes in the world of publishing that made Austen's novels readily accessible.[19] Janeites, Johnson's discussion suggests, may come from all social classes, with varying degrees of access to cultural capital, a point one might also draw from Rudyard Kipling's story, "The Janeites."[20] Janeitism, as Kipling's story (and the quotation with which this essay begins) shows, can transcend class, but not without difficulty and distortion: "Once [Austen's] reputation thrived beyond a small circle of enthusiasts, Austen's appeal has been wide enough to be a worry, for it reaches beyond the authority of those who consider themselves entitled to adjudicate not only who but how it is proper to enjoy 'great' literature."[21]

Supported by academic studies throughout the last century, the officially sanctioned characteristics most commonly associated with Austen's name relate to a high culture aesthetic that values literature; history; class hierarchies; an appreciation of irony and satire at the expense of class hierarchies; anglophilia, or at least a tolerance thereof, with a latent or implicit nostalgia attached to it; dialogue-driven narratives delivered in an elevated language; and the repression of foul language and overt sexuality. The adaptations, in turn, have bought into this persona. They are, as Fay Weldon puts it, "something that you can take the kids to, and hope to educate them just a bit." "A little dose of English heritage [love, as well as personal responsibility, long-term goals, and delicacy of response] as an antidote to CNN...O.J. and Bruce Willis."[22] The BBC's "older and more literal" adaptations were "usually transmitted on Sunday afternoons for the improvement of the young"; Janet Maslin's tongue-in-cheek rating for *Emma* captures a different aspect of the same thought: "*Emma* is rated PG...It includes violence of the discreet conversational variety, which perfectly suits the film's idea of polite society."[23]

The 1940 MGM version of *Pride and Prejudice* set the pattern. MGM had worked hard for years to cultivate a reputation as a studio associated with prestige projects. MGM films were characteristically big-budget, star-studded projects with high production values. It was in keeping with

MGM's profile that Aldous Huxley, a novice at scriptwriting but a recognized British author of literature, was hired to adapt Austen's novel. Louis B. Mayer, head of MGM, was proud of making wholesome family entertainment, films in line with conservative (US) Republican values, but entertaining – and commercially successful – nonetheless. Huxley's version of Austen contains some of the most egregious changes to be found in all the adaptations. For example, Elizabeth challenges Lady Catherine, but there's no clash of values since Lady Catherine is playing Cupid for Darcy. All's well that ends well, and everyone comes out of it happy. Greer Garson as Elizabeth may have stood around in a modest suit of underwear, but it was all very tastefully done.

This is the pattern that Austen adaptations currently follow, also with great success. Since *Pride and Prejudice*'s success in 1995, Lisa Mullen writes, "The megabucks classical adaptation has been the definition of profitable flagship programming – gobbling up budgets, sure, but paying out bigtime in overseas revenue and global prestige."[24] Because the Austen novels are in the public domain, costs for adaptations are that much lower. High production values usually translate into money for locations and costumes. Locations are probably most important these days, for a part of what these adaptations offer is the lure of cinema from its origins in travel films and actualités; the ability to take us to another world, a place that we can go to only vicariously, but which the images on screen help us to experience more intensely. If the performers in these adaptations haven't always been internationally recognizable before their appearances, they are definitely stars after the fact.

In short and to generalize hugely, film and television adaptations of Austen's novels offer an inoffensive experience to middle-class whites who like to think of themselves as discerning and endowed with the good taste of cultural capital. "Posthumous queen of genteel cinema" that Austen is, her name alone is enough to make the connection between viewers and cultural capital.[25]

Cultural capital/commercialized culture

Culture, as used herein, refers to "the works and practices of intellectual and especially artistic activity" and "to signifying or symbolic systems" (that is, to "symbolic" rather than to "material" production), which, since Matthew Arnold's time, has been "associat[ed] with class distinction": "It is significant that virtually all the hostility . . . has been connected with uses involving claims to superior knowledge . . . refinement (culchah) and distinctions between 'high' art (culture) and popular art and entertainment."[26] Cultural Studies has recognized the connection between culture and class distinction – "the use of culture as a means of class differentiation, a mark of distinction" – since Pierre Bourdieu's sociological studies of the function of taste in French society.[27] To have culture, to be cultured, can be materially beneficial, and the attainment of culture is rarely achieved in the absence of material comfort. Culture and economics are connected. Cultural status may or may not affect social interactions so directly as does money, but the effect is there, obvious or not. Through clever marketing, Austen's cultural status, her cultural capital, translates into commercial success and economic capital for producers such as the BBC, or Columbia, or Miramax, or A&E.

The cultural capital in question now differs from the sort of cultural capital that Austen had in her own day. *New Yorker* film reviewer Martin Amis's amusing and generally spot-on article "Jane's World" explores how the Austen canon has fared critically over time, concluding that "for every generation of critics, and readers, her fiction effortlessly renews itself."[28] That is how Austen-the-author has accrued cultural capital over the years. In her own day, Austen was a single woman without distinctions significant enough to attract the sort of attention and respect that Austen-the-author can now take for granted. This does not mean that Austen had no cultural capital to draw on in her own time. As Lovell notes, Austen and the other daughters of Church of England clergymen who made careers of writing tended to be "better educated and better supplied with 'cultural capital' than other women" of their day.[29] Their social superiority rested on cultural rather than material wealth. One need hardly look further than Mrs. and Miss Bates to see both the value and the vulnerability of cultural capital in the absence of material wealth.

Cultural capital, as a term available for analysis of the individual's standing in society, can help us to understand Austen in her time, as well as the characters she created. It can also help us understand the appeal of her novels to individual readers over time. As a term connected with and derived from economic and sociological analysis of social structures, cultural capital can also help us understand group phenomena, such as the popularity with collective audiences of Austen's novels and their adaptations.

For example, many of the Austen adaptations have been produced by the BBC, the British Broadcasting Corporation (see the Filmography). Often, these productions occur in association with WGBH, a Boston affiliate of PBS, the (national US) Public Broadcasting Service. PBS was known in an earlier incarnation as NET, or National Educational Television. NET became PBS in 1969,[30] roughly the same era that Masterpiece Theatre began to air on US television (via public television). As "Franklin-2" notes in a user comment included in the Internet Movie

Data Base page on *The Forsyte Saga* (1967),[31] this series "inspired the creation of PBS's 'Masterpiece Theatre' and the birth of the U.S. mini-series" in imitation of the British model. Masterpiece Theatre, with sponsorship eventually from the Mobil Oil Corporation, was originally introduced by Alistair Cooke, a British-born institution whose *Letter from America* still airs weekly on National Radio in Aotearoa New Zealand, and in the United Kingdom. Boston has maintained associations with its British origins and to some extent with class hierarchies and concepts of high culture associated with those origins. Thus, WGBH's association with the BBC in producing material for Masterpiece Theatre to be broadcast over PBS looks "natural" rather than the result of mutually supportive ideological confluences working within the media. To the cynical, the leftist, and those not particularly inclined to anglophilia and its Boston equivalent, Masterpiece Theatre (satirically referred to as "Master Race Theatre") has often seemed more like a venue for "quality" television imported from Britain – where they really have culture – because the US couldn't produce its own.[32] In relation to cultural capital, what this information suggests is that when producers and distributors such as the BBC, PBS, WGBH, and Masterpiece Theatre have already branded themselves in association with a certain level of cultural capital, the audiences they reach can be assumed to have some common characteristics vis-à-vis cultural capital.

Cultural capital's value as an analytic tool has helped it to become a relatively familiar phrase. It has even entered the vocabulary of bureaucrats and politicians. For example, the New Zealand Film Commission has used the concept in arguments to persuade the government to increase funding for the production of New Zealand films.[33] The point being made is that films identifiably from this country represent a branding opportunity that draws tourists and potential investors to consider Aotearoa New Zealand as an attractive place, part of the attraction being that it offers a sophisticated, talented, and gifted pool of artists who enhance the cultural experience of an otherwise superbly endowed natural landscape. That is, the development of culture – now defined as a marketable commodity – forms a part of, contributes to, and enhances a nation's economic capital. Other countries making the same argument through their highest levels of politicians include Ireland (especially when Michael D. Higgins carried the ministerial portfolio for culture and the arts) and even Britain (through Tony Blair's "Branding Britain" campaign).

Culture – that is, things usually, or at least historically, considered within a frame of reference controlled by aesthetic criteria – is now being recognized and acknowledged as an economic factor. In the usual run of things, economic criteria for evaluation differ hugely from aesthetic criteria. For example, these days a book's presence on the best-seller list or reports of a film's opening weekend gross is likely to be as effective as a good critic's review for drawing people to read or watch. In effect, once culture takes on an economic role, distinctions between high and low culture grow difficult to maintain.

Adaptation: authentic or real?

One way the Austen adaptations have tried to maintain high culture status while achieving mass popularity and hence commercial success is to claim authenticity, an authenticity that manifests itself through location, costume, and casting. As Julianne Pidduck notes, realism is the least that one can anticipate from such films, in contrast, supposedly, with Hollywood productions such as the 1940 MGM *Pride and Prejudice*.[34] The video copy of the A&E *Emma* prefaces the feature with previews of *Pride and Prejudice*, touted as "filmed entirely on location" in England, while the film's production designer proclaims the goal "to recreate [Jane Austen's] vision." The A&E website on *Pride and Prejudice* boasts that its production "is filmmaking as only the BBC and A&E can do it," a "stunning production" that "captures all the celebrated beauty of the English countryside and its glorious, stately manors."[35] Location is thus equated with realism, as if shooting in original edifices and landscapes some two centuries after the fact guarantees authenticity, a return to an uncorrupted visual essence somehow related to literary-cinematic effect.

Realism, of course, is only one style among a range of choices. As a style, realism alters with time and in relation to technical developments within a medium. It can be evaluated in terms of its effectiveness (measurable by its persuasiveness that it is genuine), which of course may also alter with time. For this essay the first point of interest is the relation between realism and adaptation. The novels exist, and most audiences for their adaptations anticipate some degree of adherence to this source material as a first degree of authenticity. Authenticity in this case depends on what we think was real in Austen's time. Thus, adherence to source material involves finding a convincing representation of what we think of as Austenian.

Consider, for example, the possibility that one "can rustle something up from *The Jane Austen Cookbook* (all ingredients have been modernized)."[36] What does it mean to modernize in accord with changing times or to adapt for a different medium? Do changing times and different media make a literal adherence impossible? Lest we forget, adherence to source material and realism do not necessarily go hand in hand, although, says Pidduck, "costume dramas by definition transport the viewer into historical settings."[37] So realism of the sort associated with settings, costumes, language, behavior, and so forth becomes one aspect of adherence to source material when adaptations of Austen are at issue.

Are we, though, talking about a literal realism, or a psychological realism, a letter of the law or a spirit of the law approach? It has to be a matter of degree. Literal, word-for-word adherence to Austen's texts is beyond an adaptation to another medium, for it would generally exceed reasonable time limits, apart from technical constraints belonging to the specificities of the different media (the most obvious issue for adaptations of the novels being the presence in the novels of an authorial voice). Such literal adherence would also be undesirable because it would amount to copying. To quote Lloyd Michaels, part of what's involved in making films from novels "is the distinction between copy and imitation, in the latter of which (Coleridge wrote) 'a certain quantum of difference is essential . . . [*sic*] while in a copy, it is a defect, contravening its name and purpose."[38] That quantum of difference, the element of discrepancy, raises doubts about any adaptation's authenticity – its "being what it professes in origin or authorship," its very "genuineness," to quote the *OED* on authenticity.

Disputes about the authenticity of period pieces based on novels usually begin with anachronisms: mistakes of costuming, setting, linguistic usage, even body types, and so forth. These would seem to be relatively simple disputes because the underlying facts would seem to be discoverable. For example, the use of Chopin's music as background accompaniment in *Persuasion* (1995) is manifestly anachronistic, as it hadn't been written before Austen died. By contrast, the similar use of Bach in the same film is debatable, because, while the music had been written, it wasn't necessarily in favor with Austen or with the sort of people about whom she wrote. Such small choices contribute to how tenuous the "accurate" representation of history can be. The choice to highlight one aspect of an historical period over another can be as controversial as speculations into (the legitimacy of) reasons why.

Austen herself has been criticized for neglecting details of historical significance in her time – Napoleon, for instance. Counterarguments include observations that Napoleon was no more important to Austen's social sphere than the events she takes as subject matter, or that her social sphere constituted the world to the eighteenth-century mind, or that her ahistoricity has its value.[39] In a similar light, the Nick Dear/Roger Michell *Persuasion* (1995) has attracted comment for the extent to which it forefronts the economic underpinnings of Austen's socialite protagonists, while Janet Maslin sees it as one of Douglas McGrath's "little jokes to seldom depict servants here, even though an absurd set of props appears on the manor lawn" so frequently.[40] Another counterargument is that some history present as a backdrop would have been recognizable to Austen's contemporaries while they read her novels but is lost to us.[41]

Appreciating satire

To some extent, reader/viewer competence is at issue here: the more we know, the more subtleties of detail we can appreciate, perhaps to a point where we might see the interconnectedness of events, be they intimate domestic or public sphere in nature. Austen appeals to people with various tastes and skills because we all seem to find something satisfying there. At ten or fourteen when I failed miserably to persuade a friend to share my initial appreciation of the glories of *Pride and Prejudice*'s opening sentence, I may have been precocious; several decades later I may have more competence as a reader, but in each reading I have always taken pleasure from the same sentence.

Or is it the same sentence? There has to be some common ground, something that is the bedrock Austen, that we all identify and acknowledge, whatever our competence as readers and viewers of Austen. Consider, in this context, *Clueless* (1995). Writer and director Amy Heckerling hasn't mentioned Austen in the film's credits, but neither does she try to hide her story's original. Elton, for example, is a dead giveaway. Is a handful of names good enough to constitute an adaptation? Of course not. James asks, "What is character but the determination of incident? What is incident but the illustration of character?"[42] If action is character and character action, then it is what Austen's characters do and how they behave that matters. Most of all, it's how they respond to the situations they find themselves in. Could those situations be anything at all that one might imagine? Again, no. What Austen's characters do, they do on a domestic scale. The story's resolution connects with the public affirmation (implicit or otherwise) of a couple where previously there had been two (possibly even antagonistic) protagonists. If a little social satire gets thrown in – as when *Clueless* manages a few digs at aspects of US culture through its references to pop culture (Cher/Dionne) and consumerism (malls) – all the better.

What sort of social satirist was Austen? Did her eye rove more – using the language of our day – toward social structure or gender relations, or perhaps some combination of the two? If Austen were writing about the interrelation of social structure and gendered relations, did she write as a feminist?

Although frequently discussed as a satirist whose novels cast a shrewd and critical eye on her own society, Austen was also a professional writer with an eye toward sales, especially when publishing her novels was self-funded. She sought to please the book-buying public. Consequently, we can read Austen both as a protofeminist and as a supporter of her day's most conservative British thinkers. Amis notes, "Each age will bring its peculiar emphasis, and in the current Austen festival our own anxieties stand fully revealed," and Johnson confirms: "Reading Austen is a social practice contingent upon our desires, needs, and historical circumstances."[43]

Adaptation: letter or spirit of the law?

Thus, current adaptations may emphasize different aspects of the Austen novels such that her intentions may seem less debatable than in the novels themselves. For example, the Emma Thompson–Ang Lee *Sense and Sensibility* (1995) makes the legalities of inheritance and genteel women's lack of access to paid work more bluntly explanatory for the story we see on screen than Austen does in her novel (presumably in part because of what she could assume her readers would already know). Did Austen mean to write a tendentious piece on women's rights or a commentary on the tendency of her era's romance novels to advocate willful behavior over sensible consideration for the feelings of others?

If literal realism turns out to be more nebulous than denotative, how much more so must be the spirit of the law approach? Consider, for example, the fact that both *Pride and Prejudice* (1995) and *Persuasion* (1995) contain anachronistic alterations pertaining to sexuality. Do these episodes – for example, the public kiss on a Bath street with which *Persuasion* concludes and the scene in *Pride and Prejudice* in which Mr. Darcy cools his ardor with a dip in the pond – heighten the realism of Austen's stories, as contemporary romance author Jo Beverley would argue (in private correspondence), by introducing an element sadly lacking in the original? Or are these changes marketing devices and capitulations to the conventions of late twentieth-century visual storytelling? Amis argues that such alterations reveal "much more about the blatant sensuality of our own" imagination than about "the latent 'sensuality' of Jane Austen's imagination," while Weldon writes that "if Captain Wentworth and Anne Elliot need to fornicate in Milsom Street, and not just kiss, for the sake of a satisfactory ending to a brilliant film, that would be OK by me."[44]

A letter of the law approach can at least pretend to have factually based guidelines to which to adhere. What holds a spirit of the law approach to the straight and true? The answer cannot be so clear-cut as one might wish. What we expect of characters' behavior, what gives the impression of psychological realism in our day may seem far different from that of Austen's era, especially to those who consider themselves able to identify

2. A thwarted romance rekindled: Anne Elliot (Amanda Root) and Captain Wentworth (Ciaran Hinds), from *Jane Austen's Persuasion*, a Sony Pictures Classics Release, 1995

what might accurately reflect her time. What would constitute a realistic representation of the psychology of Austen's day, the frame of reference through which her characters operate?

Courtesy, manners, and personal beliefs: use-value vs exchange-value ethics

Austen's novels suggest an understanding of the world in terms of people's connections with each other. Most if not all of those connections are regulated by determining economic factors. Much of Austen's irony and satire originate in her perception of the distribution of power between and among people at a time when England's social structure was changing in response to pressures from various historical factors, including the Industrial Revolution, developments within capitalism, and the French Revolution followed by the Napoleonic Wars.

Many of the consequent changes in social structure, particularly those relating to social hierarchies, had been in train for a while. One response to those changes had been the rise of the conduct book. Nancy Armstrong has detailed the historical development of conduct books as they moved from instructing aristocratic males to middle-class females. She also distinguishes between the component parts of a body of educational material, some parts dealing with domestic economy, some parts turning

into novels of manners, while others "aspired to be courtesy literature."[45]
Penelope Fritzer distinguishes between courtesy or conduct books, on the
one hand, and books of etiquette, the latter being more pragmatic and
specific than the former:

> Courtesy literature is concerned with manners and society, but unlike simple
> etiquette, it is based on morality and inner development rather than on fashion
> and expedience. Courtesy books are deeply concerned with morality and with
> the reader's relationship to his [*sic*] conscience as well as to his God. There is a
> definite flavor of earnestness about the courtesy books that is lacking in books of
> simple etiquette: the writers are terribly concerned that their readers do the right
> thing, not as dictated by fashion, but as dictated by goodness.[46]

Austen was familiar with the conduct books that had developed as a
way of teaching people how to behave in a changing society. She was
also familiar with novels that were thinly veiled conduct books under the
veneer of fiction.

Comparing and contrasting Austen's novels and the courtesy book literature, Fritzer finds "a direct correlation between courtesy advice and
the behavior of Austen's characters in the areas of conversation, keeping secrets, laughter and wit, flattery and letter-writing" and notes that
"Austen's best characters generally adhere to courtesy advice, while the
less admirable ones stray from it, often in significant ways,"[47] observations Bradbrook confirms.[48] Fritzer goes on to note:

> The courtesy books of Austen's period recommended certain behavior, some
> of it in accord with simple etiquette, but most of it directed toward the improve-
> ment of character . . . Austen does not codify particular actions or thoughts, but
> in general she advocates duty, charity, chastity, modesty, honor, humility, educa-
> tion, good nature, and activity (rather than idleness), the same virtues that appear
> throughout the courtesy books.[49]

Fritzer concludes, "Jane Austen's system of values in many ways matches
that of the courtesy writers, as shown by the remarkable congruence of
the values in their writings and hers."[50]

Austen's values and those of the conduct books reject the ethics of
capitalism, of exchange-value as a factor interfering with relationships,
which leads to exploitation and self-interest as a basis for personal relationships. Josephine Donovan explains the opposition between use-value
and exchange-value, in Marx's terminology:

> Marx stipulated that the inherent value of a product varies according to whether
> it is produced for use or for exchange. Use-value implies a qualitative appreciation,
> whereas "exchange-value . . . presents itself as a quantitative relation" . . . Subse-
> quent Marxists have suggested that a base in use-value production provides a
> standpoint from which to critique the exchange-value ethos – that which com-
> modifies people as well as products in terms of their exchange-value identity.[51]

Armstrong describes a debate between two different discourses, one from a public sphere dominated by men in which exchange-value increasingly determines behavior, but notes, in contrast, "domestic fiction mapped out a new domain of discourse as it invested common forms of social behavior with the emotional values of women."[52]

Exponents of use-value ethics champion qualitative over quantitative values, and they measure an individual's worth on his or her ability to appreciate the qualities espoused by conduct books rather than those materialist aspects fostered by capitalism. "The novels I write," asserts romance author Judith Arnold, "don't revolve around material achievement, domination, or conquest – the standards by which we tend to gauge success in our male-dominated society...Women assess their worth by other criteria: how much they contribute to the well-being of others; how successfully they navigate the complex world of relationship."[53]

A reassuring world

To return to the added scenes of "blatant sensuality" in current Austen adaptations, how does the addition of such arguably inauthentic material affect the cultural value of the Austen experience? Is it an addition or a betrayal? Several authors in Linda Troost and Sayre Greenfield's *Jane Austen in Hollywood* (1998), a treatment of films based on Jane Austen's novels, evaluate it as a negative addition. "Harlequinization," in this instance, is derogatory. Yet Amis manages a sketch of the Austen novel structure that reads like a tip sheet for writing the Austen category romance: "There is a Heroine, there is a Hero, and there is an Obstacle."[54]

In Austen's novels, domestic settings and the romantic entanglements of her principal protagonists become vehicles for the expression of values associated with good behavior and the promotion of happiness among members of intimate communities: "Austen's novels display the serene conviction that decency, civility and common sense will be rewarded. Not by the hand of God, but simply because they lead to warm and lasting relationships and lives free of turmoil, dissatisfaction and debt."[55] If "private life" was "the dominant social reality" of nineteenth-century life, as Monaghan writes with reference to Armstrong's discussion of "that important domestic novel, *Emma*,"[56] then the interpersonal relations of men and women within the domestic environment take on keen interest.

These settings and situations are familiar to millions of readers of Harlequins, Mills and Boons, Silhouettes, and so forth. That in itself delivers millions of potential viewers in the form of readers who can recognize, in the cover art and other marketing devices promoting the adaptations, a promise of the sort of narrative experiences they enjoy.

Others, too, can derive comfort from Austen. Laura Miller finds "the social climate" Austen describes not that far from our own, with authority resting "in the hands of a dubious elite, prosperity...precarious and, most of all, parents...just not doing their jobs."[57] Despite all this, Austen delivers a happy ending. Virtually a genre unto herself, Austen works, according to Amis, within the genre of classical comedy, which "itself guarantees consummation."[58] As Radway discovered in her study of romance readers, reassurance through the familiarity of a happy ending contributes to a novel's success. Because we know what to expect, we can derive comfort and security from the experience. As Amis describes his own initial experience with *Pride and Prejudice*, Austen can dangle uncertainty in front of us,[59] but her characters always get their just reward, which satisfies our desire.

The sort of reassurance Austen provides that the powerless can be happy is the same source of satisfaction romance author Doreen Owens Malek describes: "In a reality where a pitiless, random fate had buffeted me almost beyond endurance, [romance novels] offered a universe in which fate is under control, because in the end it is always the heroine's friend and always gives her exactly what she wants."[60] This sounds much like Michael Holquist's discussion of the English detective novel of the 1930s, a world in which logic was absolute, but an artificial world set up against the chaotic world of horrors experienced during WWI.[61] Johnson records that Austen's novels have had therapeutic effects on readers, and they were even prescribed therapeutically for shell-shocked veterans.[62]

While "Austen's characters resist the ministrations of the therapy age,"[63] their stories, as Austen tells them in their own age, minister to the therapeutic needs of various ages or, as Kipling's Humberstall says, "You take it from me, Brethren, there's no one to touch Jane when you're in a tight place. Gawd bless 'er, whoever she was."[64]

Ideologically, as Ira Konigsberg observes, Austen's novels deliver "a world in which the individual and society are ultimately in harmony, in which they both share the same decent values, and in which the needs and desires of one are satisfied by the other." From this harmony comes "the strength and stability which they finally depict at their conclusions," he further notes, conclusions based on "a belief in individual capacity and in a stable, civilized society, a belief in a knowable, practical system of morality and conduct."[65] This same world, by and large, carries over to the adaptations. This aspect of the adaptations contributes largely to their ability to participate in current development of the concept of culture, and its value within society. These adaptations particularly lend themselves to the sort of contrast between high and low culture parodied, for example, in the "Sneakin' in the Movies" episode of *Hollywood Shuffle*.[66] In that episode, the parody of *Amadeus* stands out among the crude mimicry of the *Dirty Harry*, *Indiana Jones*, and "blaxploitation" films both for its difference from them and for its utterly incongruous mismatch with a pair of uneducated urban African American "bros" standing in for Siskel and Ebert.[67] One can imagine that any of the Austen adaptations might take the place of *Amadeus* were *Hollywood Shuffle* to be made today.

What's in a name?

There are some audiences that Austen's name can't deliver, either to marketers who can use the adaptations to move their own products or to the producers profiting directly from the success of their adaptations. Nonetheless, the economic value of Austen's name is sufficient to see announcements of further adaptations in the pipeline and yet to come. One reason Austen can deliver so many members of her potential audience is that the ideological worldview that she offers can be presented, however modified, in our own terms. Even when we may seem to have conflicting worldviews – among ourselves, or with Austen – her stories manage to offer something that appeals, as Kipling's story shows. The irony of Austen's current status is that an exchange-value culture is profiting from her expression of a use-value ethics, even to the extent of converting Austen-the-author into a commercial commodity.

From an economic point of view, Jane Austen's name seems to authorize greenlighting, i.e., approval for adaptation productions. In effect, we are in a decade in which her name functions like a license to print money, to paraphrase what was said of publishing romance novels in the late 1970s and early 1980s. From a consumer's point of view, anxious for a viewing experience that comfortingly meets expectations (like Holquist's mystery writers and readers of the 1930s or more recent readers of category romances), Austen's name promises sense over sensibility, where the former stands for behavior determined by concern for the well-being of others. Good manners is not a matter of *pro forma* behavior, according to some rulebook, for sometimes rules must be broken. In such cases, the guiding principle for behavior is its effect on others. One may go against the rules, for example, to relieve another's discomfort.

These are use-value ethics. In contrast, to act out of self-interest is always suspect, in Austen's world and in her adaptations. Exchange-value ethics can be joked about, but only when it is clear that the benefit referred to is not a real factor, for example, when Elizabeth jokes with Jane about Pemberley's effect on her feelings for Darcy.

"Jane Austen" does not authorize all things for everybody. Her name represents a certain approach to issues framed within a certain context.

The ambiguities inherent therein are acknowledged, once again, by Kipling: "There must be a lot more to this Janeite game."[68]

NOTES

My thanks go to Mrs. Phyllis Harding, Sue Thomas, Harry Ricketts, Paul Emsley of the Victoria University of Wellington Library's Audio-Visual Suite, and Aro Street Video for providing access to primary source material essential to this essay.

1 In *Debits and Credits* (London and New York: Macmillan, 1927): 174.

2 Jane Nardin, "Jane Austen and the Problem of Leisure," in *Jane Austen in a Social Context*, ed. David Monaghan (Totawa, NJ: Barnes and Noble Books, 1981): 123; Penelope Joan Fritzer, *Jane Austen and Eighteenth-Century Courtesy Books* (Westport, CT: Greenwood, 1997): 96.

3 See the "Introduction" to Linda Troost and Sayre Greenfield's edition of *Jane Austen in Hollywood* (Lexington, KY: Kentucky University Press, 1998): 1–2 and Martin Amis, "Jane's World," *The New Yorker* 71 (January 8, 1996): 83 on the commercial success of Austen adaptations.

4 *The Kentucky Fried Movie*, Director John Landis, 1977; *Jane Austen's Mafia*, Director and writer Jim Abrahams, Touchstone, 1998.

5 See Terry Lovell, *Consuming Fiction* (London: Verso, 1987): 8–11, 28; Fritzer, *Courtesy Books*: 20; Frank W. Bradbrook, *Jane Austen and Her Predecessors* (Cambridge: Cambridge University Press, 1966): 25–26; Margaret Anne Doody, "The Short Fiction," *The Cambridge Companion to Jane Austen*, eds. Edward Copeland and Juliet McMaster (Cambridge: Cambridge University Press, 1997): 94–96; and Fanny Burney, "Author's Preface," *Evelina* (London: Dent, 1958): xiii.

6 See Janice Radway, who in turn repeats the eighteenth- and nineteenth-century moralizers' criticism by asserting the negative impact of reading novels on the reader's response to life itself in *Reading the Romance: Women, Patriarchy, and Popular Literature* (Chapel Hill, NC: University of North Carolina Press, 1991): 220.

7 Troost and Greenfield.

8 "Home1 Discusses Writing, Editing, Marketing Harlequins," *Encompass: Alumni Newsletter of the Comparative Literature Program* 2.2 (1987): 4 (Bloomington, IN: Indiana University Alumni Association).

9 The echo of Molly Haskell's words on the woman's film is deliberate, to call attention to similarities across a diversity of media and genres ("The Woman's Film," in *From Reverence to Rape: The Treatment of Women in the Movies* [Chicago: University of Chicago Press, 1987]: 153–188). Penny Gay uses similar language to defend Austen's novels against Dr. Johnson's criticism of novels (*Jane Austen's "Pride and Prejudice"* [Sydney: Sydney University Press, 1990]: 7).

10 Jennifer Crusie Smith, "Let Us Now Praise Scribbling Women," on Romance Writers of America website (October 10, 1999): www.rwanational.com/crusiearticle.htm

11 In his "Introduction" to *Jane Austen in a Social Context*: 2.

12 John Wiltshire, "*Mansfield Park, Emma, Persuasion*," in *Cambridge Companion*, eds. Copeland and McMaster: 75.

13 Deborah Kaplan, *Jane Austen among Women* (Baltimore, MD: Johns Hopkins University Press, 1992): 178.

14 In response to Deborah Kaplan (ibid.), consider Claudia Johnson's critique of Harding's elitism, which saw "Austen's admirers . . . [as] her worst readers" ("Austen Cults and Cultures," in *Cambridge Companion*, eds. Copeland and McMaster: 219). More direct support comes from Doody's discussion of Austen as a Regency writer, with direct reference to the queen of Regencies, Georgette Heyer ("The Short Fiction": 87). Heyer is clearly the mother of current manifestations of the Regency, some of which are published by Harlequin.

15 *You've Got Mail*, Director, writer, and producer Nora Ephron. Warner Brothers, 1998.

16 *Star Wars*, Director and writer George Lucas, Twentieth-Century Fox, 1977.

17 Lynda Obst, *Hello, He Lied & Other Truths from the Hollywood Trenches* (New York: Broadway Books, 1997); Jesse Algernon Rhines, *Black Film/White Money* (New Brunswick, NJ: Rutgers University Press, 1996).

18 Christina Lane, "From *The Loveless* to *Point Break*: Kathryn Bigelow's Trajectory in Action," *Cinema Journal* 37.4 (1998): 59–81.

19 Claudia L. Johnson, "Austen Cults and Cultures" (Chicago: University of Chicago Press, 1988): 211.

20 Harry Ricketts notes in his discussion of Kipling's own mixing of the sort of values associated with class differences and aesthetics in *Debts and Credits*, "There were no firm boundaries between high culture and low cultures, no fixed categories" (*The Unforgiving Minute: A Life of Rudyard Kipling* [London: Chatto and Windus, 1999]: 363). *Debts and Credits*, Ricketts tells us, was not one of Kipling's great successes in his own time.

21 Johnson, "Austen Cults and Cultures": 212; see Fay Weldon, "Jane Austen and the Pride of Purists," *New York Times* (October 8, 1995): H24.

22 Weldon, "Pride of Purists": H15.

23 Janet Maslin, "So Genteel, So Scheming, So Austen." Review of *Emma*, *New York Times* (August 2, 1996): C15; Charles Wenz, "BBC Video," www.pemberley.com.janeinfo/jabbcvid.html (April 12, 2000).

24 Lisa Mullen, "Fair Game," *Time Out* (October 28–November 4, 1998): 24; see also Weldon, "Pride of Purists": H15.

25 Maslin, "So Genteel": C1.

26 Raymond Williams, *Keywords: A Vocabulary of Culture and Society* (New York: Oxford University Press, 1983): 90–92.

27 "Just as different social classes and groups are defined in terms of their differences in their access to economic capital, and hence material power, so Bourdieu agrees they must be seen to possess correspondingly unequal cultural capital and symbolic power" (Tim O'Sullivan, *Key Concepts in Communication* [London: Methuen, 1983]: 62). See also Pierre Bourdieu's *Distinction: A Social Critique of the Judgement of Taste*, 1979 (London: Routledge, 1984), and Lawrence Levine, *Highbrow/Lowbrow: The Emergence of Cultural Hierarchy in America* (Cambridge, MA: Harvard University Press, 1988).

28 Martin Amis, "Jane's World," *The New Yorker* 71 (January 8, 1996): 34.

29 Lovell, *Consuming Fiction*: 42; see also Johnson, "Austen Cults and Cultures."

30 See www.pbs.org/insidepbs/facts/faq1.html

31 Franklin-2, "The Best Dramatic Series in Television History." http:llus.imbd. com/Title?006 1253, September 25, 2000.

32 Discussing the relationship between public service broadcasting and local content, the authors of a study on local content and diversity commissioned by New Zealand On Air (a government-supported funding agency) write that "for some countries, especially those where English is the first language, quality programming need not be local . . . In the United States, the public broadcaster PBS also uses large quantities of imported programming, especially from the BBC. Indeed, New Zealand could be seen as an extreme case in this regard, instanced by the reliance of its public broadcaster TVNZ on the BBC for quality drama, and the promotion of its flagship Sunday evening programme [Montana Theatre, the local equivalent of Masterpiece Theatre, where many of the Austen adaptations have aired] under the rubric 'quality British drama'" (Paul Norris, "Introduction," *Local Content and Diversity: TV in Ten Countries*, eds. Paul Norris, Brian Pauling, and Geoff Lealand, with Henk Huijser and Craig Hight [Wellington: NZOA, 1999]: 13).

33 Sources for this point and the following outline of the argument include Kathleen Drumm of the New Zealand Film Commission (Victoria University of Wellington class presentation on the cinema of Aotearoa New Zealand), the New Zealand Film Commission's press releases and reports, and back issues of *OnFilm* (Aotearoa New Zealand's trade publication for local film, television, and television commercial production).

34 Julianne Pidduck, "Of Windows and Country Walks: Frames of Space and Movement in 1990s Austen Adaptations," *Screen* 39.4 (Winter 1998): 385.

35 www.aetv.com/scenes/pride (April 12, 2000).

36 Amis, "Jane's World": 32.

37 Pidduck, "Of Windows": 393.

38 Lloyd Michaels, Review of James Griffith's *Adaptations as Imitations: Films from Novels* (Cranbury: University of Delaware Press, 1997) in *Screen* 39.4 (Winter 1998): 426.

39 Monaghan, *Jane Austen in a Social Context*: 1–2; Johnson, "Austen Cults and Cultures": 217; Ira Konigsberg, *Narrative Technique in the English Novel: Defoe to Austen* (Hamden, CT: Archon Books, 1985): 214.

40 Maslin, "So Genteel": C15.

41 See Edward Copeland and Juliet McMaster's "Preface" to *The Cambridge Companion* on what contemporary readers are unlikely to understand: xi.

42 M. H. Abrams, "Plot," in *A Glossary of Literary Terms* (6th ed., Fort Worth: Harcourt Brace Jovanovich College Publishers, 1993): 159.

43 Amis, "Jane's World": 34; Johnson, "Austen Cults and Cultures": 224.

44 Amis, "Jane's World": 34; Weldon, "Pride of Purists": H24.

45 Nancy Armstrong, *Desire and Domestic Fiction: A Political History of the Novel* (New York: Oxford University Press, 1987): 61.

46 Fritzer, *Courtesy Books*: 4.

47 Ibid.: 79.

48 Frank W. Bradbrook, *Jane Austen and Her Predecessors* (Cambridge: Cambridge University Press, 1966): 112–114.

49 Fritzer, *Courtesy Books*: 107.

50 Ibid.: 111.

51 Josephine Donovan, "Women and the Rise of the Novel: A Feminist-Marxist Theory," *Signs* 16.3 (1991): 445.

52 Armstrong, *Desire*: 29.

53 Judith Arnold, "Women Do," in *Dangerous Men and Adventurous Women: Romance Writers on the Appeal of the Romance*, ed. Jayne Ann Krentz (Philadelphia: University of Pennsylvania Press, 1992): 138.

54 Amis, "Jane's World": 32.

55 Laura Miller, "Austen-mania," www.salon.com/02dec1995/features/austen. html

56 David Monaghan (ed.), *Emma: Jane Austen* (New York: St. Martin's Press, 1992): 12.

57 Miller, "Austen-mania."

58 Amis, "Jane's World": 32–33.

59 Ibid.: 33.

60 Doreen Owens Malek, "Mad, Bad, and Dangerous to Know," in *Dangerous Men*, ed. Krentz: 78.

61 Michael Holquist, "Whodunit and Other Questions: Metaphysical Detective Stories in Post-War Fiction," *New Literary History* 3.1 (1971–2): 135–156.

62 Johnson, "Austen Cults and Cultures": 217.

63 Amis, "Jane's World": 34.

64 Kipling, "The Janeites": 173.

65 Konigsberg, *Narrative Technique*: 214–215.

66 *Hollywood Shuffle*, Writers Robert Townsend and Keenen Ivory Wayans, Director Robert Townsend, 1987.

67 See my "Sneaky Re-Views: Can Robert Townsend's Taste for Stereotypes Contribute Positively to Identity Politics?" in *Performing Gender and Comedy*, ed. Shannon Hengen (Newark, NJ: Gordon and Breach, 1998): 199–218.

68 Kipling, "The Janeites": 156.

3 "Such a transformation!": translation, imitation, and intertextuality in Jane Austen on screen

Jocelyn Harris

What can audiences expect of Jane Austen on screen? Should directors "faithfully" translate her novels, or should they imitate her, capturing the spirit of the text through a new and familiar medium? I shall argue that translation is actually impossible because even those directors who try primarily to "translate" her diverge from her every time they cut or re-arrange a scene. Others more aggressively appropriate her, displace her, and make of her something new. Then too the very nature of translation makes "fidelity" to Jane Austen unlikely, while such characteristics of cinema as spectatorship, commercialism, visuality, idealism, realism, velocity, and a perceived need for "relevance" open up even wider distances from her texts. Furthermore, every adaptation, whether it incorporates the earlier prose text or departs from it, must necessarily acknowledge the existence of its predecessor. This inevitable intertextuality, or what Jonathan Culler describes as a complex vraisemblance in which "one work takes as its basis or point of departure [another work] and must be assimilated in relation to it,"[1] affects all the onscreen versions. The most successful cinematic versions derive not from translation but from the eighteenth-century theory of imitation which inspired Jane Austen herself. That is, they copy the essence of the text but at a distance. They highlight difference rather than sameness between the two texts, they comment on Jane Austen's pastness, acknowledge shifts in our thinking about the world, or satirize modern times. This essay will examine questions of translation, imitation, and intertextuality in the onscreen versions of Jane Austen's novels, with Emma Thompson's and Ang Lee's *Sense and Sensibility*, Patricia Rozema's *Mansfield Park*, and Amy Heckerling's *Clueless* providing its main examples.

Translation

All of the Jane Austen movies "translate" her novels from the language of print culture into the sign-system of cinema. But can they do so "faithfully"? When poetry is translated from one language to another,

44

say the theorists, original meanings must turn to new idioms if they are not to sound stilted and bizarre. As the modern translator David Constantine puts it: "The translation is a metaphor of the original, a various, differentiated living equivalent of the original."[2] The original must "estrange" itself into a foreign tongue so that it is "palpable" to new readers. To Gayatri Chakravorty Spivak, translator of Jacques Derrida's *Of Grammatology*, translation is therefore a reading that "*produces* rather than *protects*."[3] So too cinematic translations of Jane Austen will express her in cinematic terms, rather than her own.

John Dryden, the seventeenth-century critic, would have understood, he who remarked that when Ben Jonson based his tragedies on the ancients, he "learnedly followed their Language" but "did not enough comply with the Idiom of ours."[4] Jane Austen's mentor Samuel Johnson explains the matter further in *Lives of the English Poets* (1781):

When languages are formed upon different principles, it is impossible that the same modes of expression should always be elegant in both. While they run on together the closest translation may be considered as the best; but when they divaricate each must take its natural course. Where correspondence cannot be obtained it is necessary to be content with something equivalent.[5]

So, too, cinematic directors of Jane Austen must translate her prose into their own language, answering her in an idiom that is equivalent rather than closely corresponding. Demands for fidelity are therefore inappropriate because the shift from one language to another, from a verbal sign-system to a visual one, inevitably creates difference.

In any case, when we speak of fidelity to Jane Austen, whose Jane Austen are we talking about? Jane Austen's Jane Austen, or the individual reader's? We cannot know her mind. To guess at an author's original "meanings" is to be labeled a liberal humanist, a cultural hegemonist, and to fall beyond the pale. The author, said Roland Barthes, is dead: long live the reader.[6] Yet different readers, say some, respond according to their own material conditions, locations, histories, and genders, as Donna Haraway explains: "All readings are also mis-readings, re-readings, partial readings, imposed readings, and imagined readings of a text that is originally and finally never simply there."[7] If it is true that readers construct meanings, even meanings that an author may never have "intended," how can directors possibly be "faithful" to every one of them? Jane Austen's "meanings" are, in fact, particularly slippery because her texts are founded on dramatic conventions (the novel derives significantly from drama), which means that readers read them like play-texts, peopling, clothing, and organizing these fictional worlds at will. As Graham Hough has shown, dialogue is Jane Austen's staple form, together with other narrative forms such as colored narrative and free indirect speech that stand in for dialogue.[8] When we read, then, we play out different scenarios in the theaters of our minds. If no one reading can be "right," whose reading should directors follow? They might as well cleave to their own.

Film theorists similarly debate whether spectators participate in creating meaning by responding in accord with their own construction and experiences, whether they hold together all the traces by which the text is constituted,[9] or whether they are controlled by the "apparatus" of cinema, that is the very mechanics of representation, the camera, the editing, the immobility of the spectators before a screen.[10] Is our imagination preempted by the director's control of our gaze? Do directors impose on us interpretations that prove canonical to the point of tyranny, especially when stamped "BBC"? Does the fact that films can be endlessly repeated in an age of mechanical reproduction, transmitted across time, space, and cultures to a multitude of viewers, make them immortal, imperious in the imposition of meanings? Whichever camp is correct, directors indisputably modify Jane Austen into versions that will be modified in turn by spectators. This distancing at two removes from the text once again renders any notion of "fidelity" illogical.

Aspects of modernity such as commercialism, visuality, idealism, realism, velocity, and intertextuality likewise foil directors' attempts to translate Jane Austen directly into film. The same imperatives that attract filmmakers to her prestigious texts make faithfulness problematic, for in order to sell, directors must defer to the twentieth-century tyranny of visual culture. Films swerve again from their originals when movie screens are filled from edge to edge. Lady Russell sports glamorous toques and taffetas in Roger Michell's *Persuasion*, and Emma Thompson unblushingly appropriates what David Monaghan (Chapter 10 in this volume) calls the prestigious aura and authenticity of heritage houses for *Sense and Sensibility* – in her preliminary notes to the screenplay she writes that they are connected with famous people and crammed with artwork by named artists: they are original, priceless, spectacular, magnificent, unparalleled, magnificent, spectacular, sumptuous, and again magnificent. Two of them, we are told, belong to the National Trust, and in another, the World War II Normandy invasion (the 1944 Allied attack on Germany) was planned.[11] But even without her prompting, the sheer materiality of the movie distracts from Jane Austen.

Then, too, the idealizing culture of Hollywood demands the wan perfection of a Gwyneth Paltrow in Douglas McGrath's *Emma* or the manly vigor of a Colin Firth in Andrew Davies's *Pride and Prejudice*. Neither may fit our imaginings of Jane Austen. And if cinema is idealistic, it is

3. Emma (Gwyneth Paltrow) watches as Mr. Knightley (Jeremy Northam) engages in target practice with bow and arrow in Douglas McGrath's *Emma*, a 1996 Miramax Films release.

also famously realistic. Roger Michell makes his mud-stained, weather-beaten protagonists innocent of make-up in *Persuasion*, as if their imperfection guaranteed their "real" existence. Anne has a sad little mouth and shell-shocked eyes, Captain Harville splayed teeth, Captain Wentworth lank hair, Captain Benwick a spotty face, and Mrs. Clay protruding teeth and a bosom to match (Regency dresses flatter only the flat). But it is a sleight of hand to suggest that the authenticity of realism guarantees authenticity to Jane Austen. Thus, both the idealism and the realism of cinema make fidelity to her texts impossible.

Further signs of the modern world such as velocity, feminism, and the carnivalesque leak into the movies, "contaminating" what Jane Austen wrote. For instance, the Vorticist obsession with velocity to which early filmmakers responded with jump-cuts and speeding cars makes feathers flutter, horses gallop, feet twinkle, and arrows fly about in McGrath's *Emma* as they never could in Jane Austen's *Emma*. In the same movie, modern expectations for women transform her into an Amazonian huntress, while Mikhail Bakhtin's theory that the carnivalesque overturns hierarchies precipitates a circus into the sober streets of Bath in Michell's *Persuasion*. If these episodes gesture knowingly to us, others do so inadvertently. The Hollywood star system with its attendant gossipy knowledges means for instance that Hugh Grant's portrayal of the "amiable and worthy" Edward Ferrars,[12] as Thompson calls him in *Sense and Sensibility*, is disconcertingly "ghosted" by his real-life dalliance with a whore on Sunset Boulevard. All these markers of modernity necessarily occur in movies, for if, as Bakhtin says,[13] the novel is polyphonic, a microcosm of social, historical, and literary voices, then films are equally multi-voiced. These voices, however, may be entirely out of control.

Finally, the Jane Austen versions cannot be considered faithful translations if the scriptwriters mangle her words, though some slips may be blamed on the carelessness of actors. No one can possibly use everything she wrote, but accurate quotation is surely preferable to bad substitution. Here is Jane Austen's Miss Bates arriving in full flow at the Crown:

"Well! – This is brilliant indeed! – This is admirable! – Excellently contrived, upon my word. Nothing wanting. Could not have imagined it. – So well lighted up. – Jane, Jane, look – did you ever see any thing? . . . This is meeting quite in fairy-land! – Such a transformation! Must not compliment, I know – (eyeing Emma most complacently) – that would be rude – but upon my word, Miss Woodhouse, you do look – how do you like Jane's hair? – You are a judge – She did it all herself. Quite wonderful how she does her hair! – No hairdresser from London I think could . . . A little tea if you please, sir, by and bye, – no hurry – Oh! here it comes. Everything so good!" (III.iii)

Even this arbitrary selection from a long, bravura speech resonates suggestively for *Emma*'s characterization and plot. Miss Bates's incomplete sentences expose her trick of dashing distractedly from one thought to another, while the welter of delighted exclamations proves her to be indeed a "standing example of how to be happy" as Mr. Knightley puts it (II.xi) in her appreciation of small joys. Self-abnegation and gratitude are typical of her, as is her devotion to Jane. But when she praises Jane at Emma's expense, she innocently irritates Emma's sense of jealousy and displacement that will inflame her to exasperation at Box Hill. Just as unconsciously she tortures her beloved niece when she says that "no London hairdresser could," for that must remind Jane of Frank's lie that he went to London for a haircut. Though "fairy-land" seems an exaggeration typical of Miss Bates, it links *Emma* to its originating text, *A Midsummer Night's Dream*.

Any scriptwriter would conflate and compress these prolix meanderings, but McGrath's version alters and even adds:

(*To Emma and Mr. Elton*) "And we're so obliged to you for having us tonight, very much indeed. I was just saying to mother, 'we should be invited' and indeed we are. Doesn't your hair look pretty? Just like an angel. (*To Mrs. Bates*) ANGEL, mother, (*to Emma and Mr. Elton*) Oh, speaking of angels, Mr. Elton, your sermon on Daniel in the Lion's Den was so inspiring, so powerful in all its particulars, it left us speechless. Quite speechless, I tell you, and we have not stopped talking of it since. Oh isn't this a lovely party? Lovely, lovely, lovely!"

These sentences are too complete, too complex for Miss Bates, while lame repetition replaces her wonderful variety of exclamations. Furthermore, because Emma's hair is praised instead of Jane's, neither jealousy nor torture can carry on the plot. Daniel in the Lion's Den alludes to no obvious originating text, while the gag about Mrs. Bates being deaf, being left speechless, then "not stopped talking of it since" is weak indeed. Although Miss Bates carries on for two whole pages, Jane Austen's free indirect speech gives the impression of selectivity and speed. By contrast, the scriptwriter plods. For all film's reputation for quickness, then, it cannot always move at fiction's pace. Cinema's narrative methods must often be less subtle and flexible than Jane Austen's.

Cinematic techniques can, however, erase the need for words altogether. Thompson's detailed screenplay for Lee's *Sense and Sensibility* shows images happily replacing words. For instance, Fanny Dashwood's deduction of a coin from the landlord's tip displays her meanness, and her checking of the hallmark on the butterknife her snobbery. Then again, a significant shift in Elinor's response to Edward is signaled by the stage directions: *The use of the Christian name – and in such a loving tone – stops* ELINOR's *breath altogether*. Or images supply objective correlatives to a mood, as when the cottage looks cold and bleak. On these and many other occasions when visual sign-systems successfully supplant verbal ones, cinematic techniques quickly convey complex information. They speak a language parallel to prose, that is, the familiar idiom of film.

Such examples result in justifiable difference. But improper difference derives from unselfconscious, even ignorant lapses of tone, register, or felicity, as when Mr. Martin says, "Oh, blast!" or Emma calls Mr. Knightley "overqualified" to contribute a riddle in McGrath's *Emma*. In Michell's *Persuasion*, Captain Wentworth bursts out indecorously to Sir Walter Elliot in the middle of a card party that he has come with a proposal of marriage to his daughter, and Anne and Captain Wentworth kiss in the street like modern teenagers. Too modern also is Captain Wentworth's "I bet you had little idea of the consequences when you sent Captain Benwick for a surgeon"; equally unlikely is Sir Walter's "'Please God let them not snub us," that he says of Lady Dalrymple and Miss Carteret. Anne would never blurt out at the dinner table that Mrs. Smith is not the only widow in Bath with no surname of dignity, nor would she run after Wentworth at the concert and beg him to stay, like Marianne. Why did

Captain Wentworth catch Anne at breakfast instead of lifting the boy from her back, as he ought? Why is Elizabeth Elliot shrewish, slouching, and always stuffing her face with bonbons? Why the caricatures of Lady Dalrymple, her jammy mouth like Bette Davis's, and Miss Carteret, whose red cheeks look like Petrouchka's? Why dip into the chapter wisely canceled by Jane Austen, where Wentworth asks Anne on Admiral Croft's behalf whether she plans to return to Kellynch Hall? Worst of all, when Captain Wentworth drops not the pen but the sand-shaker, Michell misses the vital point that although the pen, with its power to define, has always been in the hands of men, a man now drops it in order that a woman may speak. Such moments make one wish for more fidelity to Jane Austen rather than less.

Cinematic versions of Jane Austen are inevitably intertextual since the films build on the books. However, references to other texts can also enter by mistake. For instance, in Davies's *Pride and Prejudice* Darcy strays into the television version of *Little Dorrit*[14] when he seeks Lydia in the London fog, an effect compounded by the excessively curly brim of his hat. Mrs. Bennet smacks of Miriam Margoyles playing Dickens's Flora, all fluttering ribbons and agitation, while Lady Catherine de Bourgh plays the witch from Disney's *Snow White* with her black peaked hat and her stick and her bony fingers.[15] Colin Firth as Darcy broods, smolders, and glowers like a true Byronic hero, his tousled hair brushed forward, his stock holding his proud head high, and his coat-front cut away to reveal the interesting trousers. Glimpses of him in the bath prepare the viewer for the moment when he wrenches open his shirt and jumps into the pond. Then, at the end of Michell's *Persuasion*, a shot purloined from *The Mutiny on the Bounty*[16] wrenches us disconcertingly from one movie context into an inappropriate other. Let's hope that Captain and Mrs. Wentworth make it to Pitcairn Island.

Such modernizing moments appeal to familiar stereotypes. If conscious, they bridge Jane Austen's world and ours. If unconscious, they are ridiculously anachronistic. Ideally, intertextuality engenders metatextual commentary, because the context imported by an allusion prompts further reflections. But allusion shorn of context is mere echo, and may even mislead the viewer. Whenever directors elide boundaries between one film and another like this, their allusions confuse rather than clarify the matter.

Onscreen versions of Jane Austen cannot, then, for a multiplicity of reasons, be faithful translations. Is the attempt worth making anyway? Since modern film audiences include many young people ignorant of Jane Austen, directors often try to make their films universally attractive through visual detail and occasional modern reference, as we have seen. But if they try to please us by making their versions "relevant," if they mirror back to us our own reflections, they may render the interpretation not so much "wrong" as solipsistic and self-perpetuating. Only Amy Heckerling's *Clueless* operates successfully in the recognition of that youthful ignorance; only *Clueless* "translates" the fictional world that young people do not know into the one that they thoroughly do, the world of Hollywood teenage soaps and school melodramas. Like John Dryden imagining that an ancient poet, had he lived in our age, would have altered many things "that he might accommodate himself to the Age in which he liv'd,"[17] or Samuel Richardson using the same word "accommodate" to explain how he shaped his novels to the understanding of youthful and uneducated female readers,[18] so too Heckerling legitimately "accommodates" Jane Austen to a young and equally unlearned clientele, as we shall see.

What all this means is that the relationship of the Jane Austen versions to Jane Austen's texts can never be purely mimetic. "Faithful translations" of her works cannot exist, for as soon as they are carried into that other medium of film, their difference means that they displace their originals in a kind of metaphoric or even metonymic maneuver. Far better to make the alteration deliberate and wholesale, that is, to create an imitation.

Imitation

Unlike translation, an imitation stresses its difference from the original in order to showcase the inventiveness of the author. Dryden explains: "Imitation of an Author is an Endeavour of a later Poet to write like one who has written before him on the same subject: that is, not to Translate his words, or to be Confin'd to his Sense, but only to set him as a Pattern, and to write, as he supposes, that Author would have done, had he liv'd in our Age, and in our Country."[19] Imitation differs from translation because here the creating mind, instead of attempting to follow the predecessor's words and sense, works from a more general notion of characters, themes, and plots. By highlighting differences between the old text and the new, the imitator constructs a commentary that poststructuralists would call "metatextual."[20]

The imitation, which flourished after the Restoration, depended on two assumptions: that human nature was always the same, and therefore that to copy the classics was to copy general nature. But as soon as an author set out to write for "our Age" and "our Country," he inevitably modernized the older text. Thus imitations both echoed and diverged from their originals. When Johnson called imitation a "method of translating looser than paraphrase, in which modern examples are used for ancient, or domestick for foreign,"[21] he missed its essential feature, the pleasure of recognizing how images and thoughts borrowed from a respected predecessor have been ingeniously, self-consciously transformed by the contemporary author.[22] The delight is in the difference. So too, I suggest, with the cinematic versions of Jane Austen. Our delight lies in seeing the old from a new perspective, in viewing it in a new context that opens up possibilities previously overlooked.

The relationship of texts to texts is as ancient as literature itself. A whole cluster of words such as emulation, plagiarism, translation, allusion, and imitation describes its varieties. The Romans were proud to rewrite the Greeks, while medieval literature, says Bakhtin, was a tissue of quotations all talking dialogically with one another, in a history of "appropriation, re-working and imitating of someone else's property."[23] Renaissance writers similarly crammed echoes and allusions into their work, the "inventio" appearing not in the originality but in the selection and recombination.[24] The habit of citing named "authorities" certainly preceded Jankyn's in the Wife of Bath's tale,[25] while "beauties" of older literature were commonly quoted, with or without acknowledgment, to illustrate or to confirm a general truth. Intellectual property rights were unheard of, as eighteenth-century dramatists proved when they cheerfully appropriated Shakespeare. The very root ("*ludere*") of the word "allusion" promises play, the witty yoking of two different things together as in metaphor. (Robert Folkenflick even argues that allusiveness and realism are antithetical.)[26] Through allusion an author also builds up a sense of shared heritage, a community of mind. All these practices made relationships between texts seem natural, normal, and actually creative.

Longinus believed that imitators who emulated their predecessors were "ravished and transported by a spirit not their own."[27] Creative imitation was therefore symbolized by the nectar-gathering bee or by filiality. But parallel tropes of competition and hierarchy meant that the imitation actually produced great uneasiness in eighteenth-century poets. What William Kinsley calls the "anxiety of imitation"[28] became more and more acute in the eighteenth century. Here he echoes Harold Bloom's phrase "anxiety of influence," for Bloom, his eyes so bedazzled by the Romantics that he cannot see beyond them, speaks of the shame of belatedness, of coming after powerful predecessors, of an Oedipal struggle to defeat the parent poet.[29] Nonetheless, because great authors are invariably great readers, there can be no such thing as originality. As Bakhtin puts it, every word arrives "from another context which is saturated with other people's interpretations."[30] Notions of literary hostility must disappear when Dustin Griffin talks about the deliberate and companionable challenging of predecessors, rewriting of other authors, creation as re-creation, ideas of imitation, translation, and improvement, an absence of anxiety – and thus of competition.[31] Such reassuring concepts might apply to the onscreen imitators of Jane Austen.

What this means is that before the Romantics promulgated their notions of originality so widely, everybody knew that books were made out of other books in a spirit of benign or competitive emulation. We have recently circled back to that earlier perception, for modernist, postmodernist, and poststructuralist ideas of creativity depend in their various ways upon intertextuality, or the relation of books with books. All the Jane Austen versions, whether they set out to be a translation or an imitation, necessarily stand in an intertextual relationship to her novels. Yet, only some directors seize the chance to thicken up their intertextual possibilities. I believe that Thompson's *Sense and Sensibility*, Rozema's *Mansfield Park*, and Heckerling's *Clueless* reinstate the honor, the creative potential of the imitation.

Imitation, which works from the most prestigious and well-known of classical authors, invites the reader to hold both the old text and the new simultaneously in the mind. This quasi-metaphorical maneuver depends for its effect on intelligent and informed readers, whose pleasure compounds with the flattery. Kinsley defines literary allusion as the technique whereby a writer echoes and brings an earlier text to the reader's awareness in a way that significantly affects the meaning of the later text. His terms "target text" and "alluding text" stress the intentionality of the maneuver, and distinguish allusion from passive submission to external influence – the assumption that lay behind the old pastime of source-hunting. Instead of setting up hierarchies of texts, this to-and-fro movement resembles the Aeolian harp, Coleridge's image for creativity, which answers the wind with a new sound generated by wind and harp together. The essence of the matter is not just novelty but deliberation. As the imitating author stops, compares, and develops, the well-read reader recognizes sameness along with difference.[32] When film directors similarly re-create that prestigious and well-known "modern classic" Jane Austen, the well-read spectator likewise enjoys the rewards of recognition.

Jane Austen herself looked back to the English classics as well as to her contemporaries.[33] Sometimes silently refashioning, sometimes imitating and modernizing, she moved in what Howard Weinbrot calls an "imitative spectrum"[34] from parody in the juvenilia to wholesale appropriation in the later novels. Her intertextual practices include translation, parody, imitation, allusion, and metatextual commentary, all of which show her mind creatively engaged with the paradigms and particulars of other authors. Thus, as Spivak puts it, her "original text" itself is "that palimpsest of so-called 'pre'-texts that the critic might or might not be able to disclose and any original inscription would still only be a trace."[35]

Jane Austen discovered her own voice in dialogue with her predecessors. Her early parodies especially resemble imitation, which depends upon readers recognizing the relation between copy and archetype. For instance, knowing that her family would know Richardson's *Sir Charles Grandison* (1753–1754) as well as she did, she exaggerated him to make those readers laugh. Sometimes she reminded them explicitly, as when she spoke of Lady Williams as being like "the great Sir Charles," who scorned to "deny himself when at Home, as she looked on that fashionable method of shutting out disagreeable Visitors, as little less than downright Bigamy." (Here the metatextual commentary remarks on the uncomfortable fact of Sir Charles being in love with two women at once.) Sometimes she simply assumed knowledge of Richardson, as when she parodies his account of Sir Charles as so god-like that a sunbeam from his eye seems to play on Beauchamp's face and "dazle" his eyes, making him withdraw behind a chair. Jane Austen exaggerates very little when Charles Adams attends a ball dressed as the sun, a man "of so dazzling a Beauty that none but Eagles could look him in the face." Ludicrously, "The Beams that darted from his Eyes were like those of that glorious Luminary tho' infinitely superior," so that no one dares to venture within half a mile of them.[36] Here the joke depends largely on knowing the original, on watching the tone change from serious to totally ridiculous.

As a mature writer, Jane Austen moved from parody to an appreciative deployment of Richardson, using for instance his device of the entry into a noble house four separate times. Almost always she reworked her source, a rare exception being where she too literally "translated" his *Clarissa* into the brief and confusing story of the two Elizas in *Sense and Sensiblity*. The consequence is that the *Clarissa* fragment remains unassimilated, a piece of bricolage that does not fit – Thompson sensibly changes the name of the younger one to Beth to avoid confusion, and shows her pregnancy in silhouette. When Sir Walter Elliot's clock striking eleven with its silver sounds recalled Belinda in Pope's *Rape of the Lock*, Jane Austen implied that it is not only women who are vain, for the vanities of person, rank, wealth, and possessions of this old man have already been amply demonstrated (Virginia Woolf would similarly attack men's vanity of rank, appearance, and wealth in *Three Guineas*). Later, Jane Austen appropriated *A Midsummer Night's Dream* for *Emma* and the Wife of Bath for *Persuasion* with a silence that suggests complete approbation.

Thus, the onscreen versions of Jane Austen stand to her in the same intertextual relationship as she stood to her predecessors. These are texts which allude to other texts. Because her novels are as well known to modern readers as the earlier English classics to eighteenth-century ones, directors can confidently invite spectators to construct Spivak's "palimpsest," to layer a cinematic text over the printed text and to hold them simultaneously in the mind in a kind of resonating doubleness. This confirms that they are imitations more than they are translations.

Even in versions which seem primarily to translate, one finds intelligent expansions approximating imitation. For instance, when the camera brings Margaret, the shadowy third daughter in *Sense and Sensibility* quite literally to light, Emma Thompson endows her with a presence, an education, and a future. This precocious, curious girl-child seems to have wandered in from the *Arcadia* of Tom Stoppard, whose young mathematician had herself recalled Byron's sister Ada Lovelace, inventor of the computer and a contemporary of Jane Austen whom the author never knew – in Thompson's screenplay John and Fanny Dashwood plan to build a hermitage as if paying homage to Stoppard's. This bravura development reveals the gaiety of the girl-child before it is cramped by convention, like a gentler, kinder, more genuinely curious Catherine Earnshaw. As fearless physically and mentally as Carroll's Alice, she prefigures the modern world where girls can do anything. No wonder she insists on keeping the atlas, for the world of adventure, empire, and exploration will soon be hers. As if anticipating Mary Kingsley and all the other intrepid women travelers of the nineteenth century, she identifies the source of the Nile as Abyssinia, stares at Mrs. Jennings as if she were some thrilling form of wildlife, examines a foxhole, and discusses routes through China with Sir John. Quivering with fascination when she hears that Colonel Brandon served in the East Indies, "I like Colonel Brandon," she says, "he's been to places." No wonder that Elinor threatens to give her to the gypsies, those archetypal, undomesticated wanderers.

Mrs. Dashwood half-laughs, half-sobs that Margaret will become a pirate, transgressive and different. Margaret's voice is "disembodied and truculent," divorced from her female body and decidedly unfeminine. A disheveled tomboy who spends all her time up trees and under furniture, she learns sword-fighting from Edward and makes her tree-house into a room of her own. Her petticoats, symbolizing womanhood, snag and tear as she tries to climb an impossible tree; she lacks decorum and discretion, and she likes the energy of the Middletons. Freer in spirit than her sisters, she asks awkward questions and exhibits more spontaneous feelings than they. In a further expansion of her role she accompanies Marianne on that fateful walk, bravely squares her shoulders and tries to sense the direction when told to seek help. At the end, she has built herself a new tree-house, a room of her own from which to gaze godlike upon Edward's proposal to Elinor.

When Thompson prophetically modernizes Jane Austen and compares the life of late eighteenth-century women to the greater freedom of ours, her metatextuality is entirely characteristic of imitation. Her multiple layers of allusion comment on Jane Austen's text, for Thompson signals that this third child will take a different path from her sisters. Margaret need not marry, for as the early English feminist Mary Astell said in *Some Reflections Upon Marriage* (1700), the service that woman is become obliged to pay to a man is only her "Business by the bye, just as it may be any Man's Business and Duty to keep Hogs'"[37] – "By God," said Virginia Woolf, echoing Astell's weary stoicism, "I will not look upon marriage as a profession."[38] Like Byron's sister Ada, Margaret will become a Chloe, an Olivia such as Woolf writes about in *A Room of One's Own*, a scientist, an astronomer like Caroline Herschel in Adrienne Rich's poem "Planetarium," lost in the galaxies like the stars, the marginalized women, and now found. But for all these allusions to resonate, Thompson depends on her spectators to join joyfully in the production of her text.

Thompson calls up intertextual allusion to convey a meaning, as when her Marianne identifies with those doomed heroines Juliet, Guinevere, and Heloise. Again, where in Jane Austen we only hear that Marianne and Willoughby read Cowper, Thompson has Edward recite lines from "The Castaway" that indicate (perhaps via Mr. Ramsay in Woolf's *To the Lighthouse*) the depths of his despair. And when Willoughby recites a Shakespeare sonnet about constancy (perhaps via Mrs. Ramsay in the same book), hindsight reveals the irony of his choice. Willoughby cuts off a lock of Marianne's hair in a "strangely erotic moment," says Thompson, that looks back to the more sexualized and sinister connotations of Pope's *Rape of the Lock* (as Penny Gay remarks in Chapter 5 of this volume), while he himself becomes a Romantic villain-hero, powered by the gleaming haunches of his steed. Thompson prepares us for this reading in her opening scene: "Marianne is sure to find her storybook hero," says Mrs. Dashwood. "A romantic poet with flashing eyes and empty pockets?" suggests her husband. Sure enough, when Willoughby first appears, *Crash! Through the mist breaks a huge white horse. Astride sits an Adonis in hunting gear*, says the stage direction. *He gallops off into the mist – we almost expect Bedivere to sprout wings*, and will surge away at the end like an embittered Heathcliff. Marianne calls Catherine-like to Willoughby as though he were near, and "The effect is eerie, unworldly," writes Thompson. Like the irresistible force of Shelley's "Ode to the West Wind," he lifts her as if she weighed no more than a dried leaf, while his offering of wild flowers links him to untamed nature in contrast to the hothouse bunch of his rival. The stage direction when Marianne is ill, *The dead are coming for the dying*, confirms that we are in Brontë-land. But Thompson's intertextual allusions when Colonel Brandon has "melancholy, brooding eyes," his "unfathomable look of grief and longing," and his cape billowing out behind him as he rides promise more strongly than in the book that his "more relaxed and sexually confident body," as Gay puts it, will be more than an adequate substitute for Willoughby's.

Thompson also gestures to other Jane Austen texts. Fanny Dashwood's plan to replace the walnut grove with a Grecian temple recalls the reprehensible plan to "improve" the avenues by cutting them down that a very different Fanny sighs over in *Mansfield Park*, while Edward's reply, "How picturesque," looks back to Henry Tilney's lecture on the picturesque in *Northanger Abbey*. If John Dashwood's fear that Marianne will "lose her bloom" comes straight out of Anne's similar anxieties in *Persuasion*, Charlotte's voice-over that "I dare say" Miss Grey's bridal gown "was a sorry affair, scalloped with ruffles" recalls Mrs. Elton's opinion of Emma's wedding. Marianne's transgressive entry through a gate into Cleveland Park to the sound of thunder sounds like Maria Bertram pushing past the locked gate into prohibited ground at Sotherton, though her piano must surely derive from *Emma*. It is as though all Jane Austen's texts were one text, in which meanings slide about readily to confirm meanings.

Patricia Rozema ranges just as freely over all the Jane Austen novels in *Mansfield Park*, as well as dipping intertextually into the juvenilia, letters, and recent biographies. David Nokes's idea that the novels may be fruitfully mined for autobiography has clearly inspired her, for she merges Fanny Price with Jane Austen the writer. The opening titles suggest as much when she backs her close-up shots of textured paper and pens by loud sounds of crackling and scratching. As soon as Fanny arrives at Mansfield Park, Edmund gives her a thick stack of paper upon which to write, just as Jane Austen's favorite author Samuel Richardson made similar arrangements for Pamela – Virginia Woolf would surely agree that women must have paper of their own as well as a room of their own if they are to write. Fanny has both, even if her little garret room is stuffed with the detritus of a great house, even if she too is unwanted. Far from being the creep-mouse of the novel, she turns into the "wild Beast" of the letters that Nokes admires. The juvenilia she recounts to Susan are anarchic, sexual, and violent. "Your tongue is sharper than a guillotine," says Henry Crawford ruefully, recalling D. W. Harding's controversial accusation of Jane Austen's "Regulated Hatred."[39] "The effect of education," replies Fanny mockingly, a phrase Jane Austen actually used of Mary. Unlike Jane Austen, though, who never enjoyed the intellectual support of her family, Fanny is encouraged by her cousin Edmund, who says he has talked to Egerton the publisher about printing her "Effusions of Fancy by a Very Young Girl in a Style Entirely New." She laughs, perhaps at the old-fashioned, gendered, apologetic title such as Jane Austen herself abandoned, or perhaps at his naïve promise of 10 percent, for Jane Austen never got anything so grand.

Rozema expands episodes of Fanny's attraction to Henry into her full and whole-hearted acceptance of his proposal, then models her subsequent rejection of him on Austen's acceptance and rejection the next day of Harris Bigg-Wither.[40] She draws on the life and the letters once again when she builds a scene of Fanny dancing exuberantly with Henry Crawford on Jane Austen's account of dancing with Tom Lefroy. Jane had asked Cassandra to "imagine everything most profligate and shocking in the way of dancing and sitting down together" and added that "I *can* expose myself... only once more," as Tom would be leaving the country soon after the next ball. Claire Tomalin observes that her remark about his morning coat resembling that of Tom Jones shows that Jane Austen "doesn't mind talking about a novel which deals candidly and comically with sexual attraction, fornication, bastard children and the oily hypocrisy of parsons, and roundly states that the sins of the flesh are of little account, and much to be preferred to the meanness of spirit of sober, prudent people." By telling Cassandra that she and Tom Lefroy have talked about the book together, says Tomalin, "she lets her know just how free and even bold their conversation has been."[41] This interpretation allows Rozema's characters to speak far more openly and frankly than in the published novels, compared to the letters, and encourages her to develop *Mansfield's Park*'s intense sexual undercurrents.

Just as Thompson alludes to other Austen novels for *Sense and Sensibility*, Rozema transfers her praise of novels in *Northanger Abbey* to Edmund. Similarly, Fanny utters Catherine Morland's radical attack on history as violent, tiresome, and exclusive of women, as well as the narrator's bitter comment on the attractiveness of imbecility in women. When Sir Thomas admires Fanny's improved countenance and figure he recalls that other patriarch Sir Walter Elliot remarking on Anne's second spring of health and beauty, while Henry proposes to Fanny on a stone pier suspiciously like the Cobb in *Persuasion*, where a fine wind restored Anne's bloom and freshness of youth. These allusions act as a kind of shorthand to direct our understanding.

Rozema also inserts recent influential readings of the eighteenth century into her movie when, like Felicity Nussbaum and Laura Brown,[42] she places gender, race, and class at the very heart of her enterprise. Women confined by patriarchy she images as caged birds, based on the starling who cries "I can't get out," in Laurence Sterne's *Sentimental Journey* (1768). When Henry reads that passage expressively to Fanny, he seems to understand what it means to live in a patriarchal house. But he is only an actor, and his response is both inauthentic and untrustworthy.

Trapped in a loveless marriage, Maria repeats the starling's words "can't get out, I can't get out." Escape results in eternal enclosure with Mrs. Norris.

The trapped bird is a common literary trope for women – Anne Finch for example writes in "The Bird and the Arras" (1713) of a bird who, seeking to soar like tapestry birds, dashes her head upon the ceiling. Turning to the window, she is thrown back by the clear panes until a kind hand releases her into the air, the only heaven of birds. Within the century separating Anne Finch from Charlotte Brontë, recurrent imagery links women to birds and the freedom to fly in the air of Jane Eyre's name. In *Mansfield Park* caged parakeets comment on the life of women, doomed to gaudy imprisonment and mimicry. The feathers peeking out of Mary's hat suggest the freedom of a bird, but even she is trapped by convention and the need to marry well. Henry sends fireworks, a barrel-organ, and a basket full of cooing doves to Fanny at Portsmouth, but the lone dove heading steadily in the direction of Mansfield Park is rather a homing pigeon, a symbol that Rozema picks up from the ending of *Jane Eyre*. Fanny, declares the image, will fly back home. In fact, not just women but men are trapped behind the grand window-frames of patriarchal dwellings. Sir Thomas watches Fanny leaving for Portsmouth from behind large panes, and the windows of Wimpole Street similarly bisect the Rushworths and the Crawfords. But after Mary alienates Edmund by expatiating on the advantages of Tom's death, Fanny turns to watch a flock of birds wheeling up and away. The camera bursts out through the window into open air, rising up high over estate and countryside in a panning shot that points to liberation and freedom beyond the panes of patriarchal custom.

This trope of women as caged and liberated birds merges with another pervasive eighteenth-century discourse of women as slaves. "If *all Men are born free*," wrote the early feminist Mary Astell unanswerably, "how is it that Women are born Slaves?"[43] Gender, race, and class underpin Rozema's reading of *Mansfield Park*, with its analogy between the economy of slaves and of women. Her postcolonial lens magnifies Jane Austen's hints about the slavetrade, for she represents Sir Thomas's dual functions as slave-owner and patriarch as indistinguishable. Attracted himself to Mary Crawford, he pushes Edmund to enjoy her as it were by proxy, and when the "potential brutalizer" that Jan Fergus speaks of elsewhere in this volume gloats over Fanny's figure and countenance on his return, she turns away with a slight recoil of distaste. He speaks of the beauty of "his" slaves, especially mulattoes, while asserting that like mules they can't breed. Fanny resists his degradation of humans to animals, and asks if they would be freed in England. (Here she echoes Justice Mansfield, after whom Mansfield Park may be named, who had famously

4. Fanny Price (Frances O'Connor) confronts Sir Thomas Bertram (Harold Pinter) in Patricia Rozema's 1999 Miramax Films' *Mansfield Park*.

ruled in 1771 that as soon as any slave set foot upon English ground he became free.) When Sir Thomas plans a ball for her, she says to Edmund that she will not be "sold off like one of your father's slaves" and rides away furiously in the rain – horse-riding was also seen in the eighteenth century as emblematic of freedom for women. To name her horse Mrs. Shakespeare hints similarly at her liberation through reading the English classics. But Edmund lends Mary the horse, and Fanny loses her sole chance to feel free.

Edmund speaks of "problems" with the slaves that force Sir Thomas to go to Antigua, for the abolitionists are making inroads. "We all live off the profits, even you," he says to Fanny. In Rozema's reading of *Mansfield Park* this knowledge literally sickens Tom, who is driven mad and bad by the "dis-ease" of being his father's first son and heir, complicit by birth in this ugly trade. Sir Thomas calls his expressionist self-portrait "morbid," its haggard face doubled by the figure of Death, but Tom blackens himself for the rehearsal as if in sympathy with the slaves. His vividly realized sketches expose the horrors of rape and murder, with Sir Thomas a violent oppressor to his slaves. Tom's coverlet of watered orange silk, that gorgeous product of empire, cannot save him from empire's effects.

Faced with the possibility that his son might die, Sir Thomas grieves that Tom had a mission, a noble mission. Give him time, says the doctor, while an orrery stands reassuringly nearby. Tom does indeed recover, and Sir Thomas gives up his interests in Antigua to grow tobacco. In a final vivid example of the empire striking back, Lady Bertram's lassitude is caused by opium. Through the Opium Wars Britain weakened the resistance of China and opened it up to trade. The drug that destroyed a nation now blights a British noblewoman.

The song of a "black cargo" wafts from a slave-ship when Fanny leaves Portsmouth, and again during the closing credits. The same black ship reappears ominously in the background as Henry proposes to Fanny. Edmund is right to say that the wealth and status of Mansfield Park is built upon slavery and the imperial project, including their vast, moldering and oddly unfurnished house where they live out their lives of lavish idleness. Fanny is right to point out that it matters how wealth is acquired, but nobody is exempt from its enjoyment. Sir Thomas decorates his study with drums, a worked metal casket and a sculptured African head, Fanny displays shell necklaces in her little room, and Mary wraps herself in an opulent black and silver shawl from India. All are the beneficiaries of empire.

Class too is highlighted when Lindsay Duncan plays both Lady Bertram and Mrs. Price, one surrounded by luxury, the other by maggoty plates and filth. The sheer accident of marriage makes one pampered and pretty, the other worn and plain. "Remember, Fanny, I married for love," says Mrs. Price warningly. But the siren's harp and reaper's scythe silhouetted together on the skyline remind us that even the young and beautiful must join in the dance of death.

Modern preoccupations with bodies make Rozema's *Mansfield Park* more explicitly sexual than Jane Austen's could ever be. To mark the arrival of the Crawfords, the camera acts as the family's eyes when it pans slowly from their feet to their handsome heads, not overlooking everything that lies between. As objects of the cinematic gaze, the sexualized bodies of the Crawfords perform their gender and class. No need for the subplot about Henry helping William Price, when sexual attraction alone does the trick. The celebrated nudity of Maria and Henry, offstage and literally "obscene" in Jane Austen, is made visible for our modern times. Rushworth has invited a journalist from a London paper to write about his "improvements," but what the journalist sees is a rumpled and enseamed bed recently abandoned by the lovers. He licks his pencil excitedly in anticipation of a scoop. As Jane Austen's favorite novelist Samuel Richardson had warned, a reformed rake does not make the best husband, and Fanny says repeatedly that she cannot trust Henry. At the end,

Rozema suggests that the betrayers are betrayed when their two spouses exchange conspiratorial glances. Unlike Jane Austen, she shows no sympathy for Mary, who speaks, not writes, her arguments for anticipating Tom's death. It seems unlikely, however, that such an intelligent creature would expose herself so openly. Mary is portrayed as advanced, playing billiards and smoking a cigarillo like a suffragette. She extenuates Maria's fault by exclaiming "It is 1806 for heaven's sake" but the appalled faces of the family show that they cannot accept her moral relativism even in the name of modernity.

Mary's spiderwoman sleeves reveal her predatory nature in this speech, as in her first appearance, while at the ball scene she circles hungrily in black around Edmund. Fanny, by contrast, dresses in white, but with a décolletage quite unlike her schoolgirl pinafores of dark blue – cinema conveys meaning through the semiotics and color of clothing. Tipsy and staggering slightly as she weaves her way from the ballroom, Fanny exults in her newly discovered sexuality. At cards, Mary stakes her last like a woman of spirit, but Fanny trumps both king and queen with the ace of spades, the black ace that in Pope's *Rape of the Lock* signifies the woman's pudendum. After this remarkable display of agency on Fanny's part, the narrative voice-over declaring it "quite natural" for Edmund to learn to love Fanny quite naturally devolves to her. Edmund is a man of sensibility to match Fanny, that devoted reader of Sterne's *Sentimental Journey*. He approves of her tears when she arrives at Mansfield Park, cries when she goes to Portsmouth, and weeps when Mary speaks. Rozema offers a new proposal scene in which this modern Edmund declares to Fanny, "I have loved you all my life." To her indulgent "I know," he replies, "I love you as a man loves a woman." Fanny smiles merrily into the camera as Edmund embraces her, incandescent and triumphant. In all these ways, Patricia Rozema's *Mansfield Park* declares itself an imitation by its intertextualities, its developments of Jane Austen's hints into fully realized scenes, its attention to these dominant modern paradigms of gender, race, and class.

Amy Heckerling's *Clueless* is, however, the most thoroughgoing revision of Jane Austen and therefore the most fully creative imitation – Weinbrot writes that the imitation is "not a restrictive but a liberating form which enlarges the [writer's] possibilities for metaphor and insists that the reader be aware of his moment in history and its relationship to other moments."[44] As if acting on Dryden's advice, Heckerling abandons Jane Austen's actual words and sense altogether while appropriating almost all of her characters and situations. She writes, to use his words, "as [s]he supposes, that Author would have done, had [s]he liv'd in our Age, and in our Country."

Cher, like Emma, is a spoilt, educationally challenged rich kid. She drives a white jeep, chooses her clothes by computer, and is meddling, pretty, and smart. Motherless, for her mother died of a fluke accident during a routine liposuction, she is not exactly likeable, but her solicitude about her hard-working father's diet, like Emma's patience about Mr. Woodhouse and his gruel, shows that her heart is good. This brilliant and funny movie endows Cher with a rich black friend, Dionne, a combination of Mrs. Weston and Jane Fairfax who gives her someone to talk to (her rapping "homie" boyfriend, hitching his baggy pants up to half-mast, delivers a quick and savvy sermon about street slang as an increasingly valid form of expression). Mr. Knightley becomes Josh, her Granola-breath, Nietzsche-reading stepbrother. When he rebukes her for her 90 percent selfish life, she responds defensively that she plans to brake for animals. Her consequent realization that "it is a far far better thing doing stuff with other people" sets her off on a path similar to Emma's.

Just as Emma takes credit for the marriage between Miss Taylor and Mr. Weston, she tricks two teachers into falling in love ("old people can be so sweet"), and confidently undertakes the makeover of her friend and lost soul Tai ("under your tutelage she's exploring the challenging world of bare midriffs"). She makes Tai do aerobics to give her buns of steel, and advises her to enlarge her vocabulary by using new words in a sentence. "Sporadically," says Tai, to her teacher's pride. Cher's main thrill in life is a makeover, for it gives her a sense of control in a world of chaos. After Cher takes Tai's photograph ("doesn't she look classic?") and their "way popular" classmate Elton pastes it in his locker, Tai has to believe he loves her ("I noticed him scoping you out"). But after throwing her souvenirs of Elton on the gas fire, Tai learns to appreciate the devoted Travis, whom she once thought a slacker. On his own domain of the skateboard ramp, he shines as brightly as Mr. Martin on his English farm. Mr. Elton's actually making violent love to Emma in the carriage becomes sexual harassment in a car ride through Sun Valley, while Emma's rudeness to Miss Bates transforms into an offensive assumption that the San Salvadorean maid speaks Mexican. Cher fails her driving test and goes down a shame spiral ("Josh thinking I was mean was making me postal"). Really, she is totally clueless and a virgin, she thinks miserably, confronting like Emma the barrenness of her declining life.

The revelation that Christian, the Frank Churchill figure, is gay provides a particularly rich reading – he dances narcissistically on an empty floor, flirts with the bartender, and prefers watching Tony Curtis to going all the way with Cher ("Maybe my hair got really flat," thinks Cher). Nonetheless, he makes a great shopping companion. As in all the Austen versions, the visual displays of dancing provide the preliminary to the

5. Christian (Justin Walker) fools the clueless Cher (Alicia Silverstone), who is blind to his sexual preferences, in the Paramount Pictures release *Clueless*.

marriage choice, permission to touch flesh experimentally. To a background of high-school students puking into the swimming pool, Cher rubs provocatively up against Christian, and Josh plunges about gallantly to rescue Tai from the humiliation of having nobody to dance with. But Josh watches Cher, for he is not Cher's brother, no indeed, no more than Mr. Knightley is Emma's father. Instead of Emma realising with the speed of an arrow that Mr. Knightley must marry no one but herself, "Oh my gosh," says Cher, "I love Josh. I am majorly, totally but crazily in love with Josh." After they declare their love, she says, "You can guess what happened next. As if. I mean I am only sixteen, and this is California, not Kentucky." The final surprise is that the glitzy wedding is the teachers', not their own, but Cher gets the bouquet, after a brief and vicious scrum.

Heckerling goes even further than Thompson and Rozema when she works not only from Jane Austen but from a multiplicity of printed, filmic, and musical texts. As a product of the late twentieth century, she can assume an intertextual awareness in modern audiences, who are trained, as David Lodge citing Umberto Eco puts it, to hear the filmic archetypes "talk among themselves" and "generate an intoxicating excess of signification." As Eco argues, "Works are created by works, texts are created by texts." What *Casablanca* did unconsciously, says Eco, "other movies will do with extreme intertextual awareness, assuming also that the addressee is equally aware of their purposes"; he calls these "post-modern" movies, "where the quotation of the topos is recognized as the only way to cope with the burden of our filmic encyclopedic expertise."[45] In *Clueless*, for just one example, Christian's admiration of Tony Curtis in *Spartacus* hints at bisexuality long before Christian turns out to be gay.

Clueless is as knowing, as deliciously intertextual and postmodern as *Casablanca* in Eco's reading of it. Cher knows that it was Polonius not Hamlet who said "To thine own self be true," but remembers the quotation only because of Mel Gibson, just as she recalls "the darling buds of May" only through the mediation of *Cliff's Notes*. Watching *Ren and Stimpy* with Josh, Cher remarks that it's way existential. "Do you know what on earth you are talking about?" says Josh. "No," says Cher sadly, feeling more clueless than ever. Even the music adds extra layers. The strains of *Thus Spake Zarathustra* swell out for an ominous close-up of the black cellular phone, a witty look-alike for the monolith at the start of *2001*, while the theme from *Gigi* follows Cher's slow, Scarlett O'Hara-like descent of the staircase wearing the tiny Calvin Klein dress that her father calls underwear, and which dazzles Josh.

The charm of *Clueless* lies in its cheek, its transformation of high culture into low, its gleefully transgressive disestablishmentarianism, its cast of young and culturally hybrid actors reflecting the ethnic makeup of Los Angeles, its thoroughgoing relocation and dislocation of Jane Austen to the New World and the end of the twentieth century. References to Mr. Woodhouse's work-induced stress, Mrs. Woodhouse's liposuction and Knightley's Granola all anchor it both in our time and in the universal dreamscape of California. *Clueless*, though located at the furthest distance from Jane Austen's text, is the closest to Dryden's idea of imitation. That is, it draws its essential elements from Jane Austen, but renews them completely, deliberately, within and by means of their new context. Of all the cinematic versions, *Clueless* proclaims its own most comprehensive and self-contained life. It stands on its own feet as imitations were meant to do. Bloom may argue that in the violent Oedipal struggle "strong" authors displace their poetic progenitors, but imitations (uniquely) do not obliterate the parent text. They recall it. Jane Austen is both absent and present in this movie, as if "under erasure," in Jacques Derrida's formulation[46] (much like James Joyce's relocation of Homer into 1920s Dublin in *Ulysses*). *Emma* is alive and well in *Clueless*. But if you want to read Jane Austen, you can always read Jane Austen. Her aura and authenticity remain intact, however often she appears on screen.

To cite Dryden for one last time, the imitator "assumes the liberty not only to vary from the words and sense, but to forsake them both as he sees occasion: and taking only some general hints from the Originals, to run division on the ground-work, as he pleases."[47] Variations on a theme are acknowledged to be creative in music or art, so why not in cinematic texts? Jane Austen, who transported the English classics into her own age and country, has now become that oxymoron a "modern classic" upon whom, as we have seen, movie directors stamp their markers of modernity. To define the onscreen versions of Jane Austen as imitations rather than as translations allows us to appreciate those moments of genuinely creative divergence from her texts.

So-called fidelity to the text cannot, then, guarantee a successful transition from novels to films. Quite the opposite. The most satisfying Jane Austen movies are not just "translations" but "imitations" rejoicing in their difference. Just as Jane Austen defended that upstart and "low" form, the novel, in *Northanger Abbey* (i.v), so we may praise *Sense and Sensibility*, *Mansfield Park*, and *Clueless* in Miss Bates's words, "Such a transformation!" Only a movie each may be, but like a novel each displays a thorough knowledge of human nature, delineates its varieties, and conveys the liveliest effusion of wit and humor to the world in the best chosen language. These innovative and creative works suggest new paths for future adaptations of Jane Austen.

NOTES

Elements of this essay first appeared in *Eighteenth-Century Fiction* 8.3 (1995): 427–430.

1 Jonathan Culler, *Structuralist Poetics: Structuralism, Linguistics, and the Study of Literature* (London: Routledge and Kegan Paul, 1975): 140.

2 David Constantine, "Finding the Words: Translation and the Survival of the Human," *The Times Literary Supplement* (May 21, 1999): 15.

3 Gayatri Chakravorty Spivak, "Translator's Preface" to Jacques Derrida's *Of Grammatology* (Baltimore, MD: Johns Hopkins University Press, 1974): lxxv.

4 John Dryden, *An Essay of Dramatick Poesie*, 1668, ed. James T. Boulton (London: Oxford University Press, 1964): 90.

5 In the edition by George B. Hill (Oxford: Clarendon Press, 1905): I, 422.

6 Roland Barthes, *Image–Music–Text* (New York: Hill and Wang, 1977): 142–148.

7 Donna Haraway, *Simians, Cyborgs, and Women: The Reinvention of Nature* (London: Free Association Books, 1991): 124.

8 Graham Hough, "Narrative and Dialogue in Jane Austen," *Critical Quarterly* 12 (1970): 201–230.

9 See Judith Mayne, *Cinema and Spectatorship* (London: Routledge, 1993): 36, who cites Barthes, *Image–Music–Text*: 148.

10 Mayne, *Cinema and Spectatorship*: 45.

11 Emma Thompson, *The "Sense and Sensibility" Screenplay and Diaries: Bringing Jane Austen's Novels to Film* (London: Bloomsbury, 1995).

12 Ibid.: 53.
13 Mikhail Bakhtin, *Problems of Dostoevsky's Poetics*, trans. R. W. Rotsel (Ann Arbor, MI: Ardis, 1973).
14 *Little Dorrit*, Director Christine Edzard, 1987.
15 *Snow White and the Seven Dwarfs*, Director David Hand. Walt Disney, 1939.
16 *The Mutiny on the Bounty*, Director Frank Lloyd, 1939; Director Lewis Milestone, 1962.
17 Dryden, *Dramatick Poesie*: 63.
18 See the Letter to Aaron Hill, October 27, 1748 (*Selected Letters of Samuel Richardson*, ed. John Carroll [London: Oxford University Press, 1964]: 98).
19 *The Poems of John Dryden*, ed. James Kinsley (Oxford: Clarendon Press, 1958): I, 184.
20 See Udo Hebel's comprehensive introductory survey in *Intertextuality, Allusion, and Quotation* (Westport, CT: Greenwood, 1989): 14–17.
21 *Dictionary*, 1755. Johnson was remembering Dryden's definition from his own "Life" of the older poet: "Translation . . . is not so loose as paraphrase, nor so close as metaphrase" (see *Lives of the English Poets*, 1781, ed. George Birkbeck Hill [Oxford: Clarendon Press, 1905]: I, 422).
22 See Howard Weinbrot, *The Formal Strain: Studies in Augustan Imitation and Satire* (Chicago: University of Chicago Press, 1969) for elucidating examples.
23 In *Problems*: 146.
24 See William Kinsley, "'Allusion' in the Eighteenth Century: The Disinherited Critic," *Man and Nature; L'homme et la nature* 3 (1984): 22–45.
25 See *The Wife of Bath's Prologue and Tale* from *The Canterbury Tales* by Geoffrey Chaucer, ed. James Winny (Cambridge: Cambridge University Press, 1971).
26 Robert Folkenflick, "'Homo Alludens' in the Eighteenth Century," *Criticism* 24 (1982): 218–231.
27 Weinbrot, *Formal Strain*: 6.
28 Kinsley, "'Allusion'": 35.
29 Harold Bloom, *The Anxiety of Influence: A Theory of Poetry* (New York: Oxford University Press, 1953; repr. 1970).
30 Bakhtin, *Problems*: 165.
31 In the Afterword to *Regaining Paradise: Milton and the Eighteenth Century* (Cambridge: Cambridge University Press, 1986).
32 Kinsley, "'Allusion'."
33 See my *Jane Austen's Art of Memory* (Cambridge: Cambridge University Press, 1989) and my "Jane Austen and the Burden of the (Male) Past: The Case Re-examined," in *Jane Austen and the Discourses of Feminism*, ed. Devoney Looser (New York: St. Martin's Press, 1995): 87–100.
34 Weinbrot, *Formal Strain*: 16.
35 Spivak, "Translator's Preface": lxxv.
36 Samuel Richardson, *Sir Charles Grandison*, ed. Jocelyn Harris (London: Oxford University Press, 1972): vol. II, 388.
37 Reprinted in *Astell: Political Writings*, ed. Patricia Springborg (Cambridge: Cambridge University Press, 1996): 11.
38 Letter, May 1, 1912. Quentin Bell, *Virginia Woolf: A Biography* (New York: Harcourt Brace Jovanovich, 1972).

39 "Regulated Hatred: An Aspect of the Work of Jane Austen," *Scrutiny* 8 (1939–1940): 346–362.
40 See Claire Tomalin, *Jane Austen: A Life* (London: Viking, 1997): 180–182.
41 Ibid.: 113–115.
42 Felicity Nussbaum and Laura Brown (eds.), *The New Eighteenth Century: Theory, Politics, English Literature* (New York and London: Methuen, 1987).
43 Astell, *Some Reflections upon Marriage*, in *Astell*, ed. Springborg: 18.
44 Weinbrot, *Formal Strain*: 219.
45 David Lodge (ed.), *Modern Criticism and Theory* (London and New York: Longman, 1988): 445.
46 Ibid.: 447, 454.
47 *Poems*: I, 182.

Jan Fergus

Response to the 1999 Miramax film of *Mansfield Park*, as well as to the 1983 BBC television series, reflects the negative critical response to *Mansfield Park* the novel. Easily Jane Austen's most controversial work, *Mansfield Park* has been least appreciated among the six novels by Austen's readers during this century, although critics have recently received it more favorably as her most politically radical work, dealing with imperialism and the slave trade.[1] Austen's choice of the self-conscious, oppressed, anxious adolescent Fanny Price as heroine, however, has never met with much approval, starting with Austen's own friends and family, some of whom found her as "insipid" and unlikable as many moderns do.

The 1999 film met such views and objections head on and, partly as a result, was well received by most reviewers. Written and directed by Patricia Rozema, this version flaunted a connection between gentry life at Mansfield and the brutality and exploitation of slave plantations; more radically, it grafted Austen herself onto Fanny. The rebellious and assertive Austen of the juvenilia addresses the camera and the audience directly, satirizing male versions of history and female stereotypes; this Fanny Price is so strong that no viewer can doubt her eventual triumph. By contrast, the 1983 television series,[2] directed by David Giles, predated a general critical focus on Sir Thomas as a slave owner in Antigua. This version does not mention slavery, offers a self-conscious, oppressed, anxious Fanny Price, and sticks close to the text. Never aired on public television in the United States, it was not widely reviewed when first shown in England, and its reception was lukewarm. *Observer* reviewer Julian Barnes was most critical, citing a "National Trust approach to literature: lots of raked gravel, background music, mob-capped actors vaguely familiar from previous classic serials, and a deceptive deference to the surface of the text."[3] That is, the 1983 version shared the novel's and the heroine's status as "poor relation" among adaptations mounted at about the same time: the 1979 BBC *Pride and Prejudice* and the 1971 *Sense and Sensibility*. Giles's version, with Ken Taylor's screenplay, however, deals more

successfully than any other adaptation with the central problem of filming Austen: the problem of finding an equivalent for the narrative voice.
Ironically, then, for Austen "purists" – those who appreciate the language,
the subtle and comic rendition of character, and the author's narrative –
the 1983 BBC screenplay of this least-loved novel (now in danger of receiving too narrowly politicized readings) sets the standard for adapting
Austen's novels to the screen. Indeed, the virtues of this rendition could
heighten some viewers' appreciation of the novel itself, for it vividly realizes the essential qualities of ironic narrative that set Austen apart from her
contemporaries and that attract Austen purists. This essay will delineate
standards for a "purist" or perhaps "neopurist" approach to rendering the
pleasures of Austen's narrative and will illustrate them with particulars
from the Giles BBC production (as edited and preserved on two videotapes, issued in 1986), contrasting both with less effective postmodern
choices made in Rozema's 1999 production.

Patricia Rozema's postmodern 1999 *Mansfield Park*

Rozema's version constructs a postmodern pastiche of Austen's novel.
Brenda R. Silver has suggested, in studying versions of Virginia Woolf's
works, that "adaptations should be conceived as versions of the work:
texts with the same status as any other text in the ongoing, historical
construction of a composite, palimpsestic work."[4] Silver insists that an
adaptation is not merely "a form of editorializing" on a particular text:
"it does more than comment on or interpret an original . . . an adaptation,
like a critical essay, claims legitimacy for its perspective, its own political
agenda, through the construction of its text."[5] This postmodern view of
adaptation as intervention is consistent with many of the rave reviews that
the film received, most notably that of Claudia Johnson in the *Times Literary Supplement*, who called it a "stunning revisionist reading of Austen's
darkest novel . . . more of an intervention than an adaptation" and particularly admired the "superb" scenes at the end "that freeze the action
and break the illusion of realism to call attention to the intervention of
her art."[6] Although such breaks in "the illusion of realism," including
Fanny's direct addresses to the camera, may seem postmodern, in fact
they echo narrative comments at the end of *Mansfield Park* – as Johnson
implies. The most notable is "Let other pens dwell on guilt and misery.
I quit such odious subjects as soon as I can, impatient to restore every
body, not greatly in fault themselves, to tolerable comfort, and to have
done with all the rest" (III.xvii).

Postmodern pastiche is more insistently present in the film when Rozema incorporates elements of the Gothic, as if the Brontës had collaborated on the screenplay. Mansfield Park itself is dark, gloomy, empty – barely inhabited and decaying to ruin at the margins. Harold Pinter's Sir Thomas is presented as a brutalizer and rapist not only of slaves but potentially of Fanny herself, as Rozema acknowledged in an interview.[7] His response to Fanny, played by Frances O'Connor, is incestuous: he appears menacingly and unrecognized in darkness before her on his return from Antigua and, more fearsomely, looms over her in her bedroom when he enters, ostensibly to announce Henry Crawford's proposal. These Gothic elements slide nicely into modern political and social trendiness: sexual abuse, racism, violence, family dysfunction, even addiction (Lindsay Duncan as Lady Bertram swills opium). In fact, Rozema evokes all modern shibboleths and produces a heroine-artist capable of resisting them all. This Fanny is unfazed, too, even receptive, when Mary Crawford (Embeth Davidtz) comes on to her sexually in two scenes. Partly as a result of Fanny's strength, the role of Edmund, played by Jonny Lee Miller, is weakened. A strong Fanny scarcely needs Edmund's advice and support, after all. Rozema even adds the first nude sex scene in an Austen adaptation, for Henry Crawford and Maria Rushworth copulate at Mansfield itself, detected by Fanny. Consistently, what is latent in the novel – from sex to the Bertrams' reliance on slave plantations – is made blatant.

Any adaptation of a novel for film or television certainly must make some of what is latent blatant (or "dramatic"), must render some verbal content visual, and many Austen critics believe that her narrative is particularly resistant to such transformations. One is Roger Gard, who argues in Chapter 1 of this text that "The camera has no narrative voice." As a result, film "can't establish an ironic context."

Pictures can tell only of the surface of things . . . they can't condense, they can't moralise, they cannot conduct sustained arguments without cluttering the mind with irrelevant visual detail – that chair, that dress, that tree . . . their bold definiteness and specificity . . . leaves no room for mystery, for imagination about, for example, someone's appearance, or for reflection about the nuances of their actions and motives.

Gard explicitly cites the "bravura opening" of *Mansfield Park*, "with all its rich implications – how lumbering, how impossibly drawn out, an attempt to film this would be." Nevertheless, Giles's BBC version achieves much of what Gard says cannot be achieved. Gard specifically argues the impossibility of a filmic "ironic context" that "leaves room . . . for reflection about the nuances of . . . actions and motives." Yet, such ironic nuances are actually rendered by the opening of the BBC version.

The BBC's 1983 purist *Mansfield Park*: speaking "as they ought"

Obviously, the television adaptation does not precisely try to film the opening lines in detail. It is selective, and it pays special attention to performance in a manner faithful to Austen's own notions of her voice and her characters. We know, for example, that when *Pride and Prejudice* was first published, the Austen family at Chawton read it aloud on successive evenings to themselves and a neighbor. The first night's installment pleased Jane Austen enormously; she had probably done most of the reading herself. She confessed (on February 4, 1813), however, to "some fits of disgust" or distaste on the next night: "I believe something must be attributed to my Mother's too rapid way of getting on – & tho' she perfectly understands the Characters herself, she cannot speak as they ought."[8] Clearly, Austen imagined her own characters' voices in her mind. She heard her characters in performance, their words properly enacted, speaking "as they ought." Furthermore, when her mother read the text, Austen suffered some of the same discomfort that many modern readers experience when adaptations of the novels violate their sense of the characters and the stories.

Austen's formulation, however, tells us how a performance can satisfy Austen purists. In such performances, the characters will speak "as they ought," as I believe they do in Giles's BBC adaptation. Yet, even if characters' speeches are rendered appropriately, the narrator's voice can pose problems. Other versions of the novels wrench the narrator's comments into the mouths of characters who would not, or could not, or should not utter such words, as when Charlotte Lucas is given the opening line of *Pride and Prejudice* in the 1979 BBC version: "It is a truth universally acknowledged, that a single man in possession of a good fortune, must be in want of a wife." The multiple ironies of that sentence cannot be encompassed by Charlotte's voice, nor even by Elizabeth Bennet's, though the A&E version gives her part of that line. Giles's BBC *Mansfield Park* succeeds with the narrator's voice because it is willing to abandon it. Here, narrative is not, as in the versions mentioned, inappropriately allotted to characters. The screenplay finds a number of much more effective techniques for incorporating important elements in the narrative and thereby creating powerful ironic contexts; a close examination of the opening scenes shows these devices at work.

Narrative techniques

Visual equivalents for narrative

First, Giles's adaptation finds a visual equivalent for significant words or phrases. Take the first sentence, as Gard did:

About thirty years ago, Miss Maria Ward of Huntingdon, with only seven thousand pounds, had the good luck to captivate Sir Thomas Bertram, of Mansfield Park, in the county of Northampton, and to be thereby raised to the rank of a baronet's lady, with all the comforts and consequences of an handsome house and large income. (I.i)

Arguably the most important word in this sentence is "captivate," since Maria Ward's captivation of Sir Thomas outlines the predatory relation between female beauty and male money that Austen dissects in her novels. How is such a word or concept to be rendered visually? I suggest that it is done by making Lady Bertram both beautiful and static at the start and in the majority of succeeding scenes. She is decidedly an object of the gaze, in Laura Mulvey's well-known formulation,[9] and nothing else. Sitting like a spider on her sofa, she draws others inevitably to her in most scenes: in the first, Mrs. Norris bustles in to sit facing her and Sir Thomas, who stands nearby. The camera too seems captivated: like Mrs. Norris, it cuts closer to the corner where the sofa stands. Although Mrs. Norris's "spirit of activity" (I.i) in the text is represented visually and aurally by her movement, by her words in voice-over as the camera shows us Fanny's voyage, and by her subsequent presence in the carriage that takes Fanny from Northampton to Mansfield, her homing instinct takes her back once more to perch before Lady Bertram's sofa – as does the camera. On this occasion, Mrs. Norris brings Fanny to sit by Lady Bertram, whose husband and four children stand before her, while the more privileged Pug occupies her lap. In the next scene, after the children have withdrawn, Sir Thomas and Mrs. Norris discuss the "point of great delicacy" (how to keep Fanny from thinking herself a Miss Bertram) over Lady Bertram's head, yet they do so before her sofa.

In one sense, then, Lady Bertram seems successfully to captivate not just Sir Thomas but Mansfield itself; yet in another sense she is herself the captive – her stasis, her inertia, indeed her marriage to her sofa serving as a fine visual equivalent for the limited options women face in her world. Not that she rebels, of course: she embraces restriction. Although Lady Bertram is shown standing up and actually moving in her next appearance, at Mr. Norris's graveside and in the entrance hall to Mansfield just after the funeral (added scenes), as in most such instances,

6. Fanny Price (Frances O'Connor) and Henry Crawford (Alessandro Nivola) in Patricia Rozema's 1999 Miramax Films' *Mansfield Park*

she is supported by Sir Thomas. In any event, she is clearly in search of her couch. A nice touch of visual comedy occurs through Lady Bertram's despairing glance up the staircase that she must ascend in order to achieve her sofa; she seems a genuine mourner at that point (and as she climbs). After these scenes, Lady Bertram and her sofa (and Pug) are fixtures in most of the sequences at Mansfield. In fact, she tends to sink deeper into it, dozing and snoozing like Pug, more supine as the story progresses. For example, in her next appearance, she is lying on her sofa, her feet up, shoeless, a finger stroking her nose – almost as if she is sucking her thumb. In this scene, Mrs. Norris energetically rejects the notion that Fanny should live with her. When Mrs. Norris pleads poverty among other excuses, Lady Bertram significantly exerts herself to remind her sister, as in the novel, that "Sir Thomas says you will have six hundred a year" (I.iii). That is, Lady Bertram is not wholly a cipher. Though she generally does not initiate topics, she sometimes does in both the novel and the film (as when she tells Fanny that she will live with Mrs. Norris in the White House). Nonetheless, her words here and elsewhere generally have no real weight, no real consequences: Mrs. Norris has her way. In the film, then, Lady Bertram's sofa visually represents not simply her inertia but her lack of agency – and again, women's limited options in the world Austen described.

Altogether, Lady Bertram lies back on the couch with her feet up in thirteen further sequences, in many of which Pug dozes on or by her, and in three of which she herself sleeps, accounting for about eighteen and a half minutes of screen time. Though the camera does not focus on her at all times in these sequences, it continually returns to show us her recumbent form and her comically absent (or surprisingly apt) responses to what is occurring around her. In addition, she does sit again after the two initial scenes: she is shown seated at dinner twice, and she sits up on her sofa once to welcome Sir Thomas home from Antigua; however, as soon as he leaves to inspect his room, she puts her feet up again. Altogether, we are shown Lady Bertram sitting rather than lying on her sofa for more than nine minutes, and sitting two more minutes at the dinner table. These nineteen scenes outweigh in frequency and duration her twelve standing or moving sequences, which take up less than thirteen minutes and are primarily devoted to arrivals, departures, and ceremonies, like the first two instances arising from Mr. Norris's funeral. Subsequent upright moments include Maria's and Fanny's weddings, Sir Thomas and Tom's departure for Antigua, her withdrawal from the card table at the Grants', the receiving line for the ball at Mansfield and then the promenade with Sir Thomas to the ballroom, her removal from the breakfast-room as Henry Crawford arrives, Tom's return ill, a kneeling stint at Tom's sickbed, from which she is removed by Edmund, and Edmund, Fanny, and Susan's joint arrival at Mansfield. Again, she tends to stand or move in these scenes with support from her husband or Edmund; while Sir Thomas is in Antigua, Lady Bertram is couchbound except for meals.

Narrator's voice assigned to character

To return to the ironic contexts supplied in the first scene: Lady Bertram's beauty and bland mindlessness complicate our understanding of Sir Thomas there, clarifying his limitations (as do other elements in this scene). Lady Bertram's stasis is also verbally suggested when she laments the distance by coach from Northampton – "full eight miles." Even though the phrase occurs nowhere in the text, it plausibly characterizes her and reminds those familiar with the text of the "ten miles of indifferent road" (I.iv) that Mrs. Norris forces Lady Bertram to traverse in pursuit of Mr. Rushworth's fortune for Maria. Yet even this inert and inane Lady Bertram can be made to do narrative work: the screenplay's second technique for incorporating important significant narrative elements gives characters phrases that belong properly to the omniscient narrator but that the character could very well utter. Lady Bertram quavers that her sister Mrs. Price married a Lieutenant of Marines, without fortune or education, very close to the narrator's "Lieutenant of Marines, without education, fortune, or connections" (i.i). These are among the very few subjects that the former Maria Ward shows herself capable of reflecting upon, after all. Readers of the novel will remember that the only "rule of conduct" that Lady Bertram ever gives Fanny is that "it is every young woman's duty to accept such a very unexceptionable offer" as Henry Crawford's (iii.ii). For her to be given this phrase of narrative, indicating just the offer a young woman should not accept, does not violate a performance or "reading" of her character, any more than does her dismay at the thought of traveling eight miles anywhere.

Voice-over narrative

A third technique is conventional: voice-over narrative, but intelligently assigned. In the first scene, Mrs. Norris, as noted earlier, details in voice-over the ways in which Fanny Price, brought up and educated at Mansfield, will be settled (that is, married) "without farther expense to any of us," as we see the child Fanny on her lonely journey in a carrier's cart then abandoned at a Northampton inn, waiting for Mrs. Norris to arrive. Her pictured isolation and abandonment ironically counterpoint Mrs. Norris's verbal praise of her own generosity and her management of Fanny's destiny ("she will never be more to them [the Bertram brothers] than a sister"). Fanny's confidential letters to her brother William at sea are also given in voice-overs. Her letters to William are important in the text, and they allow the adaptation to offer more of Fanny's voice (put down as she is by everyone but Edmund) than we would otherwise obtain, and even more of the comedy. She quotes in a letter, for instance, Tom Bertram's hopeful notion that Dr. Grant is "a short-neck'd, apoplectic sort of fellow," implying that he will soon "pop off" as the novel has it (i.iii). When she writes with enthusiasm to William about the mare that Edmund has obtained for her use, "almost every day," the phrase is repeated to lead nicely into the next scene in which Mary Crawford monopolizes the horse as Fanny looks on from indoors, harassed by her aunt.

However, Fanny's final letter to William creates the most subversive ironic contexts, rivaling the text itself. While Fanny's voice describes the disastrous outcome of Maria's marriage, including Rushworth's divorce and Maria's banishment with Mrs. Norris, and recounts Julia's reconciliation with her family after her only slightly less unpromising marriage to Yates, the camera offers us another marriage, that of Fanny and Edmund, witnessed by – among others – that horrible model of a matron, Mrs. Price. While Fanny's marriage is most likely to be read as a positive counterweight to the others, a more jaundiced reading is possible – and is reinforced when the camera cuts to a view of Fanny and Edmund settled at the parsonage. In voice-over we hear a convoluted, highly ambiguous final sentence, hoping for a visit from William, "through all the years to be – happy – as we remain together, within the view and patronage of Mansfield Park." Both the happiness and the togetherness seem undercut by the pauses around "happy" and by "as." Similarly, the final eight words – almost the final words in the novel – are loaded: the view and patronage of Mansfield has been poorly exercised, as Sir Thomas's and his daughters' marriages suggest. This verbal ambiguity in the voice-over is visually reinforced by the camera's view of Fanny carrying her own Pug to a bench outdoors, then sitting with Pug at her feet and Edmund by her side. Again, although a conventional "happy ending" can be read here, any association between Edmund, Fanny, Pug, and a seat creates a powerfully ironic visual context, recalling the marital couch and the limited options of Lady Bertram and echoing the corrosive verbal ironies of the last chapter of the novel.

Character narrative

Still another technique involves taking advantage of Austen's mature style, in which narrative slides into and out of different characters' perspectives. The most obvious way in which Austen blurs the distinction between narrative and dialogue occurs when she casts a character's words into the third person – as indirect speech – but places quotation marks around the words, as if they represented direct speech. Such passages can very easily be retransposed into a character's direct speech, as is Mrs. Norris's self-congratulatory pronouncement on the adoption of Fanny: it appears in the text as "The trouble and expense of it to them, would be nothing compared with the benevolence of the action" (I.i) and in the screenplay, condensed but in the first person, as "The burden will be as nothing to our benevolence."

However, Austen has a more complex method of blurring the distinction between narrative and dialogue, much discussed among her critics, and nicely exploited here: the technique most frequently described as "free indirect discourse." Through this technique, what may seem at first to be objective third-person narrative, especially in *Mansfield Park*, *Emma*, and *Persuasion* (to a lesser extent), often proves to be actually one character's view or words – particularly Emma's, of course, in that novel.

Without any punctuation, the omniscient narrator of *Mansfield Park* in the very first chapter slides into the words of Mrs. Price's despondent letter to Mansfield, into a condensed version of Sir Thomas's deliberate objections to adopting Fanny, and into Mrs. Norris's deft evasion of Sir Thomas's notion that Fanny will reside with her. Such passages are always written in the third person, but they do not include quotation marks: it is up to the reader to determine the point of slippage from omniscient reportage to biased account. For instance, the text tells us that Sir Thomas

had been considering [Fanny] as a particularly welcome addition at the Parsonage . . . but he found himself wholly mistaken. Mrs. Norris was sorry to say, that the little girl's staying with them, at least as things then were, was quite out of the question. Poor Mr. Norris's indifferent state of health made it an impossibility; he could no more bear the noise of a child than he could fly; if indeed he should ever get well of his gouty complaints, it would be a different matter: she should then be glad to take her turn, and think nothing of the inconvenience; but just now, poor Mr. Norris took up every moment of her time, and the very mention of such a thing she was sure would distract him. (i.i)

The shift to Mrs. Norris's words occurs in sentence two; transposed into the first person, the remaining sentences occur almost word for word in the screenplay. What this technique means for an adapter is that an omniscient narrator seldom intervenes to comment on the action; narrative is frequently what J. F. Burrows has called "character narrative,"[10] and can therefore be comfortably assigned to a speaker. In the first chapter of *Mansfield Park*, for example, about 55 percent of the lines (or 175 out of 317 lines in Chapman's edition) may seem at first to be narrative, the rest dialogue; but on examination, more than a fifth of those 175 lines of "narration" turn out to be character narrative. Thus, more than half of the first chapter is expressed in voices: those of Mrs. Price, Sir Thomas, Mrs. Norris, and even Lady Bertram. By this means, Austen's mature style, her delight in troubling the distinction between narrative and dialogue, affords adapters more of the characters' words to press into service as dramatic or revealing speech.

In her favorable review of the Miramax *Mansfield Park*, Claudia L. Johnson singles out Rozema's rendering of Austen's authorial voice for special praise. Although she dislikes adaptations that translate Austen's free indirect discourse into voice-over, presumably Johnson would not object to the assignment of the passage cited above to Mrs. Norris, as in the BBC version. More surprisingly, however, Johnson finds that the film delivers "Austen's presence as a narrator" in the words of Fanny, both directly uttered and in voice-over: "By weaving in Austen's uproarious early writings, Rozema transforms Fanny into a version of the Austenian narrator we love" and allows Fanny to take over the narrator's acerbic lines ("her aunt tried to cry").[11] My own feeling is that we can only sense the Austen narrator we love on film by relishing the sort of ironic juxtapositions of characters' speeches that the novels offer; these ironies, augmented by expressive visuals, are present in the BBC version but not, to my ear or eye, in Rozema's film.

Because the adapters of BBC version mine the novel's free indirect discourse for characters' speeches and because they are sensitive to comic and ironic possibilities in juxtapositions, the opening scene, in which Mrs. Norris is about to set off to meet Fanny at Northampton, conveys a surprising amount of the narrative as well as the dialogue of the novel's first chapter. Although the decision to adopt Fanny has been made beforehand, Mrs. Norris is quite in character when she recapitulates the decision as she bustles into the parlor at Mansfield. Her speeches outrageously flatter Sir Thomas ("you are everything that is considerate") and herself ("the trouble to myself you know I never regard"). Both Sir Thomas's erect stance by the fireplace (Mrs. Norris sits, and Lady Bertram is of course seated throughout) and his complacent acceptance of such speeches indicate his power as well as his limitations, expressing a good deal of the ambiguity of his character evident in narrative comments like, Sir Thomas "had interest, which, from principle as well as pride, from a general wish of doing right, and a desire of seeing all that were connected with him in situations of respectability, he would have been glad to exert for the advantage of Lady Bertram's sister" (I.i).

Above all, the scene dramatizes verbally and visually the great distance between Mrs. Norris's idea of her benevolent self and the reality of her selfishness and miserliness. The novel's narrator expresses this distance perfectly, of course: "it was impossible for her to aim at more than the credit of projecting and arranging so expensive a charity; though perhaps she might so little know herself, as to walk home to the Parsonage after this conversation [in which the adoption is planned] in the happy belief of being the most liberal-minded sister and aunt in the world" (I.i). Yet this same distance is beautifully rendered in the film by the discrepancy between Mrs. Norris's complacent voice-over arrangement of Fanny's destiny after the adoption (adumbrating her longer speech in the novel – I.i) and images of the harsher reality. The camera cuts to a front view of young Fanny being cheaply conveyed on a carrier's cart while Mrs. Norris begins, "Indeed, Sir Thomas, and with such opportunities." Although in the text Sir Thomas pays for more expensive travel than Mrs. Norris would choose, this lowly transport visually represents Sir Thomas's notion that Fanny is "not a *Miss Bertram*." A cut to a side view of the cart accompanies Mrs. Norris's next words: "Give her an education, an introduction into society under such favorable circumstances, and ten to one but she has the means of settling well without further expense...". By the end of this important phrase about expenses, we see a back view of the cart, and then the camera cuts to an inn yard at Northampton, with Fanny completely invisible though in fact the camera is actually directed toward where she sits on her luggage. However, animals and people cut off the view. These gradually move aside but still obscure Fanny as Mrs. Norris continues, "to any of us – though I should be the last to withhold my mite on such an occasion." As she concludes this sentence, a horse passes across the screen, nearly filling it, as if to suggest the magnitude of Mrs. Norris's occluded view of her own generous nature. The suggested obliquity in her view of herself is visually reinforced, for at the end of her next six words, "A niece of yours, Sir Thomas," the camera itself tracks obliquely to the right in order finally to reveal and zoom in on Fanny, isolated, dwarfed by people and luggage, frightened, abandoned, while Mrs. Norris concludes, "will not grow up in this neighborhood without many advantages." "I do not say she will be as handsome as her cousins, [camera zooms] but in all probability she will make a creditable match. And you need fear nothing for your two sons upon this account. Even suppose her to have the beauty of an angel, brought up together she will never be more to them than a sister." Then the camera cuts to Mrs. Norris's obsequiously smiling face as she suggests the White Attic for Fanny – and obviates the notion that Fanny might stay with her in the long speech already quoted. Our view of Sir Thomas's minutely tightened lip and quick glance at Mrs. Norris adds a final touch to the distance this scene conveys between Mrs. Norris's idea of herself and the reality: he evidently deplores Mrs. Norris's rejection of any responsibility for Fanny, yet his sense of his own dignity does not permit him to say so.

Narrator's ironic context made visual

Such subtleties of class and character are precisely those that the narrator of the first chapter dwells on in the opening sentences and that establish an "ironic context" of the sort that Roger Gard thinks cannot be conveyed in a visual medium. Space does not permit analysis of the ways in which the novel's brilliant set pieces – the dinner party in which "improvement" is discussed and the decision to visit Sotherton is reached, the visit to Sotherton, the enacting of *Lovers' Vows*, the dinner at the Grants, the Mansfield ball, and the scenes at Portsmouth – are all presented with comparable complexity in the BBC version: again, the combination of faithful dialogue, incorporated narrative, and visual shorthand works remarkably well. A brief analysis of one simpler sequence, the impromptu dance at Mansfield, can suggest what might be done for the more complicated ones. I will argue later that stage management is an important element in the central conception that drives this production – particularly the desire, held by many, to stage-manage Fanny, to "put you in and push you about," as Tom later says he will do to Fanny if she will play Cottager's Wife. In the impromptu dance sequence, about three minutes long, Tom Bertram and Mrs. Norris are briefly set up as rival "pushers" or managers, with different attitudes toward the spectacle of visible sexuality that is played out before them in the dance and with different agendas for managing their own pleasures. In the text, this sequence closes a chapter whose focus is on sexual murk; Edmund tells Fanny that she is wrong to suppose that Henry admires Maria, and Fanny does not know what to think. Although these particular elements do not appear, the impromptu dance does emphasize murky sexuality and people's selfish blindness to what is before them. As a matchmaker, Mrs. Norris has a proprietary investment in the spectacle, rejoicing in the dance coupling of Maria with Rushworth (her match) and Julia with Henry Crawford, whereas Tom is condescending and worldly, using words close to those in the text: "They must all be in love, to find any amusement in such folly – and so they are, I fancy, if you look. All but Yates and Mrs. Grant, and she, poor woman, must want a lover as much as any of them. A desperate dull life hers must be with the doctor." His casual attitude toward Mrs. Grant's possible adultery as well as toward love is fashionable, like his dress and his adroit management of Dr. Grant's having possibly heard his insult (he asks him about the news from America). Both Tom and Mrs. Norris see Julia and Henry as a couple; Tom but not Mrs. Norris views Edmund and Mary as lovers; neither sees the dance spectacle clearly, and the sequence exposes parallel forms of selfish management in both.

The dance sequence begins with a voice-over: Fanny writes to William that Tom has returned unsuccessful from the races, bringing Yates, and that a dance might occur in the evening. During her voice-over, the camera cuts to a close-up of Tom fashionably coiffed, very much the eldest son of the house, then cuts back to reveal him standing by the fireplace, where we first saw Sir Thomas, with Mrs. Norris at left in a chair watching the dancers beside Lady Bertram, half-visible with her feet up on her couch; Dr. Grant is seated right. Tom and Mrs. Norris are visually central, then, and their rivalry is underlined in the sequence by other visual cues. When Mrs. Norris asks Tom to play bridge with her, Lady Bertram, and Dr. Grant, just after Tom has skillfully managed matters so that he does not have to join the dance with Fanny, the camera cuts to a close-up of Mrs. Norris – the only other close-up in the sequence beside the first one of Tom. In order to avoid her management, however,

Tom outdoes her as stage manager: he asserts that he is about to dance, accusing Fanny of dawdling and leading her off rather abruptly – pushing her in and pulling her about, as he later proposes to do. The sequence closes as Tom voices his indignation at Mrs. Norris for asking him to play "so as to leave me no possibility of refusing," but of course he has no notion that he behaved similarly to Fanny, having sat beside her and asked her to dance while he opened a newspaper – so that Fanny was forced to decline. The presentation of both Tom and Mrs. Norris underlines their relative class positions, Mrs. Norris as an arriviste at Mansfield, Tom as the heir with aristocratic associations (the Honourable Mr. John Yates, "the younger son of a lord with a tolerable independence" – I.xiii) and aspirations: visually, Mrs. Norris is seated throughout, while Tom ranges more widely, sitting and standing; verbally, Mrs. Norris views the visible sexuality of the dance in terms of marriages, Tom in terms of folly and illicit amours. The comedy in this sequence arises largely from their mutual blindness, but a wonderful touch of the visual comedy that expresses character occurs when Mrs. Norris brags to her sister about the Bertram sisters' likely marriages: as she speaks, Lady Bertram taps her hand to the music – completely off the beat.

Other visuals in this adaptation express class and character also, especially the fine gradations in fashions that show the relative Londonness of the Crawfords, Yates, and Tom Bertram as opposed to the dowdiness of Edmund and Fanny. By contrast, the Rozema version maintains its postmodern approach even in costume design: Fanny's dresses are simple and, with their empire bodice cut and loose, flowing style, visually close to some modern evening wear, as are some of Mary Crawford's, but most other characters sport conventional period dress. The BBC version, however, finds ways as the Rozema version does not to make the visual pleasures of costume drama express character and comedy. Lady Bertram's headdresses are startlingly elaborate confections, as if to proclaim the emptiness within. Hairstyles are particularly revealing: Lady Bertram's hair is always fashionably arranged, but Sir Thomas adheres throughout to an old-fashioned wig, either brown or a more formal white. Fanny's curled front hair coincides with her "coming out" at the Grants' dinner party (and attracting Crawford's attention), yet she never sports the fully cropped and tightly curled head of Mary Crawford. Tom Bertram has straight hair and a queue to start with, but his return to Mansfield with cropped, curled hair, first seen in the impromptu dance sequence, signals his fashionable aspirations and slightly dissipated character, while Edmund retains his long straight hair, his country clothes, and his Mansfield allegiances. The Hon. Mr. Yates's topknot of curls proclaims his dandyism, as do his exaggeratedly cut coats and hats. Henry

Crawford's hair and dress are emphatically more tasteful than Yates's but still appropriately modish.

Even the claustrophobic rendition of the Portsmouth scenes is effective. When Fanny emerges from the small, dark rooms of her parents' home, she attains only a view of an evidently fake sky and ocean with Henry Crawford – who is not aware how far his performance as devoted suitor is staged. The staginess of the scene emphasizes not only the horrid confinement of poverty and vulgarity in the absence of affection for Fanny among the Prices, but also the stage management of Sir Thomas, who has brought this performance about: in this sense, his "medicinal project upon his niece's understanding" (III.vi) parallels the *Lovers' Vows* sequence, authorizing Fanny's and Henry's performances as pursued and pursuer. Again, this staginess is central to the concept that drives this production. By contrast, the large, luxurious interiors and exteriors at Mansfield and (briefly) Sotherton emphasize Fanny's isolation in some scenes, her exploitation in others. Yet this adaptation does not aspire to present a "heritage" England as some do. Nor does it linger on period costumes and sets, just as it does not strive for the spurious "realism" of the film *Persuasion* by allowing dirt to appear on hems and shoes.

In general, decisions about setting are vital because they establish the parameters of the heroine's world and provide a sense of its limits. The argument by relatively recent critics that *Mansfield Park* can exist only on the basis of slavery in Antigua and (to some extent) Fanny Price's slavery at Mansfield, for example, though important, does not lend itself well to representation in an adaptation: in the Rozema version, the focus on slavery sacrifices complexity of character for a sensational representation of Sir Thomas as colonial sadist and rapist. To follow Sir Thomas to his Antigua estate even by sketches, however, as Rozema does, is just what Austen does not and would not do ("You would be in danger of giving wrong representations," as she wrote to a niece writing a novel, if her niece followed her characters to Ireland).[12] Both the Rozema and the BBC screenplays emphasize the domestic setting as limiting or even trapping the heroines. The BBC version, however, brings splendid irony to bear on the domestic trap at the end, showing Fanny with her own Pug. Although Rozema's film insists on this trap, especially at squalid Portsmouth, she subverts her own vision by inventing images of escape and flight (especially the doves at Portsmouth, the birds at Mansfield) to suggest that domestic limitations can be overcome by romantic aspiration (the artist-writer) or romantic closure (union with the beloved).

Altogether, then, a purist approach to adapting Austen's novels should rely upon the means discussed above to incorporate narrative into the screenplay, using visual devices among others to create ironic contexts that parallel those created by the texts. This approach might better be termed "neopurist," however, in that its respect for the text does recognize a need to translate it to a visual medium. A neopurist approach, then, will find visual equivalents for significant words, phrases, and themes in the novels; it will make intelligent use of voice-overs; it will only rarely assign the omniscient narrator's words to characters – that is, when the character suffers no violence as a result; it will take advantage of Austen's mature style, wherein what at first might appear to be omniscient narrative is actually "character narrative," registering a character's thoughts or speech – thus making more of the text adaptable for dialogue; and it will find visual means of representing the novels' themes, both in smaller sequences and overall, as discussed in the previous section.

Voice effects

Finally, without excellent actors, even a good screenplay would fail to allow the characters to speak "as they ought." The casting for the BBC *Mansfield Park* seems close to perfect. Angela Pleasance is splendid as Lady Bertram, with fluting, threadlike voice punctuated by coos, hums, and vague, vacant smiles. Bernard Hepton renders Sir Thomas's complexity wonderfully, his coldness and his warmth, his integrity and dignity along with his willingness to starve Fanny into accepting Crawford: it's a fine touch that he asks Edmund's advice about sending Fanny to Portsmouth while the two men are out shooting, planting his shotgun butt down on the ground and holding it like a standard as Edmund accedes. Anna Massey as Mrs. Norris is a revelation. I had always imagined Mrs. Norris as abrasive in manner and voice, but Massey's saccharine rendition seems exactly right: her obsequious smiles, her unctuous tones, her eager posture (always stretching forward, as if to attend to every word – or to mow down opposition) mix servility and assertiveness in a nuanced portrait – showing a more irritating abrasiveness along with greater pathos, the pathos of a character who depends on others' status and position to bolster her own. All these characters are reduced to caricatures in the Rozema screenplay; Mrs. Norris snarls, Lady Bertram sits in a drug-induced stupor, and Sir Thomas rages and ravens.

The other parts in the BBC version are equally well cast. The Crawfords (Jackie Smith-Wood and Robert Burbage) have precisely the right sort of charm and worldly shallowness; Tom, Maria, and Julia Bertram (Christopher Villiers, Samantha Bond, and Liz Crowther) the proper degrees of unquestioned, arrogant selfishness and privilege (Julia's share being the least and compensated for by a more explosive, angrier presence). Mrs. Price (Alison Fiske) displays a fine, relentless querulousness;

Mrs. Grant (Susan Edmonstone) a good-humored, sensible matronliness in stark contrast to all the other married women; and Mr. Rushworth (Jonathan Stephens) a corpulent natural vapidity and vanity exceeded only by Yates's more artificial version of both (Robin Langford).

The most difficult parts are, of course, those of the hero and heroine; indeed, critics of the novel often express grave reservations about both. My own reading of the novel assumes that Austen wanted her audience to be caught between the different orders of attraction presented by Fanny Price and Edmund Bertram on one hand and Henry and Mary Crawford on the other. That is, readers are to be attracted against their will, as the Crawfords are, to the goodness of Fanny and Edmund, and moved, as Fanny and Edmund are (against their will also), by the Crawfords' charm. Goodness is never easy to represent, and some viewers have objected in particular to Nicholas Farrell's stiffness as Edmund and to the way the actress Sylvestra Le Touzel plays Fanny Price as "neurotic." I understand those objections, particularly to Le Touzel's performance, but her interpretation is faithful to the sort of adolescent excess Austen attributes to Fanny. In the novel, Fanny feels too much. She lives in an adolescent world, without perspective. Le Touzel is accordingly tense, edgy, anxious, even furtive in early scenes as well as quiet and repressed; her body expresses discomfort, a sense of not belonging that works in terms of the novel but also in this particular production, which takes stage-management as its central metaphor. In this version, Fanny moves from being uncomfortable and peripheral to Mansfield in early scenes (like a stagehand, a helper who, in an interpolated scene, lights candles as others dine) to being an actress who takes a central role; this movement is present in the novel as well. The young woman who is "not out" comes out. From speaking little, she speaks out. The production's central conception is metadramatic, drawn in part from the novel's exploration of what it means to "act" in *Lovers' Vows*: Fanny learns to "act" so as to resist direction.

Conclusion: the postmodern versus the purist

In the early scenes of the BBC's metadramatic *Mansfield Park*, Fanny complies readily with others' demands although from the sidelines. However, when *Lovers' Vows* is being produced, she is wanted onstage, as an actress: her cousins, Mrs. Norris, and even Edmund try to "direct" her. Her first real act of non-compliance is the surprisingly loud cry of "no" that she utters when Tom demands that she enact Cottager's Wife; from this point she stages resistance in essentials along with compliance in nonessentials. Fanny complies at last with the management of her peers when, center stage and in fact elevated on a ladder, she yields to the pleas of all to come down and stand in for Mrs. Grant. Later, she resists the attempted management of Henry Crawford, Mary Crawford, and Sir Thomas, all of whom wish to direct her marriage, though she complies with lesser demands: Mary Crawford's suspicious insistence that she take a necklace or Sir Thomas's order that she retire early from the ball. That is, changing combinations of acts of compliance and acts of resistance express Fanny's growth in moral stature. Compliance costs her relatively little from the start, but learning resistance is a major struggle. The most painful example occurs, as in the book, in the East Room with Sir Thomas. There her resistance in Giles's version causes near-hysterical sobbing, almost a breakdown. Nonetheless, by the time she stages her resistance to Sir Thomas's stage-managed "medicinal project" at Portsmouth, that is, her resistance to Henry Crawford's courtship there, she has at last become more comfortable in her own body and with her own wishes. She is calm and direct.

A parallel, more filmic representation of this development from compliance to resistance is registered by close-ups of Edmund and Fanny together over the course of the film. In the first shots of both grown up, Fanny's face dissolves from child to adult as Edmund reads poetry to her in voice-over, his voice changing also; her silence and her intense stare across the table express her admiration and submissive compliance, as do her words of gratitude when she finally speaks. He is empowered at this point. But later when Edmund speaks to Fanny before the Mansfield ball about his pain at Mary Crawford's manner and leads Fanny upstairs, apparently still empowered in their relation, a slight alteration occurs. Eventually, a two-shot positions both at a balustrade, Edmund looking off screen right, slightly behind Fanny who faces off screen left: their eyes, staring straight ahead, don't meet, though their profiles confront each other. Fanny recognizes that their viewpoints differ; she tensely and resistantly intervenes, warning him not to say anything of Mary Crawford that he will later regret, and in effect he is silenced. At the end, however, when Edmund joins Fanny in a two-shot to recount the callousness that Mary has fully revealed at last, they sit beside one another, both staring left (as Fanny has done earlier). They appear darkened, almost in silhouette, against a window with rain pouring down outside, Edmund now having come to share Fanny's perspective, as he did not earlier, and having come to admit his dependence on her.

Ironically, then, Le Touzel's Fanny Price has some of the spunk and power that Frances O'Connor's Fanny shows in the Rozema film, but these qualities are expressed more subtly, by gradual development, by a "coming out" of what was latent before. Her performance and her role

7. Fanny Price (Frances O'Connor) and Edmund Bertram (Jonny Lee
Miller) in Patricia Rozema's 1999 Miramax Films' *Mansfield Park*

in the production seem driven by an early 1980s conception of selective
resistance and choosing one's battles, a political and social conservatism
appropriate to the Thatcher years in England and the Reagan years in
America. Giles's *Mansfield Park*, in other words, like Austen's, acknowledges the difficulty that rebellion against those in power entails, the small
victories that must be hardly won. Ideologically, young viewers in the
1990s often think that all the battles, especially feminist ones, have been
won; it is hard to persuade them that their capitalist consumer culture
disempowers them in any way. As one consequence, they expect individual resistance to be unremitting as well as uniformly successful – as
Fanny's is in Rozema's *Mansfield Park*. Their (and the film's) uncritical
focus on Fanny's personal success tends to undermine Rozema's insistence that Mansfield itself is supported by slave exploitation – the film's
strongest "take" on the novel. In part because they responded so positively
to Rozema's Fanny Price, many of my students found it hard to perceive
Fanny's resistance in both the novel and the BBC version, conflating it
with passivity. Those who saw both versions much preferred Rozema's.

For them, the slow pace and low production values of Giles's *Mansfield Park* were unappealing, even soporific. These students found the stars' performances in Rozema's film compelling, and they appreciated a romantic tale that focuses on a central couple, Fanny and Edmund, involved thanks to the Crawfords in two love triangles. Yet Austen's novels, when reduced to romantic plots, are caricatures of themselves, and for all its lively intervention and innovation in the genre of Austen films, Rozema's *Mansfield Park* is reductive in this way. By contrast, Giles's BBC *Mansfield Park,* like the novel itself, bestows interest almost equally among a number of other characters: Sir Thomas, Mrs. Norris, Lady Bertram, Tom, Maria, Julia, Mr. Rushworth, Mr. Yates, Mr. and Mrs. Price, Susan and William Price, and even Dr. and Mrs. Grant. Romance is not central; stars are not central; character is.

The lessons that the two versions of *Mansfield Park* offer for future adapters of Austen's novels are, however, somewhat disheartening. A neopurist adaptation, one that retains as much of the narrative voice as possible, will choose to rely on Austen's words and on visual nuance rather than romance and spectacle, as the BBC *Mansfield Park* does, but it may have trouble attracting a young audience. After all, Giles's adaptation requires (and rewards) precisely the close attention to words as well as to nuances of structure and presentation that the novel does, a sustained visual and verbal attention that the quick cuts of modern advertisements or MTV shows discourage. Nonetheless, Rozema's very different approach to Austen's narrative pleased neither most Austen fans nor a general audience. Despite her concessions to postmodern tastes and ideology, and despite attempts to market its "hot young stars," the film did not succeed at the box office in the United States. Before it dropped off *Variety*'s listings in the issue of March 13–19, 2000 (11), it had last been shown to gross 4.68 million dollars in fourteen weeks – a far cry from Ang Lee's *Sense and Sensibility,* starring Emma Thompson, which grossed well over 100 million dollars. Perhaps the best approach for a future adapter of *Mansfield Park* would be to follow Amy Heckerling's lead in *Clueless* to abandon Austen's narrative voice and set the characters, suitably modernized, in contemporary situations. This approach would produce what Jocelyn Harris's essay (Chapter 3) describes as an "imitation" rather than a "translation," and it might well be as entertaining as well as somewhat more disturbing than *Clueless,* given the darker nature of *Mansfield Park* in relation to *Emma.* However, we are fortunate to have Giles's faithful translation, which in giving Austen's characters a great deal of the novel's language, does as much justice to the comedy and the complexity of the narrative as any filmed version can do.

NOTES

I am grateful to many friends whose discussions helped me produce this essay, particularly Ruth Portner, Jan Thaddeus, Ruth Perry, Linda Lipkis, Dorothy Cockrell, and students of Austen on screen: Erika Borg, Bud Brennan, Giraud Lorber, Rebecca Nemiroff, Jaime Pumphrey, and Colleen Watts. Special thanks are due to my colleague Alex Doty, who permitted me to sit in on his course in Feminist Film Theory and advised on practice, and to Gina and Andrew Macdonald, whose editing is ideal: inspiring and supportive.

1 Jane Austen, "Opinions of *Mansfield Park*," ed. R. W. Chapman. *Minor Works*, *The Works of Jane Austen*: VI, 431–432.

2 Originally the series was aired on Sunday evenings from November 6 to December 11, 1983, in segments of 50 to 55 minutes; a newspaper strike during the weekend of November 27 means that the length of that episode is undeterminable, but the total must have come to well over five hours. The two videotapes take up four hours 21 minutes. One review favorably mentioned an episode that was cut, for it does not appear in the videotape: Anthea Hall felt that "Sharon Beare as young Julia, singing plaintively and slightly off key [*sic*] was a delight" ("Jane's People," *The Sunday Telegraph*, November 13, 1983: 15).

3 Julian Barnes, Review of *Mansfield Park*, *The Observer* (November 13, 1983): 48.

4 Brenda R. Silver, "Whose Room of Orlando's Own: The Politics of Adaptation," in *The Margins of the Text*, ed. D. C. Greetham (Ann Arbor, MI: University of Michigan Press, 1997): 58.

5 Ibid.: 60.

6 Claudia L. Johnson, Review of *Mansfield Park*, *The Times Literary Supplement* (December 31, 1999): 16–17.

7 James Berardinelli, "The Darker Side of Jane Austen: Patricia Rozema Talks about *Mansfield Park*" (November 15, 1999). http://movie-reviews.colossus.net/comment/111599.html

8 Deirdre Le Faye (ed.), *Jane Austen's Letters* (Oxford: Oxford University Press, 1995): 203.

9 Laura Mulvey, "Visual Pleasure in Narrative Cinema" (1975), reprinted in *Visual and Other Pleasures* (Bloomington and Indianapolis: Indiana University Press, 1989).

10 J. F. Burrows, *Computation into Criticism: A Study of Jane Austen's Novels and an Experiment in Method* (Oxford: Clarendon Press; New York: Oxford University Press, 1987).

11 Johnson, Review: 16.

12 Le Faye, *Letters*, August 10, 1814: 269.

5   *Sense and Sensibility* in a postfeminist world: sisterhood is still powerful

Penny Gay

The history of filming Austen's and other classic novels in the twentieth century indicates that such films are as subject to the fashions of their own time (both material and intellectual) as any other cultural work is. At the most obvious level, think of Greer Garson's crinolines in MGM's *Pride and Prejudice* (1940), of the bouffant hairstyles of the young women in the BBC's 1970s literary adaptations. Laughable to viewers today, these fashions in their day were simply the normal look for youth and beauty. Arguably, the same may be said of the thematic shaping in film of Austen's stories of families and courtship: that is, that each shift in cultural history will draw from the novels the emphases that readers of that time naturally look for in them. Their images of the nation, of the family, of gender behavior, courtship and sexual desire, will be delineated according to contemporary agendas – whether intellectual, political, or commercial. For the film to succeed, however, it must achieve a double effect: it must create the impression of keeping faith with the original text (by not straying *too* far from the plot), and it must engage the audience with the sense that the story speaks to them of their own concerns. This essay will examine the ways in which late twentieth-century liberal feminism informs one such film, Ang Lee's *Sense and Sensibility* (1995), scripted by Emma Thompson, who also played Elinor Dashwood.

Textual intersections

> She was not going to say: "I love my dear sister; I must be near her at this crisis of her life." The affections are more reticent than the passions, and their expression more subtle. If she herself should ever fall in love with a man, she, like Helen, would proclaim it from the house-tops, but as she only loved a sister she used the voiceless language of sympathy.
>
> (E. M. Forster, *Howards End*, 1910)[1]

When Emma Thompson won her Academy Award for Best Actress for *Howards End* in 1992 she thanked, among others, "E. M. Forster for creating Margaret Schlegel," the sensible older sister, whom Thompson played. She dedicated the Oscar to "the heroism and the courage of women" and hoped "that it inspires the creation of more true-screen heroines to represent them." She was, of course, already in the throes of making her own contribution to this potential, by working on her script for the 1995 film *Sense and Sensibility*. There are many striking similarities between Forster's 1910 novel and Austen's 1811 precursor,[2] similarities which carry over into the two films that were made of these classic English novels, both starring Emma Thompson. Both focus on two sisters, the elder sensible and staid, the younger passionate and unconventional, and their respective relationships with men in a patriarchal and antifeminist English society. Both novels signal their awareness of the necessity of money to a civilized lifestyle; both are very conscious of the emotional importance to the main characters of the English landscape and a country home, which of course only men can provide. Above all, there is the author's fundamental commitment to making the most important thread of the story the love between the two women, sisters not simply by virtue of the familial relationship but in their profound emotional dependence on one another (for Austen, this was the most important relationship in her life; for Forster, the fictional sisters' love represented his own utopian desire to find acceptance of same-sex passion).

It is not surprising, then, that traces of "Margaret Schlegel" played by Thompson in *Howards End* can be found in Thompson's script for *Sense and Sensibility*. For example, Elinor's habit of addressing her sister with the epithet "dearest" (notable in Forster, not found in Austen). On one fraught occasion Elinor says to her younger sister, "Meg, dearest, please ask Betsy to make a cup of hot tea for Marianne."[3] "Meg," the pet form of Margaret, is used consistently in *Howards End* between the sisters, but never in Austen's novel; in *Sense and Sensibility* the name is altered back to Margaret. Finally, there is Thompson's note – in the script but not followed in the film – that Marianne is becoming more like Margaret Schegel: her "sickness has left her slightly short-sighted and she uses a pince-nez that makes her look like an owl,"[4] echoing the pince-nez of *Howards End*.[5] Significantly, *OED* indicates that the word (and therefore the object and its accompanying semiotic significance) is not recorded before 1880.

What all this demonstrates is that the Thompson/Lee *Sense and Sensibility* is not simply an "adaptation" of Jane Austen's novel but a reworking into a different textual form of material supplied by Jane Austen. As Barthes reminds us, a text is "a tissue of quotations drawn from the innumerable centres of culture," and no "author" is an independent creator.[6] Thompson's script is one text, redolent of her own sensibility, her own cultural and biographical luggage; Ang Lee's film is another, redolent of his:

many critics have seen the similarity between Lee's precise and affectionate examination of social codes and sexual mores in the Taiwanese community in his earlier films (*The Wedding Banquet*, 1993; *Eat Drink Man
Woman*, 1994) and Austen's depiction of Georgian England. Further, the
film genre also operates as a site of multiple textual intersections for film
audiences to make meanings from, not all controllable by the director
or *auteur*: the Austen industry, the genre of English Heritage film, the
foreknowledges of the film's stars (their previous roles, their private lives)
that audiences will have. For example, audiences watching the film some
years after its making will be aware of the offscreen relationship begun
there between Emma Thompson and Greg Wise (Willoughby) – thus
deliciously supplying what Thompson was unable to include in her final
script, the strong erotic attraction that Austen records between Elinor
and Willoughby when he comes to Cleveland to tell his side of the story:
"[Elinor] felt that his influence over her mind was heightened by circumstances which ought not in reason to have weight; – by that person of
uncommon attraction, that open, affectionate, and lively manner which it
was no merit to possess; and by that still ardent love for Marianne, which
it was not even innocent to indulge" (III.ix). Audiences might further reflect on the quasi-incestuous nature of film casting which has Kate Winslet
(Marianne) going on to play Ophelia in Kenneth Branagh's film of *Hamlet*
(1999) – Branagh having in the meantime broken up with his wife Emma
Thompson, and established a relationship with Helena Bonham Carter,
the Ophelia of Zeffirelli's *Hamlet* (1990) and the Helen of *Howards End*
(1992).[7] Mental gossip and speculation such as this will circulate on the
edges of the filmgoer's mind, and cannot be discounted as an element of
the experience of watching – as Austen herself demonstrated in her examination of a "theatre" of the little world, the claustrophobic community
of Highbury in *Emma*.

Women's lives

Thompson writes the script of the film *Sense and Sensibility* as a late twentieth century, English, middle-class, Cambridge-educated feminist. She
and her producers, to their credit, were quite clear that the film kept
the story "focused on the relationship between the two sisters, so that
it wouldn't seem like a movie about a couple of women waiting around
for men."[8] As a politically aware writer Thompson further ensures that
her text spells out the conditions of women's lives in the early nineteenth
century, by inventing the early dialogue for Edward and Elinor in which
she says to him that she cannot earn a living – "You talk of feeling idle
and useless – imagine how that is compounded when one has no choice

and no hope whatsoever of any occupation";[9] and by structuring it so that it is "bookended" by patriarchal images – the death of the father at the beginning (and the women's consequent loss of their home) and the triumph of the soldier-landowner-suitor Brandon at the end, tossing a handful of sixpences into the air for the disempowered (here represented by children and the laboring class) to scramble for. The camera, in slow-motion, almost freezes on that rain of silver – certainly it is the most striking image at the end of the film, overshadowing the rejoicing community procession which briefly follows it, and the image of the defeated beta male, Willoughby, gazing wistfully at the church from afar before wheeling off with yet another jejune theatrical gesture.

Into the interstices between men's significant and decisive actions Thompson threads her late twentieth-century reading of Austen's story of women's lives. In the course of the film this hierarchy of power and agency is represented by a topographical trope, what Julianne Pidduck calls "gendered" space:[10] men are seen outdoors, confidently inhabiting, riding over, using, the wide and fertile landscape which they in fact do own; the women of the film are for the most part indoors, framed and contained by walls, doors, windows from which they gaze longingly at that which they can make no move to own. Unless, of course, they indulge, as Marianne does, in dangerously transgressive behavior – the landscape turns wild and threatening when she walks out into it to enjoy her romantic sensibility ("You always say that [it's not going to rain] and then it always does," complains Margaret). Elinor, properly, only goes out into the landscape accompanied by a man.

The gendered body in (and out of) place

Thompson records that Ang Lee said of the entry of Willoughby into the women's house bearing the wet and injured Marianne, that he "wanted the camera to watch the *room*, sense the change in it that a man, that sex, had brought. For Ang, the house is as important a character as the women"[11] – because, we might extrapolate, the house is a female space, it symbolizes the women. In an extraordinarily sensitive collaboration with Thompson's script,[12] Lee fleshes out her feminist analysis. His direction of the actors, his choice of the way the camera looks at them and his *mise en scène*, calling into play proxemics, kinesics, lighting, set, and costume texture, gives the audience a complex but easily readable narrative of the characters' experiences *as bodies*.

I have already commented in general on the ease with which the male characters inhabit the landscape, and the sense of enclosure that accompanies most of the scenes with the women indoors: they sit, doing fairly

8. Willoughby (Greg Wise) bringing the injured Marianne (Kate Winslet) a bouquet of wild flowers, while her sisters Margaret (Emilie François) and Elinor (Emma Thompson) look on, in a scene from Columbia Pictures/TriStar Pictures' 1995 *Sense and Sensibility* (note the foregrounding of the couple with the family hovering in the background)

meaningless "work," i.e. decorative embroidery – with the exception of Elinor, who is seen agonizing over the family budget; they gaze out of windows and doors, waiting for a visitor; they pace like caged tigers. Scenes 58–60[13] offer a fine example of this gendering of space and place in the film. As the women realize their disappointment that Edward has not brought the atlas himself, the grayness of their lives is reinforced by the plain gray walls behind them. Elinor changes into her housework apron in the utilitarian little entrance hall of the cottage; Marianne and Margaret push past her to the barely glimpsed green outdoors, but the camera follows Elinor and her mother as they move with a sense of dreary habit into a Vermeer-like interior room, lacking only – but vitally – the striking areas of color that enrich a Vermeer interior (Elinor is in white, Mrs. Dashwood in black). As Elinor articulates the disappointment of her hope of escape – "We are not engaged, Mamma... I am by no means *assured* of his regard for me... a woman of no rank who cannot afford to buy sugar" – the camera pulls back so that the two women occupy

9. Elinor (Emma Thompson) and Marianne (Kate Winslet) with their mother Mrs. Dashwood (Gemma Jones) in front of their country cottage, in a complex emotional scene from Columbia Pictures/TriStar Pictures' 1995 *Sense and Sensibility*

progressively less than half the frame, the rest being taken up by the inner door lintel and an outer empty room notable only for its heavy confining verticals. Elinor's conclusion to the scene is a determined acceptance of the inevitable rather than an objective decision on the merits of sense versus sensibility: "In such a situation, Mamma, it is perhaps better to use one's head." It is spoken in a virtual prison cell.

The alternative is a deceptive illusion of escape into the natural world. The camera cuts to a wide shot of Marianne and Margaret climbing briskly up a brilliant green incline, but the moment of exhilaration is brief, for the next image is a long shot of the two girls struggling on the horizon against increasingly strong wind and fast-developing rain and mist. After a brief – and somewhat forced – exclamation of ecstasy from Marianne – "Is there any felicity in the world superior to this?" (they are already obviously wet and cold), Marianne's fall, both physical and spiritual, is enacted in a natural world by now downright punitive toward the transgressive girls. In strong contrast to the image of the immobile, helpless, and distressed females, a galloping horseman is seen approaching through the mist, his cape swirling, his face invisible. The horse rears in frightening close-up, Margaret screams, the man slides off and reveals himself to be human and charming – but also impudent, a taker of the liberties that opportunity offers him: "May I have permission to – ascertain if there are any breaks?" An extreme close-up of the encounter between male hand and female ankle – no faces – pulls back to reveal a Marianne "almost swoon[ing] with embarrassment and excitement mixed,"[14] and then crosses to a full-length shot of Margaret gazing with astonishment and incomprehension at this primal scene.

Transgressive sexual behavior is resolved into conventional romance imagery as Willoughby lifts the sodden and helpless Marianne to carry her back to her proper place, the cottage. Nevertheless, Marianne's now sexualized body does not disappear into this romantic cliché – the seminal rain continues to pour down and her naked limbs are clearly visible through the wet and clinging muslin as Willoughby (unembarrassed by the rain in his sturdy hunting gear; he is clearly accustomed to such natural phenomena) bears her back into the cottage. The earlier shot of Elinor and her mother, enclosed in the room, is now broken up by the incursion of an excited Margaret, and, incontrovertibly, with Willoughby sex does change the room. With it come the light and color that were missing from the earlier sequence: the gray walls reflect (impossible) sunshine; we see a blue striped cushion, a spray of green leaves in a vase as Marianne is laid on the sofa and Willoughby moves smoothly into the exaggeratedly polite behavior of the young courting gentleman. Austen would have enjoyed the fleshing out of this seminal sequence in her text, which has its own carefully coded awareness of the sexual connotations of this fall. In Austen, of course, it is not necessary for Willoughby to arrive *en gothique* on his rearing charger – his masculinity is clearly signaled by his being merely out walking with his dogs and gun. However, Thompson is writing a script for an audience familiar with the much more obviously dangerous masculinity of *Jane Eyre*'s Mr. Rochester, whose first encounter with Jane this so gleefully mimics (at least until the point where it is Rochester who falls and needs to be assisted by the diminutive but heroic Jane). Thompson's remark that Willoughby is "an Adonis in hunting gear"[15] indicates her own postmodernist assumption that her audience will take such romantic moments with a strong grain of irony. Film audiences, in my experience, laugh at Willoughby's arrival, though they may well within a few seconds be swooning with Marianne at the matinée-idol charm of Greg Wise.

As this sequence demonstrates, much of the narrative of the film is conveyed through the visual images of bodies in space and place – and in varieties of costuming codes. Costume operates in the "period film" primarily to distance the audience from a complex moral engagement with the narrative – to guarantee escapism. All the evidence of Thompson's diaries suggests that pandering to the escapist impulse was far from her (and producer Lindsay Doran's) intention. She is interested in recreating the experience of being a woman, an embodied gendered individual, in a period which is historically different from the audience's but which clearly operates within a very similar discursive field as far as women are concerned (Amy Heckerling in *Clueless* has developed the same intuition about *Emma*, with impressive results). We read, for example, of Thompson's relief on the days when she doesn't have to wear corsets.[16] There is a substantial sequence in the *Diaries* in which Thompson comments on the cast's training in eighteenth-century body language:

The bow is the gift of the head and heart. The curtsy (which is of course a bastardisation of the word "courtesy") a lowering in status for a moment, followed by a recovery. She [Jane Gibson, the movement coach] speaks of the simplicity and grace of the time, the lack of archness. The muscularity of their physique, the strength beneath the ease of movement. She reminds us that unmarried women would not necessarily have known about the mechanics of sex. We search for a centre of gravity. Everyone suddenly feels clumsy and ungainly. As Jane says, we don't know how to behave any more . . . Riding side-saddle is bizarre . . . The saddle has two leather protuberances [*sic*]. You wrap your legs around and hold on tight. Very good for the thighs. I wobble about, trying to be brave.[17]

In fact, in the horse-riding sequence and conversation with Edward, we see a considerably more elegant and fashionable Elinor than appears in the rest of the film. Her riding costume, complete with a tricorn felt hat, is a tailored three-piece garment, much more sophisticated than her everyday dresses with the occasional shawl or pelisse. (The younger and more conventionally pretty Marianne still manages fashionable touches in the cut and fabric of her simple dresses at Barton.) The message is clear: at Norland, Elinor had the means to be, if she wished, as fashionable a female as her sister-in-law Fanny Dashwood. Further, she had access to the pleasure of riding (at a sedate pace) for her outdoor exercise: Thompson invents a scene (Scene 37) in which she is sadly saying farewell to her horse – she cannot afford to take it with her to Barton Cottage – and uses it as the setting for the abortive explanation and farewell that Edward attempts before he is dragged off by the overbearing Fanny. The last frame of the scene has Elinor, alone, gazing sadly toward the departing Edward, recognizing that she is to be deprived of so much social and, perhaps, physical pleasure.

In this scene Edward Ferrars's (Hugh Grant's) repression is literally signaled by his buttoned-up look. Throughout the film he is never seen without his coat and a high collar and stock, so that the only naked skin visible is that of his face and his hands. Colonel Brandon (Alan Rickman) is a more interestingly costumed figure; Thompson and Lee, in conjunction with costume designers Jenny Beavan and John Wright, worked to develop the image of his experienced and dependable masculinity. Having begun in funereal black, looking as repressed as Edward, he is soon seen in fetching sporting gear – first in corduroy coat and slouch hat silently offering Marianne the use of his hunting knife, then in his shirtsleeves in Sir John's gun-room. There is nothing namby-pamby about Rickman's Colonel Brandon – his waistcoat (certainly not flannel,[18] for the flannel waistcoat was in fact a protective undergarment: see *OED*, 2nd edition, "waistcoat") is as elegant as the smart item which Willoughby wears with a red brass-buttoned coat at the picnic. Most notably, Brandon is transmogrified into the image of the romantic Byronic hero in the scene in which he waits outside Marianne's sickroom at Cleveland: coatless, his shirt unbuttoned at the neck, his cravat hanging loose and untied. After this his habitual black costume, on a more relaxed and confidently sexual body as he becomes Marianne's successful suitor, looks positively fashionable rather than dour. Finally, he is splendidly virile in his red-coated colonel's dress uniform for his wedding ceremony. Thompson combines an interesting but tragic history and a flattering wardrobe to win viewer approval.

Marianne's story

If *Sense and Sensibility*, as I have suggested, is primarily the story of the love of two sisters, Marianne's story (like Helen's in *Howards End* which climaxes with her pregnancy) is inscribed on her body. Here the film offers satisfying visual equivalents of what we can find in a close reading of Austen's text. I have already commented on the physical, bodily conscious, desiring emphasis that Thompson and Lee give the first meeting between Marianne and Willoughby. The dramatization of the powerful attraction between these two beautiful young people continues more tellingly, not so much in the recitation of poems and speeches of eighteenth-century "sensibility" (true to the novel, but a somewhat uncomfortable form of expression for modern actors and their audiences), as in more readily comprehensible fast movement: the manic curricle-rides, the impromptu whirling dance at the picnic which almost brings forth a declaration of love from Willoughby. Moreover, the episode of the cutting of a lock of Marianne's hair is treated with an erotic intensity which produces – properly – a kind of embarrassment in the viewer; this fetishistic fascination with a trivial body part seems mawkish, as Willoughby kisses it lingeringly. Part of our embarrassment is because the hair is also a metaphor (as Alexander Pope's Belinda cries in *The Rape of the Lock*, "Oh hadst thou, cruel! been content to seize/ Hairs less in sight, or any hairs but these!" – Canto 4, 1.176).[19] Most importantly, the transaction in the film is witnessed by Elinor, unwilling but fascinated (as the audience is): the camera cuts between her and the object of her and our gaze, the whispering lovers: "ELINOR *is transfixed by this strangely erotic moment.* WILLOUGHBY *senses her gaze and looks over. She snaps her head back to her sums and is astonished to find that she has written 'Edward' at the top of the sheet. Hastily she rubs it out and writes 'Expenses'.*"[20] Although Elinor's Freudian slip does not make it into the final cut, the directions in the script emphasize the importance of this moment for her own repressed life of the body. Austen makes a different choice in her rendering of the event: it is told to Elinor at second hand by Margaret, the sexually ignorant child, who interprets it naïvely as a conventional public signal of intention to marry, like an engagement ring. Thus Austen's novel, directed to a more conventionally chaste readership than today's film audience, escapes any accusation of impropriety while at the same time allowing the more knowing of her readers to infer the strong sexual content of the episode.

That this is a conscious acknowledgment of the power of physical desire on Austen's part – that "sensibility" is a code word in this text for the behavior of the unruly body – is borne out by her subsequent rendering of Marianne's collapse after Willoughby's desertion: "She was awake the whole night, and she wept the greatest part of it. She got up with an headache, was unable to talk, and unwilling to take any nourishment... Her sensibility was potent enough!" (I.xvi). Marianne's state in London is similarly registered on the body: her near-faint when Willoughby publicly rejects her at the ball; and the morning after, Elinor wakes to see "Marianne, only half-dressed... kneeling against one of the window-seats... and writing as fast as a continual flow of tears would permit her" (II.vii). Austen's text positions Marianne obsessively in the bedroom, as though unable to drag herself away from the barren bed and its failed promise of bliss:

Marianne, seated at the foot of the bed, with her head leaning against one of its posts, again took up Willoughby's letter... no attitude could give her ease; and in restless pain of mind and body she moved from one posture to another, till growing more and more hysterical, her sister could with difficulty keep her on the bed at all. (II.vii)

Austen's imagination is working theatrically here; like Thompson, she is writing directions for a character's movement in yet another confined room: we might say she "sees" an embodied performance of physical and mental agony, such as Kate Winslet was to give, in a different medium, two centuries later.

Marianne's inability to sleep or eat of course weakens her physical strength, so that she easily falls seriously ill following her chill at Cleveland. According to a March 1996 interview in *Sight and Sound*, for

Lee, "The climax is the Cleveland sequence, the most cinematic in the movie."[21] Lee had a serendipitous advantage in rendering Marianne's dissolution of mind and body: "a strange, twisted hedge which the film-makers nicknamed the 'Brain Hedge.' Deformed long ago by a freeze, and deliberately maintained in this shape ever since":[22] the hedge, shot in eerie blue light, is a nightmarish symbol of Marianne's collapse. At Cleveland we enter a Gothic landscape as Marianne suffers the fate of the foolish literary heroine who indulges her sensibility without regard for decorum or common sense. Austen takes the opportunity for a last satirical glance at such literary conventions: "from [Cleveland's] Grecian temple, her eye . . . could fondly rest on the farthest ridge of hills on the horizon, and fancy that from their summit Combe Magna might be seen. In such moments of precious, of invaluable misery, she rejoiced in tears of agony to be at Cleveland" (III.vi).

Yet, Thompson and Lee again pick up what we might dub the "Brontë option" of later nineteenth-century Gothic in order to signal to their twentieth-century audience the state of Marianne's mind and body. Atop the hill, in pouring rain and wind just as at her first meeting with Willoughby, "through frozen lips she whispers" Shakespeare's Sonnet 116: "Then she calls to Willoughby as though he were near. The effect is eerie, unworldly" (Thompson conflates scenes from *Wuthering Heights* and *Jane Eyre*).[23] Thompson's investment in such romantic imagery naturally brings forth an answering hero: Brandon reprises the romantic gesture of Willoughby and carries the now collapsed and hypothermic (rather than sexually excited) young woman back into the house. The difference between the images of the two men, however, tells us all we need to know about the difference between romance and reality: instead of the charming courtesy of Willoughby's subsequent behavior in the cottage, Rickman shows us an exhausted, soaked, trembling man incapable of speech. For him this has been an extreme experience, marked on the body.

A healthy man, the film's Brandon soon recovers and is seen waiting in great anxiety (and, as noted earlier, in Byronic dishabille) for his next opportunity to help the dangerously ill Marianne. This occurs when Elinor asks him to fetch their mother. In the novel, Brandon remains a man of eighteenth-century sense:

He, meanwhile, whatever he might feel, acted with all the firmness of a collected mind, made every necessary arrangement with the utmost dispatch, and calculated with exactness the time in which she might look for his return. Not a moment was lost in delay of any kind. The horses arrived, even before they were expected, and Colonel Brandon only pressing her hand with a look of solemnity, and a few words spoken too low to reach her ear, hurried into the carriage. (III.vii)

In the film, Brandon, having won his heroic spurs, literally wears them. We see him fling himself on his horse, black cape billowing, and gallop off into the sunset.

The film then moves into the long sequence of Marianne's near-death, which Lee sees as the "climax" of its narrative. Marianne's body has still to suffer more, to be purged before she can be admitted back into normal (patriarchal) society. In a detail not found in the published screenplay, though the language of the diary entry ("adds to edge") implies it was Thompson's own rewrite,[24] Marianne is bled by the doctor in grisly close-up; and "Elinor carries a bowl of her sister's blood into the darkness."[25] The doctor's part is the single biggest difference between published screenplay and final film, and the sacrificial connotations are impossible to miss: Marianne must pay with the body for the transgressions of the body. Lighting and camera angles further emphasize this reading: after Elinor's broken plea to her sister not to leave her (which I look at in more detail below) the camera pulls back toward the ceiling, in a visual maneuver which tropes the soul leaving the body. We look down on Marianne's still body lying like a sacrificial victim on the virginal white of the bed. Everything in this shot suggests to the viewer that Elinor's worst fears have been fulfilled. The dissolve out to the garden with its weird hedgerow and funereal urns in the eerie morning light continues the dominant metaphor of the flight of the soul from its earthly tenement. We can hardly believe our ears when we register that the faint sound on the soundtrack is that of a lark's morning song: life will, after all, return. Back in the bedroom, Elinor wakes from her stooped position at the side of Marianne's bed, and goes to the window: as she looks out (yet again) into that world of impossible promise, of benign nature, there is a whisper from behind her on the bed. Marianne is awake: reborn.

Elinor's story

There is no doubt that Elinor is the protagonist of the film – and, indeed, of the novel. In the novel it becomes clear relatively early that her voice is the closest to Austen's own: it is she who sees through the foolishness of her beloved sister's exaggerated sensibility ("It is not everyone who has your passion for dead leaves," III.v); she who behaves with the most admirable combination of personal restraint and determined common sense in the face of the family's difficulties. Although Marianne's experiences are the more extreme, eventually our empathy with her is displaced onto Elinor, who remains fully conscious as she suffers the novel's events – there is no escape into hysteria or illness for her.

Critics like Patrice Hannon argue, "The film nicely captures what is funny in the *situation*, but the greater humor in the narrative voice – again, mostly at Marianne's expense – is lost."[26] Although Lee's film may be unable to supply the exact equivalent of the author's ironical narrative voice (a standard critical complaint),[27] it can and does compensate for this with a visualization and virtual embodiment of Elinor's suffering. We may be deprived of Austen's tart comment about the happy marital establishment of Elinor and Edward – "They had in fact nothing to wish for, but the marriage of Colonel Brandon and Marianne, and rather better pasturage for their cows" (III.xiv) – but we are offered instead a version of the story that, we might say, early in her career Austen did not allow herself to tell. It is almost as though she had the opportunity to rewrite *Sense and Sensibility* after she had experienced creating the emotional vulnerability of *Persuasion*'s heroine Anne Elliot.

Thus, from the very beginning of the film we are given images of Elinor alone – not out in the fields indulging a romantic solitude, but indoors, making the best of the conditions of her confinement (just as Jane Austen, the writer, did). She does the budget calculations, writes the letters looking for a new home, says farewell on her family's behalf to the large servant establishment of Norland. This loneliness begins to be relieved when Edward Ferrars arrives (a new acquaintance in the film; already an old friend in the novel): he imaginatively and with unforced charm helps Margaret deal with her grief and anger (the atlas, the fencing lesson), watched by an appreciative Elinor; and their first private conversation without this intermediary figure begins with his perception of her sadness: "EDWARD *comes into the doorway and sees* ELINOR *who is listening to* MARIANNE *playing a concerto.* ELINOR *stands in a graceful, rather sad attitude, her back to us. Suddenly she senses* EDWARD *behind her and turns . . . He comes forward and offers her a handkerchief, which she takes with a grateful smile.*"[28] Devoney Looser sees Edward, with his "pleasing manner" and "nurturing qualities," as a model of the "New Man."[29] When Edward is forced to depart from Norland by the imperious Fanny, Elinor is once again left alone. We see that only she has an objective perspective on the fevered courtship of Marianne and Willoughby (as for example in the lock of hair scene). Her separation from her family's wholehearted involvement in this affair is brilliantly depicted in the scene after Willoughby's precipitate departure: Marianne, Mrs. Dashwood, and Margaret all retire to their rooms, sobbing audibly; Elinor is left perched on the stairs, drinking the cup of tea that was refused by Marianne. The high camera angle looking down on Elinor, who occupies only the top right corner of the screen – the rest of the frame being the gray uncarpeted stairwell – in this absurd but heart-rending scene says more than any expostulation of

Elinor's could do. Our view of her – her gray-clad back and bonnet, no face visible – echoes the position of the "other" sketch of Jane Austen by her sister Cassandra (whether consciously or unconsciously on the part of the filmmakers). Yet Jane was depicted sitting in a fertile landscape and looking outward; her fictional alter ego is once again in a virtual prison, her only view three closed doors.

Lucy Steele's arrival at Barton Park serves further to draw out Elinor's isolation and emotional distress at the blighting of her hopes for a continuation of the relationship with Edward. At the card party at Barton both Elinor and Marianne are separate from the noisy party, Marianne brooding in a corner, Elinor reading on a sofa. We see the predatory Lucy approaching Elinor to confide her secret engagement, and the dialogue is filmed in a series of head-shots, so that we cannot miss the triumph in Lucy's eyes and Elinor struggling to keep her composure. As they take a turn around the room Lucy clings maliciously to Elinor's arm, pursuing her when Elinor breaks away to a chair. A similar series of close shots is used a few minutes later, as Lucy and Elinor sit in the carriage that is taking them to London: Lucy drives home her advantage, Elinor is imprisoned with her torturer. Between these two scenes comes a short scene (Scene 93) in Elinor and Marianne's bedroom, in which the camera is fixed in close-up on Elinor lying in bed, her face turned toward the viewer, away from her sister who rattles on about her excitement at the proposed visit to London. At the conclusion of the scene we see Elinor struggling to hold back tears as she replies to Marianne's cheerful question, "What were you and Miss Steele whispering about so long?" – "Nothing of significance." Here the transfer of audience empathy is total: Marianne seems a heartless egoist who does not even suspect what we see in heartbreaking clarity.

The scene in which Edward finally visits the Dashwood sisters in London, only to find that Lucy is at that moment paying a call on Elinor with yet more triumphs to report – a scene of mixed comedy and discomfort – is bookended by almost identical shots of Elinor, alone in the room, sitting with her head bowed. These images are an important counter to the much more violent and active scenes of Marianne's distress during and after Willoughby's rejection of her at the ball. They prepare us to receive Elinor's first emotional outburst in the film, "What do you know of my heart?". There is a peculiar pleasure in watching that repressed surface break up – it is not shock, since viewers have been privy to Elinor's feelings as no one within the cinematic narrative has – but rather relief and a sense of justification: we *want* Elinor to speak out; we know her cause is just. Furthermore, we are rewarded doubly for our emotional commitment to Elinor by Emma Thompson's searing bravura performance. The speech is largely Austen's, though the opening line is Thompson's: the force of the whole scene is founded on Thompson's brilliant cutting and reshaping of Austen's writing.

Thompson achieves a comparable artistic triumph in her writing and performing of the scene in which Elinor has the difficult task of conveying to Edward Colonel Brandon's offer of a living so that he may marry Lucy. The end of the scene is Thompson's dramatically apt expansion of Austen's hints about the emotional temperature: "they parted, with a very earnest assurance on *her* side of her unceasing good wishes for his happiness in every change of situation that might befall him; on *his*, with rather an attempt to return the same good will, than the power of expressing it" (III.iv). The film's audience is watching an unspoken love scene: the yearning closeness of the two actors' bodies as they sit, the pregnant pauses in their speeches, the slight movement of Edward's hand toward Elinor as they stand up to make their farewell, as though he would lift her hand to his lips – but he denies even this contact, and the scene ends with the stiff formal bows of any acquaintance. (That hand kiss is achieved only in one of the film's last frames, as the now-married couple come out of the church.) Samuelian makes a fine, though disapproving, analysis of this scene, pointing out that Thompson has "chose[n] to shift much of the passion and complex emotions generated in and by" the interview with Willoughby at Cleveland "to a pair of scenes between Elinor and Edward – reassigning the power to arouse and influence Elinor to the man she is destined to marry."[30] She points to verbal similarities between Austen's text in the Cleveland chapter and Edward's speeches in the film. The second scene in question is of course the final *éclaircissement* between Edward and Elinor: "Thompson seems once again to have taken the passionate speeches of one lover and put them, slightly altered, into the mouth of another to render him more interesting than Austen deemed necessary."[31]

However touching the first of these two scenes is, it does not have the emotional power of Elinor's appeal to Marianne as she lies apparently dying. For a good reason: the sisters' love is an allowed relationship within the moral landscape of Austen's world; both Elinor and Edward know *and accept* that their love is disallowed. Elinor's emotional life must all be channeled toward her sister. For Lee, this is the defining shot of the film *Sense and Sensibility*: "Desperate Elinor discovers that Marianne's her soulmate; and if Marianne dies, she'll die, too. I told Emma to show pure fear and remove every other emotion."[32] This is the impulse behind the lines that Thompson invents for Elinor here: "Marianne, please try – I cannot – I cannot do without you. Oh, please, I have tried to bear everything else – I will try – but please, dearest, beloved Marianne, do not leave me alone . . . *She falls to her knees by the bed, gulping for breath, taking* MARIANNE's *hand and kissing it again and again.*" Not only does Elinor shower kisses on her sister's hand, she unselfconsciously and passionately strokes her whole body, as if trying to warm it back into life through this loving contact. It is undoubtedly the most physically passionate scene in the entire film. There is passion in Elinor's final hysterical sobbing at the news that Edward Ferrars is not married, but Lee's decision to cut from the film the scene after this dénouement, in which Edward and Elinor kiss, reinforces the sense that the sisters have the strongest emotional relationship in the narrative. Patriarchally sanctioned heterosexual marriage – in which, as Austen *and* the filmmakers make quite clear, money and property have their incontrovertible place – is emotionally shallow compared with the bond of sisters who have (potentially) nothing but one another.

Romantic solutions

This is not to deny the filmgoer her or his satisfaction in the happy marriages achieved at the film's end. But the imperatives of the romance genre of the Hollywood film do deny the viewer (and particularly the reader of Austen's text, who knows what is missing) an even more complex heroic image of Elinor. Thompson was uncomfortable with the loss of the scene in which Willoughby arrives at Cleveland and makes his confession to Elinor: "a wonderful scene in the novel which unfortunately interfered too much with the Brandon love story. I wrote hundreds of different versions and it was in and out of the script like the hokey-cokey."[33] Not only does this scene in the novel awaken in Elinor an erotic sense, a realization of the uncontrollability of desire, it also allows her to become for a moment the symbolic representation of the writer of these stories (a theme which Rozema's later *Mansfield Park* forcefully develops). Austen makes this unusual (for her) equation in the course of the chapter following Willoughby's visit:

Willoughby, "poor Willoughby'" as she now allowed herself to call him, was constantly in her thoughts; she would not but have heard his vindication for the world, and now blamed, now acquitted herself for having judged him so harshly before. But her promise of relating it to her sister was invariably painful. She dreaded the performance of it, dreaded what its effect on Marianne might be; doubted whether after such an explanation she could ever be happy with another, and for a moment wished Willoughby a widower. Then, remembering Colonel Brandon, reproved herself, felt that to *his* sufferings and *his* constancy far more than to his rival's, the reward of her sister was due, and wished anything rather than Mrs. Willoughby's death. (III.ix)

Austen is here deflecting criticism of her anti-romanticism by showing how tempting and easy the regeneration of Willoughby and defeat of Brandon would be – and having her heroine Elinor show the superiority of her moral imagination by rejecting it. Thompson, faced with the demands of a more economically powerful genre – the Hollywood romance film – simply opts for making Brandon more attractive: a hunter and horseman, like Willoughby; a poetry-lover and a musician; a man with a worldly past who is no stranger to passion. The casting of Alan Rickman, who brings to the role a brooding sexual presence derived from such previous performances as Valmont in the Royal Shakespeare Company's *Dangerous Liaisons* and the revenant lover of Juliet Stevenson in Anthony Minghella's *Truly, Madly, Deeply*, fills the bill and solves the problem perfectly.[34] It will be difficult for subsequent readers of Austen's novel to return Colonel Brandon to the decidedly asexual persona that Austen gives him.

The viewer and history

If, then, our reading of Austen's text is unavoidably nuanced by having viewed the powerful visual images of Ang Lee's film, we are simply acknowledging our inevitable place in the process of history (comparably, readers of 100 years ago saw the characters as Hugh Thompson's 1890s drawings – so convincing were they in their time that the Thompson illustrations are still reprinted and prized by Austen lovers). Emma Thompson builds into the film a metafictional awareness of the historical distance between all texts and their readers through her development of the character of the youngest sister, Margaret Dashwood. Margaret, born let us assume on the cusp of the century (Thompson makes her eleven rather than the novel's thirteen; the novel was published in 1811), will grow up into a world which does countenance solo female travelers, as her intrepidity, her fascination with geography, and her disregard of gender norms suggest she will become.[35] She will perhaps settle down in London once the establishment of such feminist enterprises as the Langham Place Circle (1858) guarantee her some like-minded company. Perhaps, in that parallel fictional world, she will become the great-grandmother of that intellectually adventurous, well-traveled feminist and passionately devoted sister, E. M. Forster's Margaret Schlegel.

If Emma Thompson rewrites Margaret Dashwood for an audience generally aware of the last two centuries' developments in the status of women, Patricia Rozema's more recent (1999) film *Mansfield Park* is even more forthright in its feminism, rewriting Austen's story of nervous and self-effacing Fanny Price by audaciously replacing her with the figure of the young Jane Austen, the "wild beast" of recent biographies (e.g. David

Nokes's use of extravagant phrases from Austen's letters and juvenilia).[36] In fact, Rozema told film reviewer James Berardinelli that she wanted to make a "collage" that was "an accurate portrait of Austen and her work" and that counteracted the current "period piece romances that make Austen out to be more sentimental than she actually was."[37] The result is a young woman who writes (and reads to an audience) comically violent satires of contemporary women's fiction, and to her sister acute and witty letters describing the goings-on at Mansfield Park. Fanny's narrative, rather than being that of Christian patience, becomes a *Bildungsroman*, its triumphant conclusion being the knowledge that her stories are to be published as the work of "a new and original writer." Even as she kisses Edmund in the film's romantic dénouement, we observe her ink-stained fingers. This is an Austen heroine for the twenty-first century, who will manage to have both love *and* work.

Rozema signals her enlistment of Austen in her own feminist project – that of giving voice to women's lives through her art – by noting in the credits her role as both writer and director of a film "based on Jane Austen's novel *Mansfield Park*, her letters and early journals." That is, Austen herself is the raw material of "history" as it is now reconfigured to include women's lives and perspectives. To reinforce the point, Rozema even puts into Fanny's mouth Catherine Morland's proto-feminist critique of "real solemn history" as written by men: "the men all so good for nothing, and hardly any women at all" (*Northanger Abbey*, I.xiv). Thus, instead of the hermetic world of costume drama[38] (as for example in Douglas McGrath's *Emma*, where – as David Monaghan points out in Chapter 10 – it seems to be virtually always summer), we are shown a decaying great house and its owner, Sir Thomas Bertram, enmired in the murky economics of the West Indian slave trade. Rozema's Fanny, picking up from Austen's line "Did not you hear me ask him about the slave trade last night?" (*Mansfield Park*, II.iii) has "been doing some reading about" this topic[39] – so much so that she dares to challenge Sir Thomas on the moral and legal issues. Tom's graphic pictures and her own hearing of the slaves' eerie songs as she travels from Portsmouth give a grim realism to this question.

Postcolonialism undoubtedly enters into the whole project of the film: Rozema is a Canadian; her Fanny (Frances O'Connor) is Australian; her Mary Crawford (Embeth Davidtz) was educated in South Africa. Frances O'Connor comments in an interview that Rozema perhaps cast her "because casting someone from outside that [English] culture created an interesting dynamic. Fanny Price is an outsider too."[40] All the actors nevertheless perform with impeccable British accents, as if to signal that "Englishness" is just one more mask for the performer on the global stage. Rozema's postcolonialist, feminist rewriting of Austen's novel for the film is based on current critical readings by, for example, Kathryn Sutherland and Claudia Johnson.[41] Johnson, in turn, in her review of Rozema's *Mansfield Park*, praises it as "a stunning revisionist reading of Austen's darkest novel" and notes that "Rozema emphasizes and augments the unseemliness unquestionably present in the novel."[42] Her film at all points – like Austen's novels – assumes an intelligent, even intellectual, audience. Thompson and Lee's *Sense and Sensibility* assumes a more general audience (that may, for example, need instruction about the precise situation of women in the early nineteenth century); its principal radical appeal is its demand for the audience's emotional involvement in its story of sisters' love. Rozema's ebullient and witty Fanny rarely requires our sympathy, and her close relationship with her sister (replacing the "dear brother William" of the novel) is no more the most important thing in her life than is her love for Edmund. Rather, it is her writing, her self-determination as an artist, that centers her.

Like Amy Heckerling's *Clueless*, Thompson/Lee's *Sense and Sensibility* and Rozema's *Mansfield Park* have the courage to be their own creation rather than attempt "faithfully" to illustrate Austen's novels. Is it significant that the scripts of all three were written by women, two of whom also directed? Certainly any woman brought up in the liberated atmosphere created by the feminist movement of the last third of the twentieth century will be likely to approach these stories of love leading to marriage in a way that tends to undermine the apparent self-sufficiency of such closures. But Austen's texts do provide the clues for these subversive gestures. The process of adaptation, like any reading, demands a recognition of the historical distance between the original text and its new audience. The challenge for filmmakers is to find the visual language and a reading of the original that allow the story to speak to that new audience.

NOTES

1 In the Harmondsworth: Penguin edition of 1989: 24.
2 See also Graham Fuller, "Cautionary Tale," *Sight and Sound* (March 1996): 21.
3 Emma Thompson, *The "Sense and Sensibility" Screenplay and Diaries: Bringing Jane Austen's Novel to Film* (London: Bloomsbury, 1995): 118.
4 Ibid.: 190.
5 Forster, *Howards End*: 118.
6 Roland Barthes, *Image–Music–Text*, trans. and ed. Stephen Heath (New York: Hill and Wang, 1977): 146.
7 Director James Ivory, Merchant Ivory Productions, 1992.
8 Lindsay Doran, Introduction to Thompson's *Diaries*: 14.

9 Thompson, *Diaries*: 49. Compare *Howards End*, in the same conversation in which Margaret's pince-nez are mentioned: "Work, work, work if you'd save your soul and your body. It is honestly a necessity, dear boy" (118).

10 Julianne Pidduck, "Of Windows and Country Walks: Frames of Space and Movement in 1990s Austen Adaptations," *Screen* 39.4 (Winter 1998): 381.

11 Thompson, *Diaries*: 237, author's emphasis.

12 This analysis of the film's emphasis on "sisterhood," both literal and metaphorical, counters the arguments of critics like Kristin Flieger Samuelian ("Piracy Is Our Only Option: Postfeminist Intervention in *Sense and Sensibility*," in *Jane Austen in Hollywood*, eds. Linda Troost and Sayre Greenfield [Lexington, KY: University of Kentncky Press, 1998]: 148) who claim that the film, "while seeming to legitimize feminist discourse, is more in line with postfeminism and effectively erases the implicit feminism of Austen's novel" by overinvesting in the romance plot. Thompson's rewriting of the courtship behavior of Brandon and Edward to attract a twentieth-century film audience does not constitute a "foreground[ing] [of] the very passion and romance that Austen condemns" (151). The film's most passionate relationship is that between Elinor and Marianne (see my discussion of Marianne's "death-bed" scene). Rebecca Dickson, however, considers this too "antifeminist": "it is the strong woman who breaks, not the immature, malleable one . . . she is also more dependent on men than Austen's Elinor . . . When Thompson offers us an Elinor who must come emotionally unglued in the film, she erases much of Elinor's achievement" ("Misrepresenting Jane Austen's Ladies: Revising Texts (and Histories) to Sell Films," in *Jane Austen in Hollywood*, eds. Troost and Greenfield: 55–56).

13 Thompson, *Diaries*: 81–88.

14 Ibid.: 86.

15 Ibid.: 85.

16 Ibid.: 278.

17 Ibid.: 212 and 214.

18 Eileen Sutherland points out that in complaining about Colonel Brandon's mention of a flannel waistcoat Marianne "displays her naiveté and ignorance of the world. . . . She should have connected it with danger, endurance and courage, a kind of military uniform." Sutherland concludes, "Fops and dandies and town beaux might consider their silk, striped or brocaded vests as the epitome of sartorial splendour, but *Real Men Wore Flannel Waistcoats*" ("That Infamous Flannel Waistcoat," *Persuasions: Journal of the Jane Austen Society of North America* 18 (December 1996): 58, original emphasis).

19 Compare Elinor's remark apropos Marianne's speedy intimacy with Willoughby, "you have received every assurance of his admiring Pope no more than is proper" (i.x) – Austen clearly knew his work and understood his double entendres.

20 Thompson, *Diaries*: 103.

21 Fuller, "Cautionary Tale": 24.

22 Thompson, *Diaries*: 286.

23 Ibid.: 177.

24 Ibid.: 274.

25 Ibid.: 275.

26 Patrice Hannon, "Austen Novels and Austen Films: Incompatible Worlds?" *Persuasions* 18 (1996): 29.

27 Unlike Jan Fergus, I find voiceover narrative strikingly successful in Rozema's *Mansfield Park*; as Claudia Johnson argues, "By weaving in Austen's uproarious early writings, Rozema transforms Fanny into a version of the Austenian narrator we love" (Review of *Mansfield Park*, *The Times Literary Supplement* (December 31, 1999): 16). In fact Rozema's observant Fanny eventually uses many narratorial passages from *Mansfield Park* itself.

28 Thompson, *Diaries*: 45.

29 Devoney Looser, "Feminist Implications of the Silver Screen Austen," in *Jane Austen in Hollywood*, eds. Troost and Greenfield: 159, 172.

30 Samuelian, "Piracy": 153.

31 Ibid.: 154.

32 In Fuller, "Cautionary Tale": 24.

33 Thompson, *Diaries*: 272.

34 *Truly, Madly, Deeply*, Director Anthony Minghella. Independent Films, 1991.

35 See "Travel Writing," in *The Feminist Companion to Literature in English*, eds. Virginia Blain, Patricia Clements, and Isobel Grundy (London: Batsford, 1990). Pidduck points out that "[s]ignificantly, the figure of the (kinetic) female child as a torchbearer for a feminist future recurs in other contemporary feminist costume dramas such as *The Piano* (Jane Campion, 1993), *Orlando* (Sally Potter, 1993)" ("Of Windows and Country Walks": 391).

36 David Nokes, *Jane Austen: A Life* (London: Farrar, Strauss and Giroux, 1997).

37 James Berardinelli, "The Darker Side of Jane Austen: Patricia Rozema Talks about *Mansfield Park*" (November 15, 1999). http://movie-reviews. colossus.net/comment/111599.html

38 Although I entirely agree with Jan Fergus about the excellence of the 1983 BBC version of *Mansfield Park*, it is unfair, I think, to compare adaptations in different genres: the television adaptation has the luxury of nearly four hours more than the film in which to develop its subtle and detailed narrative. Interestingly, the films *Sense and Sensibility* and *Mansfield Park* shared a cinematographer, Michael Coulter, suggesting that he has developed a specialty in effectively filming this "new wave" of Austen movies.

39 Kathryn Sutherland, in her Introduction to the Penguin Classics edition of *Mansfield Park* (1996: xxxii), points out that Austen was familiar with Thomas Clarkson's *History of the Rise, Progress, and Accomplishment of the Abolition of the African Slave-Trade by the British Parliament* (2 vols., London, 1808).

40 "Frances O'Connor Talks to Film.com about her Role in *Mansfield Park*." http://us.imdb.com/Trailers

41 Claudia Johnson, *Jane Austen. Women, Politics, and the Novel* (Chicago: University of Chicago Press, 1988).

42 Johnson, Review.

6   Regency romance shadowing in the visual motifs of Roger Michell's *Persuasion*

Paulette Richards

Commentators on Roger Michell's 1995 film adaptation of *Persuasion* have criticized the incongruity of Captain Wentworth and Ann Elliot embracing in the street and the marketing strategy that placed on the cover of the video-cassette a "still" of a torrid embrace that never occurred in the film. Inevitably, recreation and "purity" of text becomes tangled with questions of "purity" of motivation: can productions based on the profit motive do justice to the aesthetic value of a literary text or do they reshape and distort the text to appeal to the values, prejudices, and expectations of the mass audience? Some commentators answer no to the first question and bewail the manipulations referred to in the second. For example, Amanda Collins laments the nostalgic propensity of recent Austen adaptations to rewrite history as a reflection of the present and of the present's distorted view of the past.[1]

Yet, twentieth-century filmmakers standing at a historical and cultural distance from Austen's world must translate Austen's intent into filmic representations that carry significance for modern filmgoers. As Harriet Margolis suggests in Chapter 2 of this text, Coleridge's distinction between faithful copies and imaginative imitations of literary masterworks is most pertinent to this debate about the value of recent Austen adaptations. No matter how well-crafted and entertaining a near-as-possible duplication is, a "purist" copy that seeks total fidelity to text will never be faithful enough simply because of the difference between written art and filmic art. Therefore, filmmakers do better to recreate Austen, to convey the spirit of her work on screen through visual means to which modern filmgoers can respond. Nonetheless, the purist viewer will always find disturbing incidents of "misinterpretation" that seem to do violence to Austen's novels.

Modern costumes and Regency fantasies

The most obvious evidence of the problem facing filmmakers lies in the costuming. Austen assumes her readers know the fashions of her world and need only information about rank and title to conjure up in their imaginations the appropriate attire. The rare instances in which she does describe attire are clearly for satiric purposes or to establish eccentricity. Yet, this assumed knowledge clearly does not apply to modern readers of Austen, unfamiliar with the sartorial conventions of the time, and, in fact, with our increasing distance over time, our ability as readers to imagine the society Austen describes diminishes. More significantly, this assumption cannot apply to moviegoers, whose visual experience must include clothed characters. The cliché that "clothes make the man" (or woman) becomes irrefutable fact on the screen. Since Austen provides no or minimal directions, costumers and directors are left to their own devices.

Amy Heckerling's decision in her modern recreation of *Emma*, entitled *Clueless*, was to simply throw convention out the window, opt for a modern setting, and translate Austen's eighteenth-century world into a comparable modern one where she could explore questions of maturation, socialization, classism, and materialism. The most famous sartorial scene therein is Cher's dressing room, a walk-in closet with interchangeable clothing and accessories, available through a motorized delivery system such as dry-cleaners employ, and Cher (the Emma figure) at the computer mixing and matching for the most appropriate fashion statement of the day. The scene is devastating satire in the spirit of Austen, though clearly far removed from Austen's experience and particular intention. Costuming in the 1949 *Pride and Prejudice* was driven by the need to please a star, Vivien Leigh, hence the numerous and varied Hollywood gowns (glamorous nineteenth-century-style fashions!) to show her figure to best advantage. The BBC Austen productions have been, predictably, far more conservative about clothing, but they too have involved compromises between period accuracy and viewer expectations. Critical comments about the predominance of "wonderbras" to make eighteenth-century fashions better fit modern concepts of breast display have already called attention to this disjunction between period accuracy or "museum quality" costuming and inventive film costuming to fit modern sartorial taste and expectation. In many modern adaptations of Austen's novels, filmmakers draw on the conventions of dress familiar to readers of Regency romances (modern stories set in Austen's time) to establish the "historical accuracy" of the film. The choice of costume actually performs a number of functions, for example, establishing character and class differences, allowing for an eroticism absent in Austen but expected by modern viewers, and satisfying "imperial nostalgia" fantasies even while purporting to offer a "high culture" aesthetic experience.

While Jane Austen set the standards for Regency romances popularized by such modern writers as Georgette Heyer and Clare Darcy, the

significations of Regency costume in romance novels have, in turn, inevitably influenced the readings of costume in film adaptations of Jane
Austen's novels, casting a long shadow over analogous visual conventions
and making Regency romances popular modern touchstones for film.
Regency romances attract extaordinarily loyal fans in both England and
America, fans whose influence outweighs their numbers. It is, to some
degree, on the foundation of the popular Regency romance that film
director Roger Michell reconstructs Austen's *Persuasion*.

The author most responsible for articulating the Regency romance
interpretation of Austen's world, Georgette Heyer (1902–1974), penned
almost sixty romance and mystery novels beginning with the historical
romance *The Black*.[2] She admired Austen so much that she unearthed an
entire tradition of women's romantic fiction familiar to Austen and her
contemporaries. Drawing on this body of literature, Heyer almost single-
handedly created the Regency romance genre and the requisite attire that
gives it visual life.

Where Austen provides only minimal descriptions of attire, assuming
that her intended readers would already have in mind clear images of how
such characters would or should dress, the Regency romance genre which
sprang from her work dwells obsessively on sartorial details, describing
bodice cuts, petticoats, and the particulars of fashion that separate the
dowdy and the rural from the fashionable, the urban, the sophisticated.
As a result of these ready-made and highly specific period descriptions
of dress, costuming in Austen films is often read in Regency terms, with
film adaptations building on Regency romances as popular modern visual
images. Furthermore, because of the visual nature of the film medium,
costume becomes much more significant than in the novels themselves.

In Regency romances, fashion looms large as a way to shape the iden-
tities of female characters. A staple of the Regency genre is the makeover
in which the country-nobody heroine is dramatically transformed by
London modistes and hairstylists at the behest of wealthy relatives or
an indulgent new husband. In such cases "clothes make the woman"
or rather the Lady. Armed with a new wardrobe, the heroine exerts a
degree of power and influence in society which would have been unimag-
inable before her transformation. The language of desire is also expressed
through sartorial symbols in the world of popular romance. Sensual details such as the texture of silks and velvets, the transparency of light
muslins, the beguiling innocence of pale pastels or the bold display of
vivid colors reveal the heroine's awakening sexuality as surely as "charming deshabille" follows an appearance in a scandalously low decolletage.
Descriptions of clothes are therefore an important element of the erotic
fantasies romance novels portray. Even in the traditionally "sweet" genre

of Regency romance, which once saved the first kiss between the hero and heroine for the last page, such eroticism has become much more explicit than ever would have been imaginable in Jane Austen's time. The distinctive high-waisted gowns of the Regency era signify a flavor of romance readily distinguishable from the hoopskirts and pantalets of the ever-popular Civil War saga or the unyielding hooks and laces that pose such irresistible temptation to the heroic rogues who populate the eighteenth-century "bodice-ripper." Such sartorial choices loom large in modern film productions of Austen novels.

In sympathy with the unfortunates dispatched by Mme. la Guillotine, many women cropped their hair *à la victime*. Such short, carefree hairstyles like that of the heroine in Patricia Rozema's *Mansfield Park* were a welcome change from the towering wigs of the preceding era. Women arranged longer tresses in imitation of the graceful, curled tendrils which adorned Greek statues, as do the sisters in film versions of *Pride and Prejudice*, just as the high-waisted line of their gowns was inspired by the elegant simplicity of ancient Greek and Roman robes. The "empire waist" gown so visible in the BBC productions of *Emma*, *Mansfield Park*, *Pride and Prejudice*, and *Sense and Sensibility* evolved as a conscious imitation of a faded imperium, but it was most commonly made up in muslin, printed cottons, and light silks imported from the tropical outposts of the new European empires. At the same time, male attire moved away from the peacock dandyism of the past, and under the influence of Beau Brummell, toward the sober, tailored suit and white shirt which is still standard business attire today. Well-dressed men of the Regency era relinquished vivid colors, plumes, and lace but remained concerned with the cut of their jackets and the brilliant patina on their boots. This historical reality has made Regency romance heroes especially appealing to twentieth-century women immersed in a culture that dictates that real men should be blissfully unaware of fashion. *Persuasion* identifies the unreliable male as a dandy by his clothing and Anne's father with his brocade vests and startling color combinations is mocked through costume as an old-fashioned peacock. In turn, the naval officer hero of *Persuasion*, resplendent in his blue dress uniform, represents the military force which has secured a far-flung empire. In uniform he towers visually above the civilians around him, and yet, in doing so, is lonely and isolated, often depicted filmically on the edge of any significant social gathering, rather than at its center. The uniform has enabled him to better himself socially and financially and to escape class to some small degree in a class-ridden society. It speaks to viewers about British imperialism and naval might and makes its wearer a romantic but also a sad figure. Likewise, the exotic feathers and turbans of the ladies reflect the influence of empire on fashion.

10. An excursion on the waterfront at Lyme from *Jane Austen's Persuasion*, a Sony Pictures Classics Release, 1995. The navy leads the way.

Additionally, costume manipulates the signifiers of erotic desire in the same way that romance writers use sartorial eroticism. Following the approaches of contemporary Regency authors such as Catherine Coulter and Mary Balogh, who have stretched the conventions of the genre to add more erotic spice to their tales, filmmakers have prompted controversy with, for example, scenes of Darcy going in swimming in *Pride and Prejudice* – his wet male body accentuated by tight breeches and a clinging gauze shirt – or a heavily cloaked male on horseback looming out of the rain to sweep into his arms the scantily clad, rain-soaked sister in *Sense and Sensibility*.

Action and interaction: Regency romance influences

The kiss in the last frame of *Persuasion* transgresses the film's scrupulous attention to historical accuracy since such public displays of affection offended genuine Regency notions of propriety. Nevertheless, this last-frame kiss corresponds effectively to the last-page kiss which was long the staple ending of the modern Regency romance novel, and indeed the whole plot builds inexorably to this denouement just as the classic Regency romance novel was paced to build to the final embrace. Thus,

Michell's *Persuasion* offers a rich field for exploring the ways in which film changes literature to meet modern viewer expectations and film convention.

Regency readers are led to identify with the aristocratic values (or what they imagine to be aristocratic values) represented in the texts. While many Regency fans may be Jane Austen enthusiasts who ran out of Jane Austen novels to read, there are significant differences between Austen's literary texts and the Regency romance novels patterned after her works. Where Austen wrote about characters from the middle class and the lower gentry, Regency romances have traditionally invited readers to participate in a fantasy recreation of life among the ton, the "upper ten thousand" families of Britain. Germaine Greer claims that the concept of romantic love within marriage developed in conjunction with industrialization, a myth invented to seduce women into accepting their second-class status within society and to make conjugal love a cherished ideal in western society.[3] If so, all the calculating preoccupation with the "marriage mart" which marks the characters in Austen's novels and their descendants in Regency romance signifies the beginnings of this phenomenon, which reached full bloom in the early nineteenth century with a new consensus that mutual attraction, if not full-blown love, could, or even should, be an important ingredient of a successful marriage.

Austen's heroines and their popular romance counterparts struggle to balance the desire for position and wealth with the desires of the heart. It doesn't take Elizabeth Bennet long to decide Mr. Darcy is not so insufferable once she sees his palatial home. Romance readers are grateful for the fact that Austen and her descendants arrange for their heroines to "have their cake and eat it too." Yet, real-life Regency belles, draped in their fluttering East Indian gauzes, surrendered themselves to husbands who controlled their social and economic destinies as firmly as the British Raj controlled the economic and political destiny of its colonial subjects.

Yet, at the same time, Regency fashion is emblematic of important changes in gender roles under the accelerating impact of the Industrial Revolution, with the hero's fashion sense a visible sign of either his stodgy conservatism or his sensual nature. Breaking out of the hermetic society of the Austen novels, skilled writers such as Marion Chesney and Jayne Ann Krentz, writing as Amanda Quick, have even used Regency romance as a forum for exploring social issues such as the plight of the servant classes in Regency England and the relationship that popular romance bears to traditions of women's fiction. Heyer's interpretation of Austen's Regency England identifies with the nobility even though Austen was not part of the nobility and did not write about the ton. Filmmakers, following her lead, make this shift in class-consciousness. The novel *Persuasion* is precisely about the negotiation between the old landed aristocracy and the upwardly mobile members of the middling classes whose fortunes (built on manufacturing and colonial exploitation) were grudgingly assimilated into the old nobility through marriage. Sir Walter's disdain for the navy illustrates this social tension perfectly. He strongly objects to it "as being the means of bringing persons of obscure birth into undue distinction, and raising men to honours which their fathers and grandfathers never dreamt of"(I.iii).

The visual metaphor in the films for the power and prestige of the landed few is not simply the elaborate neoclassical interior sets and Georgian fronts, but also the conspicuously empty grassy lawns, decorated occasionally by a few picturesquely grazing sheep, to be sure, but mainly wasted space, unsullied by useful enterprise of any kind. This emptiness speaks loudly, balancing its Augustan notion of nature put into the order God intended with its unshown opposite, fields packed with sugar cane, slaves, servants, all the sweaty toil of enterprise that constituted the economic underpinnings of new social wealth. This iconic use of wasted space runs through the Regency romances and has its ultimate, if diminished, apotheosis in the modern suburban lawn, a final testament to conspicuous waste signifying economic power.

Furthermore, Michell's *Persuasion* is visually more aware of the "lower orders" than most recent film adaptations of Austen's other novels. It includes images of gardeners scything the lawn before Kellynch Hall, lines of footmen attending the Elliots' removal from their ancestral home, beaters rousing the pheasants that make easy targets for Charles Musgrove and Captain Wentworth's fowling pieces, and even a homeless beggar who is the beneficiary of Anne's charitable impulses. Most notably, Lady Dalrymple receives callers in a room painted to resemble the inside of an houri's tent with two black footmen flanking her as she sits on a large ottoman. This scene effectively captures the fashionable exoticism of the eighteenth and early nineteenth centuries. It also alludes to the colonial sources of wealth supporting the "great houses" of this period.

Although *Persuasion* is very much concerned with material wealth on the surface, an important lesson in the text is that being open to persuasion rather than being selfishly determined to pursue one's own desires makes for more harmonious social relations. The approved code of conduct in Austen's novels as well as in the Regency romance novels modeled on her work exhibits the use-value. In contrast, the film's reading of *Persuasion* ultimately founders in the exchange-value ethics which surround the Austen brand-name as cultural capital. Ironically, the filmmakers' scrupulous concern with historical accuracy and faithfulness to the text contribute to its misreading.

Deeply hurt that Anne had been persuaded to break off their engagement eight years before, Wentworth at first applauds Louisa Musgrove's

firmness of will. Filled with remorse after her accident, however, he learns
"to distinguish between the steadiness of principle and the obstinacy of
self-will, between the darings of heedlessness and the resolution of a collected mind" (II.xi). As a result he comes to understand "the perfect excellence of the mind with which Louisa's could so ill bear a comparison"
(II.xi). Meanwhile Anne, comparing herself to the headstrong Louisa
Musgrove, comes to value her own persuadability – "She thought it could
scarcely escape him to feel, that a persuadable temper might sometimes be
as much in favour of happiness, as a very resolute character" (I.xii). Mutual recognition of this value is the foundation of Anne and Wentworth's
reunion. The film faithfully reproduces the scene where Louisa is injured
in the attempt to jump from the sea wall into Captain Wentworth's arms
but misses the symbolic significance this incident conveys in the novel.

The text makes this symbolism clear. It explains that teasing Wentworth into jumping her from stiles had become an enthralling game for
Louisa: "the sensation was delightful to her" (I.xii). When she is injured,
Wentworth had already jumped her down from the sea wall once. She
then ran back up to be jumped down again because she loved the game.
Her compulsively flirtatious manner and the pleasure she takes in repeat-
ing her leaps of faith suggest that she is playacting and is not particularly
attracted to Wentworth for himself. She is one of those people who is in
love with love because of the emotional and sexual rush it gives her. Her
fate reminds readers of the heedless romantic risks of becoming a "fallen
woman" if the man fails to support her at the moment she chooses to fling
herself at him. It is also telling that Louisa's injury is not to her limbs but
to her head. For her the healing process entails regaining enough strength
to be in her right mind, aware of her surroundings. She has to be brought
back to reason.

Austen's opus consistently favors the rational, restrained woman over
the headlong romantic. Anne Elliot and Fanny Price, in particular, are
foils for the strong-minded female characters who appeared in some contemporary women's fictions. For example, in Maria Edgeworth's *Belinda*
(1801),[4] Lady Delacour fights a duel with another woman. The plot
of the novel forces her to suffer for this transgression against femininity
(among other transgressions) as the recoil from the gun causes an ulcerat-
ing wound to her bosom. Nevertheless, her dashing exploits allowed early
nineteenth-century women to imagine a more active and liberated role
even though such freedom was only possible in escapist fiction. Austen
consciously drew Anne Elliot as the antithesis of such hoydens. Yet,
twentieth-century romance fiction has presented more and more independent, outspoken, active heroines. For example, Serena Spenborough,
heroine of Georgette Heyer's *Bath Tangle*,[5] rides "hell-for-leather" to

11. The accident on the waterfront at Lyme with Captain Wentworth (Ciaran Hinds) and Anne Elliot (Amanda Root) attending the injured Louisa while Captain Benwick looks on helplessly, from *Jane Austen's Persuasion*, a Sony Pictures Classics Release, 1995

stop an elopement, an exploit usually left to fathers and brothers, though Austen's attitude toward such aggressive behavior is clear in her negative portrait of Lydia Bennet in *Pride and Prejudice*, who violates family trust to race headlong and foolishly into a compromising affair. Nonetheless, Patricia Rozema's Fanny Price of *Mansfield Park* is modeled on such daring women, even riding wildly at night in a visually romantic setting.

The taste for feisty, active heroines leaves twentieth-century readers and viewers less able to accept Anne Elliot's reticence. The film therefore reworks Austen's plot and characters so that the central conflict initially seems to be the battle of the sexes on the field of love, a common theme of popular romantic fiction, or at least a battle between Anne's desires and her conventionality. In the process of waging this battle, Anne becomes a twentieth-century Regency romance heroine whose initial modesty and reticence are in keeping with her sense of social place but whose growth in assertiveness and sensual awareness ostensibly wins Wentworth and opens up enlarged horizons of activity for herself as a sailor's wife sailing the high seas with who knows what brave new worlds, adventures, and responsibilities awaiting her.

Early on, the film inserts a scene in which Anne attempts to tell Lady Russell that she might have been happier had she not been persuaded to refuse Wentworth. Lady Russell silences her and the film proceeds to portray Anne as continually silenced and put upon when she goes to Uppercross. She is expected to remain self-effacing, dutiful, and useful to others. In the novel, Anne's inner musings include some small pleasure in feeling useful amongst the Musgroves when she is counted as "nothing" in her own family. However, in the film, this condition is made clearly deplorable, and, when the action moves to Bath, Anne begins to assert herself more. She stands up to Sir Walter and insists on visiting Mrs. Smith as promised rather than going to the Dalrymples.' The text reports: "She left it to himself to recollect that Mrs. Smith was not the only widow in Bath between thirty and forty, with little to live on, and no sirname of dignity" (II.v). In the film, however, she responds to his disparaging remarks about Mrs. Smith's lack of social status by openly retorting that Mrs. Smith is not the only poor widow in Bath, a pointed allusion to Mrs. Clay, his houseguest. In other words, what in the novel is covert, in the film is overt, and, in keeping with a modern Regency romance sensibility, some signs of rebellion are essential if viewers are to respect their heroine.

Therefore, the film representation of the concert evening departs most radically from the text in endowing Anne with greater assertiveness. In the novel, Anne very strongly desires to speak with Captain Wentworth and make him understand her feelings for him but she is hemmed in by social restrictions. Over the course of the chapter she anxiously watches the seating arrangements among her party. At the end of the first intermission, she has some hope:

> In re-settling themselves, there were now many changes, the result of which was favourable for her. Colonel Wallis declined sitting down again, and Mr. Elliot was invited by Elizabeth and Miss Carteret, in a manner not to be refused, to sit between them; and by some other removals, and a little scheming of her own, Anne was enabled to place herself much nearer the end of the bench than she had been before, much more within reach of a passer-by. (II.viii)

This subtle maneuvering succeeds when Wentworth does approach and speak to Anne. Unfortunately, Mr. Elliot interrupts the conversation, asking her to explain the Italian again. Wentworth leaves in a jealous huff. In the film, Anne sees that Wentworth is leaving, gets up, and hurries to the back of the hall to intercept him. This action would have been extremely forward behavior for the Bath concert room in 1814. In the film's reading of the character, however, Anne finally deserves to win Wentworth because she has learned to assert herself in face of social and familial disapproval.

In keeping with the twentieth-century sensibility of the film adaptation, a large part of Anne's growing self-assertion is her reconnection with passion. The closing is very tame compared to the norms of screen eroticism, but it is a perfectly placed and perfectly paced conclusion to an interpretation of the novel which owes so much to the Regency romance genre. Our first glimpse of the Elliot household shows the family gathered together to receive Lady Russell's advice on reducing expenses. Readers of Regency romance will instantly recognize Lady Russell as one of the ubiquitous turbaned dowagers who dispense all manner of advice on how to "go on" in society. Sir Walter, preening by the fireplace in a pewter blue coat declares: "No I will not have a sailor in my house." As it is September, only one low flame flickers on the hearth. When Anne appears, she is dressed in a light blue gown and is lit in a way which makes her look wan and washed-out. At the mention of Wentworth's name, she crosses to the window saying, "Please excuse me. The fire. I became overheated." The cool colors and nearly empty grate portray the lack of passion in Anne's life.

Changes in costume as well as action further underscore Anne's growing sensual awareness. In many of the Bath scenes she wears a pink pelisse which brings a new bloom to her cheeks. Her hair is arranged in a softer, more becoming style. Later, as she sits before a cheerful blaze talking to Mr. Elliot about good company, she becomes quite animated in her manner. His charm helps raise Anne's awareness of herself as a desirable woman. Through casting and costume, the visual narrative credibly establishes Anne as a heroine who is ready to embrace desire by the time she and Wentworth finally reach an understanding.

We first see Wentworth through the window of the Great House in Uppercross. His dark hair, rugged profile, and broad shoulders accentuated by gold epaulets are framed in an over-the-shoulder shot. Scenes of this dinner party are cross-cut with scenes of Anne, who has stayed home to nurse her nephew, gazing into the fire. The flames are low but there are several whereas there was only one tongue of flame when she became overheated before, thus visually suggesting that Wentworth's return rekindles Anne's desire.

Wentworth's subsequent screen presence owes much to the archetype of the tall, dark, and handsome romance hero set off against a smooth-faced dandy, a "curly-haired darling." Ciaran Hinds is the darkest actor in the cast. He is also the tallest, and low-angle shots give him an even more towering presence. He lacks the superficial qualities of screen beauty, but he has a rugged manliness that looks well next to Robert Glenister as Captain Harville and Richard McCabe as Captain Benwick, both of whom are described as attractive in the text. Samuel West as Mr. Elliot, in turn, is actually handsomer than his counterpart in the text. In the novel, Mr. Elliot's manners and address leave the impression that he is attractive, but the narrator explicitly states that he was not a handsome man. In the film Mr. Elliot is not simply handsome; rather he is delicately beautiful, with fair curls, finely chiseled features, and a lean, elegant figure. In the novel, he wears mourning for his recently deceased wife, but readers of Regency romance will recognize the exquisitely cut "bottle-green" coat he wears in the film as the sign of a dandy. Indeed, on screen, in keeping with the Regency romance sartorial code, his obviously padded shoulders and chest indicate his fundamental insincerity. Still, on both page and screen, a man who displays such fashion sense also exhibits a kind of sensual awareness often lacking in twentieth-century models of manhood. The Regency romance convention of the dark, even morose, brooding, and possibly dangerous male lead set off against a more conventionally attractive male, whose good looks warn of his insincerity, comes to life on Michell's screen.

At the same time the film plays an interesting game with the question of class and social acceptance. Mr. Elliot dresses well, speaks well, and moves in the right circles and, because of birth, is accepted as a suitable match for Anne, whereas the hero, as a member of the rising middle class, has seemed unsuitable and has been rejected as a man of limited possibilities. Mr. Elliot clearly is at home in a drawing room; Captain Wentworth is not. However, the navy has afforded him the opportunity to prove his mettle and to rise above his birth, whereas Mr. Elliot depends on his charm to win him a rich wife. The film plays the silent, brooding Wentworth off against the glib and socially adept Mr. Elliot. Yet, in the end, Austen points out: "Captain Wentworth, with five-and-twenty thousand pounds, and as high in his profession as merit and activity could place him, was no longer nobody. He was now esteemed quite worthy to address the daughter of a foolish, spendthrift baronet" (II.xii). In the film, it is Wentworth's unspoken agony and blunt, honest manliness that distinguish him from the two-faced Mr. Elliot. The film reflects its modern roots by its celebration of the clear comeuppance of the man who would deceive a woman to gain her worldly goods and the victory of the plain sailor who loves his country, his military career, and his wife.

The first time Anne sees Wentworth in Bath, she is sitting in a teashop taking shelter from the rain. Spying Wentworth's approach in the street, she separates from her sister and Mrs. Clay and moves toward the front of the shop in time to intercept him. After an exchange of greetings, Anne indicates her intention to walk home in spite of the rain. Wentworth then offers to lend her his new umbrella. At this moment, however, Mr. Elliot, who had been securing places for Elizabeth and Mrs. Clay in Lady Dalrymple's carriage, returns to escort Anne home. Not having read Freud, Austen did not develop the umbrella as a phallic symbol, but the film adds an awkward moment when Anne hands Wentworth's umbrella back to him and takes up Mr. Elliot's instead.

In both the novel and the film, Captain Wentworth's jealousy of Mr. Elliot increases from this scene in the teashop until he overhears Anne disputing the relative constancy of men and women with his friend, Captain Harville. Her declaration that women love longest when all hope is gone moves him to declare his own undying love for Anne in a letter that he leaves on the desk hidden under the blotter. He quits the room with his friends but returns a moment later, claiming to have left a personal article behind. This ruse gives him the opportunity to silently point out the letter to Anne. In the film, he claims to have forgotten his umbrella. Since the umbrella has already been established as a phallic symbol, it conveys his anxiety about being rejected as a man. In the novel, Wentworth claims to have forgotten his gloves. Since gloves are a mark of the gentleman, his remark in the text betrays his anxiety about being rejected as a social inferior. This is why Mr. Elliot's attentions to Anne threaten him so much more than her poetical exchanges with Captain Benwick. Benwick shares his common origins and is junior to him in rank. Mr. Elliot, on the other hand, has a fortune and will inherit the title. It is difficult for the film audience, particularly the mainstream American film audience, to understand how Captain Wentworth could remain ineligible in the eyes of Anne's family after he has made his fortune, but as a woman of color, these nuances are much more salient to me. A black man could be worth twenty-five million in today's terms and still be unacceptable as a son-in-law in many white families.

Readers of "sweet" romance know to expect a kiss in the last chapter as confirmation of the happy ending. Thus, the passage of the carnival players through the street at the moment of Anne and Wentworth's kiss creates a liminal space in which propriety may believably be suspended. The street players also constitute an effective metaphor expressing the jubilation of love, while the fire motif (building on the flickering flames in the earlier fireplace scenes) gives the kiss more erotic force than such a tame salute could otherwise have by catching the fire-eater in the frame at the same moment. The tongues of flame shooting from his mouth allow viewers used to more explicit eroticism to recognize the intensity of Anne and Wentworth's passion. Yet according to the film, this passion comprises more than sexual desire. As a seafaring man Wentworth also represents Anne's longing for broader vistas of experience just as Anne represents Wentworth's longing for home and hearth. Throughout the film, boats and the ocean function as a symbolic leitmotif. The first frame is filled with the ocean. Then, Admiral Croft appears in a rowboat. A little later, as Anne is packing up Kellynch Hall, she finds mementos of her romance with Frederick Wentworth in a trunk. Among them is a paper boat folded from a letter. When Admiral Croft calls on Anne's sister Mary in Uppercross, he indulges Mary's sons by showing them how to fold a paper boat. At the same time, he lets it drop that Wentworth is coming. Thus, the paper boats symbolically convey him closer and closer to Anne after eight years' separation. In the next scene, Anne sails the boat with her nephews and as they are cheering it on, Henrietta Musgrove runs up with the news that Captain Wentworth is coming to dinner. His presence in the neighborhood soon provides the impetus for a visit to Lyme. Here Anne has the opportunity to walk along the seashore. She does not burst forth in raptures of admiration for the men in uniform as does Louisa Musgrove, but Wentworth and his brother officers make a strong impression in their nautical garb. Regency romance abounds with such metonymic romanticization of military figures like stalwart cavalry officers in their scarlet regimentals and naval officers in their tall, three-cornered hats. The film's representation of Wentworth as "an officer and a gentleman" similarly reinforces the sartorial significance of his marine blues as the gateway to broader horizons for Anne, a male world of action and of national importance. Evidence from *Mansfield Park* suggests that it was not the custom for half-pay officers to promenade off-duty in their uniforms:

William had obtained a ten days' leave of absence to be given to Northamptonshire, and was coming the happiest of lieutenants, because the latest made, to shew his happiness and describe his uniform.

He came; and he would have been delighted to shew his uniform there too, had not cruel custom prohibited its appearance except on duty. (III.vi)

Nevertheless, the film purposefully employs the naval uniform with symbolic intent. It also enlarges on Anne's comment that she would like to go back to Lyme because she so rarely gets to travel anywhere by adding a scene that does not appear in the novel: a honeymoon cruise with Wentworth in the final frames. Since he had earlier stated his objection to bringing women on board ship, this last scene, which is not present in the text, confirms that Anne, anticipating the romance heroines who would follow her, has embraced a new role and a new vision of herself. She is glad to have escaped the caged drudgery of her former life and pleased to accept her new status as the wife of an officer and a gentleman. Wentworth, in turn, is glad to have his wife on board, recognizing no loss in his manly status but rather a broadening of their mutual horizons. The film, unlike the novel, suggests life at sea offers an openness and possibility impossible in the constricted on-shore society. The blocks of mutual misunderstanding, meddlesome relatives, and class differences have been overcome or eliminated, and it seems to be smooth sailing ahead.

Michell's film adaptation of Austen's *Persuasion*, for all its scrupulous attention to reproducing Austen's language and the visual details of her world, offers the audience the possibility of a modern interpretation of Anne's character and of her romance with Wentworth. Though less remarked, the gratuitous addition of the honeymoon cruise and the brief clip from the 1984 film *The Bounty*,[6] a shot spliced in the final frame of the film, are much more incongruous additions than the infamous kiss. While this latter bit of cinematic intertextuality is most likely intended to suggest that Anne has carried out a successful mutiny against her family and the restrictions imposed on women of her class, the infamous story of the mutiny on the *Bounty* illustrates the worst excesses of the British navy as the executive arm of the imperialist enterprise. In the film, Mrs. Wentworth's newfound freedom rests on the commodification of Britain's relationships with her colonial subjects.

Conclusion

Deborah Kaplan has imperiously dismissed Michell's *Persuasion* as a "harlequinization" of Jane Austen, a derogatory term meant to suggest that Michell had catered to a low-brow audience attracted by sensationalism and romance over literary heights and good taste.[7] Yet, ironically, as Harriet Margolis correctly notes in Chapter 2, women's romance or domestic fiction shares the same use-value ethics Austen champions in her novels and is appreciated by women readers for these values. Denigrating these forms of women's fiction, in effect, denigrates Austen's worth. Most of these works – even Austen's novels in their original editions – are conceived of and offered on the marketplace as commercial fictions. While the romance plot culminates in the triumph of the heroine's use-value ethics over the hero's exchange-value vision of human relations, there is almost always an economic exchange between the hero and the heroine in the subtext if not the foreground of the story. Living happily ever after almost always presupposes living in material ease, and most often it is the hero who provides the wealth. Regency romance is certainly not the only mode of disseminating imperial nostalgia in contemporary popular culture, but the genre exerts an inescapable influence on film adaptations of Austen's novels because the Regency romance reinterpretation of her world has established Austen as an icon of imperial nostalgia.

Michell's *Persuasion* stands in an equivalent relationship to the spirit of Jane Austen as Georgette Heyer's Regency romance novels – it is a well-crafted, entertaining copy. Like Heyer's opus, the film's imperial nostalgia causes exchange-value considerations to overwhelm Austen's use-value ethics and prevents her deeper critical insights from emerging on screen. Instead, the resplendent naval uniforms dominate the film viewer's visual experience and lend the navy, ships, and sailors precedence over mere mortals in less splendid civilian attire.

NOTES

1 Amanda Collins, "Jane Austen, Film, and the Pitfalls of Postmodern Nostalgia," in *Jane Austen in Hollywood*, eds. Linda Troost and Sayre Greenfield (Lexington, KY: University of Kentucky Press, 1998): 79–89.
2 London: Constable, 1921.
3 Germaine Greer, *The Female Eunuch* (New York: McGraw-Hill, 1971).
4 New York: Oxford University Press.
5 London: Heinemann, 1955.
6 *The Mutiny on the Bounty*, Director Frank Lloyd, 1939; Director Lewis Milstone, 1962.
7 Deborah Kaplan, "Mass Marketing Jane Austen: Men, Women, and Courtship in Two Film Adaptation," in *Jane Austen in Hollywood*, eds. Troost and Greenfield: 177–187.

Tara Ghoshal Wallace

Early in John Schlesinger's film version of Stella Gibbons's *Cold Comfort Farm* (1994), the heroine declares that when she is fifty-three, she means to write a novel "as good as *Persuasion*"; after all, says Flora Poste (Kate Beckinsale), she and Jane Austen have much in common: neither can "endure a mess." This is a richly intertextual moment, for not only does Flora Poste go on to enact the interventionist practices of *Emma* (rather than Anne Elliot's tendency to "listen patiently, soften every grievance" [46]), but Beckinsale goes on to play Emma in the Diarmuid Lawrence film (1996).

Moreover, much of the comedy in the film derives from Flora's appalling attempts at novelistic prose, which imitate and torture the writing of D. H. Lawrence ("From the stubborn interwoven strata of his subconscious..."). Flora Poste, we realize, can never approach her dream of writing like Jane Austen, but she manages quite well as a character who could have been written by Austen. This complex set of effects is available, of course, only to a certain kind of spectator, one who is familiar with Austen's novels and who also frequents "high-culture" popularizations of British novels.[1] The pleasures of intertextual readings are, however, complicated by an inevitable sense of disappointment, as no interpretation can exactly match the reader's own imagined version of Austen's text. This essay will look at why it's so difficult to write a novel – or rather, in this case, make a film – "as good as *Persuasion*"; what strategies a filmmaker deploys to transpose Austen's narrative about two romances (one between hero and heroine, the other between nation and navy) on to the screen; and what kind of audience is implied by the choices made by the filmmaker.

Readers of Austen frequently make the perfectly correct observation that no film can hope to reproduce that characteristic narrative voice with its multilayered ironies and nuanced valences. While George Bluestone rightly argues that film adaptations cannot replicate the novel's use of "language as its sole and primary element,"[2] adaptations of other novelists have successfully provided substitutes. Bernard F. Dick gives us the example of *Barry Lyndon*: "Thackeray wrote his novel *Barry Lyndon* in the form of a memoir and hence used the first person. To give his film version the air of a Victorian novel set in the eighteenth century, Stanley Kubrick employed voice-over . . . a suave, urbane voice . . . that comments and muses."[3]

Kubrick's choice is not only workable but inspired, for that "suave, urbane voice" replicates Thackeray's own narrative mode in, for example, *Vanity Fair*. Austen's narrative discourse, however, weaves so imperceptibly in and out of the consciousness of characters that a straightforward omniscient commentator cannot approximate its subtleties. For the same reason, a first-person film voice, while it can convey Austen's use of limited viewpoint, cannot capture the multiplicities of the narrative. Besides, Austen doesn't offer the kind of theatricalized soliloquy which can be easily translated to effective aurality; there is not, in her texts, the satisfying drama of "Reader, I married him" or of "Last night I dreamt I went to Manderley again." Recent Austen films have attempted limited versions of narrative voice-over, from Patricia Rozema's controversial casting of Fanny Price as novelist/narrator to the risible spectacle of Gwyneth Paltrow as Emma Woodhouse pouring her heart out to "Dear Diary" (as if!), but none of them has replicated Austen's subtly refracted voices.

Roger Michell's decision to avoid attempting direct replication of Austen's narrative voice is bound to seem like a deficit to admirers of the novel. John Simon, in a fairly negative review, argues that while "Miss Austen's dialogue is delightful . . . no voice in all her fiction is as sparkling as the authorial . . . So a film adaptation of an Austen novel must reconcile itself in advance to a substantial amount of loss."[4] Critic Louis Menand finds it "an extremely intelligent and textured film," yet believes that "No film . . . is likely to capture the inner life of this text, because, even more than in the rest of Austen's fiction . . . the real work of the book is done in the play of the language."[5] Indeed, though Carol M. Dole rightly praises *Persuasion* for its "consistent criticism of a class system that imposed harmful barriers,"[6] nothing in the film captures some of the novel's most incisive commentaries, especially about class relations. There is no filmic equivalent to the narrative voice telling us that "Sir Walter prepared with condescending bows for all the afflicted tenantry and cottagers who might have had a hint to shew themselves" (I.v); nor the deliciously compressed account of workmen gathering around after Louisa's fall, "to be useful if wanted, at any rate, to enjoy the sight of a dead young lady, nay, two dead young ladies, for it proved twice as fine as the first report" (I.xii). Such subtleties are replaced by more easily decoded visual clues: the stony faces of the array of servants and tenants silently standing by as the Elliot carriage takes Sir Walter and Elizabeth to Bath; a working-class boy running freely and at full speed along the Cobb at Lyme followed by shots of the Uppercross women picking their way carefully, the camera focusing on their inappropriately delicate shoes.

As these examples illustrate, however, Michell's *Persuasion* deploys highly intelligent if intelligible filmic language. It is not to the discredit of either the film or the medium itself that its depictions of issues like class relations are more easily decoded and discerned than they are in Austen's text. As Christian Metz has argued, image discourse is inherently intelligible; films are always "more or less understandable... [unless] their diegesis contains realities or concepts that are too subtle, too exotic, or mistakenly thought to be familiar."[7] Moreover, films use cultural codes which "are so ubiquitous and well 'assimilated' that the viewers generally consider them to be 'natural' – basic constituents of mankind... The handling of these codes requires no special training – that is to say, no training other than that of living, and having been raised, in a society."[8]

However, the relative transparency of these codes does not mean that there is nothing to interpret; indeed, just as Michell uses image discourse to interpret a text and a society, the spectator interprets that discourse, reading both the narrative and the enunciation. Building on the theories of Barthes, Brian McFarlane distinguishes between what is enunciated (uttered, enacted) and enunciation itself, which is a process, "ways in which utterance is mediated."[9] Bernard Dick similarly separates "the film projected on the screen [from] the film projected from the screen."[10] Both formulations insist on the viewer's role as interpreter of text and subtext. In fact, Michell's *Persuasion* deftly uses visual intratextuality to deepen its depiction of class and family relations. Anne's low status in the Elliot family is finely represented by the visual contrast between modes of travel: Sir Walter and Elizabeth travel to Bath in the Elliot carriage attended by liveried attendants, while Anne sets off for Uppercross in a farm-cart which also transports pigs. The party at Lyme becomes interested in Mr. Elliot's identity because they admire his curricle, which Mary assumes would carry the Elliot arms. In Bath, Elizabeth engineers a public announcement that Lady Dalrymple's carriage awaits her. The interweaving of transport and status enriches the spectator's understanding of how Regency society uses class markers. "Thus," says Francesco Casetti, "... cinema appears to be a place for an elaboration of meanings that makes them perceptible, formulates them, and allows for their exchange with other people. In a word, cinema appears as the sphere of a signification and of a communication."[11]

Take, for example, the way Michell uses the language of food. In Metz's terms, food is one of those basic cultural codes we all understand. In *Persuasion*, food is a significant part of the *mise en scène*. In one of the first scenes, Mrs. Clay comments gushingly on the sorbet she is eating in September, and Elizabeth replies with triumphant sourness that there will be no more ice until the winter. Michell is compressing a good deal of information in this little exchange: the Elliots, unlike Mr. Shepherd and his daughter, have the resources (ice-house, servants) to enjoy an out-of-season luxury (think of General Tilney's pride in his hothouses); as with the estate itself, however, they have been improvident with these resources and will have to do without until a better season. The scene also shows us that Mrs. Clay's characteristic mode is one of delighted appreciation, while Elizabeth's is one of pleased but ungracious condescension, thus efficiently sketching their relative positions in the class/power hierarchy. In Bath, a similar point about consumption is made as the Elliots sit at the dining table graced by an enormous centerpiece of pineapples and other exotic fruit – this is a family which displays its importance in part by acquiring and consuming what is not easily available. Mary Elliot Musgrove, on the other hand, having fallen from the gracious world of Kellynch to the modest robustness of Uppercross, signals her transition from illness to aggrieved health by tucking into a large piece of ham. At Lyme, she displays her gentility by asking for dry toast while Captain Wentworth makes an equal display of sturdy "commonness" by gulping his tea. One could multiply such examples; the point is that this film astutely uses images of food to delineate character and situation, which the text explicates through narrative voice.

Nevertheless, *Persuasion* does not equate food and seduction as does Tony Richardson's film *Tom Jones*,[12] and the progressive courtship of Anne and Wentworth cannot be represented through images of their over-whelming appetites. Stanley Kauffmann refers to the problem when he says, "The last of [Austen's] novels is especially tough to handle because it deals with a romance that ends before the story begins and has its re-sumption just before the story ends." He adds: "This is novelistic, not film, material. Nick Dear's screenplay understands the dilemma but can't solve it."[13] Anne's internal turmoil, her intense awareness of Wentworth, and his slow recognition of his own feelings must be represented through the bodies of the actors, through facial expression and physical gestures. George Bluestone argues, "Not only has the film discovered new ways to render meaning by finding relationships between animate and inanimate objects [e.g. people and food], but the human physiognomy itself has been rediscovered . . . The face becomes another kind of object in space, a ter-rain on which may be enacted dramas broad as battles, and sometimes more intense."[14]

Amanda Root as Anne Elliot offers the kind of terrain which is nei-ther picturesque nor serene, and reviewers have not been kind. While

reviewers for *Rolling Stone* and for Film.com have called her "luminous,"
many others have objected to her looks. Here is a sampling of negative
evaluations: "She has pleasant eyes but a grim mouth – a countenance
that doesn't invite speculation";[15] "Amanda Root... seems to think she
is in a silent movie. She stares intently at everyone and exaggerates all
her movements";[16] "Amanda Root, with her pursed mouth and her shoe-
button eyes";[17] "Miss Root... has no bloom whatsoever, and seems never
to have had. A competent actress, she lacks the charm with which even
much homelier performers have been known to enchant an audience."[18]

This chorus of criticism may seem "looksist," and may in fact be provoked by the running motif of Anne checking her looks in mirrors, but
in fact it responds to a directorial decision: Michell seems to believe that
the way to represent Anne's intense inner life is to take away her control over her body. Whereas in the novel Anne reacts to the news about
Wentworth's family coming to Kellynch only when she is alone, and only
"with a gentle sigh" (i.iii), in Michell's version she hurtles across the
room, raising even Sir Walter's curiosity about her emotional display.
When she believes, just for a moment, that Wentworth is married, the
text tells us, "She could now answer as she ought; and was happy to
feel, when Mrs. Croft's next words explained it to be Mr. Wentworth of
whom she spoke, that she had said nothing which might not do for either
brother" (i.vi). Root, on the other hand, is visibly shaken and speechless. Anne's intense and almost swooning reaction to the first encounter
with Wentworth ("Her eye half met Captain Wentworth's... she heard
his voice... the room seemed full..." [i.vii.]) is nicely rendered as the
camera shows us what Anne hides from others – her hand groping for
and clutching a chair back for support – but there is no evidence here
or anywhere in the film of Anne beginning "to reason with herself, and
try to be feelingless" (i.vii). Moreover, as Jocelyn Harris observes, the
embarrassing and public pursuit of Wentworth in the concert room is
among the most egregious "lapses of register."[19] So too is the vision of
Anne prancing around Charles Musgrove, much like one of his hunting
spaniels, while she begs him to bring Wentworth to the Elliots' evening
party.

Root's performance, then, fails to meet James Griffith's standards of
adaptation. In a cogent defense of film adaptations, he says:

I would rather not view a novel as a verbal, psychological, or anonymously coded
event; each would erect rather than overcome barriers to adaptations – or simply
render adaptations irrelevant. Instead, I would view a novel as an aesthetic problem solved – or at least attempted – and communicated: an author has themes,
moods, or effects to convey, for which he or she then invents an action to be portrayed with chosen techniques in words. The author makes choices more complex

than finding a form adequate to the content. The material or medium does not signify much by comparison: the effects, actions, even some techniques may be communicated through the images and sounds of film, and communicated adequately to match the components of the novel.[20]

Amanda Root's wide-eyed, jittery, and girlish performance (this Anne seems much younger than Austen's heroine), her public displays of emotion, seem essentially at odds with the "themes, moods, or effects" of Austen's *Persuasion*.

A reading of one scene provides an example of the way Michell and Root's version of Anne works against the grain of Austen's text, while at the same time the film effectively interprets other aspects of it. In Bath, Lady Russell escorts her god-daughter to the Pump Room, where the two discuss Mr. Elliot's character and his possible reasons for rejoining the family. This intimate conversation is interrupted by Lady Russell's friends, with whom she talks over the proceedings of a Philosophical Society meeting where "the atheists were completely routed." Anne, both ignored and indifferent during this exchange, glimpses the Crofts entering the Pump Room, and scampers across to them, hands held out in glee. She thrusts herself between them, arms linked with each, as she eagerly questions them about their arrival. In this scene, Michell and Dear demonstrate the economy with which film can present and construct character, for here is a slightly coarsened version of a Lady Russell "rather of sound than quick abilities . . . [with] a value for rank and consequence" (I.ii). Dear has wittily articulated the spurious intellectualism of her circle, and Michell underlines the superficialities of Bath's attractions when Lady Russell turns from actual conversation to chat. Yet here again is the problem of the heroine, whose pleasure takes the form of indecorous display, one more appropriate to Lydia Bennet or perhaps Marianne Dashwood than to Anne Elliot. Such behavior may be what Alan Stone both criticizes and admires, part of what he calls Dear and Michell's desire to make "Austen's antiquated Cinderella into the strong, assertive, and independent woman who becomes the mistress of her own fate,"[21] but it ill suits the quiet, contained heroine of Austen's text.

Perhaps even more seriously, this representation works against the logic of the romance, which is rekindled at least in part by Wentworth's appreciation of Anne's "medium of fortitude and gentleness . . . the resolution of a collected mind" (II.xi). Ciaran Hinds's Wentworth, confident and mature (as well as very good-looking), doesn't seem like a man to be captivated by the nervous quiverings of Root's Anne Elliot. This Anne is so neurotically constituted that there is no sexual charge between her and Wentworth, none of what George Lellis and H. Philip Bolton call

12. An imposing-looking but tortured Captain Wentworth (Ciaran Hinds), from *Jane Austen's Persuasion*, a Sony Pictures Classics Release, 1995

"a convincing sense of the biological attraction between Garson as Lizzy and Olivier as Darcy (in the 1940 MGM *Pride and Prejudice*). For the visual medium can easily convey the contradiction between their tart verbal repartee on the one hand, and the glances and gestures that on the other hand suggest the underlying sensuality of their relationship."[22] Unlike many critics, I do not object to the public kiss at the end of the film;

its quiet intimacy against the carnivalesque street scene seems to express in film language the text's articulation of the pair's exquisite happiness, "heedless of every group around them" (ii.xi). However, I do find myself wondering if this Wentworth embraces Anne just to stop her compulsive movements and agree with John Simon's summation of this performance: "Amanda Root lets Anne Elliot and the movie down damnably."[23] In fact, Root's Anne made me think back nostalgically to the earlier BBC version, in which Ann Firbank gives us a mature and self-contained Anne, who can be both generous and cynical, and in fact sometimes seems like many readers' sense of Austen herself.

Devoney Looser quotes Roger Michell as praising Austen for "a clear-sighted vision of the way the world is tilted against women."[24] Yet Anne is not the only female character to be distorted and discredited in this adaptation. Rebecca Dickson, in the same volume, is quite right in objecting to Elizabeth Elliot's (Phoebe Nicholls) bad manners and shrillness: "The viewer who has read the book is wondering where this shrieking woman has come from, for she does not appear anywhere in Austen's novel."[25] It seems that Michell and screenwriter Nick Dear can represent Elizabeth's selfish disregard for Anne only by having her bully and belittle her (Sir Walter's much more culpable indifference to his daughter on the other hand is gently and comically handled, with Corin Redgrave turning in the best performance in the film). Lady Russell (Susan Fleetwood), garishly garbed in turbans and shakos and voluminous capes, seems aggressively dismissive of Anne. Michell appropriately inserts a scene in which Anne articulates to Lady Russell her present conviction that she was wrongly persuaded; Lady Russell, to whom Anne "was a most dear and highly valued god-daughter, favourite and friend" (i.i), responds by reiterating her early position and then choking off further dialogue by handing her a book of poems, adding by the way, "I don't care much for these Romantics, do you?" John Simon's witty and wicked *National Review* evaluation of Fleetwood's performance – "You feel that to stop Anne from marrying Wentworth, she might not so much have persuaded her as merely sat on her" – seems only a slight exaggeration.[26]

It may be argued that part of what Michell and Dear want to demonstrate is that Anne Elliot has no access to the supportive community of women described by Deborah Kaplan: "The affectionate bonds of the women's culture provided a respite from such prohibitions on expression, freeing women to say about themselves what they might ordinarily suppress."[27] Indeed, in this version of *Persuasion*, Anne is silenced, over and over, by the selfishness of her sisters and the dominant ego of Lady Russell. In the text, the narrative voice tells us that Anne's family "could not listen to her description of [Mr. Elliot]. They were describing him themselves; Sir Walter especially" (II.iii). In the film, Elizabeth furiously shouts down Anne's attempt to speak of him. In the text, when Mary asks what Anne could have to do to detain her at Kellynch, Anne replies at some length and in detail, even expressing her feelings: "And one thing I have had to do, Mary, of a more trying nature; going to almost every house in the parish, as a sort of take-leave" (I.v). In the film, the speech is cut off after the first sentence. Lady Russell not only prevents Anne from speaking her feelings about the past, but seems not to hear her present doubts about Mr. Elliot. Even Mrs. Smith seems less like an intimate friend than a gossipy acquaintance. Also, Fiona Shaw's Mrs. Croft, who in both text and film represents the possibility of both loving sisterhood and model for Anne, hasn't the serene authority which, in the novel, allows her to control the reins of carriage and marriage. This Mrs. Croft has been made eccentric, both in her gypsyish clothing and her theatrical whisperings when asked to describe her travels. Looking at the women who inhabit this film, one is tempted to echo Mary Ann Doane's hyperbolic assessment: "Cinematic images of women have been so consistently oppressive and repressive that the very idea of a feminist filmmaking practice seems an impossibility."[28] Yet, I have no sense that Michell and Dear are caught in "the way the unconscious of patriarchal society has structured film form."[29] Indeed, it may even be suggested that the film depicts a trap and an escape: Anne Wentworth, surrounded by women who have been distorted and demonized by the constraints of a patriarchal society, achieves liberty not only by finding personal romance, but by joining the world of "that profession which is, if possible, more distinguished in its domestic virtues than in its national importance" (II.xii).

Readers find in this ending a characteristic double-voiced discourse. This ringing endorsement of sailors, after all, inhabits the same novel which, while it indeed represents admirable sailors, also shows us the seamy side of the profession, both at highest and lowest levels. As Wentworth says, "The admiralty . . . entertain themselves now and then, with sending a few hundred men to sea, in a ship not fit to be employed. But they have a great many to provide for; and among the thousands that may just as well go to the bottom as not, it is impossible for them to distinguish the very set who may be least missed" (I.viii). At the other end of the hierarchy we have Dick Musgrove who "had been sent to sea, because he was stupid and unmanageable on shore . . . nothing better than a thick-headed, unfeeling, unprofitable Dick Musgrove, who had never done any thing to entitle himself to more than the abbreviation of his name, living or dead" (I.vi). Furthermore, neither narrator nor reader can have forgotten the "domestic virtues" of Admiral Crawford in *Mansfield Park*. Nevertheless, these dark depictions of sailors in no way obliterates the positive side of the profession – the loyal friendships, the cheerful undertaking of difficult tasks, the endurance of hardship – that the novel also provides. Indeed, it can be argued that to some extent *Persuasion* the novel contributes to the discourses of nationalism and patriotism which permeate England in this period. As Susan Morgan points out, *Persuasion* participates in the development of an ideology surrounding the navy and its role in British imperialism: "The novel offers a vision, as public and political as it is personal and romantic, in ways for nations as well as lovers to exist in the world."[30] Linda Colley argues that during the eighteenth and early nineteenth centuries in Britain, "patriotism was more often than not a highly rational response and a creative one as well . . . Time and time again, war with France brought Britons, whether they hailed from Wales or Scotland or England, into confrontation with an obviously hostile Other and encouraged them to define themselves collectively against it."[31] While disagreeing with Colley's sense of voluntary and unproblematic patriotism, J. E. Cookson too finds "The 'king and country' patriotism that developed from 1797 . . . a broad appeal for national unity."[32]

Despite multiple references to naval and other military action, despite recent critical attention to Austen's knowledge and representation of contemporary political and public life, there remains a general sense of Austen as the recorder only of "three or four families in a country village."[33] Rachel Brownstein is quite right in arguing that recent films make a point of showing the political dimension of the novels: Michell's *Persuasion*, she says, "confronts head-on, to begin with, the best known criticism of Austen, that she failed to notice the Napoleonic Wars. Here at the beginning of the movie are demobilized sailors; over there, therefore, are the Wars themselves, of which Jane Austen, you see, was richly aware . . . Austen is being improved for the 1990s, her field of vision and her sympathies widened."[34]

Michell's *Persuasion*, in fact, begins and ends with sailors and boats, and along the way emphasizes visually the centrality of the Royal Navy. Louis Menand congratulates the director on his depiction of national admiration for naval officers:

The other clever idea is to emphasize something Austen did not much emphasize, no doubt because it would have been obvious enough to readers in her own day, which is that an officer in the British Navy in 1814, the year in which the story is set, was pretty nearly the most exalted being on the planet . . . A naval officer at the time of Napoleon's defeat was the cultural equivalent of a movie star; and the film makes a point of showing Wentworth and his fellow officers parading around as masters of the universe in full military regalia.[35]

This may be somewhat hyperbolic, but certainly the film represents sailors glorying in being sailors. Wentworth is rarely out of uniform, whether eating a family dinner with the Musgroves or walking the streets of Bath. Ironically, the only times he wears civilian clothing are times when he's about to engage in the pseudo-military activity of hunting. In Lyme, when the Uppercross party visit the Harville home, both Harville and Benwick are in ordinary but perfectly respectable garb, but they both change to naval dress before embarking on nothing more than a walk along the beach. Clearly, these men (and the Admiral as well) not only take pride in their uniform, but also claim a public identity conferred by that uniform. The film underlines the significance and sufficiency of this public identity when, in the Pump Room at Bath, a footman announces to Anne that she is wanted by "a gentleman of the navy": no name is required when the uniform confers status.

However, while dialogue and *mise en scène* in this film confirm the centrality of the navy, Michell's editing procedures problematize romantic readings of naval service. In their introduction, the editors of *Jane Austen in Hollywood* argue, "Much of the indeterminacy that powers our delight in arguments about Jane Austen gets too settled by the films ... Once on film, those images are fixed in a way that Austen's writing (by virtue of its medium and her skill) avoids."[36] In this they echo Bluestone's contention that cinematic images, being "a perceptual and presentational form," reduce the possibilities of symbolic mediation.[37] Bernard Dick, too, finds that film language has no grammar, provides no difference between signifier and signified. However, he points out, film deploys other narrative devices: syntagmatic and paradigmatic relationships provide the associative links that readers find in words, and allow for indeterminacy and complexity of meaning. Dear and Michell, while they cannot on film replicate the contemptuous dismissal of Dick Musgrove, can manipulate images to achieve some of the same effects.

To begin with, they utilize to the full what Bluestone calls the rediscovery of the human physiognomy:[38] the naval officers in this film, with the exception of Hinds's Wentworth, are not physically attractive. Benwick, as Simon says, is "greasy, not only of hair, but also of performance";[39] Harville, who in the 1971 Granada/BBC Howard Baker version, is played by Adonis-like Michael Culver, is here suet-faced and gat-toothed, enormously cheery but not by any means an object of desire. John Woodvine's Admiral Croft is also so pleasant that it seems churlish to point out that his countenance validates Sir Walter Elliot's severe articulation of what seafaring does to a man's looks: "it cuts up a man's youth and vigour most horribly; a sailor grows old sooner than any other man" (I.iii). The donning of full-dress uniform, with ribbons and medals, cannot in fact disguise or re-form the man. This is a highly effective corrective to the romanticizing impulse in which the Musgrove sisters, for example, participate.

Michell goes much further than Austen does to deglamorize the brotherhood of sailors. In the novel, the only rift in the naval fraternity comes at the end, when Captain Harville gently complains to Anne of Benwick's change of heart and of his tactlessness in charging Harville with the task of converting a miniature meant for Fanny Harville (inexplicably christened Phoebe in Dear's script) into a present for Louisa. He rejects, in fact, Anne's proffered excuse that men's "business" weakens their romantic attachments, reminding her that Benwick "has not been forced upon any exertion. The peace turned him on shore at the very moment, and he has been living with us, in our little family-circle, ever since" (II.xi). This slight and perfectly understandable resentment is the only moment in the novel when the easy friendliness shared by the officers seems troubled. In the film, Michell has taken a moment which the text presents entirely positively – the visit to the Harvilles' home in Lyme – and made it speak in a different voice.

What Anne in the novel experiences as "a bewitching charm in a degree of hospitality . . . the picture of repose and domestic happiness" despite "rooms so small as none but those who invite from the heart could think capable of accommodating so many" (I.xi), is represented in the film as a much more complicated moment. Harville, flanked by wife and baby on one side, and Wentworth and Benwick on the other, seems to fill up the tiny room. The party from Uppercross mass together at the doorway, there being no space for them within the officer's home and circle, and for a moment look rather helplessly and haplessly at Wentworth and each other. There follows a universal round of laughter, slightly hysterical, and certainly not justified by any event or dialogue. It is as if, confronted with the poverty of a retired naval officer, aware of the difference in status and wealth, the country gentry can respond only with nervous hilarity. It is an exceedingly odd and jarring moment, forcing the viewer to re-evaluate the glamorous life of sailors: not all returning officers, it seems, have risen "to honours which their fathers and grandfathers never dreamt of " (I.iii) and become "quite worthy to address daughter of a . . . baronet" (II.ii); not all have made "twenty thousand pounds by the war" (I.ix). Wentworth and Harville, despite being of equal rank in the navy, occupy very different places in the non-military world. Even within the brotherhood of officers, even while a new class of wealthy Englishmen is forming itself, there are inequalities and hierarchies, and Michell's film makes these discrepancies inescapably visible.

Francesco Casetti, discussing Jean Mitry's theories on cinematic language, says, "On film the images are never isolated, but are connected to one another by similarity, by contrast, or simply by succession . . . The mere fact that one image follows another means that an image acquires precise *implications*."[40] Michell's film vividly demonstrates the validity of this argument. The first two or three minutes of *Persuasion* cut swiftly back and forth from navy to country gentry. The opening image of oars gives way to carriage wheels, and the parallel shots continue until, after Admiral Croft's officers have toasted him, the scene settles on Kellynch – on, in fact, Sir Walter complaining about the ugliness and social climbing of naval officers. This montage provides a good deal of information about the film's agenda. First, of course, is the irony directed against national ingratitude. As the officers on board celebrate the end of a war they have won, abandoning ship to return to country ("We're going home," says the Admiral), that country, in the person of Sir Walter, is making preparations to reject them. This seems to be fairly straightforward, especially given the shots of Kellynch laborers importuning Mr. Shepherd about payment for work: a bankrupt and irresponsible landlord dares to disparage the very people who have saved his property from foreign threat. Yet the montage also makes another point: the stony faces of the discontented workers at Kellynch differ not at all from the set faces of the sailors rowing the Admiral to his ship. Labor is labor, says this editorial editing; the underclass, whether on board ship or on estate, are overworked, possibly mistreated, and probably discontented.

While Paulette Richards in the preceding chapter finds the final images of Michell's film "gratuitous," they can in fact be seen as a complex intertextual commentary. Just as images of surly workers are played off against unfeeling aristocrats, so the shipboard images are equally double-voiced. They concretize, of course, the text's implication that Anne, like Mrs. Croft, will travel on board with her husband and perhaps be able to say "that the happiest part of my life has been spent on board a ship" (I.viii). Michell takes the narrative forward in time, beyond March 1815 and Napoleon's return to France, to a moment when, in Admiral Croft's words, "we have the good luck to live to another war" (I.viii). On the deck of a ship bustling and bristling with preparations for war, Anne and Wentworth stand side by side, embodying the fulfillment of personal and national romance. As the camera pulls away to an extreme long shot of the solitary ship on a vast ocean, the credits roll, implying satisfactory closure of amatory and naval narratives. This double resolution, however, must account for the image preceding the final one on deck: Anne, sitting in dark and cramped quarters, using a small square of light to write letters, a space so emphatically uninviting that its symbolic power is thoroughly undermined. Moreover, when Anne joins her husband on deck, we note that he barely acknowledges her presence, concentrating, as a ship's captain must, on the business at hand. If Anne had been exploited and marginalized at Kellynch and Bath, she is, in Michell's final image, irrelevant. Wentworth was right after all: a ship in His Majesty's Service is indeed no place for a woman.

Or even for sailors? The ship used in these last images, the credits inform us, is the one which represented the *Bounty* in an earlier film. What is Michell implying by this last moment of intertextuality? A paradigmatic reading of this tells us that Michell wants us to associate this ship with the *Bounty*, and Wentworth with Bligh. While this may be overreading and even distorting the director's intentions, it seems to me that, in his parting shot, Michell reminds us his film reaches beyond and behind Austen's text, to historical moments and fictional representations not available to readers. It is a bold move, claiming a power and autonomy for film as fully legitimate as a text's authority. Michell enacts, in the construction of this representation of Austen, what Judith Mayne describes as film's use of novels as "institutional reference. A novel is not simply transposed to the screen, but rather becomes one of the many texts to which the realist filmmaker, like the realist author, refers."[41]

There are, of course, difficulties when a director uses as "institutional reference" a text as canonical and beloved as Austen's novels. Two essays in a recent volume on adaptations make the point about Austen's place in the canon. Deborah Cartmell points out that screen versions of Shakespeare have made film academically respectable:

The first candidate must be Jane Austen, alongside Shakespeare, as a conservative literary icon. Both authors are identified by the word "heritage", and screen adaptations of their work tend to perpetuate their assumed ideology in spite of critical readings which suggest otherwise. The "fidelity debate" . . . takes a different form insofar as production values of film adaptations are seen to smother the potentially radical critiques embedded within the original text.[42]

Interestingly, a few pages later in the same volume, Julian North argues that filmed versions are in fact responsible for Austen becoming "something of a conservative icon in popular culture: a canonical author whose life and work signify English national heritage." He goes on to note, "An important part of this construction of Austen has been the peculiarly insistent discourse of fidelity that has accompanied adaptations of her work. A reverence for Austen's texts, her 'world' and her wishes has long dogged criticism of these adaptations."[43] North thus argues a kind of circularity: Austen is a conservative icon because screen versions have made her so and screen versions have to be faithful to her texts because she is a conservative icon.

Austen's own texts have always allowed for readings construing her as politically and culturally conservative;[44] equally, they have elicited readings which argue for her courageous radicalism.[45] McFarlane says the filmmaker's claims of "fidelity and authenticity" essentially amount to "the effacement of the memory derived from reading the novel by another experience – an audio-visual-verbal one – which will seem, as little as possible, to jar with that collective memory."[46] In an admiring review of Rozema's *Mansfield Park*, Alistair M. Duckworth articulates the practice of this theory: "Some Austen lovers have been mightily offended by the liberties Rozema has taken. Others, like the present reviewer, have tried with only partial success to abstract long-held views of the novel from their enjoyment of the film."[47] In our time, film versions have tended to foreground the radical Austen: feminist in Ang Lee's *Sense and Sensibility*, proto-Marxist in McGrath's *Emma*, abolitionist in Rozema's *Mansfield Park*. Passionate admirers of Austen's novels have argued about, tolerated, and survived the scholarly controversies about her texts, and of course the novels will continue to survive controversial representations on film. Critics and filmmakers can only hope, in the best of worlds, to present a version of Austen which makes us rethink and reread the novels as well as enjoy the "texts" that their efforts produce. Michell's *Persuasion*, for all its limitations in the representation of a much-loved heroine, achieves both a gratifying degree of fidelity and its very own authenticity as text.

NOTES

1 See Cartmell and Whelehan on the layered effects of casting in Franco Zeffirelli's *Hamlet*: "While Gibson's previous roles as action hero on the edge contribute to the fast pace of the normally slow play, Close's earlier parts in Adrian Lyne's *Fatal Attraction* (1987) and Stephen Frears' *Dangerous Liaisons* (1988) construct Gertrude as both sexual threat and potential homewrecker" (Deborah Cartmell and Imelda Whelehan [eds.], *Adaptations: From Text to Screen, Screen to Text* [London: Routledqe, 1999]: 33).
2 George Bluestone, *Novels into Film* (Baltimore, MD: Johns Hopkins University Press, 1957): vi.
3 Bernard F. Dick, *Anatomy of Film* (New York: St. Martin's Press, 1994): 62.
4 John Simon, Review of Jane Austen's *Persuasion*, *National Review* 45 (October 23, 1995).
5 Louis Menand, "Hollywood's Trap," *New York Review of Books* 43 (September 19, 1996).
6 Carol M. Dole, "Balancing the Courtship Hero: Masculine Emotional Display in Film Adaptations of Austen's Novels," in *Jane Austen in Hollywood*, eds. Linda Troost and Sayre Greenfield (Lexington, KY: University of Kentucky Press): 61.
7 Christian Metz, *Film Language: A Semiotics of the Cinema*, trans. Michael Taylor (London: Oxford University Press, 1974): 73.
8 Ibid.: 112.

9 Brian McFarlane, *Novel to Film: An Introduction to the Theory of Adaptation* (Oxford: Clarendon Press, 1996): 20.

10 Dick, *Anatomy*: 83.

11 Francesco Casetti, *Theories of the Cinema, 1945–1995*, trans. Francesca Chiostri, Elizabeth Gard Gartolino-Salimbeni, and Thomas Kelso (Austin, TX: University of Texas Press, 1999): 54.

12 *Tom Jones*, Writers Henry Fielding and John Osborne, Director Tony Richardson, United Artists, 1963.

13 Stanley Kauffman, "Division, Delay, Drag – *Persuasion*," *The New Republic* 213 (October 9, 1995): 26–27.

14 Bluestone, *Novels into Film*: 26–27.

15 Kauffman, "Division."

16 Pat Anderson, Review, *Films in Review* (September 1995).

17 Menand, "Hollywood's Trap."

18 Simon, Review.

19 Jocelyn Harris, Review of *Sense and Sensibility, Persuasion*, and *Clueless, Eighteenth-Century Fiction* 8 (1996): 427.

20 James Griffith, *Adaptations as Imitations: Films from Novels* (Newark: University of Delaware Press, 1997): 36.

21 Alan Stone, Review of *Persuasion, Boston Review* 20 (1995/1996): 6.

22 Lellis and Bolton, "Pride but No Prejudice," in *The English Novel and the Movies*, eds. Michael Klein and Gillian Parker (New York: Ungar, 1981): 49.

23 Simon, Review.

24 Devoney Looser, "Feminist Implications of the Silver Screen Austen," in *Jane Austen in Hollywood*, eds. Troost and Greenfield: 168.

25 Rebecca Dickson, "Misrepresenting Jane Austen's Ladies: Revising Texts (and History) to Sell Films," in *Jane Austen in Hollywood*, eds. Troost and Greenfield: 47.

26 Simon, Review: 58–59.

27 Deborah Kaplan, *Jane Austen among Women* (Baltimore, MD: Johns Hopkins University Press, 1992): 69.

28 In Constance Penley (ed.), *Feminism and Film Theory* (New York: Routledge, 1988): 216.

29 Laura Mulvey in ibid.: 57.

30 Susan Morgan, "Captain Wentworth, British Imperialism, and Personal Romance." *Persuasions: Journal of the Jane Austen Society of North America* 18 (December 16, 1996): 88–97.

31 Linda Colley, *Britons: Forging the Nation 1707–1837* (New Haven: Yale University Press, 1992): 5.

32 J. E. Cookson, *The British Armed Nation 1793–1815* (Oxford: Clarendon Press, 1997): 15.

33 *Jane Austen's Letters*, ed. Deirdre Le Faye (Oxford: Oxford University Press, 1995): 275.

34 Rachel M. Brownstein, "Out of the Drawing Room, Onto the Lawn," in *Jane Austen in Hollywood*, eds. Troost and Greenfield: 18.

35 Menand, "Hollywood's Trap": 4–6.

36 Troost and Greenfield, *Jane Austen in Hollywood*: 11.

37 Bluestone, *Novels into Film*: vi–vii.

38 Ibid.: 26–27.

39 Simon, Review.

40 Casetti, *Theories*: 69.

41 Judith Mayne, *Cinema and Spectatorship* (London and New York: Routledge, 1993): 88.

42 Cartmell and Whelehan, *Adaptations*: 24.

43 Julian North, "Conservative Austen, Radical Austen: *Sense and Sensibility* from Text to Screen," in ibid.: 38.

44 See Marilyn Butler, *Jane Austen and the War of Ideas* (Oxford: Clarendon Press, 1975).

45 Mary Evans, *Jane Austen and the State* (London: Routledge and Kegan Paul, 1987).

46 McFarlane, *Novel to Film*: 21.

47 Alistair M. Duckworth, Review of *Mansfield Park*. *Eighteenth-Century Fiction* 12.4 (July 2000): 571.

Hilary Schor

New Yorker reviewer Anthony Lane, in a characteristically intelligent review of Douglas McGrath's 1995 film production of *Emma*, offered a
rather sharp condemnation of the film, one with interesting implications
for most modern adaptations of Jane Austen's novels. The problem with
the film, Lane argues, is not that it makes no sense, but that it makes "easy,
do-it-yourself sense."[1] Reducing Emma's "artful" construction "around
the ethics of plotting" to a "thinness" of romance, McGrath has made
his film too easy to watch. Even such seeming accidents as its remarkable miscastings (he singles out, wonderfully, the "under the hill" Mr.
Knightley of Jeremy Northam) contribute to an Austen of few narrative
jolts, and of disturbingly even tone. The tensions we cannot resolve on
reading her fiction (as he phrases them, "Is she affectionate or flinty?
Does her tolerance float free, or does it exist to peg back her anger?") are
here dissolved into a patina as even as the decorations on "the lids of cake
tins," and the disturbing confusion of Emma's narration (is she in charge
of her world or in the grip of it?) is here quieted into a matchmaking
fantasy that never quite takes its heroine or its viewer by surprise. While
remarking, as have all critics in popular and scholarly accounts, on the
perfect poise and grace of Gwyneth Paltrow (her cheekbones, he asserts,
"would cut a swath through communities far plusher than Highbury"),
Lane finds in the very perfection of the filmic presentation a sacrifice
of the true spirit of Austen's fiction: like other critics, who preferred instead the poor-theater textual faithfulness of Roger Michell's *Persuasion*,
the more refined balance of Ang Lee's *Sense and Sensibility*, and even the
modern high-school community of *Clueless*, he resists the charms and
the ease of the McGrath/Paltrow *Emma*. The film seems, if anything, too
classy to have gotten Emma right.

Lane's criticism rings true in some important ways, but it leaves unan-
swered (and indeed, risks leaving even vaguer than when we began) some
of the principal terms by which we "read" an adaptation: What does it
mean to be true to a text? What is the Austen spirit? What is celebrity
and what is its relation to narrative film? And, most significantly, what is

144

a classic? In discussing the way McGrath's adaptation works at once to center and to dislocate our automatic identification of the film of *Emma* with the novel – and indeed, troubles our identification with Emma herself – I will focus less on what we see of *Emma* and far more on what we hear of it. What has made McGrath's *Emma* seem classic to most viewers is not anything on the screen at all, but something that surrounds it: its complicated use of voice-over narration, both from the unseen female narrator who opens the film and from Emma herself in ironic commentary and epistolary confession, and its equally strategic deployment of characters' voices, both to bridge individual scenes and to interrupt our easy progress from one perspective to another. While these techniques, in particular the narratorial voice-over, have added a dated quality which has led most viewers to dismiss the film as a conservative and not terribly adventurous version of Austen's most linguistically challenging novel, the varied and disruptive nature of these different kinds of voices actually forms a most interesting attempt to "do" Austen on screen. For what is more characteristic of Austen than that voice we love to call hers, the voice of the narrator coming in to tell us what to think? What is more perplexing in *Emma* than the attempt to tell the difference between Emma herself and the wiser, but somewhat cruelly withholding, narrator who tracks her moral growth? And what is more tempting, in Jane Austen as in life, than the attempt to substitute our voice for hers; to tell others how to live and whom to love? In "voicing" Jane Austen in film, McGrath has located a troubling point in our identification with and terror at Emma herself; more than that, he has fixed on the point most vexing in moving from novel to film: who will speak for the narrator?

Opening gambits

The novel version of *Emma* opens with a calm, collected, ironic voice describing its heroine ("Emma Woodhouse, handsome, clever, and rich," I.i); the film version opens with a sphere spinning in space, pictures of people and places, and a woman with a clear, elegant English accent telling us of the world of Highbury. As the novel continues, the narrator fills in the world; as the film continues, the pictures resolve into a spinning globe held by the hand of an elegant young woman, standing at a wedding. In both cases, the voice that sends us into the narrative world sets us spinning, and then deliberately slows us down – but what is it that a narrator does, and what is the relationship of that narrative voice to the story we are beginning? Taking this question seriously leads us to ideas of knowledge, character, and adaptation at the heart of this essay – and it is worth beginning by asking, what do we know about the narrator of *Emma*?

The narrator, we might joke, is there before the novel, for the novel's famous first sentence places us squarely (indeed, almost "already") in the voice of its narrator – and one of the real achievements of the McGrath adaptation is to ask a very novelistic question: just how much are we to trust that voice, or the voice of anyone telling us a story? In a novel, we rarely begin by questioning the person speaking to us: unless a narrator is in some way marked ("Call me Ishmael") or deliberately evasive, we take the narration as so much background noise, reliable, distanced, and with no personality which might distract us from the business at hand, that of getting the plot underway. The opening sentence of Emma, with its combination of irony and humor, offers us at once a strong characterization of its heroine and the security that nothing too dreadful can happen to her in the course of our novel: "Emma Woodhouse, handsome, clever, and rich, with a comfortable home and a happy disposition, seemed to unite some of the best blessings of existence; and had lived nearly twenty-one years in the world with very little to distress or vex her" (I.i). While the "seemed" qualifies the blessings with which the sentence began, and "distress or vex her" promises a plot filled with confusion and misunderstanding, the very mildness of those verbs suggests that the plot will not bring ruination or despair, and that the heroine's happy "disposition" will see her through to a comic ending.

However, the assurance of that opening sentence might lead us to trust more than we should a series of statements that arise in following chapters, diagnosing Emma's character and orienting her world. The descriptions of Highbury and the role of Hartfield, the "comfortable" Woodhouse home, within it; the discussions of her character by other characters, in particular her governess, Miss Taylor (now Mrs. Weston), and Mr. Knightley; and the long scene we witness after the offstage wedding of the Westons which sets the plot going with its first distress of Emma and her first consciousness of loss – all this in no way seems to mitigate the narrator's somewhat curt summary of Emma, that "the real evils indeed of Emma's situation were the power of having rather too much her own way, and a disposition to think a little too well of herself" (I.i). The "indeed" keeps us from questioning the narrator's veracity – at the same time that "a little too well" keeps us from doubting Emma so much that we would refuse to follow her through the novel. From its first chapters, that is, the novel is playing a complicated game, asking us at once to identify with its heroine, and to believe a voice floating somewhere above her, which knows more than she (or we) about Emma's "real" situation.

But what is involved in believing a narrator? What kinds of epistemological leaps, games of knowledge, is Emma displaying here? In a book
as involved as this one is in parading both knowledge and misinforma-
tion, in a book where everyone wants to be a narrator, how is Austen
marking her own authority and making us distrust our own? One final
example will suggest the difficulties of placing the Austen narrator – and
the challenges a film adaptation faces. This passage seems to recreate the
narrator's initial judgment of Emma's situation:

Emma had always wanted to do everything, and had made more progress in
both drawing and music than many might have done with so little labour as she
would ever submit to. She played and sang; – and drew in almost every style;
but steadiness had always been wanting; and in nothing had she approached the
degree of excellence which she would have been glad to command, and ought
not to have failed of. She was not much deceived as to her own skill either as
an artist or a musician, but she was not unwilling to have others deceived, or
sorry to know her reputation for accomplishment often higher than it deserved.
(I.vi)

We are reasonably certain that we are listening to an authoritative voice
in the first few sentences of this passage: the assurance of the diagnostic
authority of the "degree" of excellence which she would have been "glad
to command, and ought not to have failed of" suggest a superior intelligence, ready to measure in turn reality, degrees of excellence, and moral
duty – a voice we will come, in the novel, to associate with Mr. Knightley,
certain what Emma ought to "submit to." However, when we reconsider
the passage, much less of it appears to be located in some external, objective perspective, and much more in Emma's own: this paragraph knows
nothing Emma herself does not know. She is not "much deceived" (that
smidgen allows for doubt) but by the end of the paragraph, we are firmly
located in her perspective: she knows not only her own limitations, but
the degree to which these limitations are unseen by others. Typically of
the novel, the double negative of "not unwilling" makes her vanity seem
less venal than it might – whoever is announcing her self-knowledge is
willing to judge her a passive rather than an active egomaniac, willing to
accept but not actively to "will" her own overvaluation – and yet the speed
with which these sentences progress encourages us to more certainty in
the judgment than we would have if it were announced more clearly as
Emma's own. Once we trace the path of knowledge in the elegant sentences, we might be considerably less certain that authorial knowledge
rests in them, and more aware that what we are hearing is not an objective narrator, but a slightly filtered account of Emma's own judgment of
herself.

Thus, the novel encourages us, subtly, to distrust our distrust of Emma; it teaches us, perversely, as Mrs. Weston announces early, that there are limits to her foolishness. Some of the same lessons inhere in McGrath's filmic opening, but they push us even more directly than Austen's opening to distrust the way knowledge is understood and presented in the world of Highbury. The beautiful spinning globe of the beginning emerges against the background of what seems to be the Milky Way, and the characters and the places of the novel arise before us in hand-painted miniature form; these portraits in turn spin round with the galaxy, which turns out to be a painted ball (perhaps of silk) which the heroine, Emma, is spinning. It is her wedding present for Miss Taylor and Mr. Weston, and in the many varieties of work it will do for us (it establishes the smallness and the seriousness of this social whirl; it introduces us to groups of characters, doing the work of exposition; it introduces the motif of the heroine's artistic skills, and her want of serious practice) it stands most powerfully for the heroine's *imagined* relationship to the world around her. The narrator tells us, as the final picture, of Emma, appears, and as the spinning globe becomes a toy held in the heroine's hand, that in this village "there lived a young woman who knew how this world should be run."

Just as Austen's opening paragraph, with its assertion that Emma "had lived nearly twenty-one years in the world with very little to distress or vex her" cried out for a readerly insertion of "as yet," so McGrath's narrator's assertion that Emma knows how this world *should* be run conjures up our skepticism – but again, like Austen's premise of Emma's happy disposition, the smallness of this spinning globe seems to promise that (as with Emma's happy disposition) no disaster too absolute can overtake her. The combination of Gwyneth Paltrow's luminosity and her fragility strikes us as similarly vexed, offering at once certainty and vulnerability. Like the disjunction between the certainty of the narrator's confident assertion and the dizziness of the spinning world, the opening of the film seems to warn us that some gap will appear between word and image, between voice and action. This narrator, with her careful patterns of speech and cultivated accent, disappears after the film begins, leaving behind her not only the images from the revolving ball which introduce the initial changes of scene (pictures of Hartfield, Highbury, Randalls, and Donwell Abbey) but the promise of a voice that will *link* these worlds together.

Moreover, McGrath has made an interesting choice already, in choosing a female narrator for his film. Much as the beginning of the novel spins around the absence of Miss Taylor and the loss of female friendship which has centered Emma's world since the death of her mother, so the loss of that initial, comforting if slightly acerbic narratorial voice leads us to long for that absent mother – for a decidedly female intelligence who will complete Emma's moral makeover and make the world spin in the proper direction. As *Emma* moves through its various techniques of voice, suspending the narrator's own voice until the happy conclusion of the romance plot, it challenges us to listen more acutely to the vagaries of individual voice – and to listen for absent voices, as well.

Hearing voices: from free indirect discourse to voice-over

Thus, the filmmaker faces a particular problem in his adaptation: how to show the play of voices which makes up the world of *Emma*, while keeping viewers focused on the problems of knowledge that the novel highlights – and keeping them particularly focused on what Emma Woodhouse knows and how she knows it. McGrath does this quite literally by keeping us focused on voices, on what we hear and on what people say, and on the way that everyone in the story, to put it most bluntly, wants to be the narrator. If Austen's narrator makes her claim on us more directly in the striking impersonality of her opening voice, her characters wage a similar war against the text, arguing and interpreting and gossiping with a vengeance; Emma is the most imaginative but by no means the only narrator-surrogate in the novel, hardly alone in wanting her world to be more highly colored, more imaginative – in a word, more fictional, than it is. She wants, moreover, to believe that she sees the order behind the colorful events, that she can in some way both record and reorder the events of her shifting community. It is her best response to the sadness which strikes her early and hard in the novel – and it offers the relief of authority, a fiction of control which everyone in the novel longs for, and ultimately fails to achieve. Do readers long any less for such assurance? If, as Arnold Kettle has noted, "Reading *Emma* is a delightful experience, but it is not a soothing one,"[2] readers (and in particular critics) have disarmed their discomfort by trying to rid Emma of her pleasure in devising; to them (even some of the most astute), successful negotiation of the marriage plot involves an abandonment of agency, of interference, of mastery, of the desire to be a narrator.

McGrath's film attends most prominently to Emma's narratorial desire, taking it seriously, playing with her dramatic asides and ironic commentary, offering her remarkable space to comment on the action we are seeing. However, he pays careful attention as well to the games other people play with knowledge – games Austen draws out humorously, tracing from the earliest chapters the marriage plots imagined by the Westons, by both George Knightley and his brother John, and Harriet and Jane's more blighted attempts to write marriage plots for themselves. In a series of scenes, McGrath draws *our* attention to the ways the same events or documents are interpreted by different characters: in an early episode, we see person after person study a letter from Frank Churchill and pronounce upon it, these shifts of perspective conditioning us to believe that people see in their social interactions only what they are looking for – a version of themselves. Miss Bates's pronouncement that the letter is "kindly and charming" and "reminds me of Jane" expresses both her generosity and Frank's dangerous charm, as well as prefiguring Jane's engagement to Frank; Mr. Woodhouse's comment that it is "nicely expressed" but that Frank eats a dangerous amount of custard reinforces compactly his own gentleness and niceness of expression, his status as a valetudinarian, and Frank's as a young man of self-indulgent desires. Mrs. Goddard's announcement that Frank's penmanship is confident not only reminds us that she is a schoolteacher (and a fairly mediocre one, as Mr. Knightley points out) but that Frank's boldness transgresses norms of social behavior as surely as it does manuals of script.

This play of perspective gives *Emma* the feel of a larger social drama, integrating the view of the world as Highbury sees it, and reminding us subtly of the tedium and containment of Emma's life – as in the moment of the novel, when the "quiet prosings of three such women [Miss Bates, Mrs. Bates and Mrs. Goddard]" are "the long evenings she had fearfully anticipated" with the departure of Mrs. Weston. However, more than offering a comic view of the horrors of Highbury life, this dissemination of narratorial knowledge and the right to speak as a narrator suggests the problems of speaking and listening which the novel highlights throughout. It very carefully takes the problem of Austenian conversation beyond a mere dynamics of *speaking*. Consider a comparable scene in *Sense and Sensibility*, when Marianne sings for the company only to have Sir John be "loud in his admiration at the end of every song, and as loud in his conversation with others while every song lasted," and have Lady Middleton call him to order, "wonder[ing] how any one's attention could be diverted from music for a moment, [then asking] Marianne to sing a particular song which Marianne had just finished" (I.vii). Scenes of response tell us not only which characters are paying attention (as the narrator in the earlier novel says, "Colonel Brandon alone . . . paid her the compliment of attention") but which are worthy of our attention; when Mr. Knightley responds to Emma's anger at Jane's lack of forthcomingness about Frank Churchill, "why should you care so much about Frank Churchill," a wise viewer notes that he is paying attention *not* to Emma's treatment of Jane (to which he is accustomed) but to her attention to Frank Churchill; his critique of her conversation here, in short, is a sign of his deeper discontent with the distraction of her erotic attention.

Scenes of multiple perspective always threaten to make conversation not social but merely collective, an assortment of idiolects generated by characters so eccentric they cannot form any union; when characters speak at cross purposes, or when they seem to speak outside the frame, they are challenging more than the authority of the novel or film – they threaten to speak outside some larger social order. Or so theorists of speech in both film and novel have argued, which suggests that McGrath's play with voice, as this essay will explore, takes on larger questions of how we "speak" the self in novels and film – how the rhythm of narratorial authority and individual expression plays itself out in both media.[3] When that disembodied female voice opens his film; when characters, through cutting and sound bridges, seem to speak "for" the movie, taking over a narratorial function or interrupting other scenes; when Emma talks to herself and we seem to overhear – all these disruptions frame the issues of social discourse, individual expression, and narrative coherence herein highlighted.

The use of characters' voices to disrupt filmic coherence seems particularly appropriate for adapting Jane Austen, since the integration of voice, particularly through the technique literary critics have come to call "free indirect discourse," was one of the chief innovations Austen brought to the novel.[4] The technique suggests the kind of control Austen held over her characters' individual voices: it is conversation (discourse) which may be reported in summary rather than word for word or in third rather than first person (indirect) and is not always marked by quotation marks or other indicators (free); that is, it offers a kind of economy, breeziness, and directness we associate with the Austen style. More than that, its centrality, particularly to the later novels, suggests the importance Austen gave to the speech of individual characters – and particularly to the challenges of integrating individual voices to a larger whole – a problem we might naïvely think film has completely solved. However, it is worth reviewing the ways in which questions of who is speaking are central to fiction, and particularly to Austen's novels.

While direct speech, which delivers characters' voices exactly as they spoke, makes clear at every moment who is speaking and to whom, free and indirect speech, which reports speech without breaking off from a previous sentence or speech (without the helpful guides of quotation marks, and with compressions of time and space) gives a sense of rapid exchange, of greater anonymity of speech, of the characters' eccentricities of delivery – all the things we think of as characteristically Austenian. Take one example from *Emma*, for instance, where Mrs. Elton speaks in direct speech and Jane Fairfax replies in indirect, suggesting the greater loquacity of one and the greater restraint of the other: " 'My dear Jane, what is this I hear? – Going to the post office in the rain! – This must not be, I assure you. You sad girl, how could you do such a thing? It is a sign I was not there to take care of you'."

Jane very patiently assured her that she had not caught any cold (II.xvi).

This quickness of presentation might seem to us almost protocine-matic, and it is one associated largely with "flashy" characters in Austen. Frank Churchill speaks even more rapidly than Mrs. Elton, and his speech, although marked with quotation marks, offers a classic example of free indirect speech, what Norman Page calls an even more "telegraphic" style.[5] In this speech, he interrogates Emma about her interests: "Was she a horse-woman? – Pleasant rides? – Pleasant walks? – Had they a large neighbourhood? – Highbury, perhaps afforded society enough? – Balls – had they balls? – Was it a musical society?" (II.v). This redacted version of Frank's speech allows Austen to compress a great deal of dialogue as well as to congratulate us on our knowledge. Emma's answers are unnecessary because we have seen Highbury society and know exactly how much society it affords – it is Frank's arrival which promises more society, and the speed of his delivery, heightened by the use here of free indirect discourse, in which speeches are conflated and run jaggedly into one another, initially promises the pleasure Emma awaits. Yet, his speed also suggests the uncertainty of the behavior he in fact exhibits; it suggests a lack of interest in Emma's response which presages his lack of romantic interest in Emma. This is a man, we might observe from this passage, whose interest is firmly lodged elsewhere, in this case with his secret fiancée, Jane Fairfax, whose taciturnity above (remember, she is out in the rain trying to fetch his letters before her aunt sees the mail) conceals a similar duplicity.

Lest we think this is a fictional technique film has rendered superfluous, let us take one more example, and ask ourselves how it might become film dialogue. In a much more restrained moment later in the novel, which offers far more emotional impact, Mr. Knightley appears, and Emma believes he is about to reveal that he, like Jane, has conceived a secret engagement. This scene, which Emma believes will bring the knowledge of his attachment to Harriet, in fact brings a proposal to her. In this case, the rapidity of dialogue and its presentation in free indirect discourse suggests not haste but intimacy; the constraint will yield not to secrecy but to the revelation of affection:

There was time only for the quickest arrangement of mind. She must be collected and calm. In half a minute they were together. The "how d'ye do's," were quiet and constrained on each side. She asked after their mutual friends; *they were all well. – When had he left them? – Only that morning. He must have had a wet ride. – Yes. – He meant to walk with her*, she found. "He had just looked into the dining-room," and as he was not wanted there, preferred being out of doors. – She thought he neither looked nor spoke cheerfully. (III.xiii, emphasis added)

Notice that the passage integrates Knightley's speech seamlessly: he refers to himself as "I", obviously, when he speaks, but the narrator does not pause to break the rhythm of the sentences, or to disturb the focus on Emma's consciousness. Free indirect speech here allows the feeling of conversation *as it is experienced* by a character, without any break. Emma's interpretation of the conversation ("she thought he neither looked nor spoke cheerfully") is withheld until the end, and we are given no idea by the narrator if Emma's perception is accurate or not – or rather, we know that it is what she believes at the moment, but whether or not Knightley's conversation is "really" cheerful, we cannot tell. We are thrown back on Emma's responses, and forced (as she is) to interpret, or more likely overinterpret, the bits of dialogue we are given in so restrained a manner. There is a complexity of thought and speech here which a film would be hard pressed to duplicate – and the literary discourse conveys the relationship of thinking and speaking in a remarkably economical way.

These scenes have appealed to recent feminist critics because they seem to offer us a view of the characters unmediated by the interfering narrator or her imagined double, the implied author,[6] but there are ways in which they show the author's hand even more clearly than scenes where she speaks directly. However, given this range of *characters'* voices, what happens at those moments, filmic as well as novelistic, when the unseen authority is heard, and begins to speak up precisely to critique the individual voices of her characters? Here, our discussion might move from novelistic depiction of individual voices (both as dialogue and as free indirect discourse) to the film's depiction of individual voices, particularly in the unusual practice of voice-overs. This essay began with the elaborate presentation of the off-stage narrator at the start of the film, suggesting that her pronouncements work in ways more complicated than a simple transcription of the implied author's voice – that voicing a narrator in film draws our attention more directly to questions of authority than does a narrator in a novel. In similar ways, when Emma Woodhouse begins to serve as a voice-over narrator herself later in the film, we are aware that she is aiming somewhat higher than the usual character's role! In acting like a narrator, Emma is seeking that position somewhere above (outside and inside, at the same time) the community of Highbury – and these moments draw our attention to her in ways that complicate the viewer's relationship to her, and to the film. It becomes impossible "merely" to listen to her voice, aware as we are that it is moving beyond the simple role of one character among many.

Similarly, just as there is no way to make a novel's narrator or a character's seemingly autonomous conversation (however cunningly presented in free indirect discourse) "purely" natural, so in film problems of who is speaking to us when a voice-over narrator speaks resist the claims of simple transcription. We know that Frank Churchill's questions were followed by some kind of answers (the "he said/she said" reporting of dialogue), and in the same way we know that characters "in" a drama do not stop to comment on it; that when Walter Neff in *Double Indemnity* and Joe Gillis in *Sunset Boulevard*[7] narrate the events of the film to us, they are involved in thinking back, looking over, talking about events we are currently "involved" in. Being a narrator works as a powerful fantasy for characters, eager to stand above the action they are immersed in, but it is no less powerful a fantasy for readers and viewers. It is no accident that when Amy Heckerling adapted *Emma*, she chose the simpler expedient of making her heroine, Cher, the voice-over narrator, addressing the viewers directly, chiding us for our impressions and confessing her mistakes to us. That impulse (to lay bare the self; to confess all; to be seen and heard directly) is at the heart of voice-over narration. When characters usurp the role of the narrator, by speaking-over events, they imagine (and at times, so do we) that they have a mastery over the unfolding scene which we associate with narrators, and which we rarely feel with any certainty in our own lives. Yet, the films themselves frame that desire to achieve certainty and omniscience as troubling: when Walter Neff confesses his affair and subsequent criminal activities, he does so not directly but at one remove, speaking into a tape recorder; Joe Gillis, of course, can become a perfect narrator only (and we might add, "finally") by becoming a dead man.[8]

This is to say, then, that, as with free indirect discourse, filmic first-person narration or voice-over commentary is always and *reveals itself* always as a kind of trick; the more naturalistic it seems, the more completely it accounts for events, the less spontaneous, realistic, unmediated it in fact is.[9] Only by breaking the fiction of a "realist" film can a character talk to us – and nothing reveals the staginess of a film more than the presence of someone off stage talking to us. For this reason, the arguments against the use of voice-over narration are as heated as those circling around the use of free indirect discourse. Sarah Kozloff has laid out beautifully the contradictory ideas packed into these condemnations: voice-over narrators are considered both traces of the dramatic heritage of film and signs of something far too purely "literary"; they are imagined to "break the frame" of viewing in ways that disrupt our natural relations to film, and yet at the same time they offer a sign of a more "natural" (and hence, more personal) form of storytelling (see also her analysis of the vexed critiques of voice-over).[10] Like the use of dialogue in fiction, or moments when the narrator stops to insert himself into our readerly progress, voice-overs at once satisfy our desire to know who is talking to us, and break the fantasy that we are hearing something "true," real, absolute. Like the reminder at the end of Knightley's entrance quoted above, we are aware, suddenly, that it is "only" Emma Woodhouse we are hearing; we are no closer to knowing what Knightley "really" said or felt, only what he conveyed to one listener. The voice-over narrator, when it is not a character, can sustain the fantasy of omniscience a little longer – whoever that woman is who spoke to us at the beginning of *Emma*, when she comes back at the end, we feel some certainty that order has been restored, that a benevolent onlooker has granted us and the characters her blessing. We will consider some of the ambivalences of the narrator's return later in this essay but should first examine the ways McGrath plays with the possibility of voice-over narration in the middle of his film – those occasions when characters literally "speak over" scenes, moving from one to another; and in particular the scenes where Emma attempts to become the narrator of her own life, speaking like a first-person narrator, reporting not merely events but her "private" responses to them.

Hearing film

McGrath's *Emma* frames the act of listening primarily by making us hear before we see. One of the subtlest techniques in McGrath's repertoire of vocal styles is the separation of speaker and voice; it offers him a way of making literal a wider separation of voice and action, suggesting the way that characters' actions, speeches, and thoughts may pull them in opposing directions. Characters' internal divisions, as well as crises in the plot, are signaled as a division between visible and audible selves, much as the film uses physical comedy to suggest emotional unease. Throughout the film, scenes which are "experienced" novelistically as psychological conflict are staged as physical discomfort and jerky movement: the film's Mr. Knightley shares his novelistic namesake's habit of darting off suddenly and ending conversations abruptly; Mr. Woodhouse, in keeping with his nervous verbal dancing around conflict seems remarkably unsteady on his feet, quick to take the arms of others; in the carriage scene with Mr. Elton, Emma is forced to push him backward and forward, as well as to move quickly herself to avoid his romantic lunges. Her lack of mental preparedness for his advances is signaled economically by her physical surprise and her lightning reaction to his movements toward her: they end the scene frozen on opposite sides of the carriage, still, silent, and furious.

Yet, McGrath's use of voice as a sign of character is if anything more striking. Characters' voices routinely enter rooms before they do; a line of speech serves as a transition from one scene to another; voices proceed from space, only to have the body of the speaker emerge from a chair or from around a corner. Mr. Knightley's voice enters the room where Emma and her father sit, disconsolate, after the Weston wedding, asking "who cried the most"; Elton pops up out of nowhere to offer to take Harriet's picture to London for framing; when Emma is lamenting the failure of the Coles to invite her to their party, we see her father playing backgammon and hear Emma's voice without seeing her, only to have her follow her voice out from the depths of a chair. These voices serve a double function: a voice without a body has a curious authority, annexing, if only briefly, a narratorial position of speaking without being seen. When a voice enters the room with certainty, as Mr. Knightley's always does, it seems to assume power over those who hear it – diametrically opposite, we might imagine, to Miss Bates's meaningless prattle, which tends to continue after we see her leave, reassuring us (somewhat perversely) that we were right not to listen to her in the first place. But for both Emma and Elton, the inability to "be" where they "speak" suggests a deeper confusion: neither is behaving in a straightforward way, as indeed Elton's mistakes about Emma's affections for him and Emma's about her intention to refuse the Coles' invitation confirm. Scenes of confused mishearing (Emma's hope that Elton is proposing to Harriet when he is merely explaining his fondness for celery root; the lengthy scene in which Emma is prevented from hearing Mr. Weston's story about his son's arrival by Mr. Elton's obsequious attentions) suggest more of these psychological misunderstandings which the film must resolve, and these take the place of some of the novel's more complicated misapprehensions which the film cannot reproduce.

However, like the many scenes in which a sentence begun in one scene provides a bridge or transition to the next sequence, they suggest that hearing holds out not only "answers" but psychological truths; in films, McGrath seems to be saying, we trust what we hear more than what we see,[11] and if we are to learn *Emma*'s chief lesson, that her desire to hear only what she wants to hear will persistently mislead her, then hearing becomes an essential vehicle for moral education. Scenes of verbal instruction become strangely more powerful when we hear and see them than they are when we read them, and moments like Knightley's rebuking of Emma's joke at Miss Bates's expense are if anything overstaged by McGrath.[12] Because he has compressed the strawberry-picking at Donwell Abbey and the picnic at Box Hill into one event, we lose the sense of the cumulative disappointments Emma has experienced and the sense of loneliness which leads her to flirt so outrageously with Frank Churchill. In the film, her insult to Miss Bates follows not Frank's desperate attempts to provoke her into torturing Jane Fairfax, but a snub on the part of the

Eltons, who leave the picnic because of the unsuitability of games of wit. Provoked and disappointed, Emma in turn snubs Miss Bates, causing the entire party to turn silent and leading even dear Mrs. Weston to shake her head disapprovingly. Where the novel continues unbroken after Emma's comment, offering not a rebuke but Mr. Weston's ghastly pun on "m-a" "Emma," and leaving us until the end of the day and Mr. Knightley's scathing comment to realize how severe was the pain Emma inflicted, the film wastes no time and forces us to witness both Miss Bates's response and Emma's instant isolation. In part, this is the film's economy and its distrust of us, its concern that we will not notice Emma's gaffe; but it is also the film's desire that we recognize the power of speech in this tiny community. When Knightley traces the history of Emma's relation to Miss Bates, and the decline of their friendship from the days when Miss Bates's notice was "an honour to you," it encourages us to take notice of the quality of attention people pay to the speech of others. If nothing else, the film reminds us of the power any speech of Emma's will have in this world – both to wound and to honor – and makes us all the more observant of those moments of silence which fall when exactly the wrong words are spoken. As the film works to isolate Emma from her society and to make her question not only the propriety but the authority of speech acts, so the novel's chief scene of verbal damage must be even more powerfully staged by the talking pictures, and Emma's attention to her conscience (her "inner monitor") must be voiced even more loudly.

Bridging the social gap

Overall then, the film adaptation of *Emma* uses voice in three interesting ways: when the narrator speaks directly to us, at the film's beginning and end; when characters speak over scenes, forming the narrative's transitions or providing ironic commentary; and when Emma Woodhouse, in several different ways and to different ends, talks to herself. However, the latter technique in some way recapitulates the pattern of the whole, running as it does through virtually the entire film and canvassing a variety of narratorial moods. Emma's speech in itself, that is, duplicates the film's various relationships to voice: it operates as simple mockery (what can be thought but not said, as when Austen's narrator says Emma "denied none of it aloud, and agreed to none of it in private" [III.vi]); as a form between private speech and something more public, moving viewers from one, usually domestic, scene to another, usually more social; and as an attempt by Emma, usually doomed by self-blindness, to understand and enshrine her deepest feelings. Emma's private speech acts are the way the film most purely reimagines the novel's anxieties about how we are to express ourselves (reveal, conceal, and master ourselves) in public.

If they achieve this evolutionary power, Emma's first voice-over speeches begin rather more simply, in pure irony, reflecting the "clever" Miss Woodhouse of the first sentence. When she first meets Robert Martin, she says to herself, "Really, Harriet, you can do better than this"; when she sees Harriet with Mr. Elton and hopes that he is proposing (despite the suddenness of their acquaintance) she asks herself, "can this be a declaration?" These speeches become more active, both in their work of communicating Emma's distance from the social scene (that is, expressing a small form of discontent) and in doing the implied narrator's work of moving us from one scene to another, once Jane Fairfax enters the picture. Examining one such sequence of voice-over scenes, and Emma's overheard mental commentary, suggests the progression in the film's self-consciousness.

The sequence begins when Emma goes to call on Miss Bates, greeting with spoken pleasure the information that Miss Bates and her mother have news, while her voice-over self comments, "please do not let it be a letter from that ninny, Jane Fairfax." Miss Bates explains that indeed, it is a letter from Jane, in which the latter has said she is coming for a long visit. Convinced by Emma's politeness that Emma shares her joy, she announces that when Jane arrives, Emma must come to visit: she must sit just "where you are and say –." As she breaks off, the camera pans back to Emma, who is wearing a different morning dress and says, "We are so glad to have you with us." As Jane answers warmly, the voice-over Emma says, "She's more giving than I expected," but this optimism fades when Emma begins to interrogate Jane about her meeting with Frank Churchill, only to have Jane return to her customary reserve. Emma, unaware, of course, that the reserve is the sign not of Jane's coldness but of her secret engagement to Frank and her embarrassment at the concealment, interrupts Jane's response in her voice-over, saying, "I take it back. She is –." The voice-over ends the sentence with "absolutely impossible," and we fade back, discovering that Emma is now in the conservatory at Hartfield, transferring bulbs and complaining to Mr. Knightley, ever Jane's advocate, about Jane's failure to participate in what Emma considers proper social exchange.

The scene does several things for the viewers: it frames Emma's intelligence as overarching, carrying us as it does from scene to scene, and providing us with an insight we do not find in the other characters. It also conditions us, as it must for the suspense to build, to trust Emma more than any other voice we hear; its humorous changes encourage us to take the scene lightly, but like all of Emma's repartee with Mr. Knightley, it provides a different pleasure than the slower exchanges with Mr. Wood-house, Miss Bates, even Mrs. Weston. It prepares us for a giddier form of satiric commentary, and suggests the deeper connection between Emma and Knightley, who share (even when they bicker) a position of slight superiority, intellectual as well as class-based, to the other inhabitants of Highbury. However, it also sets us up for more dangerous pleasures and more serious lessons: that voice of ironic discontent ("that ninny"; "I take it back; she is absolutely impossible") is the voice she speaks in openly when she expresses herself so bitterly to Miss Bates, and a life-time of social self-suppression is lost in a moment: the same spirit that leads her to tell Miss Bates that she will be able to say only three boring things, leads her to mock Jane's lack of conversational interest. Curiously, of course, the later moment is a moment of attempted policing of Miss Bates's speech, which suggests the dangers of too much speech (a danger we might think Jane Fairfax has learned all too well), but Emma's earlier conversations convince her that no real danger will come to her from her own ironic perspective – or from sharing it with the likes of Knightley. Al-though Knightley does not approve of her comments about Jane Fairfax, his criticism is fairly light: he suggests that her dislike of Jane is related to her fear that Jane removes their collective attention from her; she re-marks that he is so comical he ought to perform in the town square; and he smiles, changing the subject to announce that Mr. Elton is engaged to be married.

His comment, rather than provoking the extended self-criticism we might expect, provides instead another filmic transition, this one even more complicated. Emma announces that she does not "know what to say except that I am –," a sentence which blurs into Harriet's saying "in a state of shock." Unexpectedly, she is in a state of shock not over Elton's engagement, but over a chance encounter with Robert Martin, which she recounts in a narrative that becomes a disembodied voice-over for a flashback scene in Ford's shop; again, Emma's irony has given way to a dramatic scene that could significantly undercut her point of view, but doesn't. This unexpected switch in perspective, which is exactly the one traced in the novel, carries us visually backward in time, but it also allows Harriet her bit of narration – suggesting, more fully than does Austen's version, which depends heavily on Harriet's ineptitude of explanation, what it means to see the world differently than Miss Woodhouse; the shock when *we* hear Harriet's distress and then realize it comes from a different source, is unbuffered by Emma's response, and reminds us more powerfully of our own failures of imaginative (fanciful) narration.

This is to take sound-bridges seriously as a redirection of our atten-tion: these aural transitions (there is one final example, when Emma is explaining that she "cannot attend" a party at the Coles', only to have her break off before that key verb, finishing the sentence "tell you how delighted I am to be invited" as she walks into the Coles' lighted house) do work comically to give the film a buoyancy that we do not always expect in literary adaptations, but they also prepare us for a continual adjustment of perspective, one which reinforces the play of focalization the novel engages in, or the kind of serial commentary we saw in the communal reading of Frank Churchill's letter. The belligerent presentation of individual perspectives in that scene threatened the social unity Austen's work seems so consciously to strive for, but Emma's initial voice-overs, moments of particularized, individual interest, do not really menace the social fabric. We take them, as I believe she understands them to be, as a kind of escape valve – a necessary self-expression which allows her to continue to sacrifice her individual desires to the household god of social gossip. However, the third kind of voice-over, that which is more truly private, is harder to integrate into the ordinary exchange of social life. For the same reason, such voice-overs are harder to integrate into filmic adaptation, suggesting why they get special (and especially filmic) treatment. They are mediated for us, for the most part, by acts of writing, suggesting already a kind of literary quality to them, and their "revelation" of Emma's inner life is similarly layered and hard to read. Yet what is interesting is the way they not only, like the earlier voice-overs, carry along dramatic points of interest, but also break through and interrupt the filmic qualities we have seen so far.

The technology of privacy

When Emma Woodhouse speaks to herself of romantic love, she writes in a diary, she brushes her hair, she sits in her garden, she prays – she in all ways behaves like a literary heroine. As Lionel Trilling has observed, "Emma believes in her own distinction and vividness and she wants all around her to be distinguished and vivid"; his claim is that this is "in its essence, a poet's demand,"[13] but it is a novelist's demand as well. Emma is a creature of books, a creature in particular of romantic novels and that peculiar strain of the Gothic in which mystery, clues, and secret passions abound.[14] Notice, she does not discourage Harriet's dismay that Robert Martin has not read the Anne Radcliffe novel Harriet recommended to him, though we might imagine that she shares the narrator's slight scorn that Harriet's only literary activity is collecting riddles she cannot understand. As the narrator comments, this solitary "literary pursuit" is "the only mental provision she was making for the evening of life"; but Emma's provisions for Harriet are the stuff of fiction:

secret fathers, missing inheritances, a marriage straight out of Samuel Richardson's *Pamela* (1740–1741), which assumes a servant girl's marriage to her master, Lord B, is a credible possibility. However, Emma wishes no such things for herself, and she is no confused heroine from a Gothic mind-trap. That she is finally not such a creature (such a ninny, to use her [filmic] word for Jane Fairfax) is suggested not only by her quick realization that she is not, as a heroine would be, in love with a man she has met only once, and not subject to the feline charms of Frank Churchill, but also by her inability to recognize the "real" mysterious courtship of Jane and Frank. We might observe that Emma's very realism keeps her from recognizing their affair, the one real "romance" before her eyes – a romance visible to, of all people, Mr. Knightley, who guesses long before Emma does, trapped as she is in her own ecstatic narcissism.

Ecstasy, of course, before it was associated purely with romantic love was also an out-of-body experience; to be ecstatic is to be beside the self, outside the self. Emma's voice-overs suggest repeatedly that her romantic dreams (of herself as a creature of heroic stature, the object of every erotic gaze) are far less important to her than her desire for understanding, her wish to see more of the world, to see outside of herself, to obtain some omniscient perspective. To put it vulgarly, Emma enjoys talking about (and in these scenes, particularly writing about) romance, but she is far more engaged in the pursuit of knowledge, both self-knowledge and the knowledge of the social order. She comes, and hence so do we, to associate that knowledge with Knightley's moral approval, but again we read too hastily if we subsume Emma's quest for epistemological clarity with the novel's quest to see her properly married. McGrath takes seriously Emma's desires for narratorial authority, but he also insists on our seeing through them. These scenes of self-analysis are at once lovingly filmed and more than a little mocking. They work to build our special relationship with the heroine, but also to help us learn to see beyond her vision. In important ways they advance the plot, telling us that she is first in love (though we can tell, it is only slightly) and then out of it with Churchill; but the longer scenes, following her out of her room and garden and back into the wider world, both move the story forward and reveal a knowledge of it she lacks. She may tell us that she loves Mr. Knightley; the film tells us (by virtue of allowing her voice as well as her actions to move the camera along) that she is finally correct. Yet, clever as all this is, it doesn't explain why a voice-over is necessary, or why it should be so "writerly" in its attentions.

When the film offers Emma's most private dialogues with herself, McGrath is not unleashing an old-fashioned version of literary consciousness – the kind that finds a book turning its pages or a pen moving across a screen as a novel literally turns to film before our eyes. True, Emma uses pen and ink and writes beside a lighted candle – no fluorescent lights buzz, no word-processors hum or cursors pulsate. Nonetheless, there is something technological, self-conscious, postmodern, in the moment when speaking and writing come together in this film, and reading this as a sentimental return to the novelist's moment of writing misses the point of McGrath's adaptation. These scenes "read" very differently if connected instead to some of the stranger, largely computer-based epistolary dramas of recent years. *You've Got Mail* (1998), which is self-consciously an adaptation of *Pride and Prejudice*, follows the structure of Ernst Lubitsch's *The Shop Around the Corner* (1939), introducing its lovers first as pen-pals, then as competitors, and finally as romantic soulmates.[15] In *You've Got Mail*, the romantic leads correspond exclusively by e-mail, often commenting in their letters on scenes they have just had (unknowingly) face-to-face. The amount of time the film devotes to watching them write to each other suggests its core belief: these sequences depend on the fantasy that our private selves are if anything even more adorable than our public selves – a fantasy McGrath seems in some ways to share. What is most interesting in *You've Got Mail*'s scenes of writing is what happens to the voices of the writing-subjects. Obviously, the film would put us to sleep if it only watched them writing. It distrusts the simple effect of merely having them "read" in a voice-over their *received* mail, so we often see the two writing to each other, as an off-camera version of their own voices reads what they have just "written" or are "writing" to each other. Yet, often, the character seen on screen interrupts the same character's offscreen voice; that is, Meg Ryan will be "speaking" (in reality, ventriloquizing) her thoughts, only to have the Meg Ryan who is close-mouthedly typing begin to speak as well, so that we hear her in two versions – indeed, in one of them she is "reading" (ventriloquizing) a letter from Tom Hanks, only to interrupt her own reading with a question. What this suggests is not only the curiously technological nature of "inner" voices on screen today, but the curiously *doubled* nature of introspection, a necessary doubling of soliloquy, as if the self generated in writing, or in particular in correspondence, and even more particularly in e-mail correspondence, requires a "voice" as duplicitous as a multiple personality.

Emma's scenes of introspection offer a similar blend of the technologically sophisticated and the naïvely self-expressive; in keeping with the pattern stressed throughout this reading of the film, they accentuate the act of writing so as to give even greater emphasis to the act of speaking, but their need to negotiate so many filmic boundaries between linguistic acts lends Emma's most impassioned moments of expressiveness a significantly self-reflexive quality.[16] Emma's voice-over comments give way to the literary device of the diary almost exactly mid-way through the film, as if the deepening ironies of the plot required more self-consciousness on the part of both the heroine and the film. The initial diary entry is fairly conventional: the screen goes black after Frank Churchill says his mysterious good-bye, leaving Emma with the impression that he intends to propose to her. We see her, her voice announces, "Well, he loves me . . ." and then the visible heroine begins to write. The scene is filmicly conventional as well: Emma is framed by a window, robed in a negligee, her hair down, lit only by candles – all in all, she seems to be playing the part of a romantic heroine. Her voice-over suggests this as well, as she says, "I felt listless after he left and had some sort of headache, so I must be in love as well." However, her immediate concession ("I must confess I expected love to feel somewhat different from this") reminds us that she is no conventional heroine, and is incapable of fooling herself for very long; the film's next diary entry (after hearing his name at a party, she repeats, "Frank Churchill . . . hmmm . . . I must own that I am not in love with Frank") suggests again her resistance to certain kinds of romantic plotting, and her willingness to confess – to "own" her emotions.

However, in the second diary scene, what she "owns" gives way to her desire to own other people's plots: she confesses that she has not thought of him since Harriet mentioned him the other day, and immediately she begins plotting again. The staging of the scene suggests the ways her confessions give way to more enjoyable romantic episodes. As she mentions Harriet, we see Emma's face in a mirror on her writing table; that face actually speaks "Harriet . . . and Frank," and the mirror suggests the play of narcissism and generosity (indeed, the "romance") in her plotting. Excited by her idea, Emma leaves the writing table and moves to her dressing table, brushing her hair in front of another mirror while the voice-over continues. The appearance of one Emma, brushing her hair while some other Emma continues to voice her diary, saying, "Happy the man who changes Emma for Harriet," suggests something uncanny at work here – as if the doubling of heroines the novel persistently suggests (and which the film usually signals through the constant interweaving of the same confused lovers through the elegant rituals of ballroom dancing) called for something more than *both* writing and speech. Despite the seeming authenticity, spontaneity, and verisimilitude of voiced confession, Emma's speaking (un)consciousness seems constantly to escape the various forms of representation the film undertakes.

For all of Emma's voice-overs have a haunted (and curiously technological) nature, at the same time that the film seems to be working to present them as old-fashioned, naïve, private, and romantic. Emma might wear flowing nightgowns and write before a candle-lit mirror, but the technology of the film (as it moves from voice-over to voice-over) makes this undressed quality seem mechanical trickery; the pattern of interruption and self-division again clues us in to Emma's psychic distress and the complexity of her situation. In the next long voice-over sequence, after she asserts to Mrs. Weston that she can easily "not think of Mr. Knightley," we follow her through a day in which speech constantly interrupts her attempt to prove that "I may have lost my heart but not my self-control." Emma's loss of control repeatedly punctuates the visual screen: her voice-over announcement that she tried not to think of Mr. Knightley while ordering the day's meals is interrupted by having the maid ask her if Knightley is coming to dinner, for she has ordered his favorite dish. As in the last diary scene, where she writes secretively under her "tent" of bedcovers of Mrs. Churchill's death and her attempts to renew her friendship with Miss Bates, only to interrupt herself to repeat "Mr Knightley... hmmm... Mr. Knightley," her voice-over repetitions and slight babbling suggest a desire to speak more than she can. In that scene, the reflection on Mr. Knightley is in fact prompted by her thought that if Mr. Knightley were "privy to my thoughts" he would see her changed heart; the disruption of her speech is, obviously, our glimpse of what is only slowly becoming less private (that is, less secret) to Emma herself. However, the technological tricks, which make her thoughts as loud as any speech in the film, suggest that her secret is not private but "out" as well as out loud; she herself is not only speaking it privately (romantically, literally) to us, but publicly, to the entire world of Highbury. It is this shared knowledge, as the plot's mistakes increase and Emma risks ruining her own happiness as well as everyone else's, that persuades us to stay by her side, to remain in the private (which is, here, to say wrong) space she occupies. The revelation of her feelings, however inadvertently, to the wider "public" whom we represent, actually works, perversely, to convince us that she *has* a private self. The technology of this (writing; speaking; ordering; dictating) suggests how layered and difficult to achieve this true self-awareness is. As the gimmickry of the filmic voice-over hints, Emma's true heart must be artificially startled out of her, and her reluctant voicing of it, disruptions and all, carries the viewer through to the end.

What the film needs to bring Emma to do is to "voice" some confession, some desire, which she cannot satisfy for herself within the candle-lit hall of mirrors she has created at Hartfield. By the film's end, as the voice-overs multiply, so does our sense of Emma's loneliness, the isolation which threatened at the film's beginnings with Miss Taylor's marriage. The scenes which precede Knightley's proposal either feature Emma alone, or feature her in confused spatial relationship to others; in the most poignant of them, as she hears Harriet's confession that she is in love with Knightley, the two friends cross and recross the room, Emma unable to occupy even the same frame as her friend. After her similarly spinning encounter with Mrs. Weston, where she moves constantly from thought to thought and from garden arch to arch, unable to rest once she has realized that she loves Mr. Knightley, we follow her through the day in which she tries not to think of him, only to end with her at prayer in a private chapel, addressing God in a voice-over, asking him, if Knightley "cannot share a life with me," to ensure that he at least will share it with no one else, but remain "always the brightest part of our lives." The voice-over concludes: "If he would just stay single, lord, that would be enough for me to be perfectly satisfied," but the composure of that sentence (the "perfectly" marking Emma's perfect use of adverbs throughout the text) gives way, at the same moment her lips begin to move: the Emma on screen speaks the final two words, "Almost. Amen." Only after that concession (an admission of desire and vulnerability Emma has been slow to make) can she encounter Mr. Knightley and greet his proposal; the coming together of voice-over and heroine suggests, at this moment, a self-knowledge which Emma has hardly had before, and which alone can make possible the romantic conclusion with its pattern of mis-speech, correction, and confession.

Listening to Mr. Knightley

Highlighting the gradual emotional and cinematic evolution (voice-over into voice, we might say) that leads Emma finally to "confess" her love in the church scene is, for McGrath, part of the larger examination of a technology of self-expression I have been stressing in drawing out the curiously and self-consciously postmodern elements of this seemingly traditional film; and the strands I have been following (the inclusion of the female voice-over narrator; the interweaving of characters' voices and narratorial intelligence; Emma's divided self-narration, which makes her, as Ian Watt noted long ago, seen from both the inside and the outside, at once character and self-narrator) come together in that most important scene of resolution, the proposal of marriage.[17] This scene draws together the elements of narration, authority, speech, and attention, but it uses them to comment on the problem of adapting Austen to modern viewers and particularly to modern feminist viewers; it works to take our contemporary discomfort with happy endings and our anxiety about what to do, here almost literally, with the outspoken heroine. The problem highlighted in this essay is one of where, again almost literally, to locate the site of female speech: the film, like the novel, asks, where is that voice coming from? whom is it safe to speak for? where can Emma "go" as an independent narrator? McGrath's version responds explicitly to the problems of authority and courtship Emma raises by playing questions of female speech against, of all things, male confession, the speech act I suggested was at the heart of film voice-over in its murky antecedents in film noir, the interweaving of speech, violence, and death in *Sunset Boulevard* and *Double Indemnity*. Yet, McGrath is placing male confession not in a scene of crime, but in a scene of romantic resolution, the moment where self-revelation and social union (all the things the marriage plot stands for) come together. By doing so, he is not only responding to the challenge to marriage the novel has offered us so far, but highlighting for us a particularly modern anxiety about the nature of speech itself.

Our modern intuition is to equate the successful fruition of love with self-expression, the moment when the soul (passion, deep feeling, sensibility, call it what you will) *forces* itself into speech. Jane Austen's version is considerably more complicated. The largest part of Emma's emotional development after realizing that "Mr Knightley must marry no one but herself!" comes from her fear of hearing him speak of his love for Harriet Smith; all of her self-knowledge leads her initially to suppress his desire to speak, to beg him to wait. His disappointment (for he intends to propose to her) touches her, and for the first time she begs him to speak in spite of the pain that it might cause her – real maturity revealed here in auditory rather than vocal presence. When he begins his proposal, Knightley makes a series of requests of Emma, the first of which, significantly, is that she "Say 'No,' if it is to be said." When Emma "could really say nothing," Knightley cries "with great animation, 'absolutely silent! at present I ask no more.'" He then begins his great speech, which begins, "I cannot make speeches, Emma," and continues with that most captivating of premises, that "If I loved you less, I might be able to talk about it more"; at the end of the paragraph, he says, "At present, I ask only to hear, once to hear your voice." What she says, apparently, is less important than that she says anything at all, and what she says is left largely unreported by the narrator: "She spoke then, on being so entreated. – What did she say? – Just what she ought, of course. A lady always does. – She said enough to show there need not be despair – and to invite him to say more himself." For Austen, at this climactic moment, the best speech is a promise to listen; this is some considerable boon to Emma, who has as much to conceal at this moment as to reveal, but it offers not only a rather deadly challenge to any screenwriter ("could you please write what Jane Austen knew better than to attempt") but a considerable challenge to the

model of expressive subjectivity McGrath rendered increasingly problematic all along. At a moment when he dare not let the offstage Emma
interrupt the visibly moved Emma, what can the heroine manage to
say?

McGrath writes a perfectly acceptable speech for Emma (one which
stresses her own unworthiness, allowing them to find each other in a chorus of self-dismissal) but the revision of Knightley's authority seems to
me to capture something far more interesting about the film's relationship to the novel. If Emma's story is marked by the subtle correction
of her thoughts, signaled in the film by the evolution of her voice-overs
from self-delusion to self-awareness, Knightley's is marked both by his
subtle domination of the film through voice, and his growing need to
confess, to express something internal. One of the film's most striking elements is its attention to Knightley's inner life: the film cannot recapture
the one chapter in the novel which is given over entirely to Knightley's
point of view, the one in which he "discovers" the relationship between
Frank and Jane and interrogates Emma about her cruel running joke with
Frank about "Dixon," but it does give a powerful sense of how much of
his life is spent following, watching, admonishing, and being amused by
Emma. One of the film's signal interpolations is of banter between the
two: when he witnesses Emma's request that Mr. Elton supply a riddle
to Harriet's album, he asks Emma why she did not ask him. "Your entire personality is a riddle," she replies; "I thought you over-qualified."
The scene where they discuss her plans for Elton and Harriet, and he (in
the face of her disavowal of any such plans) informs her of what she cannot
know, that when he is alone with other men, Elton talks only of marrying women with money, is staged as an archery match between them. As
Emma grows increasingly upset with his new information, her aim grows
worse and worse (revealing to us her own unvoiced self-doubt) and she
eventually shoots an arrow far from the target; as one of his dogs gets up,
whimpering, he casts Emma an affectionate glance and says, "Try not to
kill my dogs."

This incident is in keeping with the general comedic emphasis which
hints at characters' psychic unease; however, the archery incident suggests
in addition an emphasis on Knightley's growing awareness of his affection
for Emma, something the book cannot show with such clarity. In lieu of
asking for Emma's silence, as he did in the book, Knightley confesses his
complete misreading of the plot. In his proposal speech, he retells the
plot from his point of view – a speech that reveals, as does his earlier
comment that he could not tell from her actions how deep her affection
for Frank Churchill was, that he has been studying her and obsessed with
her romantic imaginings all along. In the novel, this speech comes after

his declaration of love and is given not directly in his voice, but in a version of free indirect discourse. It is an important speech, to be sure, but it has much less dramatic weight than if it had come before Emma was certain of his love; in a sense, it comes after the suspense, in a slight let-down of reader attention, which is no doubt why it has gone unnoticed in most Austen criticism.

However, in the film the speech *is* Knightley's proposal. His proposal is nothing other than the confession that he has been as blind and jealous and confused as the supposedly much-mistaken Emma all along; that he, too, has been blind in affairs of the heart. His "did you not guess?" does reiterate our more general sense that Emma has been seeing only half the story before her eyes, but it reminds us that he, too, has been undergoing the sentimental education Austen believes necessary to move us all from our primary narcissism. He has fallen in love only to be "mortified," to realize that there are others, perhaps more attractive, in the world, and he must base his claim on something other than his self-assurance. Like Emma's realization that what she cannot stand, even more than she cannot stand to be humiliated and rejected, is to give Knightley pain (it is that realization that brings her to run after him after urging him not to speak, that brings her to confront her fear that he will tell her he loves Harriet), Knightley's return to Highbury was prompted by the desire to see Emma and comfort her. Only that moment of self-abandonment, the willingness to appear a fool, will bring him to happiness. In the film, that confession is a necessary prelude to successful courtship; even more than the heroine's full confession (which of course never comes, as she cannot tell all without revealing Harriet's secret attachment), Knightley's self-revealing speech makes possible the resolution of the din of disparate voices we have been witnessing. Also, it gives our discomfort at our own lack of understanding a curiously prominent place; if there is one thing we have been able to center our reading on, it is that Knightley will correct and tutor Emma's vision, as he attempts to restrain her wilder bursts of fanciful narration. The critics have, universally, followed Knightley's fierce running commentary on Emma's behavior (which culminates in the "badly done" that he offers so resoundingly on Box Hill), to the exclusion of all other voices in the novel – including his own when he comments, at the novel's end, that his criticism of Emma has accomplished little but to make him love her better, focusing even more of his attention on her. When McGrath centers the proposal scene on Knightley's confession that his love has made him as inaccurate a reader as he accused her of being, he similarly reorients our own reading of the novel – and our own certainty that we will always know better than Emma, that we would make the better narrator of her life. What he accomplishes is to make us listen, directly, to a confession which can only confuse our own faith that we have been listening attentively, correctly, from above, all along.

The silence of Jane Austen

If we have not been listening from above, if we have not been admonished by Mr. Knightley, if we have learned different lessons than we thought we (and our heroine) were learning, then to whom have we been listening, after all? Where is the narrator, and how are the director, the writer, the actress, the "film" as a unit, to bring us closer to that fantasized voice of Jane Austen herself, the one the novel so famously keeps just out of our reach? The problem of framing female subjectivity in speech has for recent readers been a problem of recreating Austen's own (female, if not explicitly feminist) authority. Modern adaptations of Austen's fiction are unanimous in their desire to make Jane herself speak up; even Rozema's *Mansfield Park*, an adaptation so loose as to make the plot completely nonsensical, is absolutely loyal to the spirit of Austen as it perceives it – placing the voice of Austen's juvenilia in the person of the heroine, Fanny Price, and making ridiculous the modesty which differentiated her from the more "Austenian" (wittier and more alluring) Mary Crawford. The desire to give Austen a voice resounds in the general impulse to make *everybody* in Austen film adaptations express *more*; the films dissolve in a veritable orgy of weeping, confessing, and acting-out. Michell's *Persuasion*, which prided itself on a minimalism of dialogue and affect to mirror effectively Anne Elliot's restrained implicit narration, ratchets up its repertoire of dramatic effect and narratorial overwriting at the end: the (novel's) narrator's statement that the lovers stroll with "a most obliging compliance for public view; and smiles reined in and spirits dancing in private rapture," becomes, in the film, a parade of circus-people and fire-eaters through the streets of Bath. The scene of Wentworth's inquiry after her marriage plans which Austen excised from the original returns in the film, prompting a verbal explosion from the demure Anne Elliot, one rivaled only by her chasing after Wentworth, à la Marianne Dashwood, in the assembly rooms at Bath, and his similarly dashing entrance into the room where her family is playing at cards to demand her hand in marriage. One of the moments where Anne and the narrator nicely come together in the novel (proving that Anne has come into her own as an ironic commentator) occurs after her father's dismissal of her friend Mrs. Smith, when she thinks to herself, reminded of his friend Mrs. Clay, that Mrs. Smith was not "the only widow in Bath between thirty and forty, with little to live on, and no sirname of dignity" (II.vi); in the otherwise restrained film, this, too, becomes an outburst, as Anne astounds her family with the severity of her comment and pushes her chair away from the table, leaving them speechless.

Ang Lee's *Sense and Sensibility* similarly plays with issues of restraint and silence, needing for some reason to expand the artist's restrained palette. The film adds an astonishing (and quite moving) scene where Elinor Dashwood, lying at the foot of her sister's seeming-deathbed, cries out, "I cannot live without you . . . oh, please . . . please, dearest . . . Do not leave me alone." The sense that Elinor will be entirely alone in the world without her sister is poignantly vocalized here; but the comparable novelistic scene where the seducer Willoughby dangerously conveys his passion and confusion to Elinor, winning her sympathy and (against all our Austenian instincts) ours, cannot then be translated into film at all, and Marianne's equally poignant assessment of her own behavior, "I judge it by what it should have been, by yours" loses the dramatic weight it *must* have to make the point that "sense" is as powerful as "sensibility." In the film's rushing to a conclusion, sensibility has won yet once more. Throughout the film, Emma Thompson's screenplay has allied Elinor's sensibility with that of the narrator, putting Austen's narratorial comments in Elinor's mouth, and making Elinor's perspective almost entirely the camera's; in its eagerness to portray the passionate power of the sisters' love, in its sudden abandonment of its more "sensible" narrative authority, the film has tipped itself subtly onto the other side. The achievement this marks, of making us see the passion behind Elinor's restraint, cannot quite withstand the hurried romantic settlings of the endings: where the heroine of the novel leaves the room to cry behind a door (admittedly, so loudly that her lover and her family can hear her), by the film's end, Elinor is sobbing in front of all of them, and Edward (and we) can have no real suspense about her feelings.

In some ways, the return of McGrath's narrator frees *Emma* from such (to me at least) confusing additions; where other adaptations increase not only the instances of revelatory speeches but the crowds hanging around to hear them – Andrew Davies's adaptation of *Emma* (shown in the United States on A&E) adds an entire village wedding surely borrowed from Thomas Hardy, at the end of which *all* the new couples, including not only the Churchills and the Eltons but the Martins, join Mr. Knightley in toasting his bride and celebrating through a dance the life manorial – this *Emma* seems consciously to restrain itself. The narrator observes through a window the scene where Emma and Knightley inform Mr. Woodhouse of the marriage; as the narrator comments, "The elation Mr. Weston felt was soon shared by many," the other characters gradually fill the room, toasting the happy couple, and only the sobbing Harriet rushes from her encounter with Emma, devastated by her own disappointment. In the last extended scene, Harriet recounts to Emma the news of her marriage, and the narrator can conclude her script; it would seem that the opposition has been silenced.

McGrath, however, borrows one further trick from Austen – and again, its accentuation in film comes from a deliberate voicing, one that recapitulates the connection the film has been making throughout between film's vocal techniques and the problematic nature of subjectivity, particularly female subjectivity, in the text. His concluding scene follows film convention in adding the entire community to the "small band of true friends who witnessed the ceremony," perhaps on the theory that it takes a whole village to commence marital bliss, but he also retains and makes even more visible the one ironic commentator Austen's narrator cites, Mrs. Elton. Whereas the novel grants her only a small aside, in which "Mrs. Elton, from the particulars detailed by her husband, thought it all extremely shabby, and very inferior to her own, – 'Very little white satin, very few veils; a most pitiful business'" (III.xiv), in the film, she is allowed to attend the wedding, and to occupy the screen for a long moment, delivering her characteristic phrase (she does not profess to be an expert in the field of fashion, "though my friends say I have quite the eye") and concluding, "I can tell you, there was a shocking lack of satin." Moving from the novel's free, indirect discourse to direct address, a face and a voice confronting us ("you") with dissent, McGrath interrupts his own narrator, suggesting that even her certain vantage point (here reproduced cinematically by the camera's movement upward, toward omniscience and toward the church's steeple) is only one of the many available points of view, her voice only one of several to which we might equally well attend.

McGrath's Emma ends her final speech by stating sweetly, to Harriet Smith, "I only wanted your happiness," and his film does not, as my analysis might have suggested it would, end by rejecting either marital or closural bliss; but while it endorses romantic pleasure, it resists the idea most critics seem to endorse, that happiness comes from omniscience. The image of the steeple toward which the camera moved resolves into a painting like those of the spinning ball at the film's beginning; the camera moves down to a series of portraits, beginning with that of Emma and Knightley, and the film ends – but the ball does not turn itself back into the earth, spinning through the Milky Way. The return of that maternal voice, commenting and measuring and assessing, will not silence all other voices, any more than Emma's being "perfectly matched" can bring all other unions into harmony – in this version of the novel, there is no final reconciliation between Emma and Jane Fairfax; certainly, there is no harvest ball in which, as in the A&E *Emma*, the classes are reconciled into melodic and rhythmic unity.

What the play of voice and authority in the McGrath *Emma* has suggested is that what the seamlessness the novel's narrator seems to promise is a trick of narration, one that filmic narration can vex and disrupt, as it toys with our loyalty to Emma, our sense that she speaks for the film, our desire to see her vision of happiness and the film's brought back together. The very eccentricity and disassociation of character the use of voices highlights become the closest the novel comes to a moral center; only as the heroine expresses ambivalence is her narration reliable, and only as she learns to listen (or as we do) will her speech provide the true measure of her heart. Resisting as it does more conventional vehicles of speech, denying that romantic faith in self-expression the other adaptations highlight, McGrath's film comes closer to the complexity of subjectivity and realism (not mere naturalism or mimetic naïveté, but the struggle to learn and interpret) Austen's text provides to its canniest (and its least self-satisfied) readers; as in the novel, the less we are sure of what we are reading or hearing, the closer we will be to understanding the novel's hermeneutic instruction.

However, what is most moving in McGrath's *Emma* is what is most moving in Austen's: the powerful lesson that we are most estranged when we are talking to ourselves; the sense that however much society shapes what we think of as our individual selves, we are even less ourselves outside of it. *Emma* is a novel about how terribly hard it is to learn to need other voices; how dangerously self-sufficient our knowledge seems to ourselves. At the same time that it mocks our feelings of authenticity, surrounding the speaking selves with mirrors and haunting doubles, it holds up the possibility of some self which can self-correct; like the absent mother who returns only to dictate proper endings, internal monitors can give way to social harmony – and even more, to a world in which the heroine's sketch of the universe, the spinning globe in which we continue to believe Emma's portrait takes its proper place, can occupy not only our vision, but our best, listening selves.

NOTES

1 Anthony Lane, "The Dumbing of *Emma*," *The New Yorker*, August 5, 1996.
2 Arnold Kettle, "*Emma*," in *Jane Austen: A Collection of Critical Essays*, ed. Ian Watt (Upper Saddle River, NJ: Prentice-Hall, 1963): 113.
3 See Michael Chion, *The Voice in Cinema* (New York: Columbia University Press, 1999); Gerard Genette, *Narrative Discourse: An Essay on Method* (Ithaca, NY: Cornell University Press, 1980); Tom Levin, "The Acoustic Dimension: Notes on Cinema Sound," *Screen* 25.3 (1984): 55–68; Kaja Silverman, *The Acoustic*

Mirror: The Female Voice in Psychoanalysis and Cinema (Bloomington, IN: Indiana University Press, 1988); and most particularly Mary Ann Doane's insightful essay "The Voice in Cinema: The Articulation of Body and Space," *Yale French Studies* (issue on "Cinema/Sound," ed. Rick Altman) 60 (1999): 33–50.

4 The standard account of free indirect discourse or *stile indirecte libre* is Norman Page's in *The Language of Jane Austen* (New York: Barnes and Noble, 1972): 120–138. Banfield and Cohn summarize varieties of indirect speech in fiction: Ann Banfield, *Unspeakable Sentences: Narration and Representation in the Language of Fiction* (Boston, MA: Routledge and Kegan Paul, 1982); Dorrit Cohn, *Transparent Minds: Narrative Modes for Presenting Consciousness in Fiction* (Princeton: Princeton University Press, 1978). Casey Finch and Peter Bowen's important essay "'The Tittle-Tattle of Highbury': Gossip and the Free Indirect Style in *Emma*," *Representations* 31 (Summer 1990): 1–18 draws on similar issues.

5 Page, *Language of Jane Austen*: 124.

6 See Kathy Mezei's "Who is Speaking Here? Free Indirect Discourse, Gender, and Authority in *Emma*, *Howards End*, and *Mrs. Dalloway*," in *Ambiguous Discourse: Feminist Narratology and British Women Writers*, ed. Kathy Mezei (Chapel Hill, NC: University of North Carolina Press, 1996): 66–92.

7 *Double Indemnity*, Writer James Cain, Director Billy Wilder, Paramount, 1944; *Sunset Boulevard*, Director Billy Wilder, Paramount, 1950.

8 Amy Lawrence in *Echo and Narcissus: Women's Voices in Classical Hollywood Cinema* (Berkeley: University of California Press, 1991) notes the relationship between sound, technology and death almost from the beginning of recorded sound, in advertisements as simple as "His Master's Voice," in which Nipper, the faithful dog, sits on a coffin and listens to the horn of a Victrola, from which his master's voice emerges. She draws no explicit connection between this and her later stress on the "somewhat wishful insistence on the perfect fidelity of the new technology" which maintains "the recorded voice as holding a special, essential connection to the individual" (19), but this perfection is available, in some uncanny way, only in the already-dead voice.

9 Billy Wilder recently pointed out, "The thing about voice-overs – you have to be very careful there that you don't show what they're already seeing. *Add* to what they're seeing. I think that you can, within seconds, really seconds, you can tell things that are much better to *hear* than to see" (Cameron Crowe, *Conversations with Billy Wilder*, New York: Knopf, 1999). Wilder's account suggests again a different order of truth-statement in sound – which he goes on to connect to the voice-over in *Sunset Boulevard*, saying, "Nobody got up and said, 'Now wait a minute, a dead man speaking, *rum-rum-rum-rah*, I don't want to see that...' They listened" (108).

10 According to Kozloff, the voice-over "Naturalizes cinematic narration," creating a special relationship with the viewer, couching a film "as a conscious, deliberate communication" which depends on the illusion sound creates that participants hear something more real than real (Sarah Kozloff, *Invisible Storytellers* [Berkeley: University of California Press, 1988]: 129). See 22 for her analysis of voice-over. Lawrence notes the confusion over illusion and reality in recorded sound, pointing out, "When a phonograph listener of 1898

gazed at a flat wax disc and murmured to himself, 'That's Caruso,' he was participating in a sophisticated form of make-believe" (*Echo and Narcissus*: 21).

11 Kozloff (*Invisible Storytellers*) comments that we put our faith in the voice of a voice-over narrator, not as created but as creator.

12 Andrew Davies's depiction of the Box Hill incident in the A&E *Emma* is if anything harsher: Miss Bates's commentary to Knightley is distinctly audible and Emma looks immediately distressed, and his Mr. Knightley is far more critical (as he is throughout) of Emma's behavior. In this version, interestingly, Davies omits Knightley's final words, which are that he must prove himself her friend "by very faithful counsel," by telling her "truths while I can"; in McGrath's version, Knightley speaks these words, implying clearly that his harshness grows out of his sense that she is about to marry Frank Churchill, and he will no longer be able to speak to her in so intimate a way. Davies's version also omits the most poignant words of Knightley's speech, that Miss Bates "has sunk from the comforts she was born to; and, if she live to old age, must probably sink more." For Austen, as for McGrath, Emma's cruelty is a failure of forward-looking imagination, the inability to see that Miss Bates's life (and Emma's own), will grow more constrained, rather than richer, with time, and that comforts like companionship and faithful friendship are the only things that will endure.

13 Lionel Trilling, "Emma and the Legend," in *The Last Decade: Essays and Reviews, 1965–75*, ed. Diana Trilling (New York: Harcourt Brace Jovanovich, 1979): 40.

14 Austen employs Gothic conventions in a complicated way in her own fiction, invoking stereotypical Gothic anxieties in *Pride and Prejudice* and *Sense and Sensibility*, and even hinting at them in the besieged woman and men with mysterious secrets in *Emma*. Critics have attacked Catherine Morland, the heroine of *Northanger Abbey*, for her too-faithful belief in Gothic trappings, but Gilbert and Gubar offer a feminist reading in which the real Abbey horrors (including evil men, unhappy women, and dark secrets) are connected with women's lack of power in a not-so-Gothic world (Sandra Gilbert and Susan Gubar, "Shut up in Prose," in their *The Madwoman in the Attic: The Woman Writer and the Nineteenth-Century Liberary Imagination* [New Haven, CT: Yale University Press, 2000]).

15 *You've Got Mail*, Director, writer and producer Nora Ephron, Warner Brothers, 1998; *The Shop around the Corner*, Director Ernst Lubitsch, MGM, 1939.

16 In *Understanding Media: The Extensions of Man* (New York: McGraw-Hill, 1964), Marshall McLuhan suggests that Narcissus falls in love not with himself but with his image as reflected through a medium outside himself, so that the myth describes our attachment to new technologies which promise to extend the self (51–56). Thus, in the writing scene, Emma quite explicitly loves not herself but her mirror, and its promise of new forms of self-expression.

17 Ian Watt, "Jane Austen and the Traditions of Comic Aggression: *Sense and Sensibility*," *Persuasions: Journal of the Jane Austen Society of North America* 3 (December 1981): 14–15, 25–28.

Reimagining Jane Austen: the 1940 and 1995
      film versions of *Pride and Prejudice*

Ellen Belton

"Frequently the most narrow and provincial area of film theory," says Dudley Andrew, "discourse about adaptation is potentially as far-reaching as you like. Its distinctive feature, the matching of the cinematic sign system to prior achievement in some other system, can be shown to be distinctive of all representational cinema."[1] The 1990s' adaptations of Jane Austen's novels display an intriguing variety of relationships between the screen adaptations and their predecessors. However, the screen history of *Pride and Prejudice* provides a unique opportunity to consider the way in which an adaptation reflects its own particular historical moment.

This essay will focus on the 1940 and 1995 film versions because they were produced under different conditions and in different cultural contexts. (The 1979 BBC version, which was shot on video rather than film, is constrained by the limits imposed by the relatively primitive video techniques of the time that make it less interesting to compare with the two film versions.) The 1940 film attempts to appropriate the novel for purposes that have as much to do with the relationship between the US and Britain in pre-war Hollywood as with Jane Austen, while the 1995 version, although encouraging the spectator to envision herself as participating in an imaginative repossession of the original, is equally preoccupied with a postfeminist rewriting of the novel's central romantic relationship. Both versions offer a commentary on what George Bluestone describes as the "overtly compatible, secretly hostile" relationship between novel and film,"[2] but, because even the most putatively faithful adaptation involves a reinterpretation of the original, each version is also shaped by the particular concerns of its own time.

Film and the novel

Ever since the earliest narrative films, the novel has been a gold mine for the film industry, and ever since Sergei Eisenstein's discourse on the influence of Charles Dickens on D. W. Griffith,[3] film critics have been fascinated by the similarities between novelistic and cinematic forms.

More recently, film theorists have sought to establish a taxonomy by which to categorize and evaluate the success of film adaptations. Geoffrey Wagner, for example, identifies three possible relationships between a film and the novel on which it is based: "transposition," in which "a novel is directly given on the screen"; "commentary," in which a novel is altered for purposes of "re-emphasis or re-structure"; and "analogy," which alludes to the novel by "striking analogous attitudes and . . . finding analogous rhetorical techniques" but which "has not attempted (or has only minimally attempted) to reproduce the original."[4] Michael Klein develops a similar three-part system, consisting of "fidelity to the main thrust of the narrative"; retaining "the core of the structure of the narrative while significantly reinterpreting or . . . deconstructing the source text"; and treating the novel "merely as raw material, as simply the occasion for an original work."[5] Still another triad is Andrew's "transforming," "intersecting," and "borrowing."[6]

Although these systems claim to identify the various approaches available to the screenwriter who is adapting a source narrative, the categories themselves are somewhat subjective, and the boundaries among them are difficult to draw with precision. Even the most seemingly faithful "transposition" also functions as a "commentary" on the original, since every choice made by the filmmakers (a term that here might include all the decision makers such as producers, directors, screenwriters, actors, and artistic designers) implies an interpretative reading of the prior text. The makers of the 1995 *Pride and Prejudice* are explicitly concerned with fidelity to the original, but, as Dinah Collin, the costume designer, explains: "'Everything we're doing is an interpretation in the end – we aren't making a museum piece.'"[7] To the extent that an "analogy" between a free adaptation and its source is recognizable by a viewer, the elements of commentary and transposition are also present. In *Clueless*, for example, the freest of the recent Austen adaptations, the analogy between Austen's Highbury and the privileged youth culture of late twentieth-century Beverly Hills animates a modern reader's understanding of the anxiously defended yet subtly mutating social codes of Emma Woodhouse's world.

What these theories of adaptation also seem to ignore is the fact that the paradigms themselves are the product of their own historical conditions. The assumption that the central meaning of any text is both stable and accessible is highly problematic, as any viewer of the various film versions of *Hamlet* made in the last fifty years will acknowledge. Dudley Andrew reminds us that "in a strong sense adaptation is the appropriation of meaning from a prior text. The hermeneutic circle, central to interpretation theory, preaches that an explication of a text occurs only after a prior understanding of it, yet that prior understanding is justified by the careful explication it allows."[8] This would imply that the value of the prior text is in part generated by and therefore dependent upon the meanings revealed by the adaptation. In talking about adaptations of *Pride and Prejudice*, however, it is necessary to ask how a filmmaker approaches a text that is so highly regarded and widely read. Although not all members of a contemporary audience, particularly a television audience, will have read the novel, and not all those who have read the novel will remember it in detail, the adaptor today must begin with the assumption that a work that enjoys both continued popularity and high-culture status occupies a privileged position in relation to the text that alludes to or recreates it.

Even in the freest adaptations of an Austen novel, the metatextual commentary that occurs in the mind of the spectator involves an appropriation of the original and the development of a sense of possession. It fosters at least an illusion of privileged understanding. Whether an audience judges the adaptation in terms of its fidelity to the letter or to the spirit of the original, it assumes a special relationship with the earlier text and with its author, a relationship which is rarely and then only reluctantly granted to the makers of the adaptation. Yet the adaptation itself plays a significant role in shaping the interpretation of the work on which it is based. An adaptation is judged to be successful when it finds its own meanings in the prior text while conveying a sense of harmony and congruence with the original; however, the definition of harmony and congruence is itself a function of the culture that produces the adaptation.

In approaching an Austen adaptation, the viewer is encouraged to ask the following questions: What does the adaptation tell us about the novel? What does it tell us about the culture that produced it? Have the filmmakers found a way of reimagining the original that speaks to a contemporary audience while enriching its understanding of the prior text? These questions will inform the following analysis of the 1940 and 1995 versions of *Pride and Prejudice*.

The 1940 MGM *Pride and Prejudice*

The inspiration for the MGM adaptation is said to have originated with Harpo Marx, when he attended a 1935 performance of Helen Jerome's dramatization, *Pride and Prejudice: A Sentimental Comedy*.[9] The project was conceived as a vehicle for Norma Shearer, wife of the producer Irving Thalberg, with Clark Gable as Darcy; the production was shelved, however, upon the death of Thalberg just weeks before filming was scheduled to begin.[10] Had this version been made, it would have been "a comedy like the stage play Harpo enjoyed: a romp ... The director's aim was to keep it light, bright, and pleasant," in keeping with Austen's own description, "light," "bright," and "sparkling."[11] When the project was revived in 1939 with a new director (Robert Z. Leonard), new screenwriters (Aldous Huxley and Jane Murfin), and new stars (Laurence Olivier and Greer Garson), it was in a very different context. Aldous Huxley signed his contract for the screenplay days before the outbreak of war in Europe, and Karen Morley, who played Charlotte Lucas, recalls the disturbing effect on the actors of the unfolding news of Hitler's march through the Netherlands and Belgium during the filming.[12]

By the time the film opened, the Battle of Britain was at its height. The day Bosley Crowther's review appeared in the *New York Times*,[13] a front-page article reported "the biggest air combat to date of the 'Battle of Britain.'" The July 29 issue of *Time*, in which *Pride and Prejudice* was reviewed, featured a cover story on US preparedness in the event that Britain "should lose or surrender her fleet" and described Britain as "backed to the wall before Adolf Hitler's armies on land and in the air." The review of *Pride and Prejudice*[14] follows a review of *The Ramparts We Watch*, which tells the story of the residents of a US town from 1914 to 1918. The unspoken analogy between the American people's experience of World War I and their potential experience of World War II is clear.

Obviously, *Pride and Prejudice* was not marketed or received as a war movie, although, as H. Elisabeth Ellington points out, "allusions to Britain's wartime status pepper the screenplay." Ellington remarks that because the film "jettison[s] the novel's images of bucolic England that reinforce an American sense of what is at stake in the war and what is worth preserving about the English lifestyle," the screenwriters fail to take full advantage of the opportunities for "wartime propaganda."[15]

In fact, however, the film accomplishes the ideological project of linking the fate of Britain with that of the US in a manner that is both more indirect and more compelling. The opening sentence of the Bosley Crowther *New York Times* review demonstrates his implicit understanding of this project:

If your fancy would be for a picture of a charming and mannered little English world which has long since been tucked away in ancient haircloth trunks – a quaint but lively world in which young ladies were mainly concerned with dances and ribboned bonnets and the light in a Guardsman's eye, and matrons had the vapors and worried only about marrying off their eligible daughters – then the picture for you is "*Pride and Prejudice*," which came yesterday to the Music Hall.[16]

For a 1940 audience the film becomes an emblem of a lost and lovingly remembered world. The fact that such a world never existed either in history or in the novels of Jane Austen only adds to the poignancy of the invented memory and to the intensity of an audience's longing to recover it.

13. Elizabeth Bennet (Greer Garson) and Mr. Darcy (Lawrence Olivier) on the terrace at the Netherfield garden party, in the 1940s MGM production of *Pride and Prejudice*

The MGM *Pride and Prejudice* is thus offered and received as an icon of British culture, but the film does not merely appeal to an idea of the prettiness and quaintness of nineteenth-century English country life. Instead it sets out to reaffirm the ties between British and US society by infusing the world depicted in the film of Austen's novel with associations and values that are understood as essentially American and democratic in character.

One of the principal ways in which the film tries to accomplish this is by addressing the issue of class distinctions. The society represented in the film is a traditionally hierarchical society, but one that exhibits decidedly egalitarian tendencies. Many of the film's departures from Austen's narrative contribute to this effect.

Although in the novel Elizabeth proudly insists that as a gentleman's daughter she is Darcy's equal, the MGM film initially highlights the social divide between them. In Austen, Darcy's refusal to ask Elizabeth to dance at the assembly ball is explained in terms of her lack of physical attractiveness and her personal insignificance: "She is tolerable; but not handsome enough to tempt *me*; and I am in no humour at present to give consequence to young ladies who are slighted by other men" (I.iii). The screenplay modifies Austen to suggest that Darcy is equally put off by Elizabeth's looks and by her lack of social refinement: "Oh, she's tolerable enough . . . but not impressively handsome. And I'm in no humor tonight to give consequence to provincial young ladies with a lively wit."[17] In the film, however, Darcy says: "A provincial young lady with a lively wit. Heaven preserve us. And there's that mother of hers." Bingley replies: "It's not the mother you have to dance with, Darcy. It's the daughter. *She* is charming." "Yes," says Darcy, "she is tolerable enough. But I'm in no humour tonight to give consequence to the middle classes at play." The weight of Darcy's refusal has effectively shifted from his judgment of Elizabeth's personal qualities to her social origins.

This class barrier is erected, however, only to be demolished. In the film, to the astonishment of Austen's readers, Darcy's objection to asking Elizabeth to dance is short-lived; within moments, he has eagerly sought an introduction to her, and it is she who refuses to dance with him. While the novel concerns itself with the complex psychological processes by which first the hero and later the heroine fall in love with one another, the film visually suggests a mutual attraction that is almost instantaneous and that will ultimately overcome all external obstacles, including those of class differences.

In the novel, Elizabeth's "prejudice" against Darcy originates with the personal insult of his disdaining her as a possible dancing partner; only later is her dislike fortified by Mr. Wickham's account of Darcy's mistreatment. In the film, resentment of Darcy quickly solidifies into deep indignation when he refuses to acknowledge her introduction of Mr. Wickham at the assembly ball. She attributes Darcy's behavior to "insolence and bad manners" rather than personal animus. Later in the film, in one of the many moments when Elizabeth and Darcy seem to be on the verge of clearing up the misunderstandings between them, Elizabeth asks Darcy the following pointedly rhetorical question: "What would you think of a man who had everything the world has to offer – birth, breeding, wealth, good looks, even charm when he chose to exercise it . . . What would be your opinion of a man with such gifts who refused an introduction to another man who was poor and of no consequence?" Contrast this with the way Austen's Elizabeth refers sympathetically to Wickham as having lost the benefit of Darcy's "friendship . . . in a manner which he is likely to suffer from all his life" (i.xviii). In the film, Elizabeth's belief that Darcy's snub of Wickham is motivated by generic class prejudice is reinforced by Darcy's repetition of the offending behavior in his treatment of Mr. Collins at the Netherfield garden party. Whereas in the novel it is Mr. Collins's behavior that is reprehensible, and Elizabeth is deeply distressed by it (i.xviii), in the film it is Darcy's behavior toward Mr. Collins that upsets her. This episode is rendered even more surprising by the fact that Darcy and Mr. Collins have already exchanged some words in the garden party sequence when Mr. Collins is pursuing Elizabeth around the grounds of Netherfield and Darcy gallantly saves her by sending him off in the wrong direction.

The garden party sequence, which replaces the Netherfield ball in the film, and for which there is no counterpart in Helen Jerome's play, contributes to the film's egalitarian spirit in another way by establishing an idea of Britain that is united by common pursuits and a shared history of glorious accomplishments. Containing one of the few long outdoor sequences in the film, it is apparently predominantly shot on stage sets, with the exterior vistas often provided through back projection. Although Caroline Bingley, who is nominally the party's hostess, speaks scornfully of "entertaining the rustics" and sneers at the way "any childish game seems to amuse them excessively," the amusements that are depicted have been carefully chosen to idealize the British common people and remind the spectator of traditional British pastimes. The scene takes place on May 1, as a shot of the invitation pointedly declares, and while Miss Bingley and Darcy talk in the foreground, distant figures in the background are dancing around a maypole. The contrast between foreground and background figures (Darcy and Miss Bingley are on the terrace, while the dancers and other "rustics" are on the lawn) and the distancing effect of back projection accentuate the isolation of the supercilious Miss

Bingley, while reminding the viewer of the charm of British rural traditions. The centerpiece of the outdoor party is the archery sequence, "a fine old sport," as Darcy comments, suggesting associations with the legendary "Old England" of Robin Hood and of Agincourt. Elizabeth's skill with the bow and arrow aligns her with the renowned yeomanry of the British past; as George Lellis and H. Philip Bolton have suggested, it also provides a visual metaphor for the archness of her manner with Darcy.[18]

Writing on the Derbyshire section of *Pride and Prejudice*, Ellington is understandably disconcerted by the substitution in the MGM film of the "to-be-looked-at-ness" of Greer Garson for the "to-be-looked-at-ness" of Pemberley and the English countryside.[19] In fact, however, the absence of exterior scenes in general and of scenes set at Pemberley in particular serves the purposes of this adaptation well. The enclosed quality of the production imparts a feeling of containment and security. The artificial sets contribute to an impression of Britain as a garden perpetually in bloom. Karen Morley says this was a hallmark of a Robert Z. Leonard picture and that the prop man had a huge box of "the dirtiest paper flowers you had ever seen. And wherever the virgins went, everything bloomed. It didn't matter . . . It was spring all the time in a Leonard picture."[20] At the same time, reducing Pemberley to an offscreen referent distances Darcy from associations with pompous displays of wealth and power that might be unpalatable to a 1940 audience. Although Darcy's wealth is an important plot point in the film, its trappings are not made visible. The grand residences that are actually seen are Netherfield and Rosings, though there is one scene in the billiard room at what is presumably Darcy's London house. The effect is to displace the worst excesses of upper-class society onto other characters – specifically, Caroline Bingley and Lady Catherine.

One of the most extraordinary departures from the Austen novel is the reinvention of Lady Catherine (played by the redoubtable Edna May Oliver) as Cupid. In the novel Lady Catherine's opposition to Elizabeth and Darcy's marriage is unrelenting. Its efficacy in bringing that marriage about is an entirely unintended consequence. Austen merely indicates that at some point after the marriage Lady Catherine's "resentment gave way, either to her affection for [Darcy], or her curiosity to see how his wife conducted herself; and she condescended to wait on them at Pemberley," but the numerous references to the passage of time in this paragraph indicate the strength and duration of that resentment (i.xix). In the film, on the other hand, when Lady Catherine comes to inform Elizabeth of her opposition to her potential engagement, it is because she has agreed to act as Darcy's "ambassador." She not only gives Darcy

14. Sisters Elizabeth Bennet (Greer Garson), Jane Bennet (Maureen O'Sullivan), and Mary Bennet (Marsha Hunt) confer, in the 1940s MGM production of *Pride and Prejudice*.

her blessing before he proposes, but tells him why Elizabeth is "right" for him ("What you need is a woman who will stand up to you. I think you've found her"). This extraordinary transformation of the only titled character of real importance in the film is hard to read as anything less than the capitulation of the British aristocracy to democratization and social equality. Such an attempt to reconcile the British class structure with American egalitarianism is an essential ingredient of the argument for the US–British alliance.

A second theme that contributes to the idealization and romanticizing of Britain in the MGM film is the theme of middle-class family solidarity. Austen's two heroines are caught in the difficult situation of being alienated from the other women in their family while at the same time feeling bound to them not only by circumstances but by ties of affection and obligation. The MGM film, while acknowledging Jane and Elizabeth's personal superiority to their mother and sisters, places considerably more emphasis on family cohesiveness and unity of purpose. By means of its visual presentation of the Bennet family, the film's introductory and concluding sequences clearly establish these values as the framework for the rest of the narrative. This celebration of the Anglo-American family also promotes the general sense of shared interests in US–British relations.

The film begins with a long shot of a lively village street. The camera follows a shop boy through a doorway into a store, tracks past Jane (Maureen O'Sullivan) and stops to frame the back of Mrs. Bennet's (Mary Boland's) head, or rather of the enormous bonnet that covers it. The first image of Elizabeth is also of her bonnet, rather than her face, thus linking mother and daughter. When Elizabeth turns to face her mother and speak, there is a cut to a dynamic close-up in which Greer Garson's face is framed in an expression of inquiring surprise, identifying Elizabeth as the film's romantic heroine. Later in the scene, as Mrs. Bennet hurries through town with Elizabeth and Jane, rounding up the rest of her daughters, the camera frames them as a growing family party. First Mary, then Kitty and Lydia enter the frame to join the others and complete the grouping. The Meryton episode culminates in an overhead shot of the mother and five daughters bustling down the street in formation to reach their carriage for what turns out to be the race homeward with Lady Lucas. The unity of the family group, rather than the individual merits of any of its members, dominates this opening sequence.

The same emphasis on family cohesiveness also informs the opening scene at Longbourn. The first shot of Mr. Bennet (Edmund Gwenn) is in his library seated in a wing chair at the extreme left of the frame, while through the window we see the family carriage approaching at a gallop. The music in the background is "Flow Gently Sweet Afton," which imparts a sentimental flavor to this introduction of the paterfamilias. The interior of the library is furnished with books, a pipe rack, and a globe, speaking of comfort and tradition, but the room is rather dark, suggesting the cares of a father with five dowerless daughters, an entailed estate, and no son.

In the drawing-room scene that follows, Mr. Bennet first teases his family by refusing Mrs. Bennet's demands that he call upon Bingley, then delights them by revealing that he has not only already done so but has given him tickets for the ball. Initially, the family members in this scene appear at odds with one other, moving about the room in their own self-centered pursuits and not looking at one another. When Mr. Bennet makes his announcement, they all rush to him in the center of the frame, and they remain grouped together till the fade-out/fade-in to the ball. The vertical axis of this group is a diagonal linking Mrs. Bennet (seated) to Mr. Bennet behind her. The horizontal axis intersects an arc connecting Kitty and Mary on Mr. Bennet's right with Elizabeth, Lydia, and Jane on his left, with the diagonal connecting Mr. Bennet with Lizzy, who is positioned slightly behind him. The iconography of this conclusion evokes the traditional Victorian middle-class family portrait with its overtones of the sanctity of the home and the primacy of family life.

The film's ending is equally decisive in its endorsement of the Anglo-American family unit and its collective well-being. In this, it departs from the novel's more balanced view. Austen's final chapter strikes a delicate balance between the claims of kinship and the importance of personal fulfillment through romantic relationships. The new configurations brought about by the marriages of Elizabeth and Jane do not obliterate the heroines' ties to their family, but they produce new physical, social, economic, and moral interactions that work to the advantage and satisfaction of nearly everyone, especially of the two heroes and heroines. The balance between filial obligation and personal self-expression is represented by the fact that the final paragraph is devoted to the Darcys' relationship with the Gardiners, whose merits are based on personal qualities rather than social status but who are also Elizabeth's aunt and uncle. Thus, Austen carefully navigates the invisible boundary between Augustan self-restraint and Romantic self-indulgence, between "sense" and "sensibility."

By contrast, the final sequence of the MGM *Pride and Prejudice* focuses on the realization of the shared wishes of the Bennet nuclear family, all of whom have been shown to subscribe to the goal of marrying off all five Bennet daughters. Although Mr. Bennet refuses to shake hands with Wickham, there is less distinction than in the novel between the future happiness and respectability of Elizabeth and Jane and that of the younger sisters. Even the relationship between the elder Bennets is presented as less problematic, more companionable than the relationship in the novel. The final shot of Elizabeth and Darcy shows them kissing on a bench in the garden, but this is not the final image of the film. The camera cuts to Mrs. Bennet, who is observing this momentous event while hanging out the window in Mr. Bennet's library. She calls and beckons to her husband, who is in the background, and he joins her as the camera tracks in to frame them in the open window. As Mrs. Bennet rhapsodizes on Elizabeth's good fortune, she pats and squeezes Mr. Bennet's hand. She then rushes off to order something special for Darcy, opens the interior doors, and reveals a tableau in the drawing room: Kitty with Mr. Denny and Mary singing and playing to a Mr. Witherington's accompaniment on the flute. Mrs. Bennet again summons Mr. Bennet. The fact that Mary is finally able to hit and sustain the high note in her song (again, "Flow Gently Sweet Afton") bodes well for the relationship and for the family's future in general. Mr. Bennet remarks that "perhaps it's lucky that we *didn't* drown any of them at birth, my dear." Mrs. Bennet dispatches

Mr. Bennet (clutching his head as if in mild but ineffectual protest) to inquire about the new suitors' prospects, and as he exits, Mrs. Bennet utters the film's last words: "Think of it. Three of them married, and the other two just tottering on the brink." Mrs. Bennet has the final word as she leaves the room, closing the doors on her exit and on the film.

This remarkably un-Austenlike conclusion anticipates the romanticized ending of the many later films that apply 20/20 hindsight to the US entry into World War II. The 1940 *Pride and Prejudice* takes an approach to US–British relations that is necessarily less overt, but, just as the transformation of Bogart's Richard Blaine in the 1942 *Casablanca* repudiates the selfishness and shortsightedness of the "America First" doctrine,[21] so the emphasis on British egalitarianism and family unity in the 1940 *Pride and Prejudice* offers a powerful subliminal argument for Anglo-American solidarity in times of crisis. By stressing the common values of US and British society, the 1940 film implicitly encourages US support for the British war effort. By sentimentalizing the British family, the film also underscores the importance of subordinating individual self-interest to the common good, thus countering the arguments of the defenders of isolationism.

The 1995 BBC/A&E *Pride and Prejudice*

Sue Birtwistle's comment that the goal of the 1995 BBC production was "to remain true to the tone and spirit of *Pride and Prejudice* but to exploit the possibilities of visual storytelling"[22] anticipates the attitude of many of the telefilm's favorable reviews. The initial *New York Times* review, for example, describes it as a "splendid adaptation, with a remarkably faithful and sensitively nuanced script."[23] Other critical responses are equally congratulatory.[24] Although the impression of faithfulness to Austen's novel is an important factor in the BBC production's success, this impression is not entirely accurate. This section of the discussion will show how the BBC production creates the illusion of fidelity to the original by presenting an interpretation of Austen's narrative that is also attuned to the sensibilities of a 1995 audience.

Austen's novel ends with a careful discrimination among relationships and a weighing of personal inclinations against moral and social obligations. The MGM adaptation ends with a serio-comic vision of the fulfillment of a collective family goal. The BBC/A&E adaptation ends with the long-awaited kiss between Elizabeth and Darcy. This ending confirms the primacy of the romantic relationship over other claims and valorizes the drive toward individual self-fulfillment and gratification. In the decade that produced Bill Gates and overnight dot.com tycoons and that culminated in the success of the popular quiz show *Who Wants to Be a Millionaire?* (not to mention the short-lived and less popular *Who Wants to Marry a Millionaire?*) on US television, the 1995 *Pride and Prejudice* is more comfortable with the idea that self-advancement and self-enrichment through a variety of means, including marriage, are legitimate objectives for both men and women. The opening words of the BBC adaptation, "It's a fair prospect," spoken by Bingley as he gazes at Netherfield, echoed by Mrs. Bennet when she first visits him there and subtly alluded to when Elizabeth first catches sight of the magnificent house at Pemberley, function as a kind of epigraph for the film. At the same time, cultural acceptance of the idea of the New Age Man requires a romanticizing and softening of Darcy, while the translation of his character from the page – where his physical being is barely described – to the screen – where he is endowed with what Cherly Nixon calls "a new physical vocabulary"[25] – heightens his attractiveness. The 1995 audience wants Elizabeth to have it all, and the BBC production is happy to oblige.

George Bluestone points out that Austen's novel "possesses the essential ingredients of a movie script," namely, "a lack of particularity, an absence of metaphorical language, an omniscient point of view, a dependency on dialogue to reveal character, an insistence on absolute clarity."[26] The "understatements of the camera," he says, "are exactly suited to those epigrammatic understatements we have come to associate with Jane Austen's style."[27] For Bluestone, writing in 1957, the success of the MGM film resides in its faithful embodiment of "the dialectics of Jane Austen's central ironies" and in its use of the dance paradigm as a visual equivalent of narration and psychological exploration.[28] In the six-hour BBC adaptation, however, a greater expansiveness and explicitness enable the development of another kind of dialectic that helps to establish the privileged status of the film's central relationship at the expense of the "central ironies" that Bluestone admires.

The BBC adaptation attempts to find a cinematic equivalent for the interrelated processes of moral development and falling in love that are vital elements in Austen's narrative. It does this by establishing a physical distance between the hero and heroine that can only be bridged through what Austen sometimes refers to as the "regard." Austen's attempts at describing what is unspoken through looks, glances, and facial expressions read like stage directions for her "actors." Gene W. Ruoff touches on this aspect of Austen's technique when he refers to a "dramatic dimension" in *Pride and Prejudice* that is in tension with the episodes of meditation and reflection and that makes this novel "very nearly two works interleaved."[29] As Birtwistle's earlier comment indicates, the BBC film sets out to translate these episodes of meditation into the visual and the dramatic.

Lisa Hopkins sees the BBC production as "unashamed about appealing to women – and in particular about fetishizing and framing Darcy and offering him up to the female gaze."[30] Her argument concentrates on the ways in which "Darcy looking at Elizabeth becomes a recurrent and compelling image, used both to provide a crucial insight into his character and to build up a powerful erotic charge, of which he is clearly the center."[31] Although there is much merit in this analysis, it is in fact the reciprocal gaze of Elizabeth and Darcy, rather than the privileged female gaze alone, that actualizes their relationship and makes visible the phases of its development. The almost solipsistic quality of this relationship stands in striking contrast both to Austen's novel and to the MGM film.

In the BBC production, Elizabeth (Jennifer Ehle) and Jane (Susannah Harker) are visually bracketed together and distanced from the other women in their family. In many shots they are either alone together or framed separately from their sisters and from Mrs. Bennet (Alison Steadman). Even in scenes where they are grouped with the others, the differences between them and the rest of their family are underscored. For example, in the scene where Mr. Collins (David Bamber) comes to condole with the family over Lydia's disgrace, Elizabeth, Jane, and Mary (Lucy Briers) are shown sitting side by side. But although Elizabeth and Jane receive Mr. Collins's insulting professions of sympathy with unspoken indignation, Mary seems to welcome and appreciate them and to seek his good opinion. When Elizabeth and Jane stand up to encourage him to leave, Mary remains seated, as if wishing him to stay. When he finally does prepare to depart, Elizabeth and Jane rise first, and Mary only rises reluctantly a moment later. At one point Kitty, who ran away when she saw Mr. Collins's chaise arriving, appears in the background looking in through the window over Mary's shoulder and then moving out of the frame. This visual separation of the two heroines from the rest of their family underlines the distinctness of their point of view and imparts greater significance to their feelings and desires. It also implies that they will only find their rightful places in the world through fortunate marriages.

In contrast with the treatment of Jane and Elizabeth, Elizabeth and Darcy (Colin Firth) are hardly ever framed together until well into the second half of the film, and when they are shown in the same shot, the effect is to emphasize the obstacles between them. In the private interview at Hunsford that precedes the first proposal scene, Elizabeth and Darcy rarely look directly at one another. In the one shot in which both their faces are seen, Elizabeth is seated on the left, Darcy on the right, each

15. Elizabeth Bennet (Jennifer Ehle) and Mr. Darcy (Colin Firth) in the 1995 BBC production of *Pride and Prejudice*

framed against a different window and each looking toward the camera. A tall cabinet/writing desk between the windows in the background dominates the center of the shot. In the proposal scene itself, Elizabeth and Darcy's faces are never seen in the same frame until Elizabeth rises to hasten Darcy's departure. Yet, their connection to one another begins at their first meeting, and the telefilm audience can be in no doubt (as a reader of the novel may be) as to the inevitability of their eventual union.

The progress of their relationship is charted through a movement from sidelong glances to direct contemplation to mutual admiration. Their gradual discovery of one another and of the new selves they become in relation to one another is enacted through looking rather than through physical proximity or even through dialogue; their looks often speak more truthfully and completely than their words.

In the first half of the BBC film (which concludes with Elizabeth's refusal of Darcy's first proposal) Darcy's gaze functions not as a form of communication with Elizabeth but as a means of making visible to the viewer the evolution of his attitude toward her. Here is how Austen describes the beginning of this process:

Occupied in observing Mr. Bingley's attentions to her sister, Elizabeth was far from suspecting that she was herself becoming an object of some interest in the eyes of his friend. Mr. Darcy had at first scarcely allowed her to be pretty; he had looked at her without admiration at the ball; and when they next met, he looked at her only to criticize. But no sooner had he made it clear to himself and his friends that she had hardly a good feature in her face, than he began to find it was rendered uncommonly intelligent by the beautiful expression of her dark eyes. To this discovery succeeded some others equally mortifying. (I.vi)

The emphasis on eyes – both of the beholder and of the beheld – in this passage becomes for the filmmakers a set of perfectly intelligible cinematic instructions. When Darcy rejects Bingley's suggestion that he should ask Elizabeth to dance, he does not even glance in Elizabeth's direction, in spite of the fact that Bingley urges him to do so ("But look, there's one of her sisters. She's very pretty too"). Only after Bingley gives up and moves away and Elizabeth stands up and walks past Darcy, do Darcy's eyes follow her. The camera moves in and holds on his face as he watches her talking to Charlotte Lucas. He starts to look away, but his eyes again turn in Elizabeth's direction, as if questioning his first impression.

Colin Firth talks about the significance of this moment from the perspective of his reading of Darcy's character:

I think the first trigger [for Darcy's falling in love] is the moment when Elizabeth rejects him so impertinently ... When she walks past and gives him a cheeky look, Andrew [Davies, the screenwriter] was very helpful here in writing, "Darcy was used to looking at other people like that, but was not used to being looked at like that himself." So at that moment, I think he notices her simply out of bewilderment and curiosity; he becomes intrigued by her, which, I suspect, is the first time he has ever been intrigued by a woman.[32]

These comments point to another aspect of Darcy's personality, as it is presented in the BBC version. His contemplation of Elizabeth conveys the unspoken assumption that a man in his situation who decides that a woman is desirable is certain of her acceptance. It speaks of the com-modification and objectification of women in this society, an attitude that is even shared by Mr. Collins, who has much less reason than Darcy to consider himself a desirable suitor. Clearly Darcy doesn't think he has to win Elizabeth's approval. All that counts are his own feelings and wishes.

One contemporary theme highlighted by the BBC film is that Darcy must unlearn this attitude and must begin to look at Elizabeth as an independent subject. At the same time, Elizabeth's view of Darcy must undergo an equally profound transformation. Here too the filmmakers propose a visual equivalent for a process that in the novel is entirely internal and reflective.

Mr. Darcy's letter [Austen writes of Elizabeth's reaction] she was in a fair way of soon knowing by heart. She studied every sentence: and her feelings towards its writer were at times widely different. When she remembered the style of his address, she was still full of indignation; but when she considered how unjustly she had condemned and upbraided him, her anger was turned against herself; and his disappointed feelings became the object of compassion. (I.xv)

Since it would not be plausible or appropriate for Elizabeth to voice these feelings to another character, in the film, visual effects substitute for Austen's authorial voice. Instead of literalizing Austen's image of Eliz-abeth gazing so intently at Darcy's letter that she virtually memorizes it, the filmmakers translate the contents of the letter into a series of images that implicate Elizabeth in Darcy's point of view.

These images culminate in a cinematic moment for which there is no equivalent in the novel. As Elizabeth drives away from Hunsford, she leans forward and gazes out the window of the coach, and the camera cuts to a reverse-angle shot of what she is looking at. The scenery then becomes the backdrop for a superimposed flashback of Darcy's face as he repeats the words from his proposal: "You must allow me to tell you how ardently I admire and love you." In the proposal scene, as he speaks this line, Darcy is shot from below (representing Elizabeth's point of view, since he is standing and she is seated) in medium close-up. He is framed against a corner of the room, with the patterned wallpaper converging in the corner behind him and the ceiling visible over his head; the image is somewhat claustrophobic, perhaps hinting at Darcy's feeling of being trapped by his desire. Although his full face is visible, it is turned very slightly toward his right, and his expression is angry, rather than loving. As the scene proceeds and Darcy enumerates the objections and scruples he has had to wrestle with, reaction shots of Elizabeth show her looking down or away, deliberately avoiding eye contact with Darcy. In the flashback, however, Darcy is seen in extreme close-up, and his expression and the tilt of his head show more tenderness and admiration. The musical underscoring of the flashback also contributes to this effect. The moving scenery over which his image appears connects him not with the confined indoor spaces of the parsonage but with the romantic English countryside. Since this apparition is the product of Elizabeth's own imagination, the audience understands that it is literally seeing Darcy with Elizabeth's eyes. The interchange of glances in this brief sequence indicates the beginning of a new phase of the relationship in which Elizabeth is a more active and consenting participant. It reflects the 1990s' preoccupation with equality in romantic attachments. It also privileges the romantic relationship by superimposing on the immediate social context a projection of the heroine's thoughts.

After this, sequences involving Elizabeth and Darcy looking at but not communicating with each other give way to gazes of mutual admiration and understanding. The scene at Pemberley in which Miss Bingley tries to embarrass Elizabeth by alluding to her partiality for Mr. Wickham serves as one particularly telling example. Austen's narration provides the template for this scene: as the omniscient narrator darts in and out of four characters' consciousness, their own thoughts and their understanding or lack of understanding of the thoughts of others are communicated to the reader without a single word being spoken (i.iii). The scene concludes as follows:

Elizabeth's collected behaviour, however, soon quieted his [Darcy's] emotion; and as Miss Bingley, vexed and disappointed, dared not approach nearer to Wickham, Georgiana also recovered in time, though not enough to be able to speak any more. Her brother, whose eye she feared to meet, scarcely recollected her interest in the affair, and the very circumstance which had been designed to turn his thoughts from Elizabeth, seemed to have fixed them on her more, and more cheerfully. (i.iii)

Once again the filmmakers are able to reimagine the scene in the novel as a set of cinematic instructions, but in translating the elements of Austen's narrative into visual terms they again alter the balance between internal reflection and social interaction. Davies has given this scene greater importance by setting it in the evening (in the novel it is a morning visit) and by situating Elizabeth and Georgiana at the piano, with Darcy seated at the other end of the room. When Elizabeth agrees to play, there is a cut to a close-up of Darcy looking adoringly into the distance, while music and Elizabeth's not very accomplished singing are heard on the soundtrack. A cut reveals what he is looking at in long shot: Elizabeth seated at the pianoforte with Georgiana standing beside her.

As the scene continues, the visual relationship between Elizabeth and Georgiana at one end of the room and Darcy at the other seems to establish a new family grouping. Miss Bingley, who is seated on a sofa in the middle of the room, is presented as a physical obstacle to the actualization of this new configuration. When she utters Wickham's name (in the novel she dares not actually do this in Darcy's presence), a series of reaction shots follows: Georgiana, now taking her turn at the piano, looking up in distress and breaking off from playing; Elizabeth in the middle of the room glancing toward Georgiana; Darcy starting to get up as if to go to Georgiana. Forestalling this, Elizabeth returns to Georgiana, saying that she has been "neglecting" her. This is followed by a cut to Darcy, now slowly sinking back onto the sofa. His expression softens as he watches Elizabeth. The next shot is of Elizabeth turning the page of the sheet music for Georgiana. She slowly looks up, and her gaze connects with Darcy's. The sequence culminates in a close-up of Darcy gazing at Elizabeth with a loving half-smile and a close-up of Elizabeth gazing at Darcy with the gradual suggestion of a smile on her face as well. Later, when Darcy returns to the music room during the night, there is a single flashback to a shot of Elizabeth standing at the piano. She looks up at Darcy, but he doesn't see the softening of her expression or the smile of the earlier scene. This reflects his uncertainty about Elizabeth's feelings toward him; he no longer takes her receptiveness for granted. This sequence signals the transformation of Darcy from eighteenth-century lord of the manor to late twentieth-century romantic hero. It also attaches even greater importance to the development of his relationship with Elizabeth by making visible the internal drama that in the novel is confined to the interior world of the characters.

In the 1940 and 1995 films, as in the novel, the relationship between Elizabeth and Darcy is animated by a tension between attraction and resistance, but in the MGM film moments in which attraction seems about to vanquish resistance occur from the very beginning, while in the BBC film the process of overcoming such resistance is prolonged and difficult. The MGM film's additions and changes to the relationship between Elizabeth and Darcy often call into question the notion that Darcy is proud, aloof, and mysterious. It is obvious from the outset that he is drawn to Elizabeth and makes very little effort to resist succumbing to her charms. Elizabeth is equally drawn to him, and various characters allude, if only jokingly, to Darcy as a prospective marriage partner for her throughout the film. This is a couple who seem continually to be on the verge of moving to a new level of intimacy but to be prevented from achieving it by some misunderstanding or accidental reminder of the superficial differences between them.

Darcy's accessibility and vulnerability, the minimizing of the distance between him and Elizabeth and the audience's early certainty that they are destined for one another create an interesting though problematic contradiction between the narrative elements and dialogue that are retained from the novel, on the one hand, and the MGM film's screenplay and *mise en scène*, on the other. The MGM film deliberately subordinates the singularity and unlikeliness of the relationship Austen describes to what it sees as a greater social good. Thus the MGM version indirectly comments on Austen's novel by the way it appropriates and reinterprets it as a text for the 1940s.

The BBC version, on the other hand, privileges the individual romantic relationship. The film undertakes the postfeminist project of activating the central female character's unique sensibility and linking her achievement of a greater degree of autonomy with a sense of personal entitlement. The utopian ideal realized in the final shot of the film creates a private space for Elizabeth and Darcy's passion, a space that visually excludes the intrusions of society at large and of the lovers' less congenial friends and relations in particular. Although the implication is that the expression of individualism and the drive toward personal fulfillment may contribute to the common good of the extended family, the ending reflects the late twentieth-century assumption that the needs and desires of the individual take precedence over other values.

Conclusion

A comparison of the 1940 and 1995 versions of *Pride and Prejudice* underscores the fact that no adaptation can claim absolute fidelity to the original text. The very act of translating a written narrative into cinema involves a process of selection, alteration, and reinvention. This process is further complicated when the adaptation takes place in a different cultural context from that of the original. Both the 1940 and 1995 versions offer in their commentary on Austen's novel a reflection of the historical moment in which they were conceived and produced. Although the MGM version is obviously a much freer adaptation, the BBC version's professed fidelity to the original is actually somewhat deceptive because, in its fleshing out of things merely suggested in Austen's text, it gives so much more visual emphasis to the attraction between Elizabeth and Darcy.

Roger Gard, whose essay appears in Chapter 1 in this text, argues that no adaptation can do justice to an Austen novel and that none of the recent adaptations "remains in the mind as even a minor work of art." This position poses a fundamental question for the would-be adaptor: Why undertake an adaptation of Austen, or for that matter of any respected literary work, at all? The critical and commercial success of recent adaptations, of which the BBC *Pride and Prejudice* is a notable example, is in itself a powerful argument. This success has surely been a factor in the Austen mania of the past decade. The ability of an adaptation to recruit new readers of the original may, as Gaylene Preston argues, also in this volume, offer another incentive. Beyond this, however, the task for the serious adaptor is never merely, as Martin Amis suggests, one of "artistic midwifery – to get the thing out of the page and onto the screen in as undamaged a state as possible."[33] The adaptation offers an opportunity for filmmakers to reread a narrative from another age through the lens of their own time and to project onto that narrative their own sense of the world. A successful adaptation enters into a conversation with the original that animates the viewers' pleasure in both works. The goal of the adaptation is not only to rediscover the prior text but also to find new ways of understanding it and to appropriate those meanings for the adaptors' own ends.

NOTES

1 Dudley Andrew, *Concepts in Film Theory* (Oxford: Oxford University Press, 1984): 96.
2 George Bluestone, *Novels into Film* (Baltimore, MD: Johns Hopkins University Press, 1957): 2.
3 Sergei Eisenstein, *Film Form*, trans. and ed. Jay Leyda (New York: Harcourt, 1949): 195–255.
4 Geoffrey Wagner, *The Novel and the Cinema* (Rutherford, NJ: Fairleigh Dickinson University Press, 1975): 222–231.
5 Michael Klein and Gillian Parker (eds.), *The English Novel and the Movies* (New York: Ungar, 1981): 9–10.
6 Andrew, *Concepts*: 98–104.
7 In Sue Birtwistle and Susie Conklin, *The Making of "Pride and Prejudice"* (London: Penguin, 1995): 53.
8 Andrew, *Concepts*: 97.
9 Helen Jerome, *Pride and Prejudice: A Sentimental Comedy* (Garden City, NY: Doubleday, 1936).
10 Kenneth Turan, "*Pride and Prejudice*: An Informal History of the Garson–Olivier Motion Picture," *Persuasions* 11 (1989): 140.
11 Rachel M. Brownstein, "Out of the Drawing Room, Onto the Lawn," in *Jane Austen in Hollywood*, eds. Linda Troost and Sayre Greenfield (Lexington, KY: University of Kentucky Press, 1998): 13.
12 Kenneth Turan, "Interview with Anne Rutherford (Lydia), Marsha Hunt (Mary), and Karen Morley (Charlotte Lucas)," *Persuasions* 11 (1989): 147.
13 Bosley Crowther, "'Pride and Prejudice,' a Delightful Comedy of Manners, Seen at the Music Hall," *New York Times* (August 9, 1940): 38.

14 Review of *Pride and Prejudice*, *Time* (July 29, 1940): 44.
15 H. Elisabeth Ellington, "A Correct Taste in Landscape," in *Jane Austen in Hollywood*, eds. Troost and Greenfield: 104.
16 Crowther, "Delightful Comedy": 38.
17 Quoted in Andrew Wright, "Jane Austen Adapted," *Nineteenth-Century Fiction* 30 (December 1975): 435.
18 George Lellis and H. Philip Bolton, "Pride but No Prejudice," in *English Novel*, eds. Klein and Parker: 50.
19 Ellington, "Correct Taste": 92.
20 Turan, "Interview": 146.
21 *Casablanca*, Writers Julius and Philip Epstein and Howard Koch, Director Michael Curtiz. Warner Studios, 1942.
22 Birtwistle and Conklin, *Making of "Pride and Prejudice"*: 2.
23 John O'Connor, "An England Where the Heart and Purse Are Romantically United," *New York Times* (January 13, 1996): 13, 18.
24 Martin Amis, "Jane's World," *The New Yorker* 71 (January 8, 1996): 31–35; Christopher Lehmann-Haupt, "A Film that Out-Austens Jane Austen? No, but Almost," *New York Times* (February 8, 1997).
25 Cherly Nixon, "Balancing the Courtship Hero," in *Jane Austen in Hollywood*, eds. Troost and Greenfield: 31.
26 Bluestone, *Novels into Film*: 117–118.
27 Ibid.: 146.
28 Ibid.: 117, 126–134.
29 Gene W. Ruoff, "The Dramatic Dilemma," in *Jane Austen's Pride and Prejudice*, ed. Harold Bloom (New York: Chelsea House, 1987): 52.
30 Lisa Hopkins, "Mr. Darcy's Body," in *Jane Austen in Hollywood*, eds. Troost and Greenfield: 112.
31 Ibid.: 114.
32 Birtwistle and Conklin, *Making of "Pride and Prejudice"* 101–102.
33 Amis, "Jane's World": 33.

10   *Emma* and the art of adaptation

David Monaghan

Prior to the Jane Austen boom of the 1990s, almost all film versions of her novels were made for television and conformed to the conventions of the BBC classic drama house style. Film adaptations such as *Emma* (1972), *Pride and Prejudice* (1979*), Mansfield Park* (1983), and *Sense and Sensibility* (1981/1985) are, therefore, characterized by their textual fidelity, solid acting, and use of historically accurate settings and costumes. However, pleasing as it has been to millions of viewers, the "verisimilitude" carefully cultivated by televisual renderings of the Austen canon is usually "superficial"[1] and serves as a substitute for any attempt to point up the complexities of character and theme that lie beneath the polished surface of her novels. Pre-1990 BBC adaptations also tend to make use of unobtrusive and conservative camera and editing techniques that reflect their creators' unwillingness to rethink Austen's novels in visual terms. By and large, televised versions of Austen function as illustrated supplements to the original novels rather than as independent works of art. The only exception to this norm is the 1987 feature-length production of *Northanger Abbey*, which – as its lurid dramatizations of Catherine Morland's Gothic imaginings and its willingness to take liberties with Austen's text demonstrate – is free from the kind of stultifying reverence for a classic work that, in George Bluestone's opinion, usually "inhibit[s] the plastic imagination."[2]

MGM's *Pride and Prejudice* (1940) is the only Hollywood version of an Austen novel made before 1990 and, like the film *Northanger Abbey* but in contrast to the norm of BBC adaptations, is characterized by a lack of reverence for its source text. However, the film's free and easy attitude to Austen's novel and to the period in which it is set was motivated less by artistic considerations than by the wishes of its star, Greer Garson, who thought she looked more attractive in Victorian than Regency costume, and by a desire to please an audience used to screwball comedies. Nevertheless, despite the limitations imposed on its creators by the peculiarities of the Hollywood system, the film does display some of the visual flair usually absent from television adaptations. Bluestone, for instance, praises the dance-like rhythms of director Robert Leonard's editing style[3] and Rachel Brownstein regards the carriage race between Mrs. Bennet and Lady Lucas as "a brilliant translation of the theme of *Pride and Prejudice* into the language of the horse-obsessed Hollywood."[4]

While the conventions of the BBC classic drama and the quasi-industrial practices of the American film industry have continued to play a part in shaping recent adaptations of Austen's novels, there is also clear evidence that filmmakers are becoming less reverential in their attitude to their source texts and less willing to sacrifice personal vision to commercial concerns. An exhaustive analysis of all the possibilities and problems inherent in the more relaxed approach to adaptation adopted by the makers of the many Austen films and television serials of the 1990s falls beyond the scope of this essay. However, the three versions of *Emma* that will be its subject are so varied in their treatment of a common source text that a comparison of them should contribute greatly to the reader's understanding of the complex interplay between textual fidelity and filmic integrity that develops as writers and directors begin to transform written texts into cinematic images.

The ITV/A&E co-production, *Emma* (1996), written by Andrew Davies and directed by Diarmuid Lawrence, is the only one of the three films made for television. It is, therefore, as we might expect, the most obviously indebted to the classic drama formula. However, while generally staying close to its source, Davies's script also differs quite markedly from Austen's novel at times and Lawrence plays off conservatively filmed episodes against others in which he is adventurous in his use of the camera. As a result, their film is much more than an attempt at literal translation and, indeed, possesses a considerable degree of what Giddings calls "aesthetic integrity."[5] Somewhat paradoxically, though, the achievement of the ITV/A&E *Emma* does not reside, as is often the case with successful adaptations, in an interplay between its creators' personal vision and the themes of their source text but in Davies and Lawrence's ability to use the language of cinema as a means of communicating what they judge to be the major issues preoccupying Austen as she wrote her comic masterpiece. Davies and Lawrence are thus seeking a much more significant kind of fidelity to Austen's text than other adaptations that more accurately render the surface features of *Emma*.

The second film under consideration here, Amy Heckerling's *Clueless*, made for Paramount Pictures in 1995, is very different from the ITV/A&E *Emma*, not just because it is a product of the Hollywood studio system rather than of British television but because it much more completely flouts the principle of fidelity by relocating Jane Austen in contemporary Beverly Hills. *Clueless* is, as Jocelyn Harris argues in Chapter 3 of this volume, an "imitation" of *Emma* rather than a "translation." For Harris, who is indebted to John Dryden for her terminology, an imitation is a literary work that is overtly contemporary in terms of its language and intellectual and social assumptions but takes its "patterns" of character, plot, and theme from an earlier text. Such exercises in intertextuality provide intelligent authors with opportunities to explore significant points of intersection and divergence between their own milieux and those of their literary predecessors. Thus, Heckerling's examination in *Clueless* of female maturation in contemporary American society acquires a depth generally lacking in the teen movie genre because of the way in which she plays off the problems facing a young woman seeking a firm foothold on the ever-shifting sands of a postmodern cultural landscape against those of a heroine faced with what seems at times an all too stable world of moral absolutes and established ways of behaving.

The last of our three films, *Emma* (1996), written and directed by Douglas McGrath for Miramax, is a curious hybrid in that it displays characteristics of both the BBC classic drama and the Hollywood film, most particularly *Clueless*. Of the three versions of *Emma* under discussion, McGrath's is the closest to Austen in terms of incident, plot, and character. However, it is also the furthest from engaging intelligently with its source text. Despite the frequent elegance and vitality of its visual surface, this version of *Emma* is so concerned with broadening its box-office appeal that in almost every respect it diminishes Austen's novel. Where Austen is serious, McGrath is trivial; where she is complex, he simplifies; where she is tough-minded, he sentimentalizes; and where she is subtle, he is crude. However, while the Miramax *Emma* is clearly inferior to the other recent film versions of Austen's novel, it is, nevertheless, worth consideration in the present context because it demonstrates many of the ways in which the process of adapting a novel to the screen can go awry.

While all three films are based on Jane Austen's *Emma*, the makers of each film approach their common source text from very different directions. The result is three unique works of art that offer their viewers quite distinctive experiences.

ITV/A&E *Emma*

The 1996 ITV/A&E *Emma* has always been overshadowed by the BBC's serialization of *Pride and Prejudice*, broadcast twelve months earlier to enormous popular and critical acclaim. Yet, in many respects the later film is the more significant of Andrew Davies's two Austen projects. The root of the film's artistic achievement can be traced back to the ability of director Lawrence to build on the base provided by Davies's masterly

16. The Bennets, a family grouping, in the 1995 BBC production of *Pride and Prejudice*

script by translating not only the surface of *Emma* into the language of film but also at least part of the complex social vision that underpins Austen's entertaining story of Emma Woodhouse's adventures in match-making. The result is a demonstration of the ability of visual images to render the kind of philosophical abstractions – in this case a Burkeian view of the social contract – that many critics believe can be expressed only in words.

The serious nature of the ITV/A&E *Emma*'s engagement with its source text has been obscured, however, not just by the looming presence of the monumental television film *Pride and Prejudice* but also by the commercial imperative that Davies and Lawrence shape the surface of their film in accordance with a set of conventions familiar to the typically mid-brow fans of classic television drama. Thus, Davies's script is fairly faithful to the main trajectories of Austen's plot and he puts a great deal of trust in the dramatic possibilities of her diction and sentence structures. Similarly, as Sue Birtwistle and Susie Conklin point out in their book on the making of the film, actors were chosen in part because their age and physical appearance matched those of the characters they were to play and all decisions regarding costuming, interior and exterior locations, and even food were guided by a concern with period authenticity[6] Finally, the ITV/A&E *Emma* often has the look of the BBC classic serial in that Lawrence's direction, particularly early in the film, frequently involves nothing more adventurous than establishing shots followed by cutting from speaker to speaker, usually in close-up or mid-shot.

The most obvious indications that the ITV/A&E *Emma* is, on the whole, a much more serious and innovative piece of work than the general run of television adaptations are provided by the film's script. Whereas most televised versions of Austen are content to subordinate character and theme to the ready appeal of the romance plots around which her novels are structured, Davies creates complex characters and points up what he considers to be some of *Emma*'s major themes. The specific set of circumstances that are in large part responsible for Emma's meddlesome behavior and for her excursions into fantasy are, for example, sketched out in the course of several conversations that expose Highbury's leading citizens as almost pathological enemies of change. Mr. Woodhouse repeatedly laments the alteration in his personal situation brought about by "poor Miss Taylor's" marriage and Mr. John Knightley complains loudly about having to leave the family hearth to attend the Westons' Christmas party. Davies omits Mr. George Knightley's opposition to the Crown Ball but insists in his script directions that the camera should draw attention to the refusal of this most eligible of men to become involved in the courtship ritual of dancing.[7] The connection established here between dancing and the continuing vitality of the community is reinforced by an invented conversation in which Emma, substituting on this occasion for the narrator, points out that it is many years since Highbury's only ballroom at the Crown has been used for its intended purpose. In normal circumstances, a young woman denied opportunities to dance and hence, ultimately, to court and marry would either rebel against the status quo or suffer psychological damage because of the unnatural prolongation of her childhood. Emma, however, as Davies (again following Austen) emphasizes, is no less determined than the older generation that things should stay the way they are – hence her refusal to consider marriage – and finds alternative outlets for her youthful energies and inquiring mind in fantasy and matchmaking. Without this kind of explanatory framework, it is almost impossible to judge the Emma who interferes in the lives of others as anything but a spoilt and silly young woman of the type that Gwyneth Paltrow plays in McGrath's version of *Emma*. Davies's Emma, by contrast with McGrath's, can persuade the viewer that, like Austen's original, she has the intelligence and moral capacity to overcome her debilitating "blindness" (III.xi) and achieve the kind of maturity that is claimed for her at the end of the film.

Not only does Davies create a much more complex heroine than is typically to be found in televisual adaptations of classic novels but he and Lawrence also tease out the broader social implications of Emma's personal situation. The filmmakers' decision to flesh out Austen's fictional world, which deals almost exclusively with the leisured and professional classes, by introducing some of the many servants and laborers upon whom the personal and economic well-being of the landed gentry depended provides the most obvious visual clue to their interest in the historical context within which the action of *Emma* is located. Shots of work-worn and discontented-looking villagers and, even more, of the miserable hovels in which they live suggest that Davies and Lawrence intend to bring something of a post-Marxian perspective to their presentation of early nineteenth-century English society. This impression is reinforced by two scenes shot in such a way as to draw attention to the number of servants required to help members of the gentry, whom Davies describes in his script as "the idle rich,"[8] make the short journey from front door to drawing room. The presence of liveried footmen charged with moving the brocaded kneeling cushions of Mr. Knightley's strawberry-picking guests is particularly pointed because it momentarily transforms Donwell Abbey into something like Versailles in the days preceding the French Revolution. The fact that it is the vulgar newcomer Mrs. Elton who takes on the role of Marie Antoinette by claiming to be a "simple and natural ... shepherdess"[9] does not entirely deflect the scene's implied critique away from the more genteel members of the party.

Taken in the context of the whole film, however, scenes such as the Donwell visit serve more to flesh out Austen's own sometimes critical portrayal of the gentry rather than to sustain the notion that Davies and Lawrence are, except incidentally, intent on viewing a novel written in 1816 through the lens of late twentieth-century egalitarian social values. On the contrary, they are much more concerned to encapsulate Austen's view of her society – as they interpret it, of course – than to create a critical interplay between early nineteenth- and late twentieth-century attitudes toward class. Consequently, the introduction into the ITV/A&E *Emma* of the lower orders – whose discontents, we must remember, greatly alarmed their social superiors in the wake of the French Revolution – should probably be regarded, not as a sign of Davies and Lawrence's desire to expose the dirty underbelly of Austen's England, but as a sharp warning of the price to be paid at the macrocosmic level should the rulers of that fictional microcosm, Highbury, fail to shake themselves out of their complacent lethargy and take on a more active role in preserving the status quo. The role of servants and laborers in the ITV/A&E *Emma* thus supplements those played in novel and film by Mrs. Elton, whose bourgeois values offer a serious threat to the established order, and by unmarried women such as Harriet Smith, Jane Fairfax, and Miss Bates, whose vulnerable position points up a major flaw in the patriarchal structure of gentry society.

Davies and Lawrence are even more emphatic than Austen about the challenges facing the ruling classes in early nineteenth-century England, because they want to make sure that a modern audience recognizes the larger drama that lies beneath the surface of Austen's comic exploration of the manners and morals of the gentry. It is particularly important that they do this because of the danger that viewers will identify what is, by the end of the film, an affirmative and even idyllic evocation of Highbury society with the nostalgic, English Heritage version of the British past that most film and television adaptations substitute for the richly nuanced world that Austen actually creates.

Davies and Lawrence's understanding of Austen very much resembles that of critics who read her as ideologically aligned with nineteenth-century England's ruling classes, particularly with the gentry. The key elements of the dominant ideology of early nineteenth-century England were a belief in patriarchy and hierarchy and in the essentially moral function of the nation's rulers. Far from being considered "the idle rich," the aristocracy and the gentry were admired precisely because the income they earned from land ownership provided them with the leisure and the disinterested perspective necessary for the cultivation of the socially useful virtues. As might be expected in a society organized according to a system that combined rigid social distinctions with the idea that the different ranks share common interests and perform complementary duties, the most important of these virtues were judged to be those that clustered around the concepts of duty and concern for others.

The moral emphasis that runs through this classically conservative view of a society's function has its roots in the belief that the state is not a crude contrivance of human ingenuity but a divine creation. Like God's other creations, society is not frozen into a state of immutable perfection. Rather, it is, as Edmund Burke, the great philosopher of the landed interest, puts it, a living organism.[10] This organism must either grow or wither and die. Burke compares the process by means of which a society develops to the growth of a plant. It might grow straight and true for a while but eventually it will encounter problems. Perhaps the social organism will deviate from its main stock, or it might become deformed. It might even flourish excessively and become unwieldy. Worst of all, it might become diseased. A society's leading citizens must therefore be vigilant and intervene whenever some kind of correction is needed.

However, it is essential that all interventions – pruning would be Burke's metaphor – be aimed at restoring the social organism to its proper shape. For Burke, a vital society is one that functions around a dynamic interaction between the forces of change, correction, and conservation. In no circumstances are citizens justified in tearing up the original stock by its roots and replacing it with a new structure of their own design. The misapprehension that human reason, which is at best abstract and mechanical, can displace divine inspiration in the creation of social structures is, in Burke's view, the essential error of the revolutionary forces in France. The inevitable consequences of such hubris are expressed even more powerfully by Mary Shelley than by Burke when she describes the monster that results from the attempts of the man of science, Dr. Frankenstein, to usurp the role of God by creating human life.[11]

According to conservative ideology, so long as the landed gentry exercised responsible leadership and the lower orders accepted their subordinate but nevertheless essential roles, England's network of rural communities was unlikely to deviate too far from a state of equilibrium. Generational change, however, served as a continually destabilizing force, especially during the period when children were in the process of displacing their parents. Generational change is, of course, the issue that preoccupies Austen throughout her literary career. Her focus, though, is chiefly on the transition into adulthood of daughters rather than sons and it might therefore seem that her novels are not well equipped to deal with the central dramas of a patriarchal society. Such an assumption would be incorrect. According to Burke a young woman's maturation and marital choices were no less crucial to the continuing health of society than a man's inheritance of his father's estate because of the family's role as the core social unit and because of the moral function of polite behavior and social rituals.

There is something of the timelessness of myth about the concept of society as a living organism that is constantly in flux but according to a cyclical pattern that guarantees ultimate stability. As a social realist and a satirist Austen does not foreground the mythic dimensions of her repeated dramatizations of the process of generational change within the sphere of gentry society. However, in *Emma* at least, she arranges the chronology of her story so that it covers precisely one year. As a result, albeit in a most unemphatic way, Austen transforms what happens to Emma Woodhouse in the period leading up to her marriage to Mr. Knightley into something akin not just to the myth of the eternal return but even to the fertility rituals from which this myth derives.

As briefly demonstrated earlier, Davies's script skillfully encompasses the major thematic threads outlined above. A film, though, is more than a script and any analysis of the ITV/A&E *Emma* that fails to take into account the contribution made by Diarmuid Lawrence's acute visual imagination can hardly hope to do full justice to this remarkable adaptation of Austen's novel. It is, therefore, appropriate at this point to focus on several new scenes that are introduced at the beginning and the end of the film. These scenes afford a much greater role to editing and *mise en scène* than to dialogue and rely on cinematic devices to foreground the seasonal cycle that is almost subliminal in Austen's novel.

The ITV/A&E *Emma* opens with a sequence of four scenes, three of them invented by Davies, that introduce the film's major personal and social conflicts and that establish a vital link between visual style and the issue of social vitality. In the first of these scenes, Davies and Lawrence replace the leisurely passages of narrative commentary that get the novel underway with a dramatic raid on the Woodhouse's chicken house. The episode combines several key elements: an initial *mise en scène* comprising a dark night sky and a partially covered but brilliant white moon; a rapidly edited montage of shots taken from a range of distances and angles during the raid; and a sound track featuring wildly clucking hens, a gunshot, and a cock crow. In combination these visual and aural devices generate intense energy and a sense of danger. Paradoxically, the scene is also quite beautiful. The atmosphere of the similarly invented wedding scene that follows is quite different. Dark night gives way to sunny day and perilous improvisation is replaced by predictable ritual. Yet this second episode, with its pre-wedding bustle, sudden cuts away from the interior of the church in mid-ceremony, and final crane shot of the Westons' carriage speeding down Highbury's main street, is no less energetic than the first.

The only breaks in the rapid flow of the two scenes involve Emma and her father. The raid on the chicken house concludes with a close up of a sleepy and bemused looking Emma peering out of her bedroom window and the Woodhouses are part of the primarily elderly group that remains frozen in the church doorway while the Westons hasten to their carriage and then drive quickly out of town. The loss of energy that is associated with the appearance of the Woodhouses is even more pronounced in the third in the film's opening sequence of scenes. The episode in question, which takes place a few hours after Miss Taylor's wedding and has its origins in the novel, begins with a long shot and fairly lengthy take of Emma and Mr. Woodhouse seated at each end of a large table situated in the gloomy dining room at Hartfield. A cut then moves the action into a drawing room lit only by candles and a flickering fire. The tempo of editing slows down considerably during this scene and a rather deliberate and mournful piano piece replaces the jaunty music that ran through the first two episodes.

Much of the first half of the ITV/A&E *Emma* is characterized by slow-paced and fairly routine editing similar to that employed in the Hartfield scene. The look of this part of the film is thus very much that of the standard television adaptation. However, we have already seen that director Lawrence is not wedded to televisual conventions. Neither does he vary his editing techniques purely to avoid monotony. Instead, Lawrence is seeking to develop a complex visual style capable of communicating the film's main themes. Far from being merely conventional, the Hartfield scene is filmed in a style that dramatizes the moribund character of the gentry. The very different techniques employed in the scenes that precede it suggest that the void that is opening up in Highbury society can be filled in one of two ways.

The dark energy of the chicken-house raid creates the strong impression that loss of authority at the top might encourage the lower orders to follow the lead of the French by giving violent expression to their discontents. This reading is encouraged both by the appearance toward the end of Lawrence's rapid opening montage of the symbol of France, a crowing rooster, and by shots during the Woodhouses' carriage ride to Miss Taylor's wedding of ramshackle hovels and of a group of obviously downtrodden farm laborers. By combining elements of violent disorder and beauty, most notably in his shot of the moon emerging from behind the clouds, Lawrence may also be introducing an allusion to another revolution, the one started by the Easter 1916 uprising, famously described by W. B. Yeats in the line, "A terrible beauty is born."[12] The connection established here between energy and social upheaval is reinforced later in the film by the way in which Lawrence films the arrival of the vulgar, social-climbing bourgeoise, Mrs. Elton. Just as the raid on the chicken house literally shook Highbury out of its contented sleep, so do low-angle tracking shots of the Eltons' carriage, a high-angle blurred track of the street from Mrs. Elton's point of view, and the upbeat musical score that accompanies the scene combine to give the viewer a very visceral sense of the vulnerability of a soporific status quo to the newcomer's crude vitality.

There is, however, an alternative to social upheaval, either of a revolutionary or economic/ideological kind. It is introduced into the ITV/A&E *Emma* by the energetic manner in which Lawrence films the Westons' wedding and, in particular, their exit from the village, which matches the sprightliness of Mrs. Elton's arrival. What this montage of shots suggests is that the gentry can survive so long as it grasps the Burkeian principle that change has an essential part to play in ensuring a society's long-term stability. Highbury, under the leadership of the good-hearted Mr. Wood-house, may be, as Miss Bates often notes, an idyllic place, but it will wither and die unless a new generation accepts responsibility for revitalizing the community. Despite Davies's initial privileging of the Westons, the main burden of change in the ITV/A&E *Emma*, as in the novel, falls on Emma Woodhouse who, at twenty years of age, fast approaching twenty-one, is more than old enough to make the difficult transition from adolescence to adulthood. The personally and socially invigorating effect of an appropriate marriage (or more specifically, a marriage to Mr. Knightley who is also long overdue to assume full adult responsibilities) is briefly foreshadowed during the otherwise dreary first evening at Hartfield by an elegant pan shot that follows the dance-like rhythm created as first Emma and then Mr. Knightley pass in front of the other and take a seat. With this piece of bravura camera work, the function of which is to link the harmonious interaction achieved by a dancing couple to courtship and finally to marriage, the institution that Burke views as the keystone of the perfectly balanced whole that is his ideal of English society, Lawrence finds a visual equivalent for one of Austen's central metaphors.

However, as the next scene – another invented episode set in the village church – demonstrates, once again in entirely cinematic terms, Emma is not yet ready to become involved in socially productive behavior and redirects her creative energies into fantasy and meddling. Lawrence's first shot allows the viewer to see that the church service – and by implication her role in the community – has failed to engage Emma's attention. A tracking shot allows the viewer to follow her eyes as they move from her first sight of Harriet Smith down the aisle to Mr. Elton whom she has just proclaimed as her next matchmaking target. The stimulating effect on Emma's view of the world of the romantic connection that she immediately begins to forge between Harriet and Elton is expressed by a low-angle mid-shot that transforms Elton into a towering black-cassocked figure borne aloft by his pulpit and by a tilt down from a suddenly illuminated window to Harriet transformed into an angel by the shimmering golden light in which she is now bathed.

Had Emma's attention been focused on her immediate social context rather than on constructing romantic fantasies, she might have read a different and rather more troubling text in the scene before her. The key to this text is provided by the viewer's realization that the giggling group of schoolchildren at the back of the church are Harriet's responsibility. The Harriet depicted here, the one who glances anxiously toward her young charges rather than mooning over Mr. Elton, is, as we learn almost immediately, "somebody's natural daughter" and "a parlour boarder"[13] at the school run by Mrs. Goddard. In other words, she is a vulnerable young woman lacking the firm social status and economic resources needed to guarantee a respectable marriage or indeed any marriage at all. As a spinster, Harriet can expect nothing better than a lonely and penurious old age eked out on the fringes of society. Like Miss Bates, she will serve as a daily reminder of how flawed the patriarchal hierarchy is when it comes to accommodating women who fail in the marriage market.

Emma's duty, as one of Highbury's leading citizens, is to follow the example set by Mr. Knightley in his dealings with Miss Bates by doing all she can to mitigate Harriet's situation. However, it is not in Emma's interests as a matchmaker to recognize a truth about Harriet that would disqualify her as a likely partner for the ambitious Elton. Thus, instead of protecting Harriet, Emma puts the naïve young woman into great peril by persuading her to pursue Elton rather than accept a marriage proposal from the eminently worthy but romantically uninteresting Robert Martin. Later in the novel, Emma's scandalous imaginings about Jane Fairfax's relationship with Mr. Dixon endanger another vulnerable young woman's future. The scene in the church is therefore significant not only because it gives visual expression to the seductive effect of fantasy on Emma but also because it immediately points up the negative impact that Emma's preference for personal indulgence over responsible social involvement can have on the established order.

Following this four-scene overture, the main action of the ITV/A&E *Emma* charts a course close to that of its source text. Regardless of the reactionary forces at work in Highbury, new social influences gradually begin to make themselves felt. The spirit of change introduced by Miss Taylor's marriage intensifies with the arrival in the village of a stream of newcomers who simultaneously stimulate and threaten the Highbury community. These intruders have a particularly strong impact, both negative and positive, on Emma's development. Frank Churchill, for example, encourages her selfish and fantasist tendencies while the threat posed by Mrs. Elton causes Emma to become much more assertive in affirming the positive aspects of a set of values formerly taken for granted. In order to find cinematic analogies for the process by means of which Highbury, in a textbook illustration of Burke's organicist social theories, changes in order to become itself once again, Davies and Lawrence pick up on the hints provided by Austen's chronology and base the structure of their film on the cycle of the seasons, nature's prime example of continuity achieved through constant flux.

The first part of the film, covering the late autumn and winter months, alternates mostly static and conservatively lit interior with tightly framed exterior scenes played out against gray skies and a landscape that changes from green to brown and then to the chilly, blue-white of the Christmas snowstorm. Throughout this period Emma wears heavy fabrics in various shades of dark brown, gray, blue, and green. After Christmas the landscape becomes almost colorless and Emma is seen tightly bundled up in a black coat and hat. The lifelessness of the film's *mise en scène* is a perfect objective correlative for a Highbury community that has not yet begun to shake off its contented lethargy.

As winter turns into spring, however, two newcomers, Jane Fairfax and Frank Churchill, arrive. The revitalization of Highbury effected by their entry into the community is prefigured in the white dress Emma wears for a Hartfield social evening and, even more dramatically, by the prefacing of Frank's arrival with a powerful visual statement of the Burkeian ideal of harmony between human institutions and nature in the form of a spectacular long shot of Donwell Abbey surrounded by a green and sunny early spring landscape. In the scenes that follow, which include the arrival of Mrs. Elton, the action moves between brightly colored and sunlit exteriors and interiors now frequently lit by natural light pouring through large windows rather than by dim candles and flickering fires. Emma is more and more often seen wearing white dresses made of light fabrics. At the same time, a new fluidity marks Lawrence's directorial style. This is first evident during the garden scene that follows Mrs. Elton's first visit to Hartfield. The static figure of Mr. Woodhouse, seated and wrapped in a blanket, is now confined to the background while, in the foreground, a mobile camera follows Emma, Mrs. Weston, and Mr. Knightley during their perambulatory conversation.

It is not until the Crown Ball, however, that the vitality of the spring–summer *mise en scène* is fully matched by the film's camerawork. Initially, the ballroom scene is statically framed by high-angle long shots taken from the vantage point of the musicians' gallery. A strong contrast is thereby created with the main body of the action which Lawrence films from a variety of distances ranging between mid-shot and close-up while also making extensive use of panning, tracking, and rapid cutting in order to capture the complex dynamics at work, not just in the dance, but between the evening's main participants.

The overt ritualism of the Crown Ball scene prepares the way for a transformation in the way that landscape functions in the ITV/A&E *Emma*. Up to this point in the film, Lawrence, as is the case with Austen in her novel, has been content to establish a predominantly metonymic relationship between the transition from winter to spring to summer and the opening up and energizing of Highbury society. However, beginning with the visit to Donwell Abbey, landscape takes on a much more overtly symbolic role. In his script Davies provides the director with specific instructions about the new look he wants for the establishing shot of the Abbey: "Donwell Abbey shimmers in the mist. It should be pretty breathtaking."[14] Lawrence doesn't quite manage the mist but otherwise the view he provides of Donwell's honey-colored stone exterior glowing amidst the brilliant green summer landscape is extremely impressive. The following scene, in which the camera tracks gracefully around the Abbey ruins with their colorful flower beds and emerald green lawns, has a lyrical quality that confirms a change in the film's approach to landscape.

Presumably taking their cue from the passage in *Emma* in which Austen describes the harmonious relationship between Donwell and its natural setting, Davies and Lawrence are here picking up on the suggestion embodied in the epic long shot of a springtime Donwell Abbey discussed above by proposing that the resolution of their film's conflicts will involve the creation of an accord between individual, social group, and nature. The ITV/A&E *Emma* is thus becoming, in a much more overt way than is ever the case in Austen's novel, as much Burkeian allegory and fertility ritual as comedy of manners.

However, while the natural world is held up as an ideal in both the Donwell episode and the visit to Box Hill that follows, the inhabitants of Highbury are not yet ready to become one with it. Thus, images of harmony between the human and the natural during the Donwell and Box Hill scenes are always ironic. A particularly striking shot frames Knightley and Harriet like perfect lovers in front of Donwell's beautiful formal gardens. In another, Frank and Jane are caught posed high on a terrace backed by a wooded bank. Yet, the idyllic state implied by the first shot is simply a projection of the unrealistic marital aspirations fostered in Harriet by Emma, while what the camera is actually recording in the second beautifully framed shot is a lovers' falling-out. At Box Hill, a large tree spreads its branches protectively over six members of the Highbury touring party. However, the apparent unity between the human and the natural suggested by this image is undercut by the way in which the tree trunk separates the humans into two groups. Thus, the Eltons stand to the far left of the frame while Emma, Frank, Jane, and Harriet are grouped together to the right of the tree trunk in what is actually a rather modest metaphor for the multiple conflicts that plague the visit to Box Hill.

Emma is at least partly responsible for all of the various squabbles, misunderstandings, and pieces of ill-humored behavior that prevent the Donwell and Box Hill scenes from achieving their almost Edenic potential. Idealized natural settings cannot, therefore, be free of irony until Emma has come to a better understanding of her own personal desires and social obligations. The first and most crucial of such scenes occurs in the garden at Hartfield. After a stormy night which, as is also the case in Austen's novel, mirrors Emma's despair at the prospect of losing Mr. Knightley to Harriet, the skies clear and the Hartfield garden is revealed in its summer glory. The bright weather as well as images of Emma's hand brushing a bed of lavender and of her reflection in the pond seem at first sight to be ironic since Emma still believes that the various types of enhanced self-awareness that she has recently achieved have come too late to save her from a lonely and alienated future. However, Mr. Knightley appears unexpectedly, mutual misunderstandings are dispelled, and a marriage is arranged. A condition of harmony is thus finally achieved, not only between the lovers and within a community that will undoubtedly benefit from the impending transfer of power from Mr. Woodhouse to a younger, more vital generation, but also, as the earlier parts of the shot sequence have in fact accurately predicted, between the human and the natural. A final long shot of Emma and Mr. Knightley standing amidst the flourishing vegetation of the Hartfield garden is structured in a very similar way to the earlier shots of Knightley and Harriet and of Frank and Jane but without any of their deflating irony.

The mythic dimensions of the Burkeian integration of personal, social, and natural achieved in the garden at Hartfield are reinforced by the two invented episodes with which the main action of the ITV/A&E *Emma* concludes. The first is a harvesting scene in the fields above Donwell Abbey which is shot through golden filters in response to Davies's instructions that the episode should be fully mythic: "the hay being hoisted high, natural rhythms, the poetry of work, all that."[15] In such a context there is a certain inevitability about the way in which the threat of class conflict that loomed earlier in the film is finally dissipated by successive shots that show how the laborers who toil in the fields, the gentry, in the shape of Mr. Knightley seated on his horse, and the yeomanry, represented by Robert Martin passing by on a haycart, are united around a common economic activity and a shared closeness to nature. The next scene, a harvest supper organized by Mr. Knightley for the entire community, includes a number of images of class harmony, the most notable being a tracking shot in which Emma weaves through the lower ranks in order to offer her hand to Robert Martin and invite his family to visit Hartfield. However, in this instance, the film's mythic and socially specific dimensions are more equally balanced than was previously the case. Lawrence's continued use of golden filters gives a timeless feel to the harvest supper while a very specific ideological and historical context is created by Davies's invention of a Burkeian speech in which Mr. Knightley discourses about the duties of landlord and tenant and the need to balance "stability" and "change."[16]

Following Austen's example, Davies and Lawrence defuse many of the issues they have raised about the situation of impoverished single women by finding husbands and a comfortable place within the patriarchal social order for both Harriet and Jane. By the end of the ITV/A&E *Emma*, therefore, only the bourgeoise Mrs. Elton remains as a threat to the established order. However, her carping presence at the harvest supper, like her sour comments about Emma's wedding at the end of the novel, can be no more than an irritant to a society whose leaders have shaken themselves out of their apathy and initiated a process of social regeneration. Far from usurping the traditional leaders of Highbury society, Mrs. Elton has no choice but to accept her position as vicar's wife and join the second of the ranks into which the guests arrange themselves for the great communal dance that climaxes the harvest supper.

However, while there is something intensely satisfying about this image of social harmony, it would be a betrayal of Austen and of the Burkeian ideology around which, in Davies and Lawrence's view, she shapes her novel to end at a moment of frozen perfection. Therefore, writer and director add a coda to the ITV/A&E *Emma* by cutting away from the dance to another dark nighttime chicken-house raid. The effect of this repetition of the event with which they began their narrative is not only to put the world of the film back into motion but to give it the circular shape needed to remind viewers that, according to classical conservative ideology, the wheel is always turning because the process of social conservation and correction is never completed. By marrying Mr. Knightley Emma has achieved an ending but she has also made a beginning.

Davies and Lawrence's adaptation of *Emma* is particularly satisfying. This is in part because it interacts with its source text in a much more complex way than is usually the case with filmed versions of Austen's novels. Whereas most filmmakers are content to use Austen as a source of plot and characters, Davies and Lawrence make a serious and mostly successful attempt to embody within their film the same Burkeian conservative social vision that provides a philosophical underpinning for Austen's delightful comedy of manners. Even more important, Davies and Lawrence's film strives throughout to translate what Austen expresses through the written word into the language of film. As a result, indebted as it is to its source text, the ITV/A&E *Emma* deserves to be viewed as a distinct work of art that functions effectively according to the conventions of a medium very different from Austen's.

Clueless

Clueless, which even writer/director Amy Heckerling describes as "real light and real fluffy,"[17] obviously operates at a much greater distance from its source text than the ITV/A&E *Emma*. Contemporary Los Angeles,

17. An accessorized Cher (Alicia Silverstone) in the 1995 Paramount Pictures release *Clueless*

with its perpetual sunshine, grandiose and grotesque suburban mansions, palm-tree lined streets, frantic freeways, and gaudy malls, could hardly be more different from Austen's England, especially as evoked in film and television adaptations with their foregrounding of variable English weather and seasons, architecturally impressive country houses, landscaped grounds and pastoral countryside, quiet, wooded lanes, and village shops. Similarly, Heckerling's rowdy teenagers and loud and bullying adults bear little obvious resemblance to Austen's generally refined and genteel characters, while the multicolored and endlessly varied clothes worn by the high-school students in *Clueless* clearly contrast with the muted colors and uniform style of outfits worn by the actors in filmed versions of Austen. The social life of the Los Angeles teenager, as depicted by Heckerling, consists of wild parties, free-form dancing, recreational drug use, casual sex, skateboarding, shopping, and hanging out at the mall. Austen's young people, on the other hand, mostly occupy the same social universe as their elders and, when not at home, as they usually are, go to dinner parties, musical evenings, and well-organized and elegant balls. Carriage rides under the care of a coachman and visits to the village shop bear only the palest resemblance to the reckless car driving and non-stop consumerism of the teenagers in *Clueless*.

Nevertheless, Heckerling accords a privileged place to *Emma* amongst her many sources by describing Austen's novel as the "structural tree" for her own attempt at "comedy of manners." Heckerling further claims that her film's "sense of class and social dynamic"[18] derives from *Emma*. And in fact, any reader of *Emma* who begins to look closely at *Clueless* will find that it is full of allusions to the novel. For instance, almost all of the film's major characters have their equivalents in *Emma*. The overprivileged, meddlesome but good-hearted Cher is Emma; her father, a successful and aggressive lawyer who is nevertheless totally dependent on his daughter, is Mr. Woodhouse; Mr. Hall and Miss Geist, the teachers brought together by Cher, are the Westons; Cher's rather dim, lower-class friend, Tai, is Harriet Smith; Elton, who is intended for Tai but has his eye on Cher, is Mr. Elton; Cher's rival, Amber, who ends up dating Elton, is Mrs. Elton; Tai's true love, the socially despised Travis, is Robert Martin; Christian, a newcomer at the school who is briefly the object of Cher's affections, is Frank Churchill; and Josh, a college student who is almost a brother to Cher, is Mr. Knightley. Only Cher's closest friend, Dionne, lacks a counterpart in *Emma*, although her confidante role somewhat resembles that of Miss Taylor/Mrs. Weston. Because Christian's romantic secret turns out to be a preference for males rather than a secret engagement, *Clueless* has no need to find an equivalent for Jane Fairfax.

The information provided above about the roles played by the characters in *Clueless* confirms Heckerling's claim to have taken her plot from *Emma*. Many of the film's major set-piece scenes also derive from the novel. Elton's sexual assault on Cher during a car ride home from a Christmas party is, for instance, broadly based on what happens between Emma and Mr. Elton in the carriage after the Westons' Christmas party. Similarly, the incident during a frat party in which the previously non-participant Josh partners Tai because no one else will ask her to dance owes more than a passing debt to Mr. Knightley's gallant rescue of Harriet at the Crown Ball in *Emma*.

Why, though, does Heckerling base her film on a novel that would seem to have little relevance to American teenage life in the 1990s? Obviously, as we have already seen, *Emma* is useful to her as a source of characters, plot, and key situations. The novel also provides Heckerling with the opportunity for some intertextual jokes based on incongruities between scenes set in contemporary Beverly Hills and parallel episodes from Austen's depiction of Regency England. The substitution of a rowdy teenage party held in a suburban bungalow in balmy Los Angeles for the snowy evening when the Woodhouses and the Knightleys visit Randalls for a grand Christmas Eve dinner is a particularly effective example of Heckerling's comic method.

However, despite Heckerling's description of *Clueless* as a "light" movie lacking any "real life" agenda[19] and despite the tendency of critics like

Geoff Brown to dismiss the film as "frivol[ous],"[20] "lightweight,"[21] and "disposable trash,"[22] there is more than clever but superficial humor in the interplay between film and source. Not only is Heckerling correct to label her film a comedy of manners but she shares Austen's awareness of the possibilities inherent within the genre for a subtle but unobtrusive exploration of important social/cultural issues. At its most serious, Heckerling's goal in *Clueless* is to examine how some of Austen's central concerns play out in the context of a chaotically postmodern social and cultural milieu that is radically different from the much more coherently structured society of early nineteenth-century England.

The delight Heckerling takes in collapsing some of the most monumental products of what was once called "high culture" into a smorgasbord of popular genres provides particularly telling evidence of her postmodern orientation. Not even her "structural tree," *Emma*, is allowed an obviously privileged position, and it is likely that the novel's presence in *Clueless* went undetected by many of the teenage girls who were the film's primary target audience. Heckerling's heroine, Cher, certainly shows no signs of being aware of the origins of the plot in which she becomes embroiled. Wherever great literature is inscribed on Cher's cultural map, it is always overwritten by products of the contemporary North American mass media industry. Thus, for her, Shakespeare's Sonnet XVIII is "like a famous quote" from "Cliff's Notes" and *Hamlet* is a film starring Mel Gibson. Similarly, Christian is aware of Debussy only as a source for the Pet Shop Boys.

Two popular genres are much more important than this detritus of a once dominant high culture in shaping (if that's the right word) the surface of *Clueless*. The first is the high-school movie with its emphasis on dating, drugs, clothes, and hanging out at the mall and its almost total disregard for the educational function of schools. The second is the MTV video, a form whose flashy camera techniques and hyperactive editing are frequently imitated by Heckerling, particularly in shot sequences choreographed to an appropriate backing track. One of the most notable is Tai's makeover, a nine-shot montage cut to the rhythms of Jill Sobule's "Supermodel." Other genres that make at least a fragmentary appearance in *Clueless* are the television advertisement (particularly the film's "Noxema commercial" opening montage); the ghetto movies (as reflected in Murray's "gangsta" persona); the highway chase movie (during Dionne's *Speed*-like out-of-control excursion onto the freeway); the schmaltzy romance (in the form of the fountain that suddenly lights up to the accompaniment of triumphal trumpet music when Cher realizes she loves Josh); the slapstick comedy (most evidently when Tai falls down the stairs at the frat party); and the courtroom drama (in scenes depicting

Mel Horowitz, Cher's father, working on a big case with a team of young lawyers).

In order to ensure that, in the case of *Clueless* at least, the medium truly is the message, Heckerling consistently plays up the postmodern characteristics of contemporary Los Angeles. Thus, just as the presence of a master text fails to provide the film with generic unity, so must Cher's narrative voice take its place amongst a plethora of discourses. Indeed, Cher's own speech patterns are derived from a range of discursive practices including neologisms ("Baldwin" for attractive young man and "postal" for stressed); striking metaphors ("surfing the crimson wave" for menstruation); creative grammar ("this is so dope" for "this is extremely stupid"); jargon ("aerobically effective"); and sophisticated vocabulary used in the pursuit of an eloquent style ("whimsical," "egregious," "incongruous," and "capricious"). Other teenagers are equally idiosyncratic in the way that they speak. The obviously middle-class Murray affects Black ghetto English ("Bitch, what's your problem?"); Christian, a fifties aficionado, imitates the linguistic practices of Sinatra's Rat Pack ("Hey man. Nice pile of bricks you got here"); and Travis, who has obviously watched a lot of television, makes ironic use of a variety of discourses including the Oscar speech ("I'd like to thank my parents for never driving me to school") and the movie review ("Two very enthusiastic thumbs up. Fine holiday fun"). Even Tai's unselfconscious working-class Brooklyn speech patterns ("Wow, you guys talk like grown-ups") are made exotic by her relocation to an upper middle-class Beverly Hills high school.

The outfits worn by teenage girls and the houses of the wealthy are a similarly eclectic mix of styles and periods. Amber, for instance, wears a little black hat and fake fur boa of the type fashionable in the forties over a T-shirt and blue jeans; Cher's house combines Southern plantation pillars with Italianate statuary; and Dionne's mixes mock Tudor with a Burgundian tower. A sensibility that feels at home with such discursive practices, clothes, and buildings is one that has no room for notions of authenticity and originality. Cher, for example, can understand Miss Geist's look of pleasure at receiving flowers only as "a Kodak moment" or what poststructuralists call a simulacrum – a copy without an original. Dionne similarly regards a tender exchange between Mr. Hall and Miss Geist as "a photo op." Cher denies even her own feelings a unique status. Thus, she describes her sense of disorientation at learning the truth about Elton's romantic intentions as "a *Twin Peaks* experience."

The kind of established codes and moral absolutes around which Austen's world is structured would, of course, be incomprehensible in the relativistic and contingent society presented in *Clueless*. Indeed, most of the things that matter to Austen cease to be relevant once her concept of the self as the final product of a long process of experience and reflection has given way to the idea that an individual's personality is the endlessly variable product of mixing and matching the many cultural models made available by the mass media. In Austen's novels, for instance, performance is usually synonymous with inauthenticity; hence Emma's final preference for the "decided and open" over "a life of deceit" (III.xvi.). In *Clueless*, on the other hand, performance is an integral part of daily life. Thus, Cher notes that Dionne's argumentative relationship with Murray has been "influenced by the Ike and Tina Turner movie." Adult self-presentation is equally performance-based, as evidenced by the pleasure Mel Horowitz takes in his daughter's ability to earn grades through successful pleading, a skill with which he is well acquainted in his career as a litigator, rather than by hard work.

An emphasis on performance, or what we might more generally call personal style, leaves little room for manners as conceptualized by Jane Austen. Whereas public conduct in Austen's novels is usually constructed around polite codes that serve the moral function of demonstrating an awareness of and a willingness to serve the needs of others, Heckerling's characters nearly always behave in ways designed to draw attention to themselves. As a result, group interaction in *Clueless* is much more often marked by competitive rudeness than by the self-effacing behavior that generally characterizes social intercourse amongst Austen's characters. Cher is, for example, usually verbally abusive toward Josh and sarcastic in her exchanges with Amber. They respond in similar style. Heckerling's adults are not necessarily any more mannerly than teenagers. Mel Horowitz in particular has invested far too much in creating his tough lawyer persona to consider behaving politely toward Cher's friends. He greets Tai by telling her to get off his chair and calls Christian an "asshole" before mocking his Rat Pack style of behavior. Ironically, one of the few polite characters in *Clueless* proves to be the mugger who thanks Cher for the property he has stolen from her.

Just as polite codes give way to egotistical display in *Clueless*, so are the nuances of class that preoccupy Austen replaced in Heckerling's world by distinctions between the self-aggrandizing cliques that are the only type of collectivity possible in a society dominated by considerations of personal style. Students at Bronson Alcott High, for example, form groups based on various and rather arbitrary forms of self-definition, including a belief that the school TV station is "the most important thing on earth"; a high regard for BMW ownership; a concern with being "cute" and popular; and an interest in drug use.

However, the postmodern concept of difference is not perhaps quite so dominant in the contemporary America portrayed by Heckerling as comparisons with Austen's world of common assumptions and social hierarchy might suggest. It may, for example, be impossible to discriminate by any criteria other than personal preference or aesthetic judgment between the personas constructed by Cher, Christian, and Murray. However, there is no doubt that these individuals and the cliques to which they belong are generally considered superior to Travis and the "loadies" and, indeed, despite Cher's intervention, to the working-class Tai. The basis for the distinction is, of course, economic. For all the illusion that personal choice rules in a value-free America, far more prestige accrues to those who can choose to own extensive wardrobes of designer clothes, to drive late-model imported cars, to have their hair expensively styled and their bodies professionally massaged, and to bolster their carefully cultivated presentation of the self with props such as Christian's collection of fifties movies and Billie Holliday tapes, than to those whose "choices" are limited to scruffy clothes, skateboards, and recreational drugs.

Cher and Dionne are well aware that money and what it can buy provide the only firm grounding in a world of free-floating signs. When Cher feels "impotent and out of control" and in need of "sanctuary," she goes to the mall. Doing a "makeover," that is, turning another person into a commodity, also gives Cher "a sense of control in a world of chaos." However, despite the quasi-religious connotations of terms such as "sanctuary," the pursuit of material things is, by its very nature, antithetical to any system of belief rooted in a concern with the moral and spiritual dimensions of human life. Heckerling is obviously aware of this and invites the audience to laugh at her characters' obsession with getting and spending. However, unlike Austen, who is unbending in her critique of materialists such as Mrs. Elton, Heckerling ultimately papers over the moral void that lies at the center of an American society that combines postmodern indeterminacy with universal consumerism.

Thus, whereas early in *Clueless* she repeatedly points up Cher's selfishness and the superficiality of her high-school peers, Heckerling finally caters to the values of the mass Hollywood audience by subscribing to the American myth that it is possible to flourish as an autonomous, morally aware person within a capitalist society, even one that has entered its postmodern phase. First, she suggests that tolerance as well as solipsism can flourish in a culture lacking common codes of conduct and shared values. This point is central to the debate-class speech in which Cher offers her forbearance in dealing with rude party guests who turned up unexpectedly at her father's fiftieth birthday celebration as a model for the American government's treatment of Haitian refugees. Her argument has a certain plausibility and inspires Travis to rethink his intolerant attitude toward his mother's taste for the Rolling Stones. However, Heckerling's later contention that Cher is at root a good person who has inherited a "soul" from her mother and can, therefore, easily slough off the selfish personality that everything in her culture and upbringing has combined to foster is pure Hollywood fantasy.

Clueless, then, has a lot in common with the many intelligent Hollywood comedies that ask uncomfortable questions about American society before providing a conventional happy ending. However, its own ending is ambiguous enough to provide some comfort to those viewers who admired the postmodern rigor of earlier parts of the film. The final scene of *Clueless* begins with a long-distance rear view of a bride in full wedding regalia. An audience reared on Hollywood comedies will, of course, assume that this is Cher who, in the previous scene, finally found true love with Josh. However, Cher's narrative voice suddenly interrupts to assert, "As if! I mean, I'm only sixteen and this is California not Kentucky." With this intervention, it becomes possible to interpret the action of *Clueless* as merely a phase in Cher's life, the beginning of her entry into adulthood, not its conclusion. She has her Mr. Knightley but this does not mean, as it does for Austen, that she has now achieved a settled identity. It could be argued, then, that Heckerling has succeeded in returning everything that she had begun to affirm to the realm of the provisional and the constructed. If this is indeed the case she has subverted the very conventions that shape the later parts of her film, thereby reasserting her commitment to a postmodern view of contemporary American society.

In summary, *Clueless* is an intelligent film that manages to reconcile artistic and commercial ends. Viewed from one perspective, it is a lightweight spoof on American teenage manners and mores that finally attests to the worth of both American mainstream values and the power of true love. From another, it is a subtle "imitation" that develops a rich intertextual relationship with Jane Austen's *Emma* as its way of exposing the yawning gap that exists between traditional and postmodern ways of viewing the world.

The Miramax *Emma*

Like Heckerling, Douglas McGrath, the writer and director of the Miramax *Emma*, works with a range of genres and styles. However, there seems to be little artistic or intellectual logic guiding his shifts in convention and tone. As a result, McGrath's use of his sources is far less productive than Heckerling's.

McGrath's *Emma* is obviously heavily influenced by the BBC television classic drama convention that an adaptation must remain faithful to the characters and plot of its source novel. In fact, despite its merging

18. Emma (Gwyneth Paltrow) and Mr. Knightley (Jeremy Northam) lead the dance line in Douglas McGrath's *Emma*, a 1996 Miramax Films release.

of the Donwell and Box Hill visits into a single scene, the Miramax *Emma* is truer to the original than the ITV/A&E version of the novel in that McGrath includes more of the chain of events leading up to Elton's proposal to Emma, ends his film with Emma's wedding rather than an invented harvest supper, and reintroduces the Coles. Fidelity to his source text is also evident in McGrath's camerawork and editing style which, as Lane points out,[23] often create a graceful dance-like effect appropriate to the rhythms of Austen's novel. This is particularly true of the almost balletic movements that reflect the changing power relationships that occur between the two protagonists while Harriet is telling Emma of her love for Mr. Knightley.

Once we go beyond plot and, in some respects, visual style, however, it is clear that fidelity to even the surface of *Emma* is by no means always a priority with McGrath. This is particularly evident in his clumsy and sometimes inadvertently comic handling of the small details of etiquette so important in defining the social milieu of Austen's novel. Mrs. Elton, for instance, is credited with making the sandwiches for the Box Hill picnic, a task no lady of the period would have performed, especially one who is so conscious of her status as Mrs. Elton. McGrath's uncertainty about what constitutes proper behavior amongst Austen's gentry is also revealed by Mr. Knightley's habit of calling Jane Fairfax "Jane," a solecism of the kind to be expected only of someone as vulgar as Mrs. Elton. Even sillier and, of course, utterly anachronistic, is an air kiss between Emma and Harriet.

In similar vein, the appearance and personality of the characters in the Miramax *Emma* are often at odds with the way in which Austen describes them. Emma, who is "hazel-eyed" (I.v) and therefore must be a brunette, has become a blonde who, while certainly "handsome" and "rich" (I.i), is far too given to pouting, simpering, and frowning to justify the description "clever" (I.i); Harriet Smith, described in the novel as "a very pretty girl" (I.viii), has become an awkward lump; Mr. Knightley has shed about ten years, become extremely handsome and acquired a sensitive and even bashful manner; and, most striking of all, the querulous and irritating Mr. Woodhouse now has a twinkle in his eye, rosy cheeks, and a cheery wave.

McGrath, who filmed his version of *Emma* on location in England, is obviously concerned that period architectural and landscape details should be correct. However, he seems far more interested in creating striking visual effects than in following Austen's occasional clues about the look of her fictional world. For instance, the cycle of the seasons that can be identified through a careful examination of Austen's chronology is almost completely absent from McGrath's film. The blazing summer with which the Miramax *Emma* begins seems to last almost until Christmas, at which point the snow falls, there is a brief period of obviously cold weather, and then the hot, sunny weather returns. This is a climate in which Emma can be outdoors in flimsy, sleeveless dresses throughout most of the year.

The constant sunshine that lights outdoor scenes and the apparently high-wattage candles used for interiors provide McGrath with many opportunities for constructing glowing and colorful *mise en scènes*. In order to further enhance his *mise en scène*, McGrath clothes Emma, who is usually at the center of the action, in a different brilliantly colored dress every time she appears. In both exterior and interior scenes she is frequently posed against gorgeous displays of flowers. On one occasion at Hartfield, for instance, Emma is captured in a close up with a bowl of red roses to her right and an out-of-focus glowing candelabrum behind and to her left. As a result, the look of McGrath's film is often very appealing although sometimes his pursuit of the picturesque deteriorates into a pure kitsch that Anthony Lane compares to the artwork on "the lid of a cake tin."[24] This description is particularly apt for a high-angle tracking shot

19. Mr. Elton (Alan Cumming) helps Emma (Gwyneth Paltrow) decorate, in Douglas McGrath's *Emma*, a 1996 Miramax Films release.

of Emma and Harriet walking beneath a row of blooming rose bowers. At such moments the relationship between the tone of the film and of Austen's extremely astringent and unsentimental novel is remote indeed.

Besides being visually striking, the Miramax *Emma* is also full of lively movement. Much of Austen's mainly interior action is relocated outdoors where Emma can attend an open-air wedding reception, enjoy the pleasures of a bustling Highbury street market, window-shop at Ford's now apparently high-fashion emporium, drive her carriage, play archery with Mr. Knightley at Donwell, and join Harriet in her struggle with the gypsies. Such scenes are often very entertaining but once again demonstrate McGrath's failure to engage seriously with his source text, not because they are invented but because they repeatedly put Emma in situations that dispel the sense of claustrophobic enclosure that helps so much in Austen's novel and the ITV/A&E *Emma* to explain her irresponsible behavior.

The sense that the Miramax Emma is free to do whatever she likes is reinforced by the transformation of Mr. Woodhouse from clinging hypochondriac to affable old cove. As a result, there is no way of understanding her interference in the lives of others except as an expression of childish and irresponsible high spirits. Far from being an intelligent and troubled young woman struggling to find a role for herself in a world where she is at once privileged and subject to masculine imperatives, the Emma portrayed by Gwyneth Paltrow is a silly young thing who is as lucky as the heroine of any cheap romance to snap up such a gorgeous hunk as Mr. Knightley.

McGrath's own justification for his simultaneous glamorization and trivialization of *Emma* would probably lean heavily on the function of his film's opening sequence. First, the viewer sees a vast universe. Then a spinning globe rushes toward the camera until it fills the screen. The process of shrinking is taken even further when a pan shot reveals that the surface of the globe is covered, not with a map of the world, but with stylized watercolors of Highbury and its inhabitants. The function of this montage of images is to suggest that, for the next two hours, the audience should turn away from the problems of the real world and concern itself with what is happening in a tiny make-believe realm. Later dissolves between pretty portraits of Hartfield and Donwell, framed with doves and oak leaves, and long shots of the actual houses reinforce the message that what the viewer is being offered here is a fairytale rather than a filmed version of Austen's social realism.

Considered from this perspective, not only do the aspects of the Miramax *Emma* already discussed make sense but also the film's tendency to underplay the darker dimensions of Jane Fairfax's relationship with Frank Churchill and the social threat posed by Mrs. Elton. However, a number of other features of the film exist that cannot be accommodated under the rubric of fairytale any better than they fit into the category of faithful adaptation. Most obviously, McGrath's style is not consistently delicate and ethereal. On the contrary, it is sometimes broadly comic. McGrath, for instance, introduces a number of sight gags including a shot of Emma and Harriet positioned so that they seem to be wearing the men's hats that hang in the window of Ford's and a pan that moves from Knightley describing his home as "cosy" to a low-angle long shot of Donwell Abbey in all its glory. Even broader is the physical comedy of an embarrassed Harriet knocking over almost everything she touches while visiting the peasants' cottage. The incident when Emma hangs on to a squirming boy to stop him interrupting a potentially romantic moment between Harriet and Mr. Elton is only slightly less crude.

There are also a number of occasions when the characters created by McGrath act and speak with a lack of the refinement and delicacy demanded as much of fairytale heroes and heroines as of the leading players in a comedy of manners. At Box Hill, for instance, Mr. Knightley grabs Emma by the arm and pulls her round to face him in order to express his anger at her unkind treatment of Miss Bates. Emma herself is given to heavy-handed sarcasm and crude jokes. She tells Mr. Knightley that he is so "comical that he ought to perform in the town square" and suggests to Harriet that Mr. Elton must have found his wife "while doing charitable work in a mental infirmary." Mrs. Elton, who really has to work at appearing crass in the context of such behavior, continually pokes her finger at other characters and talks with her mouth full.

Thus, in addition to *Emma*, the BBC classic drama, the historical spectacle, the cheap romance, knockabout comedy, and the fairytale all have roles to play in shaping the Miramax *Emma*. However, many aspects of the film suggest a further important source in Amy Heckerling's *Clueless*. Cher is certainly as plausible a source for Emma's blonde hair as a fairy princess. Her vast array of clothes and accessories, her pleasure in hanging out at the street market and at Ford's, her crudely sarcastic wit, her brainless demeanor, and her love of carriage driving are other attributes of McGrath's Emma that owe much more to Cher than to the heroine created by Jane Austen. Similarly, Harriet Smith's comic clumsiness has its precedent not in anything Austen's character does but in Tai's pratfalls in *Clueless*. More generally, the upbeat and colorful style and the perpetual sunshine of the Miramax *Emma* bring to mind Heckerling's teenage Beverly Hills rather than the genteel English country village of Highbury.

One could argue that, by mixing sources so promiscuously, McGrath is, like Heckerling, bringing a postmodern sensibility to bear on Jane Austen's novel. However, he fails to provide the audience with any cues that it should adopt a stance of detached irony toward the material on the screen. On the contrary, he seeks by turns to engage viewers in the pleasures of scopophilia, the high passion of romance, the enchantment of fairytale, and the easy humor of adolescent comedy. It is therefore likely that commercial rather than artistic considerations drove McGrath's decisions regarding the structure and tone of his film and that he was trying to broaden his audience by appealing not just to the middle-aged, midbrow demographic that typically attends adaptations of the classics but also to the teenagers who went to see *Clueless*. Hence the presence in the cast of Gwyneth Paltrow, Jeremy Northam, and Ewan McGregor, best known for his performance as Renton in *Trainspotting*. McGrath's hope, as the author of the blurb on the video box puts it, was presumably that, "If you liked CLUELESS . . . You'll love EMMA."

Conclusion

The three films under examination in this essay are all based on the same novel, Jane Austen's *Emma*. Yet, they are in no sense interchangeable. What they demonstrate, then, is that there is no single approach to the problem of adapting a written text for the visual medium of film. Because so many classic novels have been transformed into television serials during the last thirty years, a certain normativeness has attached itself to the BBC classic drama format. However, the limitations of the classic drama model, with its emphasis on surface fidelity, are exposed by the ITV/A&E *Emma*. In this film, writer Andrew Davies and director Diarmuid Lawrence employ skillful scripting and imaginative cinematic techniques in order to explore some of the most complex thematic trajectories of Austen's novel, in particular its Burkean conservative social vision. Whereas most television adaptations are content to show viewers how Jane Austen's characters might talk and what her fictional world might look like, Davies and Lawrence give us some insight into the kind of film Austen might have made had the medium been invented at the beginning rather than the end of the nineteenth century.

Amy Heckerling's *Clueless* is equally successful but quite different in its approach. Most notably, the film owes nothing to the conventions of the BBC classic drama. Heckerling's characters and plot have their origins in *Emma* but, far from mirroring the surface of Austen's world, her milieu is that of the late twentieth-century American high school. And yet, although it begins in a very different place from the ITV/A&E *Emma*, *Clueless* is no less successful at developing a complex relationship with its source text. In this instance, the relationship is based on an interplay between Austen's depiction of an essentially homogeneous social and cultural landscape and Heckerling's own examination of the relativism that prevails in contemporary American culture. If the ITV/A&E *Emma* is the kind of film that Austen might have made during her actual lifetime, *Clueless* is, perhaps, the film she would have made had she been alive today.

Until recent years, the makers of BBC classic dramas did not have to concern themselves with the marketplace. However, both the ITV/A&E *Emma*, a co-production of British and American commercial television companies, and *Clueless*, a Paramount Pictures film, had to reconcile their creators' artistic aspirations with the producers' concern to make a profit. Both films fulfilled this latter goal. At the same time, though, each is clearly a much more successful work of art than almost any product of the BBC drama stable. While this demonstrates that art and profit are not necessarily antagonistic concepts, there is no doubt that a studio or corporation's concern with the balance sheet can be just as debilitating for lesser filmmakers as lack of budget undoubtedly has been for many BBC television adaptations of classic novels. A case in point is the Miramax *Emma*, a film that is far more focused on providing a star vehicle for Gwyneth Paltrow and on offering the viewer pretty images, an upbeat atmosphere, and lashings of romance than on anything substantial that Austen's novel might have to offer. Whereas Davies/Lawrence and Heckerling take *Emma* seriously, McGrath commodifies Austen, extracting from her work only what he thinks will sell.

Every novel provides different possibilities and poses different problems for the filmmaker who wants to adapt it for television or the cinema. Each attempt at adaptation, even of the same novel, will, as we have seen here, address these possibilities and problems in a different way and with a different degree of success. This essay cannot, therefore, pretend to be exhaustive in its treatment of the subject. What it does claim, however, is that, contrary to the belief of many literary purists, the process by means of which a great work of fiction is adapted into the medium of film is not necessarily parasitical, with the lesser artist feeding off the greater, but can be, as the ITV/A&E *Emma* and *Clueless* demonstrate, a creative endeavor that results in a new work of art that might even enrich appreciation and understanding of its source text.

NOTES

1 Anthony Giddings, *Screening the Novel: The Theory and Practice of Literary Dramatization* (New York: Macmillan, 1990): 166.
2 George Bluestone, *Novels into Film* (Baltimore, MD: Johns Hopkins University Press, 1957): 218.
3 Ibid.: 127.
4 Rachel M. Brownstein, "Out of the Drawing Room, Onto the Lawn," in *Jane Austen in Hollywood*, eds. Linda Troost and Sayre Greenfield (Lexington, KY: University of Kentucky Press, 1998): 14.
5 Giddings, *Screening the Novel*: 10.
6 Sue Birtwistle and Susie Conklin, *The Making of Jane Austen's "Emma"* (London: Penguin, 1995): 15–21, 27–45, 47–55.
7 Ibid.: 124.
8 Ibid.: 135.
9 Ibid.: 130.
10 See John MacCuran, *The Political Philosophy of Burke* (London: Russell and Russell Publishing, 1913; reprinted 1965).
11 Mary Wollstonecraft Shelley, *Frankenstein, or the Modern Prometheus* (1818).
12 In "Easter 1916," from *Michael Robartes and the Dancer* (1921).
13 Birtwistle and Conklin, *The Making of "Emma"*: 82.
14 Ibid.: 129.
15 Ibid.: 150.
16 Ibid.: 151.
17 "Harold Lloyd Master Seminar: Amy Heckerling." http://www.afionline.org/haroldlloyd/heckerling/script.1.html
18 Matt Wolf, "Jane Austen Goes Shopping." Interview with Amy Heckerling, *The Times* (October 19, 1995): 35.

19 Ibid.
20 Geoff Brown, Review of *Clueless*, *The Times* (October 19, 1995): 35.
21 Hugo Davenport, Review of *Clueless*, *The Electronic Telegraph* (October 30, 1995). http://www.telegraph.co.uk
22 Jonathan Romney, "One Minute Wonders of the Big Screen." Review of *Clueless*, *New Statesman* (October 20, 1995): 35.
23 Anthony Lane, "The Dumbing of *Emma*, "*The New Yorker* (August 5, 1996): 76.
24 Ibid.

11 Clues for the clueless

John Mosier

> Incidentally, this outdated method of bringing all esthetic possibilities to
> the level of one's own little conceptions and capacities . . . is very amusing
> in the argumentation of some modern American critics.
>
> Vladimir Nabokov's *Nikolai Golgol*[1]

Besides providing a certain level of intellectual entertainment, the primary objective of good adaptation, like that of any good interpretative
reading of a text, is to make viewers return to the text and reconsider it
anew. Probably the most successful adaptations of literature to film are
those which cause the viewer to conclude, after having returned to the
text and evaluated the reading that the film has delivered, that the filmmakers have a point, an interpretation which deserves a hearing. This
interpretation need not be all-inclusive, for the compressed length of a
film does not permit comprehensive coverage, nor does the nature of the
medium. However, it must carry insights that together provide a valid
understanding of the original text.

The list of points or understandings encompasses all types of insights,
many of which are personal. Friedrich Dürrenmatt's *Der Richter und Sein
Henker* (1961)[2] made so enormous an impression on me when I first read
it that it is the only book from my college years that I still possess. However, until I saw Maximillian Schell's adaptation of it, *End of the Game*
(1976) – in which the author himself appears – I had no idea just how
blackly comic the novel was, most notably the funeral in the rain,[3] whose
multiple comic possibilities Schell brings to the screen. Was this a new
addition to the text? Hardly. When I reread it, the lines were right there.
In my zeal to understand the symbolism of the story (and to untangle its
German) I had simply missed them.[4] There is room in this model for
some far stretches in adaptations: Michelangelo Antonioni's complete
makeover of the Julio Cortázar short story which came out as *Blow-up*
(1966); Bohumil Hrabal and Jiri Menzel's collaborative rewrite of the
Hrabal novella which ended up as *Closely Watched Trains* (1966); transpo-
sitions of *King Lear* (*Ran* by Akira Kurosawa, 1985) and *Wuthering Heights*

(*Onimaru* by Kiju Yoshida, 1988) from England to Japan; meditations on Casanova and Petronius by Federico Fellini; and a good many lesser but equally intriguing efforts by directors like Ridley Scott (*The Duellists*, 1978, from Joseph Conrad's *The Duel*), Leon Hirszman (*São Bernardo* from Graciliano Ramos, 1971), and R. W. Fassbinder (Fontane's *Effie Briest*, 1974).

The Dürrenmatt model is important to the controversy over film remakes of Austen's novels because clearly, for many critics, seeing Amy Heckerling's *Clueless* as, in any meaningful way, a serious adaptation of Jane Austen's *Emma* is a stretch. Jonathan Romney for example, calls the film a "one minute wonder,"[5] while Melissa Mazmanian calls the world of the film "clueless";[6] John Greenfield questions whether "clueless" aptly describes *Emma*,[7] and a number of articles in *Jane Austen in Hollywood* (1998)[8] deplore the commercialization of serious novels like *Emma*. No one denies the movie's relationship with *Emma*, as a survey of reviews confirms: Taylor Bowers of *The Christian Science Monitor*, Geoff Brown of *The Times*, Hugo Davenport of *The Electronic Telegraph*, David Denby of *The New Yorker*, Libby Gelman-Warner of *Premiere*, Rozen Leak of *People Weekly*, John Leland of *Newsweek*, Amanda Lipman of *Sight and Sound*, Andrew and Gina Macdonald of *Creative Screenwriting*, Liza Schwarzbaum of *Entertainment*, Peter Travers of *Rolling Stone*, and Bernard Weinraub and Janet Maslin of *The New York Times*, to name a representative sample, all see the parallels to greater and lesser degrees. However, the general response is that this film is simply another example of auteurial reflexivity, in which the filmmaker tries to demonstrate his or her intellectual credentials (or knowledge of trivia) by inserting clever references to all sorts of things, ranging from works of art to films, to the names of film critics the director cannot stand.

The question of filmmakers taking liberties with a literary text in order to capture its essence on film better is worth taking up, however. Regardless of whatever deficiencies Schell's adaptation of Dürrenmatt might have, it has one great virtue: the filmmaker certainly understood what the author was about, because he was able to translate both the author's jokes and his dramatic moments onto the screen. Jokes are an important index of understanding: when you understand a person's sense of humor, you understand the person, and this is particularly the case when the humor is as dry and subtle as Dürrenmatt's – or Austen's. This fact suggests that one of the basic measures used to evaluate an adaptation, is, quite simply, the extent to which the filmmaker seems to understand the author. As a standard, it is considerably more important than whether or not the film is faithful to the text or cloaks itself in proper period garb: fidelity demands an understanding. *Onimaru* is one of the very best adaptations of *Wuthering Heights* because the director apprehends the extent to which the novel treats extremes:[9] it is about love and death in the sense that it is violent and fundamental. Even though set in medieval Japan, the film demonstrates an understanding of the text that is far superior to that of the general run of costume dramas that have been passed off as films based on the novel. An analysis of a film adaptation which judges its success solely or even primarily on the extent to which the film mimics or recreates a given historical period or place is as deeply flawed as one which insists on judging according to the extent to which the film plods through the novel paragraph by paragraph. This is where so many of the BBC productions of Austen novels go awry: they plod through the novels, concerned with absolute historical fidelity in minor details, for example obsessing over whether a flower included in a scene grew in the region at the time of the novel, while missing the broader picture, the ideas, the ironies, the human essence of the novels. This point suggests a second standard: is the film any good as film, or is its interest completely a function of its relation to the text? Would anyone see one of the *Persuasion* films were they adapted from a novel by Ludwig Tieck? This question leads, quickly enough, to a third question: considered as art (the art of the cinema) are film adaptations actually possible, or does the whole process inevitably degrade the text and destroy the power of the word?

Mozart's *Don Giovanni* is not a cheapening of Molière

These are not rhetorical questions. Someone who reads Austen and then sees one of the film adaptations is in somewhat the same situation as musical audiences were when the recording industry appeared. For a very long time – well into the 1950s – there were purists who insisted that recordings were no substitute for the concert hall. At the same time, from the very first there were musicians of no mean accomplishment who were enthralled by the sound issuing from the first playback machines, and who thought the reproduced music they heard was absolutely lifelike. Clearly, this was not true: early sound recordings were only a vague approximation of the sounds they recorded, and their devotees were clearly hearing not the actual sounds themselves, but an overlay. Just as a talented musician hears the music when he reads the score, so when he heard a wax disk or a 78 rpm record, his hearing was supplemented by his memory of the actual sounds themselves. Nor are those insights to be disregarded. Thus, Idil Biret, in an interview conducted by Isabelle Battione (1997), notes that even though the quality of a cylinder recording made in Vienna in 1889 is bad, listeners hearing Brahms talk and play a fragment from the First Hungarian Dance can perceive accents that Backhaus himself passed on through his own playing.[10] Not surprisingly, therefore, these same divisions appear in the Austen readership and viewership. On the one hand, the purists insist that it is impossible to translate Austen into film, because her talents are fundamentally verbal. On the other hand, partisans defend the films that have been made simply because the films in some way echo their memories of the text.

Both sides suffer from a certain intellectual confusion. Although the purists often cloak themselves as traditional littérateurs, arguing that Jane Austen had never seen a movie, they ignore the fact that she was certainly familiar with the concept of adaptation from one form to another. Indeed, the eighteenth century was the great age of adaptation and translation, the opera (which was developed in the 1630s by Monteverdi, whose stories were derived from traditional texts such as the *Odyssey*) being an excellent case in point. Moreover, from the very first, the opera employed – and still employs – many of the same transpositionary elements as the cinema (as well as the theater), a fact that explains why there has always been a certain crossover from one form to the other, as the productions of both Luchino Visconti and Alfred Hitchcock well demonstrate. One could also adduce the period's penchant for drastic revisions and adaptations in the theater, as well as the recurrent device of passing off novels as being something else entirely rather than fictions: readers who picked up a copy of Daniel Defoe's *Robinson Crusoe* (1719) or Samuel Richardson's *Clarissa Harlowe* (1747–1748) from their bookseller were given the distinct impression that the former was a journal written by a merchant sailor named Crusoe and that Richardson had simply edited and reprinted the correspondence in the latter case. This is not to say that the contemporaneous reader actually believed she was reading non-fiction; probably some did and some did not. The point is that in these early novels, and a good many of those that came after, the authors went to some pains to present the reader with that illusion. The novel, in other words, is from the first in England a species of adaptation. Austen may not have seen any movies, but she certainly was familiar with the transposition from one form into another, and thus understood pretty clearly the idea of adaptation. Moreover, she probably understood it from her childhood: witness the adaptations made of her burlesques and her own dramatization of Samuel Richardson's *Sir Charles Grandison*. As the title of this section suggests, the idea that adaptation per se is doomed to failure is simply not sustainable.

Nevertheless, the purists do have one excellent point, although they frequently fail to state it precisely, and that is this: most of the commercial films adapted from serious works of literature are notable only for their cinematic deficiencies. They cash in on the reputation of the literary work, and thus lure audiences into seeing a film which they otherwise would have no interest in seeing. Only a limited audience would have gone to see any production of *Emma* if it had been based on some obscure novel of 1816 known only to a handful of scholars, and no one would have paid any attention to it critically. The relative commercial and critical failure of Ridley Scott's first feature film, *The Duellists*, is a case in point. Although Conrad is a well-known author, *The Duel* is one of his more obscure stories – even fewer people have read it than have read *The Secret Agent*. Consequently, although Scott's film is a whole order of magnitude better than any of the Austen films, it failed to attract much of an audience. Of course, the situation with Austen remakes is more complex than this, for Austen attracts viewers for reasons other than the quality of her stories. There exists in the reading population a sizeable audience for commercially manufactured romance novels, and particularly those set in the past, like the Regency romances or the Native American romances. That audience is certainly drawn to any movie that is advertised sufficiently to generate an awareness that it conforms to this romance model, as Paulette Richards argues Roger Michell's *Persuasion* does, in Chapter 6 of this text. A smaller portion of the population only goes to films that have some extrinsic redemptive quality, such as the connection to a literary classic, or a great event. All three cases apply in considering cinematic adaptations of Austen. Yet, with precious few exceptions, the films based on Austen's novels hardly qualify to be taken seriously even as costume dramas, much less as serious instances of the cinematic art.

Indeed, the only valid point most Austen film partisans have to make rests on the fundamental difference between the novel and the cinema (or the opera or the drama). The former is a solitary enterprise, the product of one writer. However, the latter is the product of a group. Auteurist ideas have so taken hold among intellectuals that the point is sometimes forgotten, but it is no less true. A bad film may still contain an excellent performance by an actor, or it may possess technical accomplishments in set design, costume, music, cinematography, or editing, that make it intriguing. In fact, a film is rarely so awful that there is not some point of interest in it, or some achievement which deserves mention. Each of the three established commercial film adaptations of Austen's novels (Michell's *Persuasion*, Ang Lee's *Sense and Sensibility*, and McGrath's *Emma*) do offer some minor point or points of interest. Unfortunately, the three Austen films all fail at the most basic levels; their partisans are perfect analogues to the musician who listened to a wax recording and pronounced it indistinguishable from the concert hall. Nonetheless, it is possible to discern from them certain points about Austen which are by no means devoid of interest. I ignore the television productions of Austen's films here, because as works made for television they must employ different standards, and, perhaps more significantly, because it has not been the practice in serious film criticism to consider such works. Such works should not be confused with movies produced by television studios and intended for theatrical distribution: Fellini's later films were, for instance, all funded by RAI.

A dwarf is not a child

Although *Die Blechtrommel* (*The Tin Drum*) was published in 1959, for the next eighteen years Günter Grass turned down numerous requests to adapt it to film, because, as he put it in an interview in 1978, "The candidates for the adaptation had always spoken to me about a gnome, a hideous dwarf. While the subject is – and the book spells it out very clearly – a child who has ceased to grow. Who can identify himself with a dwarf? Whereas each one of us has a childhood, that we miss and would like to have been able to prolong."[11] Or, as Bertrand Tavernier put it to Volker Schlöndorff in discussing this project: "a film with a midget in the main role is reduced to a problem of midgets." Grass let Schlöndorff make the film precisely because Schlöndorff realized that problem, and looked around until he found a child (David Bennent) to play the central role of Oskar Matzerath.

The Austen filmmakers have apparently not mastered this somewhat basic aspect of the cinema. Their actors are far too old for the roles they are supposed to play. A certain sleight of hand is always to be allowed. When Jean-Jacques Annaud cast the heroine for his version of Duras's *L'Amant*, he started with the proposition that his heroine couldn't really be fifteen or sixteen years old, the most fundamental reason being that he realized a film in which an underage female has sex with an adult male would run into a host of problems. Moreover, it is a rather minor part of the novel: Duras was not much concerned with *Lolita* when she wrote her autobiographical novel, but movie audiences would have it on their minds. That being said, however, Annaud went to great pains to find someone who was visually a very young eighteen, not out of a desire to titillate his audience, but because the Duras novel is about an older woman's memories of her transformation from girl to woman, a process which is conventionally supposed to be taking place in females of this age group. The feelings and actions appropriate to age sixteen to nineteen or twenty are inappropriate if they occur after that point (or before).

Austen was quite careful to select ages for her heroines (and their future husbands) which allowed her to focus on concerns appropriate to their age. This care is hardly surprising. Women writers are more acutely aware of this than men: certainly they are meticulous in giving us the ages of their heroines, and Austen is no less so than Eliot or Colette. Colette is quite precise about the age of Claudine, of Gilberte in *Gigi*, and of Léa in the Chéri novels. The situation that Dorothea Brooke gets herself into in *Middlemarch* is one that only a young woman of Emma's age could fashion – and still keep our sympathies. (Austen establishes Emma's age as twenty in the very first paragraph of her book; she is no longer a teenager but she is "nearly twenty-one" in an age when twenty was not yet considered legal adulthood; the youthful inexperience of these pre-adulthood years, especially in a young lady who has been spoiled, indulged, and protected, are essential to our understanding and pardoning of her behavior). For the same reason, Tolstoy's characters – and his readers – excuse Natasha's blind and impetuous attempt to run off with Anatole. We not only forgive faults in the young that we censure in their elders; we also expect to encounter such behavior. To use a currently fashionable phrase, these dilemmas are *age-appropriate*. Although great artists deal in universals, these universals are patiently assembled from a mass of particulars. The frightening vulnerability of a Jane Eyre to the sexual predations of upper-class males is an issue confronted only by women of a certain youthful naïveté: Mademoiselle Bourienne in *War and Peace* and the unnamed governess of *Anna Karenina* who precipitates Anna's visit to Moscow. Although the actual course of events corresponds rather more closely to Mademoiselle Bourienne's daydreams than to reality, Brontë's readers were obviously aware of the "unspeakable" fate that could have been Jane Eyre's. That it was unspeakable does not mean people didn't know what it was. What both Annaud and Schlöndorff understood was that it was fundamental for the central character to come across as young. The basic conflicts of the novels they adapted are only appropriate to a person of that age. In other words, casting is not a trivial affair. Although routinely downplayed by film critics, from the director's point of view and from that of the writer as well, the age of the actor playing a youthful part is vitally important.

Right off the mark, the three major Austen films fail this simple but important test. Emma Woodhouse's character is endearing and comical at a youthful twenty – and indeed clearly Mr. Knightley finds it so, or he wouldn't fall in love with her. She is also, as Austen tells us in the first line of the novel, "handsome." The meaning of "handsome" when applied to a woman was in Jane Austen's time pretty well understood. A handsome woman is one of a certain physical size: "having a fine form or figure (usually in conjunction with full size or stateliness)" is how the *Oxford English Dictionary* puts it in part 6 of the definition of "handsome" (1.1281 in the compact two-volume edition). She is not simply attractive, but her figure has certain physical properties. A less refined age might indeed call her voluptuous. (Her jealous sisters might even go so far as to call her "stout.") To Jane Austen, "handsome" was high praise. "Miss Heathcote is pretty, but not near so handsome as I expected," she wrote her sister Cassandra in her letter of January 9, 1796.[12] This remark is hardly obscure: the letter in which the phrase occurs is the first letter she wrote that remains to us, and this remark has been on the first page of every edition of Austen's letters produced in the twentieth century. *The Oxford English Dictionary* is hardly obscure either, and its examples and definitions pertaining to physical beauty under the entry for "handsome" are quite clear. Although this aspect of the word has changed slightly, today frequently being used in conjunction with a middle-aged woman, a woman "of a certain age" as the French would say, the original connotations of part 6 are still very much present in the language.

That this is the case puts Gwyneth Paltrow in rather an unenviable situation. Regardless of what one thinks of her physical appearance or her acting abilities, she hardly qualifies as "handsome," and she really looks too old to be an Emma of "nearly twenty-one," as the qualifier "nearly" suggests an age less than twenty-one, not more. This is hardly Paltrow's fault. Actors and actresses are generally at the mercy of scripts, directors, and agents. Indeed, on the basis of her work in the romantic comedy *Sliding Doors*, one might argue that she was simply miscast in this movie; probably, Paltrow would make a very passable Anne Elliot, since her actual age is very close to that of Elliot, and since she plays a shy, insecure, and indecisive personality well in *Sliding Doors*. Such observations are hotly contested by Austen partisans, who seem to be obsessive about the ordinariness of her heroines, who are often seen as deglamorized.

The mis-aging of Emma and Knightley in the film undercuts the plausibility of the plot. Austen has the two with an age difference sufficient to make Knightley sexually invisible to Emma: at twenty, she thinks of likely partners for romantic interest as being in their twenties; Knightley, at six or seven and thirty, is impossibly old. Moreover, he is her brother-in-law's brother and a family friend. She clearly has ruled him out as a romantic interest, and so do we – and this ruling out is vital to the surprise being sprung on the reader in the novel. A well-bred young woman of twenty might reasonably be supposed to remain unmoved by a man who is old enough to be her father. A woman the age Paltrow appears to be in *Emma* would hardly rule him out. Indeed, the cinematic Knightley looks only a few years older than Austen's readers would have supposed Frederick Wentworth to be in *Persuasion*.

The partisans of Paltrow, and of McGrath's film, might well retort, "but the Musgrove sisters certainly find Wentworth attractive enough," and this is true. However, the Musgroves are hardly well-bred young women. Their brother Richard was enough of a juvenile delinquent to be packed off to the navy (where, to no one's surprise, he got himself killed), their mother is a hypocrite, and their behavior is scandalous. Louisa quite literally throws herself at Captain Wentworth: "In all their walks, he had to jump her from the stiles; the sensation was delightful to her" (*Persuasion*: I.xii; Amelia in Joaquim Maria Eça de Quierós' *O crime do padre Amaro*, 1875, does the same thing so excitedly that Amaro throws himself on her). The sexual symbolism of the scene is clear enough, and the behavior it represents accounts for Anne's renewed despair. Not only does she feel herself at an age disadvantage vis-à-vis the Musgroves, as women of her age are generally inclined to do when comparing themselves with their younger sisters, but she is at a keen social and moral disadvantage as well, since she is too well brought up, too moral, to throw herself at Wentworth in public.

Similarly, the trials and tribulations of the Dashwood sisters are the problems of young women. In a woman the age Emma Thompson appears to be in Ang Lee's film, their agonized infatuations, their flings and restraints, all become preposterous. However, the worst case of age miscasting occurs in Michell's *Persuasion*. Amanda Root, although unquestionably a talented, personable actress, looks far too old to be Austen's Anne Eliot, and she is far too plain for the heroine of what is basically a tale of romantic love, an observation hotly disputed by aficionados of the film in a series of exchanges on the Jane Austen web site[13] during 1999. Most of my comments about Austen readers and critics come from reading the threads on this site, and Tara Wallace, in Chapter 7 of this book, covers the controversy on Root's unsuitability. When a group of forty college women who had not read the novels were asked to estimate the ages of the heroines of these films on the basis of still photographs (that is, how old they appeared in the film), they estimated Paltrow's age at "over twenty-five" but "less than thirty," Thompson's age at "over thirty," and Root's age as "over forty." Austen says, quite specifically, that Anne at eighteen had been a pretty girl, something the film does little to help us imagine.

The dramatic is not the cinematic

The miscasting has unfortunate repercussions in a way sometimes not noted. Austen, like Fielding, is oftentimes a dramatist *manquée* in her novels, writing entire scenes which could be lifted out and put into a play with hardly any revision at all. A notable example of this quality is Anne's tête-à-tête with her sister Mary in chapter 5 of *Persuasion*. Mary, prostrate on the sofa, delivers her litany of domestic complaints to her sister, whose repartee reveals a woman of great wit. Now the emphasis in this scene, as in many others in Austen, is on the dialogue itself, which demonstrates Mary's narcissistic hypochondria as well as Anne's sharpness:

"So, you are come at last! I began to think I should never see you. I am so ill I can hardly speak. I have not seen a creature the whole morning!"

"I am sorry to find you unwell," replied Anne. "You sent me such a good account of yourself on Thursday!"

"Yes. I made the best of it; I always do; but I was very far from well at the time; and I do not think I ever was so ill in my life as I have been all this morning – very unfit to be left alone, I am sure. Suppose I were to be seized of a sudden in some dreadful way, and not able to ring the bell!

". . . it was quite unkind of you not to come on Thursday."

"My dear Mary, recollect what a comfortable account you sent me of yourself! You wrote in the cheerfullest manner, and said you were perfectly well, and in no hurry for me; and that being the case, you must be aware that my wish would be to remain with Lady Russell to the last; and besides what I felt on her account, I have really been so busy, have had so much to do, that I could not very conveniently have left Kellynch sooner."

"Dear me! What can you possibly have to do?"

"A great many things, I assure you. More than I can recollect in a moment; but I can tell you some" [a detailed account of her dutiful activities follows].

"Oh! well"; and after a moment's pause "But you have never asked me one word about . . ." (i.v)

This dialogue is a classic instance of what in modern television would be called talking heads; and indeed, nothing should distract readers or viewers from the exchanges so we do not miss the underlying sarcasm of Anne's responses, no matter how mildly delivered. Moreover, since this is one of the first scenes in which we see Anne interacting with anyone, it is just as crucial to an understanding of her character as Othello's opening words are to his. Both are highly dramatic. However, Austen's scene is not particularly cinematic in the sense that the term is generally used: certainly the two women are doing nothing in particular, the scene itself is constricted and indoors, and the whole interchange never allows us to see any of the particulars of Mary's house. It is of course ideally suited to the cinema in one significant sense: we can see the facial expressions, the subtler gestures of each actress in a way that we cannot in the theater. Furthermore, since Austen is very much a writer who concentrates on subtle details, the scene, in theory, is almost prefabricated for the camera.

That said, it is interesting to see how Michell falls into the trap the scene poses. Unlike Liv Ullmann and Bibi Andersson in Ingmar Bergman's *Persona* (1966), where the close-up is essential to establishing character, personality, dominance, and subtle psychological interaction, Michell's actresses are too limited and plain to withstand the sort of close-up scrutiny the scene demands. Likewise, unlike Bergman's powerful, directed photography, Michell's, by contrast, is too amateurish to let the scene develop statically and visually. Instead, he fills up the scene with busyness, having the actresses occupy viewers' eyes with senseless, distracting activity. Regretfully, such cinematic ineptitude at handling character and moment seems to afflict Austen's more celebrated film adaptations. The director, lacking confidence either in the script or the actors, fills up the frame by random gestures, twitches, and distractions. It is instructive to compare the handling of such scenes in Austen with Oliver Parker's modern adaptation of Oscar Wilde's *An Ideal Husband*. Parker realizes that, for the lines to have their effect, he has to make viewers concentrate on what is being said. Therefore, instead of having the actors frisk and gambol before us, he has them largely motionless. As a result, Wilde's aphorisms are delivered with full force. Is Jane Austen's dialogue any less deserving because it is more subtle? On the contrary, her dialogue, like that quoted herein from *Persuasion*, requires the listener to focus as attentively as, or even more attentively than, that of Wilde.

That is why Austen rarely bothers to describe anything. Her novels are surprisingly empty; although her characters live in a world heavily populated with servants, those of the Woodhouses and the Elliots most particularly, these servants, and the houses in which the characters live, are rarely if ever mentioned in the kind of detail necessarily conveyed by a film image. Woodhouse frets about overtasking his coachman and his horses, but both remain almost entirely invisible. Austen's characters live in the same rarefied atmosphere as Tolstoy's Prince Bolkonsky, who casually tosses his dinner plates up into the air when he tires of them, supremely confident they will be caught – by somebody. There is a crucial difference, however. Tolstoy, like Tobias Smollett, Henry Fielding, and Laurence Sterne, builds the servants into the plot. At table, the old prince sits down not only with his daughter, but also with his architect and Princess Mary's French companion, and the latter character has an important role in the story. In the British novelists who so influenced Austen, servants are indispensable to the story. What would *Tristram Shandy* be without Uncle Toby's manservant, Trim? Or *Tom Jones* without Mistress Bridget and Black George? Claire Tomalin[14] is assuredly right in her assertion that these writers were the ones who had the greatest influence on Austen (and nowhere is that influence more obvious than in her sardonic sense of humor and in her merciless portraits of idiots and fools such as Mr. Elton and Mrs. Clay). However, in this area Austen broke completely with them. Her novels have few characters, fewer minor ones, and no servants at all. To fill the frames up with characters – as Michell does in the street, Pump Room, coffee house and musical scenes of *Persuasion*, or as McGrath does in the Christmas party scene of *Emma,* or as Thompson's *Sense and Sensibility* does with its household of servants – is both a distortion of her vision and an instance of a failed aesthetic.

The same is true when it comes to descriptions of places and things. Austen's novels are full of great houses – Hartfield, Mansfield Park, Netherfield Park, Pemberley, and so forth – but they are rarely described in great detail and certainly never with the amount of precision necessary to recreate them visually for the screen. In *Mansfield Park,* for instance, Fanny Price describes her first view of the house in totally personal terms:

> The grandeur of the house astonished, but could not console her. The rooms were too large for her to move in with ease; whatever she touched she expected to injure, and she crept about in constant terror of something or other; often retreating towards her own chamber to cry; and the little girl who was spoken of in the drawing room when she left it at night, as seeming so desirably sensible of her peculiar good fortune, ended every day's sorrows by sobbing herself to sleep. (I.ii)

In this Austen is perhaps closest to Laurence Sterne, who gives us very little idea of what the Shandy home looks like, but she is the antithesis of Fielding, Tolstoy, and Smollett, or later Dickens, each of whom describes settings in such a way that we could easily recognize them if we saw them. In contrast, Austen has little interest in such matters.

Consider the two cases which provide an unmistakable parallel. In Tobias Smollett's *Humphry Clinker,* as in *Persuasion,* the main characters all go to Bath. When the Bramble clan goes to Bath, Smollett gives us descriptions of the place, critical views of its architecture, and a hilarious disquisition on its plumbing and sanitation. What was the physical and material nature of Bath toward the end of the eighteenth century? What precisely did it look like? Read Smollett and you have an excellent idea, just as Fontane gives an excellent idea of what it was like to take an excursion on the Tegel in his great novel of Berlin in the 1870s, *L'adultera.* When Anne Elliot and her father and sister go to Bath, the situation is quite the contrary. For all the description of it Austen gives us, it could be Blackpool. Instead of physical details of place, Austen sees place totally in terms of individual and group psychology. Her emphasis is entirely on what Elliot feels, on her emotions, and on what she and the other characters say. It is true that the action moves from the street to the millinery shop and so forth, but each of these locations exists simply to establish the set, and functions in precisely the same way that a change of scene would in a play. Pemberley, of course, is the exception that proves the rule, for the distinction that Darcy makes between his rank and that of Elizabeth is personified in his grand home, a show place confirming his heritage and status, and in the distance that Elizabeth must travel to be accepted in it, or, conversely, the distance that he must travel to see her place in it. Normally, however, Austen does not number the petals of the tulip, so filmmakers are left to their own devices in deciding what edifices to erect, or flowers to depict.

Moreover, the difference between Austen's relative indifference to Bath and Smollett's delight in its particulars is hardly a function of the difference between the epistolary form Smollett uses and Austen's own third-person narration. The form chosen is irrelevant. It is the author's preference that defines the difference: Proust had the same interest in particulars as Smollett, Austen the same indifference to them as Kafka.[15] Indifference does not mean ignorance: it means choice – and it is the inability to accept that choice that makes the film adaptations such failures. The lack of interest in the background, like the lack of interest in painting pictures that allow us to visualize the place, is consistent and continuous in Austen. Perhaps Sir Walter's finances are such that his house is besieged by creditors, as Michell shows us, but Austen doesn't. We have no idea whether the house is run-down or well maintained, whether the servants are few or many, happy or mutinous. Mr. Woodhouse frets about his horses, but whether they are fat or thin is not mentioned. Austen deliberately strips out all the color, the detail, the minor characters. She presents us with highly dramatic scenes, but they seem to be played on a minimalist stage, not in the world. The filmmaker who ignores this quality of her work, who tries to fill up the frame with bustling servants and stampeding sheep, is simply betraying artistic incapacity.

Austen is not a critical realist

Perhaps another reason for this curious approach to Austen is the critical concern with social criticism. It is intriguing to note how many Austen film critics praise Michell and McGrath (in particular) for interpolating various bits and pieces of social criticism into the films, as they have more recently praised Patricia Rozema's concern with sexual politics and colonialism in *Mansfield Park*. For instance, Christine Colon[16] and David Monaghan[17] share this concern, and even otherwise perceptive critics like Andrew and Gina Macdonald[18] seem obsessed with the idea that an Austen film is improved substantially by the addition of scenes which in some way emphasize or hint at the oppressive social structure which the characters are part of. The point is made less convincingly by Suzanne Ferris.[19] Doubtless when Ang Lee has his male characters stampeding flocks of sheep, it is a statement of the same sort, only made by a more competent artist, and hence perhaps too subtle to attract attention. In other words, instead of judging the extent to which the films conform to preconceived notions about how the period should be seen, critics would do better to judge the adaptations by the extent to which they develop an interpretation of the text. Doing so would mean avoiding such questionable comments as that of Claudia Johnson: "*Emma* is a world apart from conservative fiction in accepting a hierarchical social structure not because it is a sacred dictate of patriarchy."[20] On the whole, Austen's more recent critics seem to dislike her ideas and detest her social milieu.[21]

It may be countered that this is indeed an interpretation, and thus valid, so let us consider, briefly, the notion of social criticism and Austen. A good place to begin is with Engels's letter of 1888 to Margaret Harkness, which speaks precisely to this point:

Balzac, whom I consider a far greater master of realism than all the Zolas *passés, présents et à venir*, in *La Comédie humaine* gives us a most wonderfully realistic history of French "Society," describing, chronicle-fashion, almost year by year from 1816 to 1848 the progressive inroads of the rising bourgeoisie on the society of nobles that reconstituted itself after 1815 . . . He describes how the last remnants of this, to him, model society gradually succumbed before the intrusion of the moneyed upstart, or were corrupted by him.[22]

Not to put too fine an edge on it, some Austen critics are doubly mistaken, both in their reading of Austen and in their conception of serious social criticism. Although this reading (as with many readings based on Marx or Engels) is ultimately a tedious one, the fact of the matter is that Austen is an excellent social critic in precisely the sense Engels notes. *Persuasion*, in particular, is a keen portrait of the "progressive inroads of the rising bourgeoisie on the society of nobles that reconstituted itself after 1815." For what else can Frederick Wentworth be? He began life as a man too poor and humble to be thought a fitting partner for an Anne Elliot, but here it is, ten years later: he is wealthy and desirable, and the Elliot family is clearly on the way downhill.

One could develop this insight at length with regard to Austen's other novels. However, the point is made so easily that there is little need to belabor it further. Austen's insights into the changing nature of British society, and how the upper classes were adapting to this change, are revelatory of the actual social process, and transcend the need for the superficial signs which, as Engels pointed out, characterize a lesser talent like Zola (or Frank Norris). Those who are concerned with the basis of society have no need to demonstrate a concern for the trivialities of its superstructure, and may leave it undisturbed for the eccentricities of the Austenites.

The philosophical roots of cluelessness

Just as Jane Austen is a considerably keener social critic than her critics recognize, she is also a considerably more profound thinker. Her insights into characters are not based simply on her formidable powers of observation. Her insights are superior because, like those of Sterne, they rest on a sound philosophical basis. In point of fact, she shares with Sterne a common philosophical base, the ideas of John Locke, a point routinely missed by Austen's partisans and critics alike. Curiously enough, the chief merit of Amy Heckerling's *Clueless* is that making viewers turn back to Austen's *Emma* forces us to consider precisely wherein lie the differences between the two works, which in turn leads to a consideration of the philosophical roots of this interesting modern word, "cluelessness."

Superficially, the differences between the two works are so great that it is hard to find any one element they have in common. Yet, there is clearly a point in this film when anyone who knows the novel does a comic double take as the realization sinks in that a relationship does exist. In fact, there is the best of all possible relationships, and it is conveyed by the title: it is the cluelessness of Heckerling's heroine that makes her such a stand-in for Emma Woodhouse. They are both handsome, rich, clever, young, and clueless. The film, of course, amplifies these connections by taking the two main instances from the novel. On the one hand, Emma Woodhouse adopts the younger Harriet and tries to plan her life; on the other, she is remarkably unaware of the interests of the men in the story, so much so that she confuses Mr. Elton's interest in her for an interest in Harriet. Anyone can put the texts together and work out a sort of parallelism: Dionne (played by Stacey Dash) is the counterpart to Mrs. Weston, Tai (Brittany Murphy) is Harriet, Josh (Paul Rudd) is Mr. Knightley, Christian (Justin Walker) is Frank Churchill, and so on. In fact, the level of enthusiasm (or desperation) of secondary and post-secondary English teachers in the United States being what it is today, numerous papers, some of them representing the real work of real students, are widely available online detailing the interrelationships from novel to film.

Cluelessness represents an intriguing concept, and Heckerling manipulates it in such a way that it has a rather profound impact on any understanding of the novel. Because Cher's cluelessness is highly specific, primarily a deficiency which relates to things sexual, she is quite capable of negotiating grade changes with her teachers, organizing successful class projects, bringing lost souls together, and shopping. When it comes to the interests and behaviors of men, however, she is completely at sea. Thus, we might differentiate her cluelessness from simple obliviousness or lack of intelligence, and observe that it represents a blind spot with respect to an awareness of how men perceive women sexually, how they respond to them, and what they expect from them. Nor is her cluelessness gender-specific for she is also clueless about the sexual drives of Harriet/Tai. What makes the density more intriguing is that it goes hand in hand with a certain narcissistic surety as to what male (and female) sexuality really involves. Cher has complete confidence in her ability to seduce Christian, and goes through all the necessary steps, and yet she has missed the most obvious fact about him, which is that his sexual preferences disincline him to any carnal interests in women.

Therefore, although in theory cluelessness could well be ascribed to almost anything (a knowledge of computers, sewing machines, or cooking, for example), Heckerling restricts it fairly rigidly to this one area, leaving just enough spillover to keep the definition from becoming schematic (interestingly enough, the one spillover is driving, where Cher is not simply clueless, but helpless; driving, particularly on the freeway system, apparently is used to represent an exclusively male activity). Now of course this somewhat restricted definition is not at all a bad characterization of Emma Woodhouse. Although, like Cher, she has no experience with the opposite sex at all, this inexperience does not keep her from telling Harriet precisely what men expect and want in their relations with women. The humor in both film and novel is exactly the same, as it depends on an ironic and aware audience who see the situation much more clearly than does the heroine.

However, the concept, despite its colloquialism, not only takes us deeply into Emma Woodhouse, but provides a sort of touchstone for an understanding of other Austen characters as well. Indeed, the Elliot family in *Persuasion* constitutes a basic manual of cluelessness (so too the Musgroves). There too, the lack is exclusively concerned with matters sexual: Sir Walter's vanity is nicely matched by Mrs. Musgrove's emotional neediness: just as he is oblivious to how silly he is in his posturing, so is she oblivious to how comical her grief is over her son. The two families exhibit a remarkably complementary set of dysfunctional traits, all of them involving the concept of cluelessness. While in this particular novel it is easy to lose track of the heroine amidst all the posturing of the other characters, Anne Elliot, although older, has the same malady. She is completely unable to comprehend what Austen diagnoses as the schizophrenia of the single female, or the extent to which she had let herself be trapped in her role within the family. Her cluelessness is, assuredly, manifested in a completely different way, but then, she is a character in another novel. Cluelessness is a useful concept for articulating the difficulties of two other celebrated heroines, Clarissa Harlowe and

Dorothea Brooke, both of whom have posed critics considerably difficulties over the years, but both of whom share with Emma Woodhouse
youth, social class, and a similar curious blindness to male sexuality.
While a discussion of the parallelisms here is beyond the scope of this
essay, the parallels suggest that the term "clueless" is a rather useful one,
not simply restricted to one character in one Austen novel.

This is all very well, the skeptical reader might say, but the term needs
more than that to justify it, since Jane Austen was rather unaware of
American slang of the late twentieth century, and, in any event, what use
is it in evaluating film adaptations of novels? The answer, quite simply, is
that the general case had been perfectly described by John Locke in his
Essay Concerning Human Understanding:

> Our ignorance great. Our knowledge being so narrow, as I have shown, it will
> perhaps give us some light into the present state of our minds if we look a little into
> the dark side, and take a view of our ignorance; which, being infinitely larger than
> our knowledge, may serve much to the quieting of disputes, and improvement
> of useful knowledge; if, discovering how far we have clear and distinct ideas, we
> confine our thoughts within the contemplation of those things that are within
> the reach of our understandings, and launch not out into that abyss of darkness,
> (where we have not eyes to see, nor faculties to perceive anything), out of a
> presumption that nothing is beyond our comprehension. However to be satisfied
> of the folly of such a conceit, we need not go far. He that knows anything, knows
> this, in the first place, that he need not seek long for instances of his ignorance.
> The meanest and most obvious things that come in our way have dark sides, that
> the quickest sight cannot penetrate into.[23]

The young, however, frequently do make this confusion, which in Lockean terms is easily understood: if their education has been deficient, that
is, they have been deprived of enough data, then their reasoning, although
logical, will be deficient, it being the task of education not simply to teach
reasoning, but to provide the developing child with the basic information
about the world that he or she needs in order to comprehend it.

In modern times, those are insulting words, but the whole thrust of
developing eighteenth-century society in Britain (and also in the colonies
of North America) seemed dedicated to keeping women clueless, and,
to judge by a great deal of anecdotal evidence, it was extremely successful, largely because the social controls were so subtle. In contrast, as the
Viscomte Valmont and Madame de Meurteuil noted with regard to Cécile
Volanges, the attempt to ghettoize young women, by placing them in,
say, a convent, only predisposed them for any sort of vice. Obviously,
these characters from Laclos[24] are exaggerating, but the mere fact of
segregation in and of itself suggested to those at the receiving end that they
were being shut off from important areas of experience. If they did not,
as does Cécile Volanges, instantly become habituated to vice as a result,

they consciously felt themselves to be sheltered and inexperienced, and behaved accordingly (as does Madame de Tourvel; she is certainly clueless, but the context of the novel seems to suggest she is also uniquely so). "Cluelessness," in other words, is not simply ignorance, although in some senses it may seem that way, just as it sometimes seems to be the opposite of *prudentia*, and it can certainly be accompanied by a sort of general naïveté, as seems to be the case with Jeremy Melford's sister in *Humphry Clinker*. However, in all these cases it is a primarily English (or anyway Anglo-American) deficiency: Emma Bovary is young, impulsive, and self-centered. Life does not work out for her. But she is hardly clueless.

Constructing arguments based on heroines abstracted from European literature is a risky business. However, the evidence from personal experience narratives supports this idea of a relatively unique Anglo-American cluelessness when it comes to sexuality to such an extent that we may cautiously accept it as being true. The problem with Clarissa, Emma, and Dorothea is not just that they have been excluded from getting this information, it is the combination of lack of knowledge with supreme self-confidence that, on the contrary, they know all there is that needs to be known on the subject. Emma has no idea what Mr. Elton and Mr. Knightley are thinking, but she is convinced she can read them like a book. In reality, she does not have a clue as to their desires, their motivations, or their behavior. It is the combination of the two qualities, the tension between thinking one knows everything while in reality knowing hardly anything, that defines cluelessness. But is cluelessness some great defect? Austen apparently does not think so. Based on what happens to her heroines, and to Emma in particular, it would seem that she sees this as a normal part of the growth process of young women. That she actually did so seems rather clear from her advice to Fanny Knight, in her letter to Fanny of January 18, 1814.[25]

If one accepts the idea that this concept organizes the heroine's behavior, so that her development through the novel is the passage from cluelessness to cluefulness, one has a very convenient means of interpreting not only what is going on in the novels, but the degree to which the various cinematic adaptations of the novels may be said to enhance a reading of the texts themselves. Unfortunately, using this yardstick, the recent film adaptations fall rather short, as a simple illustration makes clear. In *Emma*, the first indication of this problem occurs when Emma takes to herself all the credit for Miss Taylor marrying Mr. Weston:

Mr. Weston was a man of unexceptionable character, easy fortune, suitable age and pleasant manners; and there was some satisfaction in considering with what self-denying, generous friendship she had always wished and promoted the match . . .

"...I made the match myself. I made the match, you know, four years ago; and to have it take place, and be proved in the right, when so many people said Mr. Weston would never marry again, may comfort me for anything." (I.i)

She goes on to gloat over the matchmaking, calling it "the greatest amusement in the world" (I.i). To this self-congratulatory merriment, Mr. Knightley firmly and censoriously replies:

"...if...your making the match, as you call it, means only your planning it, your saying to yourself one idle day, 'I think it would be a very good thing for Miss Taylor if Mr. Weston were to marry her,' and saying it again to yourself every now and then afterwards, – why do you talk of success? Where is your merit? – what are you proud of? – you made a lucky guess; and that is all that can be said." (I.i)

It is very clear from this passage that Mr. Knightley is quite correct, because Austen reinforces his remark through Emma's repetition of her bragging phrase, "I made the match." However, as the scene is played out in the McGrath version, although Mr. Knightley still gets his piece of the dialogue with the critical remarks in it, there is no context of authorial voice to suppose he is right and Emma is wrong; there is only the equality of dual voices competing for audience sympathy, and, by the standards of modern high school youths, he sounds "way harsh."

Both here and in the Roger Michell's *Persuasion*, a rather complex state of oppositions – cluelessness – is simplified until it become something quite different. Austen's main vehicle for character revelation is, as I have noted, dramatic, but not particularly cinematic. Cluelessness is revealed not through description or action, but through dialogue. Nor is this surprising: when Sterne used Lockean ideas of how the mind works as the basis for *Tristram Shandy*, his preferred method of revelation was dramatic. It was not, however, pictorial: we know everything about Walter and Toby Shandy except what they look like. Locke was after all primarily concerned with how the mind operates, as was Austen, and this dramatic (although not cinematic) opposition, which makes Austen much more like Hesse or Musil than Tolstoy or the Brontës, has proven to be an exceedingly tough problem for the current generation of filmmakers, although both Heckerling and Rozema seem to have some basic idea of what the intellectual issues are.

Austen still awaits

For all its considerable virtues, *Clueless* has some serious problems, the two most fundamental being the drastic change in the characters of Emma's father and of her future husband. Although several critics have pointed out that there are echoes of the Austen characters in their modern equivalents, the truth of the matter is that Cher's father is not the functional equivalent of Mr. Woodhouse, being neither sickly nor particularly doting. Cher clearly considers her father lost without her attention, but to the viewer's eye he is quite capable of getting along by himself (he is a competent businessman) and simply takes pleasures in these domestic signs of her affection. If anything, her care suggests the dutiful daughter trying to replace her absent mother. Thus, the film sets up a caring relationship, but in terms of plot needs, this relationship is nonfunctional. Nor is there any trace at all in the film of the fundamental dilemma that propels Emma's conflict. In Austen's novel, Emma has decided that she cannot abandon her father, and thus she cannot consider marriage, as he would – in her mind, and in his selfishly self-projected image – be unable to function without her. In fact, Mr. Woodhouse controls his daughters through his ailments and eccentricities. Like Sir Walter Elliot, he is a hypochondriacal monster of the type that Chekhov delineates so perfectly in *Three Years* and "A Hard Case." However, Emma, as his daughter, does not see this. She follows one typical adaptive pattern of the abused child, and simply denies herself a normal future life as a sexually active woman, mother, and wife. By turning Mr. Woodhouse into Mel, Heckerling essentially guts the psychological plumbing of the novel. She eliminates the inner conflict that accounts for Emma's cluelessness (the unconscious acting out of her father's wishes) and that explains her incessant matchmaking (clearly a reaction to her enforced bachelorhood). Mrs. John Knightley's emulative hypochondria makes clear how successful Mr. Woodhouse has been in blocking the normal development of his daughters. The absence of this extreme character as well as the absence of the father as grasping in *Clueless* turns Cher's behavior into merely a series of cute devices.

The other transformation which completely derails the workings of the novel is changing Mr. Knightley into a college student, a shift which greatly reduces the sexual tension of the novel as well as drastically alters the turning point of the plot, when Emma realizes that her jealous rage at the thought of Mr. Knightley marrying someone else means that she must love him herself. In the film, Josh's interest in Cher is telegraphed to us early on, so the element of surprise in their eventually pairing off is totally lost. In fact, the surprise at the end is for Austen cognoscenti: readers of *Emma* expect a wedding and get one, but the concluding wedding shot reveals the teachers rather than Cher and Josh as bride and groom, and Cher's direct address to the viewers: "As if! I'm only sixteen! This is Beverley Hills, not Kentucky."

By contrast, Emma's realization comes as somewhat of a surprise to the reader. As American film critic Roger Ebert, in his original 1995 review of the film for the *Chicago Sun-Times*, remarked, intriguingly, in both *Persuasion* and *Emma*, for a very long time the reader has no idea how the story will be resolved, or, in the case of the former novel, no real idea of the subject.[26] Although many Austen film critics write as though Emma's marriage to Knightley was apparent from the first page of the novel, the case is quite the contrary. Based on Austen's opening comments, and much of what follows, a reader would logically assume that the course of the novel will be one in which emphasis is on the heroine being taken down a notch or two, that, in other words, it will be more like *Evelina*, and Austen's heroine – rich, spoiled, and out of control – resonates with the heroines of Eliza Haywood's cautionary tales. Austen was, of course, well acquainted with Fanny Burney's *Evelina*, judging from her many references to it.[27] It seems probable she had looked at *The Female Spectator*, given the latitude allowed in her reading. Certainly, Emma's cluelessness has parallels with Eliza Haywood's *Fantomina*, as well as with many other of the female characters she brings up in her work. The point is intriguing because Austen has the same disregard for physical detail that Haywood has in the little tales, which are interspersed among the essays in *The Female Spectator*.

Knightley's role, as a "sensible man," seems to be that of the wiser, older debunker of youthful foolishness:

> Mr. Knightley, in fact, was one of the few people who could see faults in Emma Woodhouse, and the only one who ever told her of them: and though this was not particularly agreeable to Emma herself, she knew it would be so much less so to her father, that she would not have him really suspect such a circumstance as her not being thought perfect by every body. (I.i)

Emma's discovery of her love for Knightley, and the resulting marriage, far from being preordained and obvious, comes as a series of delightful surprises, as does Wentworth's declaration of love for Anne in *Persuasion*. However, since Knightley has become a serious college student in *Clueless*, marriage is not a natural prospect, and, in fact, the ending of the film leaves the outcome of the relationship pending, a question to be resolved by time and maturation. This loss of Austen's final focus is inevitable since the essential psychological components have all been eliminated, and the film can therefore not play to the same ending.

The other serious problem with *Clueless* is the dependence on voice-over narration. Although sanctified in film by its use in *Citizen Kane* (1941) and then in such classics as *Last Year at Marienbad* (1961), in all too many cases it is used exactly as Ridley Scott's producers envisioned it in the studio cut of *Blade Runner* (1982) – as an aid for the cinematically challenged.[28] Although it has been argued that Heckerling's use of voice-over narration is a way of establishing the essentially subjective nature of the novel, in that we only see what Emma sees, this hardly stands up to serious examination. Austen was well aware of the various subjective narrative devices, and used them. If she had wanted to write a novel in the manner of *Jane Eyre*, she would have done so. In other words, voice-over narration is the equivalent of a self-conscious first-person narrator in a story. It is appropriate in a story like *L'Amant* or *Coup de grâce* because in both stories there is a storyteller. It is hardly appropriate to *Emma*, where the whole point is that the heroine's mind is completely impervious to this sort of self-consciousness.

Moreover, the novel is hardly subjective. Even the feeblest of readers must guess that Mr. Elton's crostic is addressed not to Harriet but to Emma. Besides, from the very first, Austen as narrator is very much present in the novel, which is subjective only in the sense that Austen does not constantly whack us across the fingers with her ruler and tell us what to think, in the manner of Charles Dickens or George Eliot. In actual fact, the narrative and point of view is tightly controlled in exactly the same fashion that Colette likes to control it – in such a way that the actual unraveling of the story comes as a sudden shock.

One of the differences noted above is worth a second glance. There's no particular reason for Cher to be so clueless about sex. It is true that she has apparently been deprived of a mother's influence, but American girls in the last quarter of the twentieth century hardly learned about sex from their mothers. Emma's character, on the other hand, is sympathetic because we see rather quickly the problem with which she has been saddled. To suggest that we forgive her only because she is young and likable – or lovable, as Trilling says in his introduction to the book[29] – is to miss a key element of the novel. We forgive her because we sympathize with her dilemma, and because we realize that her misbehavior – even her mean-spiritedness – is largely a function of her attempt to cope with that dilemma.

She becomes an incessant matchmaker because that is the only form of sexuality open to her to experience. Even her maltreatment of elderly Miss Bates can be seen easily enough as a reaction to life with her aging – and equally silly – father, whom she unfailingly humors and apologizes for. So too her dislike of Jane Fairfax, who is like her in many respects, but, owing to her situation, has been forced to apply her skills. As a result, the poor young woman is a walking reminder to Emma of all her personal failings and character flaws, and, understandably enough, she detests her. Jane Fairfax is thus important: she reminds us of how

Emma could be, were circumstances to enable her to grow. Significantly, this character is missing from the film; not surprisingly, there is nothing in Cher that suggests any real talent. Emma, although she behaves badly, is not a fundamentally silly person. Cher, although good-hearted, seems fundamentally an idiot. If there is a serious and intelligent young woman hidden there, it is extremely well hidden. Consequently, *Clueless*, although highly entertaining, never really gets past its basic insights about age-appropriate behavior and the idea of cluelessness. Considered as a piece of filmmaking, it is substantially better than any of the three Austen films discussed so far, but this is hardly saying very much.

In most respects, *Mansfield Park* (1999) is the only Austen film to date that can be taken seriously on its own grounds. Rozema, like Heckerling, clearly perceives the importance of the ages of the characters, as well as the importance of a certain visual appeal for her characters. Like Heckerling, she is the only one of the group who seems to comprehend Austen's viciously comic sense of humor. Strangely, Austen's critics and partisans seem oblivious to this, although R. W. Chapman devoted a third of the preface to his edition of her letters to listing examples – back in 1933.[30] Moreover, Rozema has always been an interesting filmmaker. *I've Heard the Mermaids Singing*, her first feature work,[31] was not very good, but it was intriguing, and it suggested a director with some talent.

What in *I've Heard the Mermaids Singing* was a somewhat ingenuous undercurrent of lesbianism soon became rather overt. The college professor heroine of *When Night Is Falling* abandons her sexually acrobatic and apparently rather satisfying relationship with the man who loves her and runs off with a young woman who works in a circus. She's neither repressed nor brutalized; she simply falls in love with a woman instead of a man. Rozema's explicit approaches to woman-on-woman sexual attractions have made her an extremely controversial director. Consequently, there has been a certain shock evinced at Rozema undertaking the *Mansfield Park* project, given the rather sexually explicit nature of her films. Yet, no one objected when Martin Scorsese turned from the blood and gore of *The Taxi-Driver* to make Edith Wharton's delicately chaste love story *The Age of Innocence*.[32] Similarly, although some of Austen's more intelligent readers have been aghast at what Rozema does with the action (and the character of Fanny Price), their comments betray more a lack of cinematic sophistication than serious judgment: Pialat's life of Van Gogh is no less interesting because the director gives his subject two ears instead of the usual one. Indeed, just as Austen's readers are often literally terrified that she has sex on her mind, her viewers are even more aghast at the idea that anyone might think that she did. The problem with *Mansfield Park* actually has little to do with Rozema. The film is not all that interesting simply because the novel is not all that interesting either. Historically, the argument could be made that it has been the least read of Austen's novels. It lacks the neatly tied-up plots which characterize *Sense and Sensibility* and *Pride and Prejudice*, nor does it have the psychological sophistication of *Persuasion* and *Emma*. By reworking it, and reworking bits and pieces from Austen into it, Rozema has made an interesting film. Nevertheless, this sort of license, although intriguing, relegates the film to a special corner of the world. Admittedly, it is a corner with some valuable property in it: Federico Fellini's "adaptations" of *The Satyricon* (1969) and Casanova's *Memoirs*, together with Luis Buñuel's 1967 *Belle de Jour* (it is always interesting to find out how few people have actually read Kessel's novel) come to mind. The fact remains, however, that the only two Austen films of any serious interest are pretty far out on the periphery. Moreover, given the respectful attention accorded a film like Michell's *Persuasion*, the situation is not likely to change any time soon.

The film world still awaits a cinematic recreation of Austen that translates her satiric perceptions of society into cinematic terms a modern audience can respond to, yet without losing the heart of what has made her works endure. No film has yet been made worthy of Austen.

NOTES

1 In the corrected edition (New York: New Directions, 1961): 128.
2 Friedrich Dürrenmatt, *Der Richter und sein Henker*, ed. William Gillis (Boston, MA: Houghton Mifflin, 1961).
3 Ibid.: 58–61. *End of the Game* has been shown on TV but is not available on video.
4 In the novel itself, see, in particular, the passage beginning with "Herr Schmied is sicher in den Tropen, nicht wahr, Herr Bärlach?" (7) and also "Bärlach hatte lange im Auslande gelebt und sich in Konstanopel und dann in Deutschland als bekanter Kriminalist hervorgetan" (5), the latter of which is left out of the film, presumably because it would make no sense as the time frame has been moved from post-war to the present day.
5 Jonathan Romney, "One Minute Wonders of the Big Screen." Review of *Clueless, New Statesman* (October 20, 1995): 35.
6 Melissa Mazmanian, "Reviving *Emma* in a Clueless World: The Current Attraction to a Classic Structure," *Persuasions: Journal of the Jane Austen Society of North America*, Occasional Papers 3 (Fall 1999).
7 John Greensfield, "Is Emma Clueless? Fantasies of Class and Gender from England to California," *Topic: A Journal of the Liberal Arts* 48 (1997): 31–38.

8 Linda Troost and Sayre Greenfield (eds.), *Jane Austen in Hollywood* (Lexington, KY: University of Kentucky Press, 1998).

9 *Onimaru* (Emily Brontë's *Wuthering Heights*), Director Kiju Yoshida, 1988.

10 Johannes Brahms, *Complete Works for Piano Solo* (Naxos 8.501201) 45.

11 The quotes in this paragraph are taken from the Press Kit to the film *The Tin Drum*, and Grass's comment was verified as accurate by Dorothea Moritz, the editor of *Kino* (Berlin) during the 1979 Cannes Film Festival, where the film was entered in competition.

12 *Jane Austen's Letters*, edited by Deirdre Le Faye, New Edition (Oxford: Oxford University Press, 1995): 1.

13 www.pemberley.com

14 Claire Tomalin, *Jane Austen: A Life* (London: Viking, 1997).

15 For Proust's obsessive interest in physical particulars, see Harold Nicholson's recollections of Proust quizzing him about his work in 1919 at Versailles in *Peacemaking 1919* (New York: Grosset and Dunlap, 1965): 125–126. Kafka could hardly have done so well in his job had he not been a careful and accurate observer – see the remarks by Meno Spann, *Franz Kafka* (Boston: Twayne, 1976): 32–33.

16 Christine Colon, "The Social Constructions of Douglas McGrath's *Emma*: Earning a Place on Miss Woodhouse's Globe," *Persuasions: Journal of the Jane Austen Society of North America*, Occasional Papers 3 (Fall 1999).

17 David Monaghan (ed.), *Jane Austen in a Social context* (London: Macmillan, 1981); see also Chapter 10 in this volume.

18 Andrew Macdonald and Gina Macdonald, "Updating *Emma*: Balancing Satire and Sympathy in *Clueless*," *Creative Screenwriting* (Summer 2000): 22–30.

19 Suzanne Ferris, "Emma Becomes Clueless," in *Jane Austen in Hollywood*, eds. Troost and Greenfield: 128.

20 Claudia L. Johnson, *Jane Austen: Women, Politics, and the Novel* (Chicago: University of Chicago Press, 1988): 127.

21 See, for instance, Deborah Kaplan, *Jane Austen among Women* (Baltimore, MD: Johns Hopkins University Press, 1992); Margaret Kirkham, *Jane Austen: Feminism and Fiction* (Totawa, NJ: Barnes and Noble, 1983); Laura G. Mooneyham, *Romance, Language, and Education in Jane Austen's Novels* (New York: St. Martin's Press, 1988).

22 In *Marx and Engels on Literature and Art*, eds. Lee Baxandall and Stefan Morawski (St. Louis: Telos Press, 1973): 115. The 3rd ed. of *Great Soviet Encyclopedia* cites the Harkness letter for typicality (25.690).

23 John Locke, "Of the Extent of Human Knowledge," in his *Essay Concerning Human Understanding* (1690): IV, iii.

24 Choderlos de Laclos, *Les Liaisons dangereuses*, trans. and ed. Douglas Parmée (Oxford: Oxford University Press, 1995).

25 Letter 108 in Le Faye, *Letters*: 278–279.

26 http://www.suntimes.com/ebert/ebert_reviews/1995/10/1003853.html

27 The most suggestive one is reported by Tomalin, *Jane Austen*: 148.

28 *Citizen Kane*, Director Orson Welles. Radio-Keith-Orpheum, 1941; *Last Year at Marienbad*, Director Alain Resnais, 1961; *Blade Runner*, Director Ridley Scott. Warner Brothers, 1982.

29 Lionel Trilling, Introduction to *Emma* (Boston: Houghton Mifflin, 1957): v–xxvi.
30 *The Novels of Jane Austen*, ed. R. W. Chapman, 6 vols. (Oxford: Oxford University Press, 1933). Le Faye reprints this preface in her edition of the *Letters*: ix–xii.
31 Canadian Films, 1987.
32 *Taxi-Driver*, Columbia, 1976; *Age of Innocence*, Columbia, 1993.

Questions for discussion

GENERAL ISSUES

1 The short essays by Gaylene Preston, a respected film director and screenwriter, and Roger Gard, a noted Austen scholar, sum up the differences in attitudes toward film productions of Jane Austen novels. What is lost according to Gard? What is gained according to Preston?

2 What additional perspective does Kate Bowles add to the controversy? How does the Internet's egalitarianism change the popular interpretation of Jane Austen's works? Has Austen truly been "commodified"?

3 Do you agree with Harriet Margolis's argument in "Janeite Culture: What Does the Name 'Jane Austen' Authorize?" that Austen's novels and current women's romance novels may be compared? What reasons justify such a comparison? Do you accept her argument that both types of novels express use-value ethics?

4 Although Margolis acknowledges that a male audience exists for Austen novels and films, her essay seems to assume a predominantly female audience. How is this definition of readership related to Margolis's explanation of Jane Austen's popularity?

5 Is being a Janeite good or bad? What do you think Austen would say?

6 In " 'Such a Transformation!' Translation, Imitation, and Intertextuality in Jane Austen On Screen," Jocelyn Harris raises the question of whether or not cinematic versions of Jane Austen can ever be faithful translations. If they cannot, should filmmakers even try to be true to her, or should they choose imitation with all the freedom and creativity implied by the term?

7 How far should creativity carry filmmakers? At what point should creativity be reined in by the "patterns" of plot, character, and theme provided by Jane Austen? Give a specific example to support your answer.

8 Can ancient distinctions between translation and imitation help modern filmmakers wishing to relocate Jane Austen to the screen? If they opt for deferential translation, do they lose the chance for

intertextual referencing and modernity in all its forms? If, on the other hand, they opt for imitation, will they lose that vision of reality, that sense of community, that sheer familiarity that we enjoy in Jane Austen's work? If they reach out for "relevance," do they drift away from their original?

9 In making a film based on a novel, which do you think is more significant: what is added or what is left out? Consider examples of each in Austen films.

10 Discuss ways in which a historical perspective can be introduced into a film without patronizing the audience by oversimplifying or using clichés.

MANSFIELD PARK

1 In "Two *Mansfield Parks*: Purist and Postmodern," Jan Fergus suggests that a modernization of *Mansfield Park* parallel to Amy Heckerling's *Clueless* might work well. Do you agree or disagree? What might make updating this particular novel difficult? If you think the novel could be updated in a film, where would you set it? How would you modernize the novel's characters – especially Fanny Price? Into what social positions would you place the characters? How would you update some of the central incidents, such as the visit to Sotherton, the production of *Lovers' Vows*, Fanny's return home to Portsmouth, Henry Crawford's elopement with Maria?

2 Rozema's film gets rather brief consideration in the Fergus essay. Do you think Fergus underrates that film? In particular, does its focus on the way slave exploitation deforms those at Mansfield deserve more attention and praise as an interpretation of the novel?

3 Fergus thinks that the BBC *Mansfield Park* succeeds as no other film or television version does in finding ways to translate Austen's narrative voice faithfully to the screen, as if this criterion is the most vital for an adaptation. In your view, what are the most important criteria in adapting Austen to the screen? How does the adaptation you like best meet those criteria?

4 In the 1990 film *Metropolitan*, privileged teenaged socialites in Manhattan discuss the moral dilemmas of characters in the novel *Mansfield Park*, partly displacing their own dilemmas. If you know the film, could it in any sense be called an adaptation of *Mansfield Park*? Why or why not?

5 Fergus contends that when Austen's novels are reduced to romantic plots they are caricatures of themselves. What gets left out when

an Austen adaptation focuses on the plot elements of the central romances? Are these omitted elements really essential?

SENSE AND SENSIBILITY AND PERSUASION

1   In terms of Penny Gay's argument about the filmmaker's and the
    audience's historical positioning in *"Sense and Sensibility* in a Post-
    Feminist World: Sisterhood is Still Powerful," what is the function of
    caricatured characters such as Fanny Dashwood in *Sense and Sensi-
    bility* or Sir Walter Elliot in *Persuasion*?
2   What place does the depiction of explicit sexual activity have in an
    Austen film? Should lovers even kiss? (They don't in the novels.)
3   In "Regency Romance Shadowing in the Visual Motifs of Roger
    Michell's *Persuasion*," Paulette Richards defines "shadowing" as the
    idea that our reactions to a film are changed by our previous knowl-
    edge of other roles that the actors have played. For example, Hugh
    Grant's earlier roles inevitably shape our perception of him as a desir-
    able male character in *Sense and Sensibility*. How powerful does this
    shadowing seem to be? Do you believe that this kind of shadowing
    changes your own reactions to a character?
4   Richards also argues that films do not draw simply on the literary text
    they are based on but also on conventions, patterns, and traditions
    familiar to their audience, conventions the filmmakers hope will bring
    to life a work far distant from the viewer's experience. Richards talks
    about this phenomenon in *Persuasion*. Do you find it at work in other
    Austen films?
5   In "Filming Romance: *Persuasion*," Tara Wallace argues that Austen's
    Persuasion is about two romances: one between hero and heroine, the
    other between nation and navy. What in Michell's film exploits this
    vision? To what degree does Wallace believe *Persuasion* succeeds or
    fails in depicting these dual interests? What challenges face a film-
    maker adapting a much-loved literary text to the screen? Which Jane
    Austen do you believe is the real Jane Austen, the conservative or
    the radical? What in the BBC productions promotes the image of the
    conservative? What in Rozema's *Mansfield Park* and *Persuasion*, and
    later in *Clueless*, promotes the image of the radical?

EMMA

1   Hilary Schor, author of "Emma, Interrupted: Speaking Jane Austen
    in Fiction and Film," clearly values McGrath's adaptation for its com-
    plicated use of voice-over narration. What does she mean by this? Do

you find such degrees of complication and ambiguity in the narrative voice of other Austen films?

2 David Monaghan, in contrast to Hilary Schor, believes the McGrath *Emma* the weakest of the *Emma* productions. What is his justification for this stance? Which of the two do you find more convincing?

3 Films, by their very nature, will show more than novels. This is particularly true of adaptations of Austen's novels since they are extremely sparing in descriptions of the physical features of characters and locations. The three versions of *Emma* discussed by David Monaghan in "*Emma* and the Art of Adaptation" take very different approaches to the problems and opportunities posed by descriptive gaps in their source text. Distinguish between the films in terms of their approach to the visualization of character and location and then suggest some other ways in which a filmmaker might productively give visual form to Austen's novels.

4 Fidelity to the source text is frequently cited as a major goal for adaptators of classic novels. Considering Monaghan's discussion of the three approaches to adaptation, identify some of the major problems with the notion of fidelity. Do you agree that those who are not "faithful" to their source must inevitably betray it?

5 Monaghan is fairly unsympathetic to adaptations of Austen's novels made according to the conventions of the BBC classic drama house style. Taking into account Jan Fergus's much more positive treatment of the BBC version of *Mansfield Park* and your own knowledge of other adaptations, consider whether his essay underestimates the achievement of the BBC classic drama approach to Austen's novels.

6 Monaghan discusses some of the scenes that both Davies/Lawrence and McGrath invent in their filmic versions of *Emma*. Assuming that you were charged with adapting *Emma* to the screen, what scenes might you invent and why?

7 Monaghan is less sympathetic to the Miramax *Emma* than a number of other critics. What differing assumptions make it possible for different critics to arrive at such different views of the same film? Are some critics more "right" than others or are all interpretations equally valid?

8 Compare the dismissive comments made by Monaghan's essay about versions of Austen's novels that foreground the romance elements in her plots with Harriet Margolis's and Paulette Richards's much more affirmative approaches to those who "harlequinize" Austen. Does the Margolis essay convince you that the Monaghan essay displays a debilitating masculine cultural snobbery toward an essentially female genre?

9 Monaghan describes the Emma portrayed by Gwyneth Paltrow as "silly." Amy Heckerling uses the same term about Cher. How would you judge the intelligence and/or behavior of the two characters? Are they similar in their silliness or are there better ways of describing one or both of them?

10 What does Monaghan's essay teach you about the ways in which film-makers deal with the problems of creating social context in a visual medium?

11 Monaghan's essay touches on the relationship between commercial imperatives and artistic goals. Do you think he is correct to claim that the two goals can be reconciled? If so, can you identify some films that succeed as works of art and box office hits?

PRIDE AND PREJUDICE

1 In her essay "Reimagining Jane Austen: The 1940 and 1995 Film Versions of *Pride and Prejudice*," Ellen Belton argues that the screen history of *Pride and Prejudice* provides "a unique opportunity to consider the way in which an adaptation reflects its own particular historical moment." In light of other analyses in this volume, such as Penny Gay's discussion of *Sense and Sensibility*, is such a reinterpretation of the original an inevitable component of any adaptation? To what extent does this constitute a betrayal of the original? To what extent does it contribute to our better enjoyment and understanding of it?

2 Responding to Roger Gard's assertion that no recent adaptation of Austen's novels is a work of art in its own right, Belton poses the following question: "Why undertake an adaptation of Austen, or … of any respected literary work, at all?" Based on your own experience of literature and literary adaptation, how would you answer this question?

3 Rozema's *Mansfield Park*, like Lewis Gilbert's classic film *Alfie* (1966), relies on a roguish voice-over with a satiric wit to guide viewer response. How does this approach fit with Schor's theory of narrative voice? Would she approve or disapprove? Why?

4 Jan Fergus's analysis of the 1999 *Mansfield Park* outlines a series of strategies by which a screen adaptation may find equivalents for Austen's narrative voice. Do you agree that these strategies are the right ones? To what extent can such strategies be seen to operate in either of the versions of *Pride and Prejudice* that Belton discusses?

5 Belton argues that the MGM *Pride and Prejudice* anticipates the anti-isolationism of numerous US films that were made during World

War II. Consider how other films from this period that do not take the war as their actual subject also indirectly support the Allied cause.

6 Writing in the 1950s, George Bluestone praises the MGM *Pride and Prejudice* for its embodiment of "the dialectics of Jane Austen's central ironies." Belton says that the BBC *Pride and Prejudice* develops another kind of dialectic at the expense of those ironies. What is she referring to? Do you agree with her analysis?

7 Belton says that the 1995 version of *Pride and Prejudice* caters to its audience's desire for the heroine to "have it all." What does "having it all" in this film actually mean? How does this definition of happiness differ from the definition in Austen's novel?

NORTHANGER ABBEY

1 Given the way in which *Northanger Abbey* self-consciously comments on the culture of its own time, it is perhaps surprising that it was the only one of Austen's completed novels that was not adapted for the screen in the 1990s. Assuming that you had the opportunity of writing the screenplay for such an adaptation, how would you go about it?

CLUELESS

1 What qualities of *Clueless* and *Mansfield Park* (1999) set them apart from the other Austen films and make John Mosier in "Clues for the Clueless" declare them slightly more interesting as films? He is not a purist seeking exact duplication of the literary text. What fault does he find with them, nonetheless?

2 Ironically, Mosier attacks purists and nonpurists alike, seeking filmic recreation of Austen that translates her satiric perceptions of society into cinematic terms a modern audience can respond to, yet without losing the heart of what has made her works endure. He argues that no film has yet been made worthy of Austen. What is his basis for this argument? Why does he take exception to the BBC productions? What does he feel they lack? What would be his conception of an ideal Austen film?

Filmography

1940 (MGM): *Pride and Prejudice*
Scriptwriters Aldous Huxley and Jane Murfin
Director Robert Z. Leonard
Producer Hunt Stromberg
Cast: Lawrence Olivier (Mr. Darcy), Greer Garson (Elizabeth Bennet), Maureen O'Sullivan (Jane Bennet), Edmund Gwenn (Mr. Bennet), Edna May Oliver (Lady Catherine de Bourgh)
Category: Feature Film

1948 (BBC): *Emma*
Scriptwriter Judy Campbell
Director/Producer Michael Barry
Cast: Judy Campbell (Emma Woodhouse), Ralph Michael (Mr. Knightley), Oliver Burt (Mr. Woodhouse), Gillian Lind (Miss Bates), Richard Hurndall (Mr. Elton), Daphne Slater (Harriet Smith)

1949 (NBC): *Pride and Prejudice*
Scriptwriter Samuel Taylor
Director Fred Coe
Cast: Madge Evans (Elizabeth Bennet), John Baragrey (Mr. Darcy)

1950 (NBC): *Sense and Sensibility*
Scriptwriter H. R. Hays
Director Delbert Mann
Producer Fred Coe
Cast: Madge Evans (Elinor Dashwood), Cloris Leachman (Marianne Dashwood), Chester Stratton (Edward Ferrars), John Baragrey (Colonel Brandon), and Larry Hugo (John Willoughby)

1952 (BBC): *Pride and Prejudice*
Scriptwriter Cedric Wallis
Director/Producer Campbell Logan
Cast: Daphne Slater (Elizabeth Bennet), Peter Cushing (Mr. Darcy), Milton Rosmer (Mr. Bennet), Gillian Lind (Mrs. Bennet), Ann Baskett

(Jane Bennet), Prunella Scales (Lydia Bennet), Helen Haye (Lady Catherine de Bourgh)
Category: Miniseries

1954 (NBC): *Emma*
Scriptwriters Martine Bartlett and Peter Donat
Cast: Felicia Montealegre (Emma Woodhouse), Peter Cookson (Mr. Knightley), Stafford Dickens (Mr. Woodhouse), Roddy McDowall (Mr. Elton), Sarah Marshall (Harriet Smith)

1958 (BBC): *Pride and Prejudice*
Scriptwriter Cedric Wallis
Director/Producer Barbara Burnham
Cast: Jane Downs (Elizabeth Bennet), Alan Badel (Mr. Darcy), Hugh Sinclair (Mr. Bennet), Miriam Spencer (Mrs. Bennet), Susan Lyall Grant (Jane Bennet), Phyllis Neilson-Terry (Lady Catherine de Bourgh)
Category: Miniseries

February–April 1960 (BBC): *Emma*
Scriptwriter Vincent Tilsley
Director/Producer Campbell Logan
Cast: Diana Fairfax (Emma Woodhouse), Paul Daneman (Mr. Knightley), Leslie French (Mr. Woodhouse), Gillian Lind (Miss Bates), Raymond Young (Mr. Elton), Perlita Smith (Harriet Smith)
Category: Miniseries

August 1960 (CBS): *Emma*
Scriptwriter Clair Roskam
Director John Desmond
Producer John McGiffert
Cast: Nancy Wickwire (Emma Woodhouse)

1960–1961 (BBC): *Persuasion*
Scriptwriters Michael Voysey and Barbara Burnham
Director/Producer Campbell Logan
Cast: Daphne Slater (Anne Elliot), Paul Daneman (Frederick Wentworth), Fabia Drake (Lady Russell), George Curzon (Sir Walter Elliot), Derek Blomfield (William Elliot)
Category: Miniseries

1967 (BBC): *Pride and Prejudice*
Scriptwriter Nemone Lethbridge
Director Joan Craft
Producer Campbell Logan

Cast: Celia Bannerman (Elizabeth Bennet), Lewis Fiander (Mr. Darcy), Polly Adams (Jane Bennet), Lucy Fleming (Lydia Bennet)
Category: Miniseries. 118 minutes

1971 (BBC): *Sense and Sensibility*
Scriptwriter Denis Constanduros
Director David Giles
Producer Martin Lisemore
Cast: Joanna David (Elinor Dashwood), Robin Ellis (Edward Ferrars), Ciaran Madden (Marianne Dashwood), Richard Owens (Colonel Brandon), Clive Francis (John Willoughby), Isabel Dean (Mrs. Dashwood)
Category: Miniseries. 200 minutes

1971 (Granada [ITV]): *Persuasion*
Scriptwriter Julian Mitchell
Director/Producer Howard Baker
Cast: Ann Firbank (Anne Elliot), Bryan Marshall (Captain Wentworth), Basil Dignam (Sir Walter Elliot), Morag Hood (Mary Musgrove)
Category: Miniseries. BBCV4996. 225 minutes

1972 (BBC): *Emma*
Scriptwriter Denis Constanduros
Director John Glenister
Producer Martin Lisemore
Designer Tim Hervey
Costume Designer Joan Ellacott
Music Tom McCall
Dances Geraldine Stephenson
Cast: Doran Godwin (Emma Woodhouse), John Carson (Mr. Knightley), Donald Eccles (Mr. Woodhouse), Debbie Bowen (Harriet Smith), Constance Chapman (Miss Bates), Robert East (Frank Churchill), Ania Maarson (Jane Fairfax)
Category: Miniseries. BBCV4997. 257 minutes

1979 (BBC and A&E): *Pride and Prejudice*
Scriptwriter Fay Weldon
Director Cyril Coke
Producer Jonathan Powell
Cast: Elizabeth Garvie (Elizabeth Bennet), David Rintoul (Mr. Darcy), Sabina Franklyn (Jane Bennet), Moray Watson (Mr. Bennet), Judy Parfitt (Lady Catherine de Bourgh)
Category: Miniseries. BBCV4960. 259 minutes. Shorter video version: BBCV4331

1981 (BBC; on general release 1985): *Sense and Sensibility*
Scriptwriters Alexander Baron and Denis Constanduros
Director Rodney Bennett
Producer Barry Letts
Cast: Irene Richards (Elinor Dashwood), Tracey Childs (Marianne Dashwood), Bosco Hogan (Edward Ferrars), Robert Swann (Colonel Brandon), Diana Fairfax (Mrs. Dashwood), Peter Woodward (John Willoughby), Donald Douglas (Sir John Middleton)
Category: Miniseries. BBCV4332 (1985). 174 minutes

1983 (BBC): *Mansfield Park*
Scriptwriter Ken Taylor
Director David Giles
Producer Betty Willingale
Cast: Sylvestra Le Touzel (Fanny Price), Nicholas Farrell (Edmund Bertram), Anna Massey (Aunt Norris), Robert Burbage (Henry Crawford)
Category: Miniseries. BBCV433. 261 minutes

1986 (BBC and A&E): *Northanger Abbey*
Scriptwriter Maggie Wadey
Director Giles Foster
Producer Louis Marks
Cast: Katharine Schlessinger (Catherine Morland), Peter Firth (Henry Tilney), Googie Withers (Mrs. Allen), Robert Hardy (General Tilney)
Category: Telefilm. BBCV4378. 90 minutes

April 1995 (BBC and WGBH). *Persuasion*
Scriptwriter Nick Dear
Director Roger Michell
Producers Rebecca Eaton, George Faber, Fiona Finlay
Cast: Amanda Root (Anne Elliot), Ciaran Hinds (Captain Wentworth), Corin Redgrave (Sir Walter Elliot), Sophie Thompson (Mary Musgrove)
Category: Telefilm and a Sony Picture Classics feature film. BBCV5616. 102 minutes (less than half the length of the 1971 version)

July 1995 (Paramount): *Clueless*
Scriptwriter and Director Amy Heckerling
Producers Scott Rudin and Robert Lawrence
Cast: Alicia Silverstone (Cher), Paul Rudd (Josh), Stacey Dash (Dionne), Brittany Murphy (Tai)
Category: Feature film

September 1995 (BBC) and January 1996 (A&E): *Pride and Prejudice*
Scriptwriter Andrew Davies
Director Simon Langton
Producer Sue Birtwistle
Cast: Jennifer Ehle (Elizabeth Bennet), Colin Firth (Mr. Darcy), Susannah Harker (Jane Bennet), Benjamin Whitrow (Mr. Bennet), Barbara Leigh-Hunt (Lady Catherine de Bourgh), David Bamber (Mr. Collins), Crispin Bonham-Carter (Mr. Bingley)
Category: Miniseries. BBCV5702. 301 minutes (reportedly 10 million British viewers tuned in to the last six televised episodes and 40 percent of the UK's total viewing audience watched the last episode)

December 1995 (Mirage/Columbia): *Sense and Sensibility*
Scriptwriter Emma Thompson
Director Ang Lee
Executive Producer Sidney Pollack
Producer Lindsay Doran
Cast: Emma Thompson (Elinor Dashwood), Hugh Grant (Edward Ferrars), Kate Winslet (Marianne Dashwood), Alan Rickman (Colonel Brandon), Greg Wise (John Willoughby), Imogen Stubbs (Lucy Ferrars), Gemma Jones (Mrs. Dashwood)
Category: Feature film

July 1996 (Miramax): *Emma*
Scriptwriter and Director Douglas McGrath
Producer Patrick Cassavetti
Cast: Gwyneth Paltrow (Emma Woodhouse), Jeremy Northam (Mr. Knightley), Toni Collette (Harriet Smith), Ewan McGregor (Frank Churchill)
Category: Feature film

November 1996 (Meridian [ITV]) and February 1997 (A&E): *Emma*
Scriptwriter Andrew Davies
Director Diarmuid Lawrence
Producer Sue Birtwistle
Cast: Kate Beckinsale (Emma Woodhouse), Mark Strong (Mr. Knightley), Samantha Morton (Harriet Smith), Raymond Coulthard (Frank Churchill), Prunella Scales (Miss Bates), Olivia Williams (Jane Fairfax)
Category: Telefilm. 2 hours

1999 (Miramax): *Mansfield Park*
Scriptwriter/Director Patricia Rozema
Producers David Aukin, Bob and Harvey Weinstein, et al.
Music Lesley Barber

Costume design Andrea Galer

Cast: Frances O'Connor (Fanny Price), Embeth Davidtz (Mary Craw-
ford), Jonny Lee Miller (Edmund Bertram), Alessandro Nivola (Henry
Crawford), Harold Pinter (Sir Thomas Bertram), Lindsay Duncan
(Lady Bertram/Mrs. Price), Sheila Gish (Aunt Norris), Victoria Hamil-
ton (Maria Bertram), Justine Waddell (Julia Bertram), James Purefoy
(Tom Bertram), Hugh Bonneville (Mr. Rushworth)

Category: Feature film. 112 minutes

2000 (Bollywood): *I Have Found It* (*Kandukondain Kandukondain*), an
adaptation of *Sense and Sensibility*

Scriptwriter/Director Rajin Menon

Cast: Tabu, Aishwarya Rai, and Mammouty

Tamil with English subtitles.

India. 150 minutes

2004 (Granada): *Northanger Abbey*

Scriptwriter Andrew Davies

Producer London Weekend Television

Cast: Ioan Gruffudd (Henry Tilney), Anthony Hopkins (General
Tilney), Kate Beckinsale (Eleanor Tilney), Anna Paquin (Catherine
Morland)

Bibliography

Allen, Brooke. "Jane Austen for the Nineties." *The New Criterion* (September 1995): 15–22.

Alleva, Richard. "Emma Can Read, Too." Review of *Sense and Sensibility. Commonweal* (March 8, 1996): 15–18.

Amis, Martin. "Jane's World." *The New Yorker* 71 (January 8, 1996): 31–35.

Anderson, Pat. Review (*Persuasion*). *Films in Review* (September 1995).

Andreae, Christopher. "In Defense of the Perfect *Pride and Prejudice.*" *Christian Science Monitor* (December 6, 1995): 16.

Ansen, David. "*Emma.*" *Newsweek* 128 (July 29, 1996): 67.

"In This Fine Romance, Virtue Is Rewarded." Review of *Persuasion. Newsweek* (October 9, 1995): 78.

"*Mansfield Park.*" *Newsweek* 134 (November 29, 1999): 96.

Arnold, Judith. "Women Do." In *Dangerous Men and Adventurous Women: Romance Writers on the Appeal of the Romance.* Ed. Jayne Ann Krentz. Philadelphia: University of Pennsylvania Press, 1992: 133–139.

Auerbach, Nina. "Jane Austen's Dangerous Charm: Feeling as One Ought about Fanny Price" *Women and Literature* 3 (1983): 208–223.

"Austen Anew" in Talk of the Town. *The New Yorker* 71 (August 28, 1995): 55 (2).

Austen, Jane. *The Novels of Jane Austen.* 6 vols. Ed. R. W. Chapman. Oxford: Oxford University Press, 1933.

Ballaster, Ros. "Adapting Jane Austen." *English Review* 7 (September 1996): 10–13.

Bander, Elaine. "Jane Austen and the Uses of Silence." In *Literature and Ethics; Essays Presented to A. E. Malloch.* Eds. Gary Wihl and David Williams. Montreal: McGill-Queen's University Press, 1988: 46–61.

Barnes, Julian. Review of *Mansfield Park* (1983). *The Observer* (November 13, 1983): 48.

Beals, Jennifer. "Gwyneth Paltrow." *Interview* 25 (September 1995): 118 (4).

Bellafante, Ginia. "Sick of Jane Austen Yet?" *Time* 147 (January 15, 1996): 66.

Benedict, Barbara M. "Sensibility by the Numbers: Austen's Work as Regency Popular Fiction." In *Janeites: Austen's Disciples and Devotees.* Ed. Deirdre Lynch. Princeton: Princeton UP, 2000: 63–86.

Bentley, Hale. "The English Novel in the Twentieth Century: #3: Televising a Classic Novel for Students." *Contemporary Review* 268 (March 1996): 141–143.

"The Best Cinema of 1995." *Time* 146 (December 25, 1995/January 1, 1996): 139.

Birtwistle, Sue, and Susie Conklin. *The Making of Jane Austen's Emma*. London: Penguin, 1995.

The Making of Pride and Prejudice. London: Penguin, 1995.

Blake, Richard A. "Plain Jane." Review of *Sense and Sensibility*. *America* 174 (March 9, 1996): 20–21.

Blandford, Linda. "Beware the Insidious Grip of Darcy Fever." *New York Times* (January 14, 1996): H31.

Boggs, Joseph M., and Dennis W. Petrie. *The Art of Watching Films*. London: Mayfield Publishing, 2000.

Bowers, Faye. "No Longer Clueless about Austen's Clout." *Christian Science Monitor* (April 5, 1996): 7.

Brosh, Liora. "Consuming Women: The Representation of Women in the 1940 Adaptation of *Pride and Prejudice*." *Quarterly Review of Film and Video* 17 (2000): 147–159.

Brown, Geoff. Review of *Clueless*. *The Times* (October 19, 1995): 35.

Buss, Robin. "The Writing's on the Screen." *Times Educational Supplement* (February 16, 1996): B10 (2).

Caughie, John, and Kevin Rockett. *The Companion to British and Irish Cinema*. London: Cassill and The British Film Institute, 1996.

Chapman, R[obert]. W[illiam]. *Jane Austen: A Critical Bibliography*. Oxford: Clarendon Press, 1953.

"Cinema" (The Best of 1995). *Time* 146 (December 25, 1995): 139.

Clausen, Christopher. "Jane Austen Changes Her Mind." *The American Scholar* (Spring 1999): 1785.

"Thoroughly Modern Austen." *The Wilson Quarterly* 23 (Autumn 1999): 100.

Clerc, Susan. "Estrogen Brigades and 'Big Tits' Threads: Media Fandom Online and Off." In *Wired Women: Gender and New Realities in Cyberspace*. Eds. L. Cherny and E. Reba Weise. Seattle: Seal Press, 1996. Reprinted in *The Cybercultures Reader*. Eds. David Bell and Barbara M Kennedy. London: Routledge, 2000: 214–229.

Cohen, Rich. "High School Confidential" (Amy Heckerling Interview). *Rolling Stone* (September 7, 1995): 53.

Collins, James. "Jane Reactions." *Vogue* (January 1996): 70–72.

Colon, Christine. "The Social Constructions of Douglas McGrath's *Emma*: Earning a Place on Miss Woodhouse's Globe." *Persuasions: Journal of the Jane Austen Society of North America*. Occasional Papers 3 (Fall 1999).

Constantine, David. "Finding the Words: Translation and the Survival of the Human." *Times Literary Supplement* (May 21, 1999): 15.

Copeland, Edward, and Juliet McMaster, eds. *The Cambridge Companion to Jane Austen*. Cambridge: Cambridge University Press, 1997.

Corliss, Richard. "But I'm a Cheerleader." *Time* 155 (January 24, 2000): 69.

"To Live and Buy in L.A.: *Clueless*." *Time* (July 31, 1995): 65.

"A Touch of Class." *Time* (July 29, 1996): 74–75.

Corrigan, Timothy. *Film and Literature: An Introduction and Reader*. Upper Saddle River, NJ: Prentice Hall, 1999.

"Costume Drama in Light and Darker Guise." *London Times* (November 25, 1996).

Coughlan, Sean. "Surf and Sensibility." *Times Educational Supplement* (September 22, 1995): 2.18.

Crabb, Michael. "Another Jane Austen Novel Heads for the Big Screen." *Info Culture* 25 (May 1999).

Crowther, Bosley. "'Pride and Prejudice,' a Delightful Comedy of Manners, Seen at the Music Hall." *New York Times* (August 9, 1940): 38.

Cunningham, Kim. "Austen-tatious." *People Weekly* 45 (March 4, 1996): 106.

Davies, Andrew. "Austen's Horrible Heroine." Discussion of *Emma*. *The Electronic Telegraph* (November 23, 1996). Online at http://www. telegraph.uk
    "Picture the Scene." *Times Educational Supplement* (September 22, 1995): 2.10–11.

Dear, Nick. *Persuasion: A Screenplay*. London: Methuen, 1996.

Denby, David. *"Clueless." New Yorker* 28 (August 7, 1995): 71.

Díaz de Chumaceiro, Cora L. "Induced Recall of Jane Austen's Novels: Films, Television, Videos." *Journal of Poetry Therapy* 14 (2000): 41–50; (September 6, 2001) <http://journals.ohiolink.edu/pdflinks/010806101642238458.pdf>

Dick, Bernard F. *Anatomy of Film*. New York: St. Martin's Press, 1994.

Doherty, Tom. "Clueless Kids." *Cineaste* 21 (Fall 1995): 14–17.

Dowd, Maureen. "Will Jane Nix Pix?" *New York Times* 144 (August 24, 1995): A15, A23.

Duckworth, Alistair. Review of *Mansfield Park*. *Eighteenth-Century Fiction* 12.4 (July 2000): 565–571.

Duncan, Rebecca Stephens. *"Sense and Sensibility*: A Convergence of Readers/ Viewers/Browsers." In *A Companion to Jane Austen Studies*. Eds. Laura Cooner Lambdin and Robert Thomas Lambdin. Westport, CT: Greenwood, 2000: 1–16.

Dunlap, Lynn. "The Cinematographic Novel: Specularity and Narrative Authority in 'The House of Mirth,' 'Mansfield Park' and 'Villette,'" Dissertation: University of Washington, 1992.

Ebert, Roger. Review of *Emma*. *Chicago Sun-Times* (August 1996). Online at http://www.suntimes.com
    Review of *Persuasion*. *Chicago Sun-Times* (October 27, 1995). Online at http://www.suntimes.com
    Review of *Sense and Sensibility*. *Chicago Sun-Times* (December 13, 1996). Online at http://www.suntimes.com

Eggleston, Robert. "*Emma*, the Movies, and First-Year Literature Classes." *Persuasions: Journal of the Jane Austen Society of North America*. Occasional Papers 3 (Fall 1999).

Eisenbach, Helen. "The Clued-in Director" (Heckerling). *Interview* 29 (July 1999): 42.

"Emma Thompson: A Close Reading." *The New Yorker* 71 (August 28, 1995): 55–56; 69 (November 15, 1993): 46 (3).

Favret, Mary A. "Being True to Jane Austen." In *Victorian Afterlife: Postmodern Culture Rewrites the Nineteenth Century*. Eds. John Kucich and Dianne F. Sadoff. Minneapolis: University of Minnesota Press, 2000: 64–82.

Fergus, Jan S. *Jane Austen and the Didactic Novel: Northanger Abbey, Sense and Sensibility, and Pride and Prejudice*. New York: Macmillan, 1983.

Jane Austen: The Literary Career. New York: Macmillan, 1990.

Jane Austen: A Literary Life. New York: Macmillan, 1991.

"'My Sore Throats, You Know, Are Always Worse than Anybody's': Mary Musgrove and Jane Austen's Art of Whining." *Persuasions: Journal of the Jane Austen Society of North America* (December 15, 1993): 139–147.

"Sex and Social Life in Jane Austen's Novels." In *Jane Austen in a Social Context*. Ed. David Monaghan. New York: Macmillan, 1981: 66–85.

Ferguson, Moira. "*Mansfield Park*: Slavery, Colonialism, and Gender." *The Oxford Literary Review* 13 (1991): 1–2, 118–139.

Fields, Suzanne. "Losing it at the Movies with Jane Austen." *Insight on the News* 12 (March 25, 1996: 48.

Finch, Casey, and Peter Bowen. "'The Tittle-Tattle of Highbury': Gossip and the Free Indirect Style in *Emma*." *Representations* 31 (Summer 1990): 1–18.

Flynn, Christopher. "'No Other Island in the World': *Mansfield Park*, North America, and Post-Imperial Malaise." *Symbiosis* 4 (2000): 173–186.

Folkenflick, Robert. "'Homo Alludens' in the Eighteenth Century." *Criticism* 24 (1982): 218–231.

Forde, John Maurice. "Janespotting." *Topic: A Journal of the Liberal Arts* 48 (1997): 11–21.

Foster, Jennifer. "Austenmania, EQ, and the End of the Millennium." *Topic: A Journal of the Liberal Arts* 48 (1997): 56–64.

Fraiman, Susan. "Jane Austen and Edward Said: Gender, Culture, and Imperialism." *Critical Inquiry* (Summer 1995).

Francke, Lizzie. Review of *Sense and Sensibility*. *New Statesman and Society* (February 23, 1996): 43.

Franklin-2. "The Best Dramatic Series in Television History." Included in IMDB website for *The Forsyte Saga* (1967). http://us.imdb.com/Title? 0061253. September 25, 2000.

Fritzer, Penelope Joan. *Jane Austen and Eighteenth-Century Courtesy Books*. Westport, CT: Greenwood, 1997.

Fuller, Graham. "Cautionary Tale." *Sight and Sound* (March 1996): 21–23.

"Shtick and Seduction." *Sight and Sound* (March 1996): 24.

Gallager, John Andrew. *Film Directors on Directing*. London: Praeger, 1989.

Gard, Roger. *Jane Austen, Emma and Persuasion*. London: Penguin, 1985.

Jane Austen's Novels: The Art of Clarity. New Haven, CT: Yale University Press, 1992.

"Lady Susan and the Single Effect." *Essays in Criticism: A Quarterly Journal of Literary Criticism* 4 (October 30, 1989): 305–325.

"*Mansfield Park*, Fanny Price, Flaubert and the Modern Novel." *English: The Journal of the English Association* 38 (Spring 1989): 160, 1–33.

Gay, Penny. "A Changing View: Jane Austen's Landscape." *Sydney Studies in English* 15 (1989–1990): 47–62.

Jane Austen and the Theatre. Cambridge: Cambridge University Press, 2002.

"Theatricals and Theatricality in *Mansfield Park*." *Sydney Studies in English* 13 (1987–1988): 61–73.

Gelman-Warner, Libby. *"Clueless." Premiere* 9 (October 1995): 46+.
"Girlfriendly Fire" *(Sense and Sensibility). Premiere* 9 (March 1996): 54 (2).
Giddings, Anthony, Keith Selby, and Chris Wensley. *Screening the Novel: The Theory and Practice of Literary Dramatization.* Houndmills, NY: Macmillan, 1990.
Giles, Jeff. "Earth Angel." Review of *Emma. Newsweek* (July 29, 1996): 66–68.
Gleiberman, Owen. "A Novel Romance: An Adaptation of Jane Austen's *Mansfield Park* Gets to the Heart of a British Family's Tangled Relationships with Love and Money." *Entertainment Weekly* (November 19, 1999): 108.
Gliatto, Tom. "Pride and Prejudice." *People Weekly* 45 (January 15, 1996): 13.
Gooneratne, Yasmine. "Making Sense: Jane Austen on the Screen." *Intercultural Encounters: Studies in English Literatures.* Eds. Heinz Anton and Kevin L. Cope. Heidelberg: Carl Winter, 1999: 259–66.
Grant, Steve. *"Mansfield Park." Sunday Times* (London) (April 2, 2000): sec. 9, 8.
Grassin, Sophie. "Emma, c'est elle." *L'Express International* (February 29, 1996): 61.
Gray, Beverly. *"Sense and Sensibility*: A Script Review." *Creative Screenwriting* 4 (Summer 1997): 74–82.
Greenfield, John R. "Is Emma Clueless? Fantasies of Class and Gender from England to California." *Topic: A Journal of the Liberal Arts* 48 (1997): 31–38.
Gritten, David. "A Match Made in Hollywood." *Daily Telegraph* (October 16, 1995): 41–42.
Grunwald, Henry. "Jane Austen's Civil Society." *Wall Street Journal* (October 2, 1996): A14, A16.
Hall, Anthea. "Jane's People." *The Sunday Telegraph* (November 13, 1983): 15.
Halperin, John. "The Novelist as Heroine in *Mansfield Park*: A Study in Autobiography." *Modern Language Quarterly* 2 (June 1983): 136–156.
Handelman, David. "Through the Looking Glass." *Premiere* 10 (August 1997): 72–77.
Hannon, Patrice. "Austen Novels and Austen Films: Incompatible Worlds?" *Persuasions: The Journal of the Jane Austen Society of North America* 18 (1996): 24–32.
Harding, D. W. "Regulated Hatred: An Aspect of the Work of Jane Austen." *Scrutiny* 8 (1939–1940): 346–362.
"Harold Lloyd Master Seminar: Amy Heckerling" <http://www.afionline.org/haroldlloyd/ heckerling/script.1.html>
Harris, Jocelyn. "Anne Elliot, the Wife of Bath, and Other Friends." *Women and Literature* (1983): 273–293.
    "The Influence of Richardson on *Pride and Prejudice*." In *Approaches to Teaching Austen's Pride and Prejudice.* Ed. Marcia McClintock Folsom. Modern Language Association of America, 1993: 94–99.
    Jane Austen's Art of Memory. Cambridge: Cambridge University Press, 1989.
    "Jane Austen and the Burden of the (Male) Past: The Case Reexamined." In *Jane Austen and Discourses of Feminism.* Ed. Devoney Looser. New York: St. Martin's Press, 1995: 87–100.

"Review of *Sense and Sensibility, Persuasion,* and *Clueless.*" *Eighteenth-Century Fiction* 8 (1996): 427–430.

Hays, Matthew. "Everything's Coming up Rozema." *The Advocate* (January 18, 2000): 95.

Hearty, Kitty Bowe. "Nick Cassavetes, Doug McGrath and Billy Bob Thornton" (Breakthroughs '97). *Us* (April 1997): 78 (2).

Heckerling, Amy. "Classic Scene: *Clueless.*" *Premiere* 15 (October 2001): 102.

Heyns, Michiel. "Shock and Horror: The Moral Vocabulary of *Mansfield Park.*" *English Studies in Africa: A Journal of the Humanities* 29 (1986): 1–18.

Hoberg, Tom. "Her First and Last: Austen's *Sense and Sensibility, Persuasion,* and Their Screen Adaptations." In *Nineteenth-Century Women at the Movies: Adapting Classic Women's Fiction to Film.* Ed. Barbara Tepe Lupack. Bowling Green, OH: Popular Press, 1999: 140–166.

Hochman, David. "Gwyneth Paltrow." *Us* (August 1996): 40 (6).

Holly, Grant I. "Emmagrammatology." *Studies in Eighteenth-Century Culture* 19 (1989): 39–51.

Hopkins, Lisa. "Emma and the Servants." *Persuasions: Journal of the Jane Austen Society of North America.* Occasional Papers 3 (Fall 1999).

Hough, Graham. "Narrative and Dialogue in Jane Austen." *Critical Quarterly* 12 (1970): 201–230.

Hummel, Kathryn. "Austen's English Roses." *Meanjin* 56 (September – December 1997): 735 (3).

Hunt, Liz. "Get Down and Party with Mr. Darcy." *The Independent* (July 19 1996): s4 (2).

The International Dictionary of Films and Filmmakers. 3rd ed. Chicago: St. James Press, 1997.

Iverson, Annemarie. "Emma Beauty, Circa 1996." *Harper's Bazaar* (November 1996): 126.

Jacobs, Laura. "Playing Jane." *Vanity Fair* 59 (January 1996): 74 (6).

James, Caryn. "Austen Tale of Lost Love Refound." Review of *Persuasion. New York Times* (September 27, 1995): c18.

"An *Emma* Both Darker and Funnier." *New York Times* (February 15, 1997): 28.

"Jane Austen." *Entertainment Weekly* (Special Year-End Double Issue: Best of 1995) (December 29, 1995): 40–41.

"Jane Austen in the 21st Century Audio Archive." www.humanities.wisc. edu/archives

"Jane Austen: Nearly Two Centuries after her Death, Directors Got Some Sense and Embraced her Sensibility." *People Weekly* 44 (December 25, 1995): 73.

"Jane Austen's *Emma.*" *The Washington Post.* www.washingtonpost. com/wp-srv/ style/longterm/movies/videos/emma.htm

Jerome, Helen. *Pride and Prejudice: A Sentimental Comedy.* Garden City, NY: Doubleday, 1936.

Johnson, Brian. "Austen Powers: Rozema's Version of *Mansfield Park.*" *Maclean's* 112 (November 22, 1999): 106–108.

"*Sense and Sensibility.*" *Maclean's* 108 (December 25, 1995): 86–87.

Johnson, Claudia L. "The Authentic Audacity of Patricia Rozema's *Mansfield Park* (1999)." *Times Literary Supplement* (December 31, 1999): 16–17.

Kaplan, Deborah. "Mass Marketing Jane Austen: Men, Women, and Courtship in Two of the Recent Films." *Persuasions: Journal of the Jane Austen Society of North America* 18 (December 16, 1996): 171–187.

Katz, Richard A. "The Comic Perception of Jane Austen." In *Voltaire, the Enlightenment and the Comic Mode: Essays in Honor of Jean Sareil.* Ed. Maxine G. Cutler. New York: Peter Lang, 1990: 65–87.

Kauffmann, Stanley. "Division, Delay, Drag – *Persuasion.*" *The New Republic* 213 (October 9, 1995): 26–27.

"*Emma.*" *The New Republic* (August 19/29, 1996): 38–39.

Review of *Sense and Sensibility. The New Republic* (January 8, 1996): 34–35.

Kearney, J. A. "Jane Austen and the Reason–Feeling Debate." *Theoria: A Journal of Studies in the Arts, Humanities and Social Sciences* 75 (May 1990): 107–122.

"Tumult of Feeling, and Restraint, in *Mansfield Park.*" *Theoria: A Journal of Studies in the Arts, Humanities and Social Sciences* 71 (May 1988): 35–45.

Kennedy, Dana. "*Sense and Sensibility.*" *Entertainment Weekly* (December 22, 1995): 60–61.

King, Andrea. "How TV's *Clueless* Gets its Look." *Glamour* 94 (November 1996): 92.

Klein, Michael, and Gillian Parker, eds. *The English Novel and the Movies.* New York: Ungar, 1981.

Kroll, Jack. "Jane Austen Does Lunch." *Newsweek* 126 (December 18, 1995): 66–68.

Konigsberg, Ira. *Narrative Technique in the English Novel: Defoe to Austen.* Hamden, CT: Archon Books, 1985.

Kuhn, Annette. *Women's Pictures: Feminism and Cinema.* London and New York: Routledge, 1982.

Lane, Anthony. "The Dumbing of *Emma.*" *The New Yorker* (August 5, 1996): 76–77.

"Jane's World." *The New Yorker* (September 25, 1995): 107–108.

"*Mansfield Park.*" *The New Yorker* 75 (November 29, 1999): 140.

"*Persuasion.*" *The New Yorker* (September 25, 1995): 107–108.

Lauritzen, Monica. *Jane Austen's Emma on Television: A Study of a BBC Classic Serial.* Acta Gothenburg Studies in English 48. Göteburg, Sweden: Acta Universitatis Gothoburgensis, 1981.

Lawrence, Amy. *Echo and Narcissus: Women's Voices in Classical Hollywood Cinema.* Berkeley: University of California Press, 1991.

Lawson-Peebles, Robert. "European Conflict and Hollywood's Reconstruction of English Fiction." *Yearbook of English Studies* 26 (1996): 1–13.

Leak, Rozen. "*Clueless.*" *People Weekly* 44 (July 31, 1995): 20.

Lee, Susan. "A Tale of Two Movies." *Forbes* 158 (November 4, 1996): 391.

Le Faye, Deirdre, ed. *Jane Austen's Letters.* Oxford: Oxford University Press, 1995.

Lehmann-Haupt, Christopher. "*Pride and Prejudice.*" *New York Times* (February 8, 1997). <http://archives.nytimes.com.archives/>

Leland, John. "*Clueless.*" *Newsweek* 126 (July 24, 1995): 52–53.

Lellis, George, and Philip Bolton. "Pride but No Prejudice." *The English Novel and the Movies.* Eds. Michael Klein and Gillian Parker. New York: Ungar, 1981.

LeMahieu, D. L. "Imagined Contemporaries: Cinematic and Televised Dramas about the Edwardians in Great Britain and the United States, 1967–1985", *Historical Journal of Film, Radio and Television* 10 (1990): 243–253.

Levin, Tom. "The Acoustic Dimension: Notes on Cinema Sound." *Screen* 25. 3 (1984): 55–68.

Libin, Kathryn L. Shanks. "'–a very elegant looking instrument–': Musical Symbols and Substance in the Films of Jane Austen's Novels." *Persuasions: Journal of the Jane Austen Society of North America* 19 (1997): 187–194.

Lipman, Amanda. "*Clueless.*" *Sight and Sound* (October 1995): 46.

Litvak, Joseph. "The Infection of Acting: Theatricals and Theatricality in *Mansfield Park.*" *ELH* 53 (Summer 1986): 2, 331–355.

"Reading Characters: Self, Society and Text in *Emma.*" *PMLA* 100 (1985): 763–773.

Looser, Devoney. "Jane Austen 'Responds' to the Men's Movement." *Persuasions: The Journal of the Jane Austen Society of North America* 18 (1996): 159–170.

Lovric, Michelle. *Women's Wicked Wit: From Jane Austen to Roseanne Barr.* London: Prion, 2000.

Lupack, Barbara Tepa, ed. *Nineteenth-Century Women at the Movies: Adapting Classic Women's Fiction to Film.* Bowling Green, OH: Bowling Green Popular University Press, 1999.

Lyall, Sarah. "'Emma' No. 2 Makes Austen's Heroine Darker and Spikier." *New York Times* (February 16, 1997): F4.

Lynch, Deirdre, ed. *Janeites: Austen's Disciples and Devotees.* Princeton: Princeton University Press, 2000.

Lyons, Donald. "Passionate Prelison: *Sense and Sensibility.*" *Film Comment* (January–February 1996): 36–42.

Lyttle, John. "All Dressed up for the Movies." *The Independent* (August 26, 1996): s 2 (2).

McCarthy, Todd. "Austen City Limits." *Premiere* 10 (September 1996): 38.

Macdonald, Andrew, and Gina Macdonald. "*Emma*: Balancing Satire and Sympathy in *Clueless.*" *Creative Screenwriting* (Summer 2000): 22–30.

McGrath, Douglas. "Candid Camera." *Harper's Bazaar* (August 1996): 90.

"Raising Jane: A Diary on the Making of the Film *Emma.*" *Premiere* 10 (September 1996): 74–77+.

McGrory, Mary. "'Clueless' about Jane Austen." *Washington Post* 118 (August 20, 1995): c1+.

"Dense Insensibility." *Washington Post* (December 19, 1995): A2.

MacLesh, Rod. "Movies Just Can't Get Past Austen's Charm." *The Christian Science Monitor* 88 (January 31, 1996): 19.

Mallett, Phillip. "On Liking *Emma.*" *Durham University Journal* 53.2 (July 1992): 249–254.

Mandel, Miriam B. "Fiction and Fiction-Making: *Emma.*" *Persuasions: Journal of the Jane Austen Society of North America* (December 16, 1991): 13, 100–103.

Marshall, Christine. "'Dull Elves' and Feminists: A Summary of Feminist Criticism of Jane Austen." *Persuasions: Journal of the Jane Austen Society of North America* 14 (December 16, 1992): 39–45.

Marshall, P. Scott. "Techniques of Persuasion in *Persuasion*: A Lawyer's Viewpoint." *Persuasions: Journal of the Jane Austen Society of North America* 6 (December 6, 1984): 44–47.

Maslin, Janet. "*Clueless*." *New York Times* (July 19, 1995): c9.

"*Emma*." *New York Times* (August 2, 1996).

"*Sense and Sensibility*." *New York Times* (December 13, 1995).

"So Genteel, So Scheming, So Austen." Review of *Emma*. *New York Times* (August 2, 1996): c1, c15.

Masters, Kim. "Austen Found: Hollywood Rediscovers the 19th-Century Writer." *Washington Post* 119 (December 19, 1995): G1, G7.

Mayne, Judith. *Cinema and Spectatorship*. London and New York: Routledge, 1993.

Mazmanian, Melissa. "Reviving *Emma* in a Clueless World: The Current Attraction to a Classic Structure." *Persuasions: Journal of the Jane Austen Society of North America*. Occasional Papers 3 (Fall 1999).

Medhurst, Andy. "Dressing the Part." *Sight and Sound* 6 (June 1996): 28–30.

Menand, Louis. "Hollywood's Trap." *New York Review of Books* 43 (September 19, 1996): 4–6.

"What Jane Austen Doesn't Tell Us." *New York Review of Books* 43 (February 1, 1996): B13–15.

Mettler, Mike. "*Clueless*." *Video* 19 (February/March 1996): 65–66.

Michaels, Lloyd. [Book review.] *Screen* 39.4 (Winter 1998): 425–432.

"The 'Midcult' Film Genre." *Cineaste* 22 (Fall 1996): 1.

Millard, Mary A. "Jane Austen and the Other *Emma*." *Persuasions: Journal of the Jane Austen Society of North America* 10 (December 16, 1988): 48.

Miller, Laura. "Austen-mania." Www.salon.com/02dec1995/features/austen.html

Mitry, Jean. "Remarks on the Problem of Cinematic Adaptation." Trans. Richard Dyer. *Bulletin of Midwest Modern Language Association* (1971): 1.

Molan, Ann. "Persuasion in *Persuasion*." *The Critical Review* 24 (1982): 16–29.

Moler, Kenneth L. "'Gutter Press Voices' in Jane Austen's Narration." *Persuasions: Journal of the Jane Austen Society of North America* 13 (December 16, 1991): 7–12.

Monaghan, David, "Introduction: Jane Austen as a Social Novelist." *Jane Austen in a Social Context*. Ed. David Monaghan. Totawa, NJ: Barnes and Noble Books, 1981: 1–8.

Jane Austen, Structure and Social Vision. London: Macmillan, 1980.

ed. *Emma, Jane Austen*. New York: St. Martin's Press; London: Macmillan, 1992.

ed. *Jane Austen in a Social Context*. London: Macmillan, 1981.

Monaghan, Peter. "With Sex and Sensibility, Scholars Redefine Jane Austen: A Wealth of New Scholarship Examines the Author and her Readers." *The Chronicle of Higher Education* 47 (August 17, 2001): A10 (3).

Moody, Ellen. "A Review-Essay of Film Adaptations of Jane Austen's Novels from 1940 to 1997." www.jimandellen.org/austen

Morgan, Susan. "Captain Wentworth, British Imperialism, and Personal Romance." *Persuasions: Journal of the Jane Austen Society of North America* 18 (December 16, 1996): 88–97.

Morgenstern, Joe. *"Persuasion." Wall Street Journal* (October 6, 1995): A8.

"Sense and Sensibility." Wall Street Journal (December 15, 1995): A14.

Morrison, Sarah R. *"Emma* Minus Its Narrator: Decorum and Class Consciousness in Film Versions of the Novel." *Persuasions: Journal of the Jane Austen Society of North America.* Occasional Papers 3 (Fall 1999).

Mullen, Lisa. "Fair Game." *Time Out* [London] (October 28–November 4, 1998): 24.

Nathan, John. "Jane and Louisa May: TV, Film and Tie-in Rights for Novels of Jane Austen, Louisa May Alcott." *Publishers Weekly* 243 (June 24, 1996): 24.

Neumann, A. Lin. "Cultural Revolution: Taiwan director Ang Lee Takes on Jane Austen." *Far Eastern Economic Review* 159 (December 28, 1995): 97 (2).

Nichols, Peter M. "Literary Cycle: Bookshelf, Broadcast, Video Store." *New York Times* (September 7, 1997). Online at http.//www. nytimes.com

"Tracking Jane Austen's *Emma* vs. *Emma.*" (March 7, 1997). Online at www.pemberley.com/kip/emma/emvem.html

North, Julian. "Conservative Austen, Radical Austen: *Sense and Sensibility* from Text to Screen." In *Adaptation from Text to Screen, Screen to Text.* Eds. Deborah Cartmell and Imelda Whelehan. London, England: Routledge, 1999: 38–50.

O'Connor, John J. "An England Where the Heart and Purse Are Romantically United." Review of *Pride and Prejudice. New York Times* (January 13, 1996): 13, 18.

O'Connor, Suzanne. *"Persuasion." New York Times* (October 1, 1995): H26.

O'Sullivan, Charlotte. "Fast Foreward: *Sense and Sensibility." Observer Preview* (February 24, 1996): 4.

O'Toole, Lesley. "A Cute Accent." *The Guardian* (September 3, 1996): T8 (2).

Page, Alex. "'Straightforward Emotions and Zigzag Embarrassments' in Austen's *Emma.*" In *Johnson and His Age.* Ed. James Engell. Cambridge, MA: Harvard University Press, 1984: 559–574.

Palmer, Sally. "Robbing the Roost: Reinventing Socialism in Diarmuid Lawrence's *Emma." Persuasions: Journal of the Jane Austen Society of North America.* Occasional Papers 3 (Fall 1999).

Parker, Mark. "The End of *Emma*: Drawing the Boundaries of Class in Austen." *Journal of English and Germanic Philology* 91. 3 (July 1992): 344–359.

Parrill, Sue. "The Cassandra of Highbury: Miss Bates on Film." *Persuasions: Journal of the Jane Austen Society of North America.* Occasional Papers 3 (Fall 1999).

Jane Austen on Film and Television: A Critical Study of the Adaptations. Jefferson, NC: McFarland, 2002.

"Pride and Prejudice on A&E: Visions and Revisions." *Literature–Film Quarterly* 27 (April 1999): 142 (7).

"What Meets the Eye: Landscape in the Films *Pride and Prejudice* and *Sense and Sensibility." Persuasions: Journal of the Jane Austen Society of North America* 21 (1999): 32–43.

Parrish, Stephen Maxfield, ed. *Emma: An Authoritative Text, Backgrounds, Reviews, and Criticism.* New York: Norton Press, 1972.

Parys, Bill Van. "Ewan McGregor." *Us* (August 1996): 82 (2).

PBS Corporate Organization Web Page. http://www.pbs.org/insidepbs/facts/faq1.html (September 25, 2000).

Pearlman, Cindy. "Common Sense." *Entertainment Weekly* (January 12, 1996): 9.

Pendreigh, Brian. "Wherefore Art?" *The Guardian* (July 2, 1999): s2 (2).

Penley, Constance, ed. *Feminism and Film Theory*. New York: Routledge, 1988.

Petrie, Duncan. *Creativity and Constraint in the British Film Industry*. London: Macmillan, 1991.

Phillips, William, and Louise Heal. "Extensive Grounds and Classic Columns: *Emma* on Film." *Persuasions: Journal of the Jane Austen Society of North America*. Occasional Papers 3 (Fall 1999).

Pidduck, Julianne. "Of Windows and Country Walks: Frames of Space and Movement in 1990s Austen Adaptations." *Screen* 39.4 (Winter 1998): 381–400.

Pinion, F. B. *A Jane Austen Companion: A Critical Survey and Reference Book*. New York: Macmillan, 1973.

Poovey, Mary. "*Persuasion* and the Promises of Love." In *The Representation of Women in Fiction*. Eds. Carolyn G. Heilbrun and Margaret R. Higonnet. Baltimore, MD: Johns Hopkins University Press, 1983: 152–179.

Poplawski, Paul. *A Jane Austen Encyclopedia*. Westport, CT: Greenwood Press, 1998.

"Pride and Prurience." *The Economist (US)* 317 (November 3, 1990): 106.

Randle, Nancy Jalasca. "Jane Austen and EMMA – Women For All Seasons." *Los Angeles Times* (February 1997).

Randoja, Ingrid. "Gwyneth Paltrow Glows as Emma." *Now* 15 (August 8–14, 1996).

Rapping, Elayne. "The Jane Austen Thing." *The Progressive* 60 (July 1996): 37–38.

Rapping, Nathan. "Jane and Louisa May." *Publishers Weekly* 243 (June 24, 1996): 24.

Rauch, Irmengard. "On the BBC/A&E Bicentennial *Pride and Prejudice*." *Interdisciplinary Journal for Germanic Linguistics and Semiotic Analysis* 2.2 (Fall 1997): 327–346.

Ray, Joan Klingel. "Message from the President: Code Word Jane Austen, or How a Chinese Film about Martial Arts Teaches Life Arts." *Persuasions: The Jane Austen Journal* (Annual 2000): 7 (6).

Review of *Pride and Prejudice*. *Time* (July 29, 1940): 44–45.

Rhodes, Joe. "Gwyneth Paltrow" (Breakthrough Stars of '96). *Us* (April 1996): 68 (5).

Rice, Tania. "Persuasive Arguments (BBC Film of Jane Austen Book *Persuasion*)." *Times Educational Supplement* (April 14, 1995): 30.

Rochlin, Margy. "Like Emma, Setting her World All Astir." *New York Times* 2 (July 28, 1996): 11.

Romano, Carlin. "Members of Jane Austen Society are Divided on Whether Hollywood is Good for their Author." *Knight-Ridder/Tribune News Service* (April 24, 1996): 424κ3106.

Romney, Jonathan. "One Minute Wonders of the Big Screen." Review of *Clueless*. *New Statesman* (October 20, 1995): 35.

Rosen, Leah. "*Mansfield Park*." *People Weekly* 52 (December 6, 1999): 48.

Rosenfeld, Megan. "A & E's Take on Austen's Matchmaker Rings True." *Washington Post* (February 16, 1997).

Rosmarin, Adena. "'Misreading' *Emma*: The Powers and Perfidies of Interpretative History." *English Literary History* 51.2 (Summer 1984): 315–342.

Roth, Barry. *An Annotated Bibliography of Jane Austen Studies, 1973–83*. Norfolk, VA: The University Press of Virginia, 1985.

An Annotated Bibliography of Jane Austen Studies, 1984–94. Ohio: Ohio University Press, 1996.

Rothstein, Edward. "Jane Austen Meets Mr. Right." *New York Times* (December 10, 1995): 4.1, 4.14.

Rowland-Brown, Lilian. "Navy, Army, and Jane Austen." *Nineteenth Century and After* (July/December 1917).

Rozema, Patricia. *Mansfield Park: A Screenplay*. New York: Miramax, 1999.

Rubinstein, Elliot, ed. *Twentieth-Century Interpretations of Pride and Prejudice; A Collection of Critical Essays*. New York: Prentice-Hall 1969.

Ruoff, Gene W. *Jane Austen's Sense and Sensibility* (Critical Studies of Key Texts). New York: St. Martin's Press, 1992.

Said, Edward W. "Jane Austen and Empire." In *Raymond Williams: Critical Perspectives*. Ed. Terry Eagleton. Northeastern University Press, 1989: 150–164.

Sales, Roger. *Jane Austen and Representations of Regency England*. New York: Routledge, 1996.

Sauter, Michael. "The Seductions of *Emma*." *Entertainment Weekly* (July 26, 1996): 41.

Schatz, Thomas. *Boom and Bust: The American Cinema in the 1940s*. New York: Scribner's, 1997.

Schickel, Richard. "*Mansfield Park*: Written and Directed by Patricia Rozema." *Time* 154 (November 29, 1999): 86.

Schwartz, Amy. "'Clued in' to Jane Austen." *Washington Post* 118 (August 11, 1995): A23.

Schwartz, Stan. "On EMMA and Other Austenian Matters." *Urban Desires*. 1996. www.pemberley.com/kip/emma/urban.html

Schwarzbaum, Lisa. "*Clueless*." *Entertainment Weekly* (August 16, 1996): 54–55.

"*Emma*." *Entertainment Weekly* (August 16, 1996): 48.

"*Pride and Prejudice*." *Entertainment Weekly* (August 16, 1996): 55.

Self, David. *Television Drama: An Introduction*. London and New York: Macmillan, 1984.

Sessums, Kevin. "Never Look Back" (Emma Thompson Interview). *Vanity Fair* 59 (February 1996): 80 (11).

Shapiro, Laura, and Carol Hall. "Beyond Sense and Sensibility." *Newsweek* (August 14, 1995): 70.

Shepard, Richard F. "Serban, in Film Debut, Meets Jane Austen." *The New York Times* 129 (January 28, 1998): PC11.

Simon, John. Review of Jane Austen's *Persuasion*. *National Review* 45 (October 23, 1995): 58–59.

Review of *Sense and Sensibility*. *National Review* 48 (January 29, 1996): 67.

Simons, Judy, ed. *Jane Austen and Cinema*. London: Athlone Press, 2004.

Siskel, Gene. "*Clueless*." *TV Guide* 47 (January 30/February 5, 1999): 16.

"*Sense and Sensibility*." *TV Guide* 46 (December 19–25, 1998): 21.

Sonnet, Esther. "From *Emma* to *Clueless*: Taste, Pleasure, and the Scene of History." In *Adaptation from Text to Screen, Screen to Text*. Eds. Deborah Cartmell and Imelda Whelehan. London: Routledge, 1999.

Spacks, Patricia Ann Meyer, ed. *Persuasion: Authoritative Text, Backgrounds and Contexts, Criticism*. New York: Norton, 1995.

Stark, Susan. "Clueless No Longer." *Detroit News*. www.pemberley.com/kip/emma/detroit.htm

Stenger, Ila. "Jane Austen's England: The Film Version of *Sense and Sensibility* Takes Us to the England that Was – and, in Some Places, Still Is." *Town & Country* 150 (January 1996): 78 (6).

Stern, Lesley. "Emma in Los Angeles: Remaking the Book and the City." In *Film Adaptation*. Ed. James Naremore. Rutgers Depth of Field Series. New Brunswick: Rutgers University Press, 2000: 221–238.

Sterritt, David. "*Emma*." *Christian Science Monitor* (August 2, 1996): 11.

Stevens, Amy. "Poor Jane Austen Didn't Live to See 'Sense and Sensibility.'" *Wall Street Journal* (March 25 1996): 1+.

Stone, Alan. Review of *Persuasion*. *Boston Review* 20: 6.

Stovel, Bruce. "Emma's Search for a True Friend." *Persuasions: Journal of the Jane Austen Society of North America* 13 (December 16, 1991): 58–67.

"*Northanger Abbey* at the Movies." *Persuasions: Journal of the Jane Austen Society of North America* 20 (Summer 1998): 236–247.

"Secrets, Silence, and Surprise in *Pride and Prejudice*." *Persuasions: Journal of the Jane Austen Society of North America* 11 (December 16, 1989): 85–91.

"Surprise in *Pride and Prejudice*." In *Approaches to Teaching Austen's Pride and Prejudice*. Ed. Marcia McClintock Folsom. Modern Language Association of America, 1993: 115–125.

Sutcliffe, Thomas. "Making Sense of Miss Thompson's Sensibility." *The Independent* (February 23, 1996): s2 (2).

Sutherland, Eileen. "That Infamous Flannel Waistcoat." *Persuasions: Journal of the Jane Austen Society of North America* 18 (December 1996): 58.

Thomas, Evan. "Hooray for Hypocrisy." *Newsweek* 127 (January 29, 1996): 61.

Thompson, Emma. *The "Sense and Sensibility" Screenplay and Diaries: Bringing Jane Austen's Novel to Film*. London: Bloomsbury, 1995. Rev. ed. New York: Newmarket, 1996.

Thomsen, Inger Sigrun. "Dangerous Words and Silent Lovers in *Sense and Sensibility*." *Persuasions: Journal of the Jane Austen Society of North America* 12 (December 16, 1990): 134–138.

Tibberts, John C., and James M. Welsh. *Novels into Film: The Encyclopedia of Movies Adapted from Books*. New York: Checkmark, 1997.

Tobin, Mary Elisabeth Fowkes. "Aiding Impoverished Gentlewomen: Power and Class in *Emma*." *Criticism: A Quarterly for Literature and the Arts* 30.4 (Fall 1988): 413–430.

Todd, Janet. "Jane Austen, Politics and Sensibility." In *Feminist Criticism: Theory and Practice*. Eds. Susan Sellers, Linda Hutcheon, and Paul Perron. Toronto: University of Toronto Press, 1991: 71–87.

Tonkin, Boyd. Review of *Emma*, dir. Douglas McGrath. *New Statesman* (September 13, 1996): 39.

Travers, Peter. "*Clueless*." *Rolling Stone* (August 10, 1995): 61–2+.

Trilling, Lionel. "Emma and the Legend." *The Last Decade: Essays and Reviews, 1965–75*. Ed. Diana Trilling. New York: Harcourt Brace Jovanovich, 1979.

Troost, Linda. "Jane Austen and Technology." *Topic: A Journal of the Liberal Arts* 48 (1997): iii–v.

Troost, Linda, and Sayre Greenfield, "Filming Highbury: Reducing the Community in *Emma* to the Screen." *Persuasions: Journal of the Jane Austen Society of North America*. Occasional Papers 3 (Fall 1999).

eds. *Jane Austen in Hollywood*. Lexington: University of Kentucky Press, 1998.

Turan, Kenneth. "Interview with Anne Rutherford (Lydia), Marsha Hunt (Mary), and Karen Morley (Charlotte Lucas)." *Persuasions: Journal of the Jane Austen Society of North America* 11 (1989): 143–150.

"Introduction to *Emma* on Film." *Persuasions: Journal of the Jane Austen Society of North America*. Occasional Papers 3 (Fall 1999).

"*Pride and Prejudice*: An Informal History of the Garson–Olivier Motion Picture." *Persuasions: Journal of the Jane Austen Society of North America* 11 (1989): 140–143.

Wald, Gayle. "*Clueless* in the Neo-Colonial World Order." In *The Postcolonial Jane Austen*. Eds. You-me Park and Rajeswari Sunder Rajan. Routledge Research in Postcolonial Literatures 2. New York: Routledge, 2000: 218–233.

Wall, James M. "*Sense and Sensibility*." *The Christian Century* 113 (January 24, 1996): 67.

Wallace, Tara Ghoshal. *Jane Austen and Narrative Authority*. New York: Macmillan, 1995.

"Northanger Abbey and the Limits of Parody." *Studies in the Novel* 20.3 (Fall 1988): 262–273.

"*Sense and Sensibility* and the Problem of Feminine Authority." *Eighteenth Century Fiction* 2 (January 4, 1992): 149–163.

Webb, Christine. "Rents and Rentability in Austen's Sensible City." *The Times* (October 23, 1996): s4.

Weinraub, Bernard. "A Surprise Film Hit about Rich Teen-Age Girls: *Clueless*." *New York Times* (July 24, 1995): C10.

Welch, Jim. "The *Sense and Sensibility* Screenplay and Diaries: Bringing Jane Austen's Novel to Film." *Literature–Film Quarterly* 24 (January 1996): 111 (2).

Weldon, Fay. "Jane Austen and the Pride of Purists." *New York Times* (October 8, 1995): H15, H24.

"Star of Age and Screen." *The Guardian* (April 12, 1995): 2 (3).

"What is it about Jane Austen? Stories with Lots of Words, No Kissing, No Vulgarity Add up to Big Box Office." *Los Angeles Times* 115 (January 7, 1996): M4.

Wilmington, Michael. "Adaptation of Austen's *Persuasion* Entertains Seamlessly." *Chicago Tribune* (October 27, 1995): 1+2.

Wilt, Judith. "Jane Austen's Men: Inside/Outside 'the Mystery'." *Women and Literature* 2 (1982): 59–76.

Wiltshire, John. *Recreating Jane Austen*. Cambridge: Cambridge University Press, 2000.

"The World of *Emma*." *The Critical Review* 27 (1985): 84–97.

Wolf, Matt. "Jane Austen Goes Shopping". Interview with Amy Heckerling. *The Times* (October 19, 1995): 35.

Wood, Robin. *Sexual Politics and Narrative Film: Hollywood and Beyond*. New York: Columbia University Press, 1999.

Wooden, Shannon R. "'You even forget yourself': The Cinematic Construction of Anorexic Women in the 1990s Austen Films." *Journal of Popular Culture* 36 (2) (Fall 2002): 221–235.

Wright, Andrew. "Jane Austen Adapted." *Nineteenth-Century Fiction* 30 (December 1975): 421–453.

www.jasa.nct.au

www.aetv.com

www.movie-reviewscolossus.net

www.pemberley.com/janeinfo

www.telegraph.co.uk

Index

anachronism, battle against, 221
archery, 167, 182, 222
audience: Austen's contemporaries, 106,
117, 121, 185, 234, 235; Austen films,
106–107, 108, 111, 199, 254, 256;
egalitarian social values, 202;
expectations/tastes of, 116, 120, 121,
250, 251, 255; mass audience, 218, 224;
participatory, 10; postmodern sensibility,
224, 225; Regency romance readers,
116; television, 200; wartime values,
175, 177, 178, 182, 186, 194, 195

Bakhtin, Mikhail, 47, 48
BBC productions, 4, 7, 17, 26, 27, 29–30,
31, 46, 90, 112, 197, 219, 230, 257,
259. *See also* individual Austen titles
Birtwistle, Sue, 6, 176, 186–210. *See also*
Pride and Prejudice (1995) and *Emma*
(1996)
Box Hill, 156, 168, 210, 220, 223. *See also*
the *Emmas*, novel and films
branding. *See* use-value ethics
Burke, Edmund, 200, 203–204, 206, 207,
209, 211, 212, 225

camera, 10, 12, 55, 59, 61; in BBC
productions, 197; in *Clueless*, 62, 71–92,
201, 205, 207, 209–211, 215, 219, 220,
221, 223; in *Emma*, 161, 171, 198; in
the *Mansfield Park* films, 70, 73, 77, 79,
80, 81–86; in *Persuasion*, 122, 129, 131,
139; in *Pride and Prejudice*, 181, 184,
185, 186, 187, 188, 190, 191, 192, 193,
194; in Thompson's *Sense and
Sensibility*, 93, 94, 96, 99, 101, 102–103
Captain Wentworth, 118, 120, 121, 122,
123, 125, 132, 135, 136, 137, 138, 139,
140. *See also Persuasion* (novel),
Persuasion (1971), *Persuasion* (1995
telefilm), and Hind, Ciaran, 197
Cher, 112, 154. *See also Clueless*

children, filmic representations of in *Tin
Drum*, 233
clothes. *See* costume
Clueless (1995 film, Paramount): major
discussions, 198, 199, 212, 219, 228,
250; mentions, 4, 7, 12, 33–259. *See also*
Heckerling, Amy
collaboration, 6, 7, 14
colonialism. *See* Marxism
comedy, 74, 75, 79, 82, 103, 167, 186,
197, 203, 214, 223; comedy of manners,
210, 212, 214, 215, 223; low comedy,
223–224; sardonic humor, 238, 243;
slapstick, 215
commodification: major discussion, 15, 21;
mentions, 10, 22, 28, 92, 106, 111, 191,
198, 199, 200, 218, 219, 226, 229, 254,
258. *See also* electronic media
costume and fashion: in films, 47, 90; in
Clueless, 216, 218; costume drama, 230;
in *Emma*, 201, 209, 221; in modern
Mansfield Park productions, 82, 83; in
Michell's *Persuasion*, 111–115, 121–122,
123, 124, 125, 126, 134, 137; in *Pride
and Prejudice* (1940), 197; in
Thompson's *Sense and Sensibility*, 96–97,
98, 101
courtesy/conduct books, 35–37
cultural capital. *See* use-value ethics

Davies, Andrew, 5, 226, 257. *See also*
Emma (1996 telefilm) and *Pride and
Prejudice* (1995 miniseries)
diaries, in Austen novels/films, 163, 164
Doran, Lindsay, 5, 6, 97. *See also Sense and
Sensibility* (1995)
Dürrenmatt, Friedrich, 228, 229, 251

electronic media, Internet, 10, 15, 17, 18,
21, 254. *See also* Republic of Pemberley
Emma (novel): main discussion, 238, 250;
mentions, 10, 158, 166–167, 169, 199,

authority
class/status
recognition
branding: recognition of identifiable qualities